GUADALCANAL

GUADALCANAL
Decision at Sea

THE NAVAL BATTLE OF GUADALCANAL
November 13-15, 1942

ERIC HAMMEL

CROWN PUBLISHERS, INC.

New York

FOR AIRDALES,
OLD SALTS, AND SEA DOGS,
WITH AFFECTION

Published by Crown Publishers, Inc.,
225 Park Avenue South, New York, New York 10003 and in
Canada by the Canadian MANDA Group
CROWN is a trademark of Crown Publishers, Inc.
Manufactured in the United States of America
Library of Congress Cataloging-in-Publication Data
Hammel, Eric M.
Guadalcanal: decision at sea / Eric Hammel.
p. cm.
1. Guadalcanal Island (Solomon Islands), Battle of, 1942–1943.
2. World War, 1939–1945—Campaigns—Solomon Islands.
3. World War, 1939–1945—
Naval operations, American. I. Title.
D767.98.H326 1988   940.54'26—dc19
ISBN 0-517-56952-3
Book Design by Shari deMiskey
10 9 8 7 6 5 4 3 2 1
First Edition

GUIDE TO ABBREVIATIONS AND TERMS

A6M	Mitsubishi Zero fighter
AA	Antiaircraft
ACRM	Aviation Chief Radioman
Adm	Admiral
Airacobra	Bell P-39 fighter
Air Ops	Air Operations
AKA	Attack cargo ship
APA	Attack transport
ARM2	Aviation Radioman 2nd Class
AS	Apprentice Seaman
Avenger	Grumman TBF Torpedo bomber
B-17	Boeing Flying Fortress heavy bomber
B-26	Martin Marauder medium bomber
BB	Battleship
Betty	Mitsubishi G4M medium bomber
BGen	Brigadier General
BM1	Boatswain's Mate 1st Class
CA	Heavy cruiser
Cactus	Code name for Guadalcanal
Capt	Captain
Catalina	Consolidated PBY patrol bomber
CBM	Chief Boatswain's Mate
CCStd	Chief Commissary Steward
Cdr	Commander
CGM	Chief Gunner's Mate

CIC	Combat Information Center
CinC	Commander in Chief
CL	Light cruiser
CLAA	Light antiaircraft cruiser
Cox	Coxswain
CSM	Chief Signalman
CTM	Chief Torpedoman
CV	Fleet aircraft carrier
CVL	Light aircraft carrier
D3A	Aichi Val dive-bomber
Dauntless	Douglas SBD dive-bomber
DD	Destroyer
DP	Dual purpose
Duck	Grumman J2F amphibious scout
EM3	Electrician's Mate 3rd Class
Ens	Ensign
Exec	Executive Officer
(F)	Flagship
F1	Fireman 1st Class
F4F	Grumman Wildcat fighter
FC	Fire control radar
FC3	Fire Controlman 3rd Class
FD	Fire direction radar
(FF)	Fleet Flagship
1stLt	First Lieutenant
G4M	Mitsubishi Betty medium bomber
GM2	Gunner's Mate 2nd Class
HIJMS	His Imperial Japanese Majesty's Ship
J2F	Grumman Duck amphibious scout
kg	Kilogram
LCdr	Lieutenant Commander
Long Lance	Japanese 24-inch torpedo
Lt	Lieutenant
Lt(jg)	Lieutenant Junior Grade

LtCol	Lieutenant Colonel
M1	Metalsmith 1st Class
MAG	Marine Air Group
Maj	Major
MM1	Machinist's Mate 1st Class
MoMM2	Motor Machinist's Mate 2nd Class
mm	Millimeter
MTSgt	Master Technical Sergeant
OC2	Officers' Cook 2nd Class
P-39	Bell Airacobra fighter
P-400	Bell Airacobra export fighter
PBY	Consolidated Catalina patrol bomber
Pfc	Private First Class
PhM1	Pharmacist's Mate 1st Class
PPI	Plan Position Indicator (radar scope)
PT	Patrol torpedo boat
Pvt	Private
RAdm	Rear Admiral
RBA	Rescue breathing apparatus
RM3	Radioman 3rd Class
RT2	Radio Technician 2nd Class
S2	Seaman 2nd Class
SBD	Douglas Dauntless dive-bomber
SC	Search radar
SC1	Ship's Cook 1st Class
Seabee	Navy Construction Battalion Engineer
2ndLt	Second Lieutenant
SG	Surface-search radar
Sgt	Sergeant
SM3	Signalman 3rd Class
SOC	Curtiss observation scout
SoM3	Sonarman 3rd Class
SP	Single purpose
SSgt	Staff Sergeant
TBF	Grumman Avenger torpedo bomber
TBS	Talk-between-ships voice radio

TM1	Torpedoman 1st Class
TSgt	Technical Sergeant
USS	United States Ship
VAdm	Vice Admiral
Val	Aichi D3A dive-bomber
VB	Navy Bombing Squadron
VF	Navy Fighting Squadron
VMF	Marine Fighting Squadron
VMJ	Marine Utility (Transport) Squadron
VMO	Marine Observation Squadron
VMSB	Marine Scout-Bomber Squadron
VS	Navy Scouting Squadron
VT	Navy Torpedo Squadron
Wildcat	Grumman F4F fighter
WT1	Watertender 1st Class
Y2	Yeoman 2nd Class
YC	Yacht patrol vessel
Zero	Mitsubishi A6M fighter

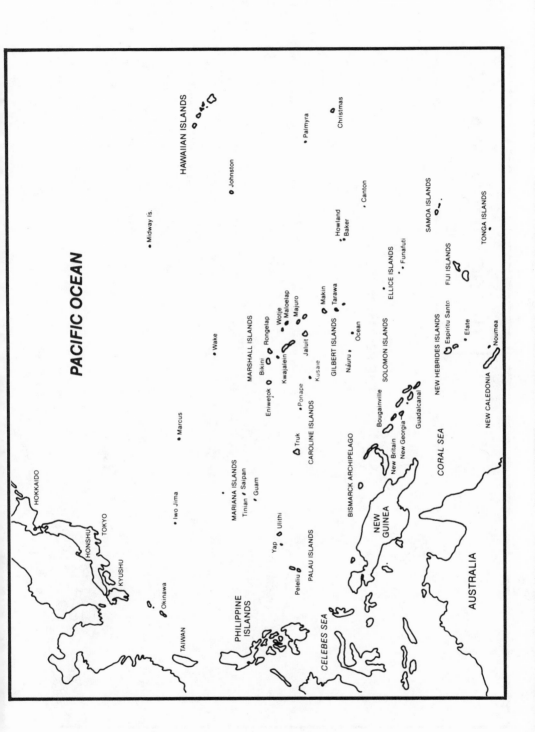

PACIFIC OCEAN

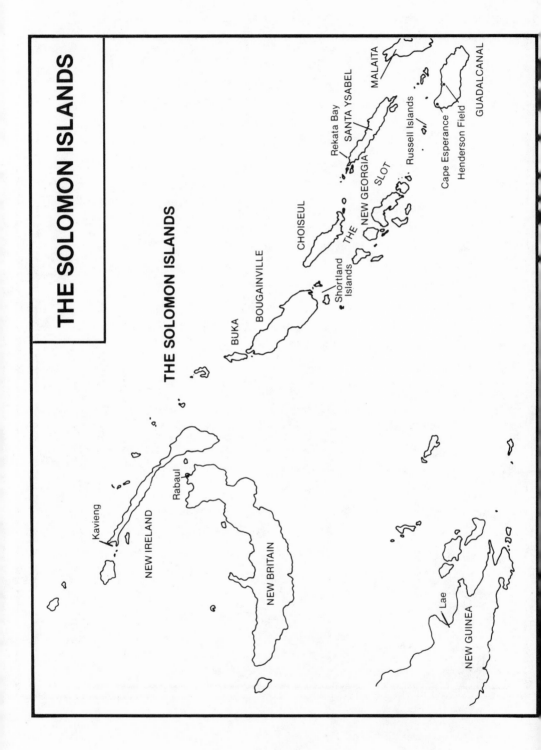

THE SOLOMON ISLANDS

THE SOLOMON ISLANDS

NEW GUINEA

Lae

NEW BRITAIN

Rabaul

NEW IRELAND

Kavieng

BUKA

BOUGAINVILLE

Shortland Islands

CHOISEUL

THE

NEW GEORGIA

SLOT

Russell Islands

Rekata Bay

SANTA YSABEL

MALAITA

Cape Esperance

Henderson Field

GUADALCANAL

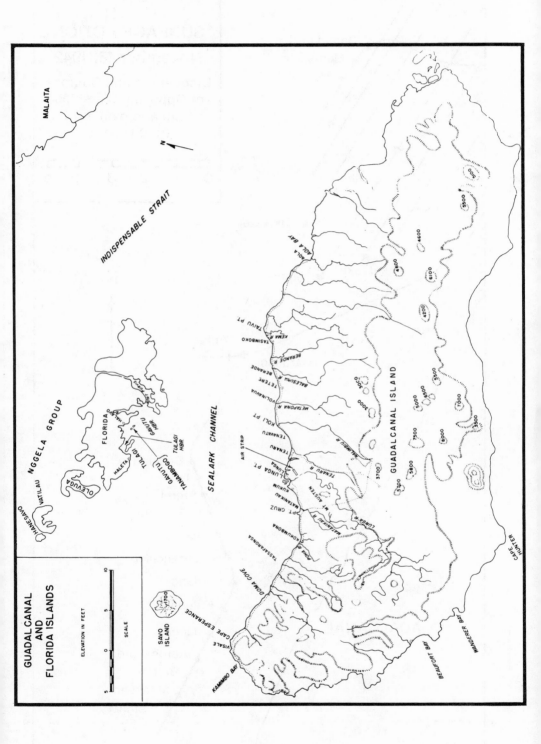

GUADALCANAL
AND
FLORIDA ISLANDS

ELEVATION IN FEET

SCALE

MALAITA

INDISPENSABLE STRAIT

NGGELA GROUP

OHANESAVO

VATILAU

OLEVUGA

FLORIDA

HALETA

TULAGIA BAY

GAVUTU

TANAMBOGO

GAVUTU HBR

TULAGI HBR

SEALARK CHANNEL

SAVO ISLAND

DOMA COVE

CAPE ESPERANCE

VISALE

KAMIMBO BAY

TASSAFARONGA

KOKUMBONA

DOMA

POINT CRUZ

MATANIKAU R

MT AUSTEN

KUKUM

MATANIKAU R

LUNGA PT

LUNGA

TENARU

TENARU R

AIR STRIP

KOLI PT

ILU R

TENAVATU

MALIMBIU R

METAPONA R

VOLINAVUA

TETERE

BALESUMA

BERANDE

BERANDE R

TASIMBOKO

KEMA R

TAIVU PT

AOLA BAY

GUADALCANAL ISLAND

CAPE HUNTER

WANDERER BAY

BEAUFORT BAY

4600

5500

5500

4600

6100

4200

5000

3000

5000

6500

3500

7500

7000

6000

5500

5800

5700

5600

N

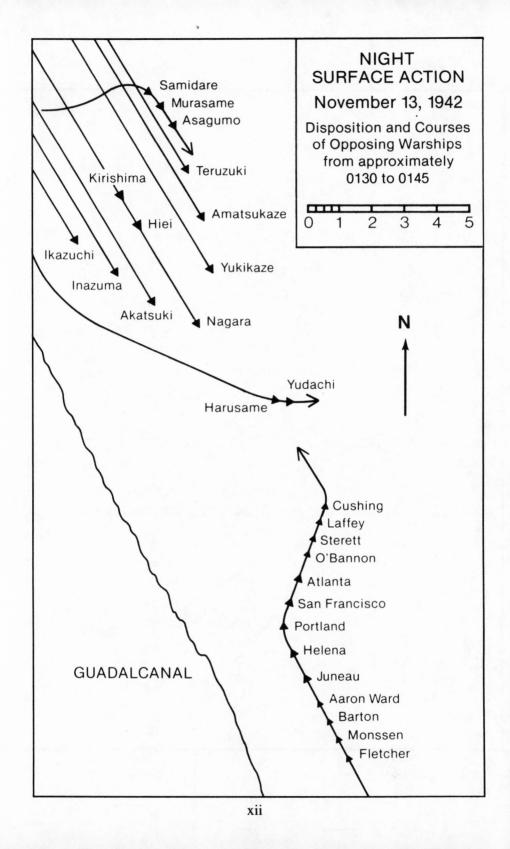

NIGHT
SURFACE ACTION
November 13, 1942
Disposition and Courses
of Opposing Warships
from approximately
0130 to 0145

0 1 2 3 4 5

Samidare
Murasame
Asagumo

Teruzuki

Kirishima

Hiei

Amatsukaze

Ikazuchi

Yukikaze

Inazuma

Akatsuki   Nagara

N

Yudachi

Harusame

Cushing
Laffey
Sterett
O'Bannon

Atlanta

San Francisco

Portland

Helena

Juneau

Aaron Ward
Barton
Monssen
Fletcher

GUADALCANAL

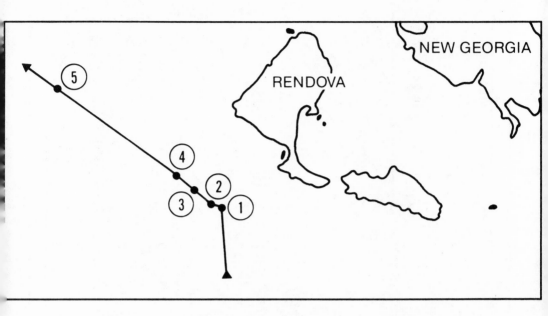

AIR ATTACKS ON MIKAWA FORCE
November 14, 1942

0	5	10	15		30		45

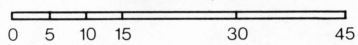

1. 0800 - Cactus bombers torpedo **Kinugasa**, bomb **Maya**.
2. 0835 - Gibson and Buchanan find Mikawa Force.
3. 0915 - Gibson bombs **Kinugasa**.
4. 0923 - Hoogerwerf and Halloran attack Mikawa Force.
5. 1030 - **Enterprise** attack group finds, attacks Mikawa Force.

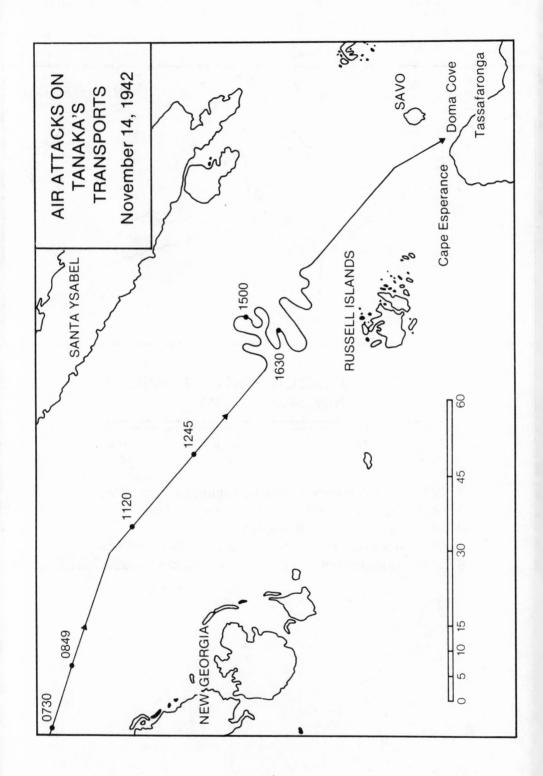

AIR ATTACKS ON
TANAKA'S
TRANSPORTS
November 14, 1942

SANTA YSABEL

SAVO

Doma Cove

Tassafaronga

Cape Esperance

RUSSELL ISLANDS

1500

1630

1245

1120

0849

0730

NEW GEORGIA

0   5   10 15   30   45   60

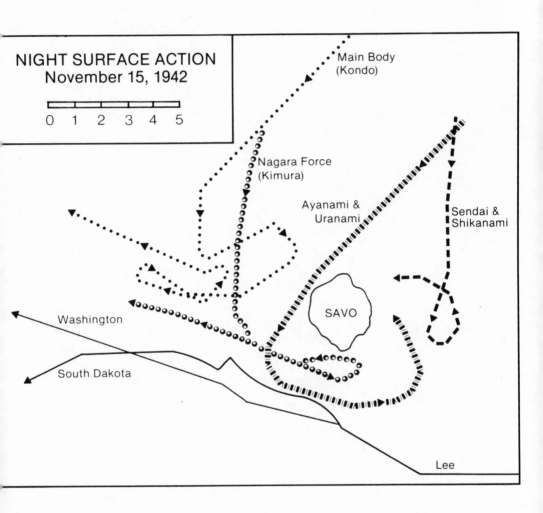

NIGHT SURFACE ACTION
November 15, 1942

0 1 2 3 4 5

Main Body
(Kondo)

Nagara Force
(Kimura)

Ayanami &
Uranami

Sendai &
Shikanami

SAVO

Washington

South Dakota

Lee

PART I

The Fleets

I

The Empire of Japan was a militaristic power. That was a matter of culture and religion. War had been the Japanese way for all of her history. Her approach to her forced opening to the West in the latter half of the nineteenth century had been to study the ways Westerners made war and to emulate them. Striving to gain a respected place among the modern industrial powers of the world, the Japanese took to the path of war to begin carving out the regional empire in East Asia she considered her own by divine right. She copied the imperialist lead of the Western powers and advanced into Korea and against China and Russia. Eventually, she was stopped in her imperial path through the diplomatic intervention of the Western powers, chiefly the United States.

Over time an enmity born of competition arose between Japan and the United States. The Japanese came to believe that an all-out war with the United States was inevitable—that winning such a war would carry Japan forward as the dominant power in East Asia and the Pacific. That she was afforded second-class status in the Five Power Naval Armaments Agreement of 1922 rankled Japanese pride. When the second-class status was reaffirmed at the London

3

Naval Conference of 1930, the Japanese were further affronted but, at the time, powerless to act.

The 1930s saw the general rise of militarism throughout the world. Despite well-intentioned but ultimately unrealistic treaties and a crippling worldwide economic depression, the world's major powers—and those who would be major—built up their armies and navies against the day a major war would certainly erupt.

Japan's military adventures were confined to China through the 1930s, beginning with her invasion of Manchuria in 1931. Alarmed by the implications of Japan's overt militarism and yet more alarmed by the militarization of Japanese-mandated former German colonies in the western and central Pacific, the United States in 1934 began a fitful series of naval modernization programs. For the first time, the U.S. Congress appropriated enough money to build warships up to the limits of the 1930 naval treaty. New classes of battleships, cruisers, and destroyers were begun.

In 1936, Japan abrogated the 1930 London Naval Conference Treaty and began building warships with an astounding zeal. An island nation, Japan required a strong maritime presence in the waters she considered within her sphere. If the threat implied by Washington's naval buildup was ever carried out in the western Pacific, the Imperial Navy would become the prime means for ensuring Japan's economic survival.

For all her zeal, Japan was unable to build the number of ships her naval leaders felt they required. Simply stated, Japan did not have the heavy industrial capacity to churn out adequate numbers of large, sophisticated warships while building up her commercial shipping fleet. On the one hand, the limited industrial capacity forced a caution upon the most rabid naval militarists, but on the other hand, innovative advances had to be made to offset weak numbers with superior quality. The Japanese steadily built up their naval war-fighting capacity in raw numbers, to be sure, but they also took the lead in such areas as propulsion and armament for new and highly improved classes of warships.

In 1937, the U.S. Congress authorized the building of two extremely modern battleships. Simultaneously, for the first time President Franklin Roosevelt and other American leaders launched a public campaign decrying Japan's out-and-out imperialist aggression in China. Japanese leaders concluded that the United States was fundamentally hostile toward their nation and, in the tenor of the time, they began to plan seriously for war.

As concerned as the United States was about the specter of war in East Asia and the Pacific, her real interests and sentiments lay in Europe and the Atlantic. Almost upon the outbreak of war in Europe in September 1939, the Roosevelt administration and the U.S. Congress joined forces to map out a prodigious buildup in all military spheres—ground, air, and naval. Although the main impetus for these moves was the war in Europe, Japan's potential threat was certainly factored into the new American military equation.

The U.S. Navy's share of the pie was huge. In addition to a massive buildup in its carrier- and land-based air arm, in 1940 the Navy received authorization to build 6 45,000-ton battleships, 5 58,000-ton battleships, 6 27,000-ton battlecruisers, 11 27,000-ton fleet aircraft carriers, 40 heavy and light cruisers, 115 fleet destroyers, 67 fleet submarines, and numerous lesser vessels and auxiliaries.

The Japanese were stunned by the size of the proposed American buildup and though many Japanese leaders realized that America's concerns were in Europe, they felt they had to map out a serious war plan to overcome the burgeoning U.S. Fleet—before it burgeoned. Thus, in its way, the onset of the Pacific War was determined by the increase in proposed new constructions of modern U.S. Navy fighting ships.

The Japanese pulled out all the stops. Virtually their entire heavy industrial capacity was turned over to the Imperial Army and Imperial Navy to build up their respective war machines. Aircraft carriers the Imperial Navy had eschewed in favor of new cruisers and destroyers were hurriedly laid down *along with* the desired floating gunnery platforms.

The final step leading to uncontained war in East Asia and the Pacific seems to have been an embargo of oil supplies to Japan imposed by the United States, Great Britain, and the Netherlands in protest against Japan's occupation of French Indochina in July 1941. The Japanese warlords looked at their nation's strategic oil reserves, determined that they had a two-year supply on hand, and reached the decision to go to war as soon as possible. Their reasoning was twofold: If there was to be a war, best to get it started while the oil reserves were plentiful, and at least one early objective of the war was to take direct control of the nearest oil fields, in the Dutch East Indies.

While the more responsible elements in power in Japan attempted to settle the extremely onerous oil-embargo crisis through diplomatic means, even they agreed to approve a drive toward the East Indies if the matter was not settled by the first week of October. The war plan grew by leaps and bounds. If it was to protect Imperial Army units bound for the East Indies oil fields, the Imperial Navy felt it had to neutralize British and American East Asia and western Pacific bases. As one plan gave way to the next, a decision to mount a series of coordinated simultaneous strikes throughout the vast region was finally promulgated. The plan was extremely complex and it placed the largest burden upon the Combined Fleet, the Imperial Navy's operational arm.

As much as the plan tempted fate, it worked. Not flawlessly, but near enough to the ideal to fool all onlookers, particularly the American, British, Australian, New Zealand, and Dutch onlookers who were defeated and overwhelmed at virtually every turn by an Imperial Navy that appeared to be everywhere at once.

The opening moves in the Japanese-instigated war in the Pacific and East Asia were the crowning achievement of the Empire of Japan. The distances and numbers of people affected were vast, the execution literally breathtaking, the results far beyond the expectations of even the most sanguine Japanese planners. But, in the final analysis, it was all a bluff—a serious and extremely deadly bluff, but a bluff nonetheless. Unless the Allies, chiefly the United States, became demoralized and gave up, Japan did not have a prayer of winning an ongoing or protracted war in so vast an arena. Her planners had not given any thought to consolidating the bases seized in the first onslaught nor to following up initial gains with a cogent policy of expansion yet farther into the Pacific or India. Japan's master plan lacked depth and greater vision, but Japan was nonetheless quite capable of giving the Western powers an amazing run for their money.

Japan launched no new battleships between 1921 and the eruption of the Pacific War. She had only two such dreadnoughts under construction on the eve of the war (one was launched on December 16, 1941), and several others she planned to build were eventually converted to aircraft carriers or abandoned.

It was in the design and construction of smaller warships that the Imperial Navy excelled. The Combined Fleet went to war with 18 heavy cruisers, 20 light cruisers, 111 destroyers, and numerous smaller fighting ships and auxiliaries. Many of the cruisers and destroyers were of recent vintage, and many of the older warships had been modernized in the final years before the start of the war. Unlike her American adversary, however, Japan had few new surface warships on the ways at the outbreak of the war. Indeed, in addition to several aircraft carriers, she would commission only one new light cruiser and seven new fleet destroyers in the whole first year of the war. Between December 7, 1941, and the first week of August 1945, Japan commissioned only 2 battleships (both nearly completed at the start of the war), 16 aircraft carriers of all types and sizes, no heavy cruisers, 6 light cruisers, and 63 destroyers (including numerous small destroyers designed for service as escorts). Except in numbers of aircraft carriers, these totals do not compare with America's 1939 authorization for new warship constructions—and they are totally dwarfed by the total of new warships that actually joined the U.S. Fleet during the course of its two-ocean war.

Japan was totally outclassed in shipbuilding capacity and all other aspects of industrial might. Her leaders knew she would be going in. Thus, her only hope—said again—was to attack the burgeoning U.S. Fleet before it burgeoned.

The Imperial Navy was an elite, elitist organization. As prone at the administrative levels as any large bureaucracy to becoming bogged down in paperwork, careerism, politics, and minutiae, the Imperial Navy nevertheless enjoyed a unique dynamic. It was driven by a sense of purpose and duty that Western naval officers could only begin to sense, much less comprehend. To be sure, Western observers saw the tangible results of the Japanese dynamism, but they did not understand its roots.

Japanese society was suffused with its devotion to the emperor and the nation's divine mission. The blood, the sinew, the heartbeat of Japan serves only one purpose, and that is paying the emperor back for his largess. When the men who stood behind the throne and guided it decreed a militarist policy in the emperor's name, when they identified the archenemy, when they articulated the goals, and when they revealed the timetable, the creative juices of the entire nation flowed in just one direction.

In a very few years, Japanese naval architects designed new high-pressure steam power plants to move larger ships faster on less precious fuel. Naval armorers devised better guns for their ships, and naval ordnancemen devised better ammunition and propellants. What the Japanese lacked in technical or industrial ability, they made up for in other ways. Japan didn't have a prayer of developing search or gunnery radars for her ships, so she found her sons with the keenest eyesight and night vision and trained them to be lookouts and spotters aboard her warships and in her observation-scout planes. They developed the finest optical devices in the world, including the world's finest marine night optical equipment.

In one extremely important area, Japan's torpedo experts improved upon the world's best 21-inch naval torpedo by developing the world's best torpedo, period—a 24-incher dubbed the Long Lance, which could go faster and was effective out to ranges over five times greater than the quirky American naval torpedo. And they installed more torpedo tubes on more classes of warships than their American counterparts. (Most U.S. cruisers had no torpedo tubes because they had been forbidden in the 1922 and 1930 naval treaties.) Unlike the U.S. Navy, the Japanese equipped their torpedo-carrying warships with extra torpedoes for reloads. Even more important, the Japanese *trained* with their torpedoes. They learned their shortcomings and improved on them over time. And they developed suitable, realistic torpedo tactics based on live-fire trials at sea. (The U.S. Navy fired few of its torpedoes in practice, and the loss of an expensive torpedo invariably led to a major investigation, a threat that itself effectively quelled experimentation.)

Likewise, the Imperial Navy sent all her ships to sea to practice group tactics in ever-changing combinations. The aim of these exercises was to test the ships and weapons to the utmost, to find faults that could be corrected. The Imperial Navy gave her officers and sailors valuable ship-handling and command experience.

Because it was relatively poor and lacked many of the modern technological systems supporting the navies of its adversaries, the Imperial Navy developed tactics based upon what modern naval tacticians and strategists now call a "standoff" philosophy. Simply stated, the Japanese sought to engage enemy surface units at night by means that would not reveal the position of their own ships. The night-vision training and aids, and the development of faster, longer-ranged torpedoes supported the philosophy, as did the development of brighter and longer-lasting starshells and relatively flashless gunpowder. All were designed to allow the Japanese to see the enemy before they were seen, and to engage him earlier and from greater distances than he could engage the Japanese.

While the Japanese were prone to operate in rigid columns of warships—a singularly uninspiring formation—they did practice the launching of successive or continuous attacks by mutually supporting formations. Above all, Japanese captains and unit commanders were taught to withhold gunfire until after their ready torpedoes had been fired and until the enemy was absolutely certain to be overwhelmingly struck by numerous initial hits. More than their adversaries, the Japanese trained to use arrays of powerful searchlights not only to locate and fix targets but also to blind and startle their adversaries.

Withal, innovations beyond these relatively simple expedients were slow in arising. The Japanese naval institutional hierarchy was extremely rigid. While subordinates were urged to speak out in practice—Japan's leading torpedo tactician, Tameichi Hara, made his greatest contributions as an aggressive young lieutenant—the men at the top ruled with an iron hand. Perquisites were distributed or withheld on the basis of family or school ties, an ultimately ruinous system that could in no way be abolished in that semifeudal society. This was not an environment conducive to change or to bringing out the best in individuals.

But for all its quirks and negative traits, in the last analysis the Imperial Navy was bred as a fighting navy. And indeed it was.

2

The ultimate mission of a navy is to close with enemy ships and defeat them with its weapons. To do that, warships must be manned by people willing and able to close with the enemy and, once that is done, equipped with armaments capable of destroying the enemy's ships.

At the close of the first half of 1942, the U.S. Navy had been in a state of unremitting shock for all of seven months. In that time its warships had eked out only two clear victories—in the Coral Sea in May and at Midway in June. Both of those battles were won by carrier-based air groups, not by surface warships. The surface warships of the U.S. Navy had lost every battle in which they engaged Japanese surface warships. *Every confrontation with Japanese warships had been a humiliating defeat.*

Some of the reasons for the execrable showing were, in a way, cultural: America had yet to be prepared for the onset of a single one of her wars. But the main reasons for the virtually unbroken string of humiliations had to do with the attitudes and mind-sets of many of the U.S. Navy's surface-force commanders at sea. They lacked a critical edge that can be called "battle awareness."

The U.S. Navy of late 1941 was a swelling bureaucracy wait-

ing for a useful enterprise. It had not fought a major fleet engagement since 1898—which means that no one then serving in the
Navy had ever been involved in a real naval battle. A very few
officers and sailors had been involved in brief skirmishes at sea in
1917 and 1918, but at ranks so low as to have no credible bearing
upon their responsibilities in 1941.

The bureaucratic aspect of the Navy's long wait for a war lay
at the heart of the unpreparedness of her leadership for the war
everyone seemed to know would eventually arrive. The U.S.
Navy's ethos simply did not prize war-fighting skills over administrative skills. Careerism was rife; most of the men who got ahead
were the ones who acquired advanced skills in keeping their heads
down. All their energies went into acquiring career survival skills.
Risk taking of any sort was totally out of vogue. By 1941, most of
the men at the top—except for a few irrepressible and brilliant individuals who simply could not be kept down by the careerist system—were experts in avoiding risk, which is to say decisions.
Since such men had gotten to the top, their careerist philosophies
were inevitably emulated by juniors who wanted to achieve similar
success.

The ancient adage *"He who runs his ship aground will suffer a fate
worse than death"* was the unspoken watchword of professional officers of the day. Taken to its extreme, this crippling tradition gutted the aggressive instincts of many fine potential combat officers.
In order to advance to a position where war-fighting instincts and
skills could have an impact, the aggressive officer had to survive.
Years of concentrating on survival took their toll; the potential warrior who could not stomach the system left early, and most of the
others were eventually worn down by it. When the opportunity
arose, many talented line officers opted for flight training, where,
along with physical risk and excitement, promotions were a bit
easier to earn and positions of responsibility were a bit easier to
attain. In the air, at least, aggressive, innovative instincts were
prized. (It is therefore really no wonder that the Navy's air arm
outperformed the surface arm early in the war.) In order to hone
and enhance his craft, the true warrior will eventually and inevitably take risks with his life, his subordinates' lives, and the equipment in his care. Many of the surface navy's few remaining natural

leaders who neither left the service nor capitulated to the system eventually "ran aground" in one form or another, their careers often ruined by black marks in their personnel files. That any natural leaders remained in the service during the frustrating interwar decades is a measure both of their sense of duty and the depth of the Great Depression.

What can be said about a military service that prizes administrative skills and career survival skills over war-fighting skills?

Admittedly, a measure of the blame rested with a parsimonious Congress, whose unyielding grip on the purse strings prevented the Navy from replacing equipment lost or damaged at the hands of both inept and combative risk-taking commanders afloat. The watchword of the era was "make do."

But all that changed in 1939, when the war in Europe lifted the last treaty barriers on naval construction and imposed an authentic sense of urgency—and relief—upon both the Congress and the naval service. Massive numbers of new men had to be acquired to man the tangible results of a crash building program aimed at bringing the sickly U.S. Fleet to a modern war-fighting standard.

Once the decision to build up the Navy was taken, strong men of clear vision quickly rose to the top of the service hierarchy. Chief among these were Adm Ernest King and VAdm Chester Nimitz, men of such consummate skill that the ennui of the prewar years had virtually no impact upon their abilities and sensibilities as commanders or as men. Others slightly less senior were pulled forward by the enormous suction created by King's and Nimitz's rise to the top.

But, for all the positive moves at the top, the Navy's infrastructure of middle managers was weak. Many of the captains of the day were superb careerists who had never taken any risks, much less the true warrior's ultimate risks. The good leaders at the top knew that the service was riddled with senior officers who could not possibly measure up in a war. Those who were easily identified were cut loose from operational commands; they were used, to be sure, but in places where they could do no harm and, indeed, might do some good. But there were hundreds of untested officers with fifteen or more years of service who could not be properly evaluated short of actually performing in combat. Some would make the grade and others would not. Some looked aggressive and competent, but only a dose of action would determine if the career-saving ethos in which they had been immersed for so long had taken a fatal toll on their decision-making powers. Only time and the unknowable outcome of battles at sea would determine the true quality of the U.S. Navy as a world-class fighting force.

☙

On the day after Pearl Harbor, LCdr Butch Parker was on the bridge of USS *Parrott*, an ancient "four-piper" destroyer of World War I vintage attached to the U.S. Asiatic Fleet. War had caught Parker's destroyer squadron in the Dutch East Indies without any plan for refueling or revictualing, so the captain called his senior storekeeper up from below to ask him what the manuals said about obtaining fuel and supplies in a foreign port during a war. When the storekeeper admitted that he didn't know, Parker sent him below to find out.

The storekeeper returned to the bridge after being away for several hours and informed Lieutenant Commander Parker that there were no special instructions in any of the paperwork he had aboard the ship. Parker simply could not believe the news.

Prior to the war, U.S. Fleet destroyers were invariably organized into standing squadrons and divisions. Such units always operated together and were serviced from tenders or supply ships. The staff of each destroyer division included a supply officer and a small staff of enlisted men to order and distribute needed supplies. That was the system. Period. Parker's question to his senior storekeeper reflected his concern that individual ships might find themselves detached from their parent squadrons, sailing alone into foreign ports at which fuel and other supplies would have to be replenished. On receiving the storekeeper's puzzling response to his inquiry, Butch Parker took the time to pore over the resupply manual. To his amazement and disgust that second day of the Pacific War, Parker discovered that the U.S. Navy had not seen fit to use the word *war* in its standing orders regarding supply of its warships.

How could the U.S. Navy be expected to conduct a serious

war effort when the departments responsible for supplying its warships did not inherently recognize the possibility of a war?

Over the next week, *Parrott* and all other U.S. navy ships in the East Indies were bombarded with extremely long messages aimed at establishing new supply procedures. Beyond tying up the airwaves, Butch Parker was certain, the new instructions were hastily contrived and undoubtedly full of bad advice.

This single experience—among many more or less frustrating—is emblematic of a military service in the hands of careerists. The modern term for such behavior is *micromanagement*. Typically, a manager of Butch Parker's stature and years—a 1925 Naval Academy graduate, thirty-seven years old, in command of a warship attached to a major fleet component—had no inherent legal authority to see to the direct purchase of vital supplies for his command. Someone in higher authority did not feel that Parker and officers of his generation could be trusted to do the right thing. Indeed, if the system denigrated and stifled the authority of commanders in such mundane areas as supply procurement, is it any wonder that the captains of many warships confronted by Japanese warships that early in the war were unable to think for themselves if forced to do so?

At the outbreak of the Pacific War, the institution was far short of being morally prepared. Commanders of warships and battle forces at sea were expected simply to switch gears after decade upon decade of conservative thinking aimed precisely at breeding out bold and aggressive traits. Most leaders were not *battle aware* and few officers or sailors had been adequately or even seriously trained to wage war.

₡

Personnel issues aside, the state of the U.S. Fleet's physical plant on the eve of Pearl Harbor was mixed. There were new ships leaving the ways almost weekly, but the bulk of the Fleet was old, not up to the demands of the time. No one in the know doubted that the new ships—many of startling new design—would bring the Fleet to the highest modern level once they were built. The doubt lay in the timing: Could the rapidly expanding shipyards turn out an adequate number of modern warships and auxiliaries soon enough to beat the clock; could the onset of the seemingly inevitable war be delayed long enough to overcome the decades of decline?

The answer turned out to be No.

It is a hard and fast rule of battle that when the fight is joined you go with what you have.

The opening shot at Pearl Harbor was Japan's way of ensuring that the U.S. Pacific Fleet did not have much with which to join the fight. At the end of an era dominated by battleship strategies, the Pearl Harbor strike crippled not only the planned means of America's war-making potential at sea, it crippled the thinking behind the potential.

The smaller U.S. Asiatic Fleet had for decades been based closest to the Japanese and was reasonably expected to be the first to meet the Japanese at the onset of war. For all that, it was filled with ancient ships such as LCdr Butch Parker's destroyer *Parrott*. While *Parrott* was guarding the western Pacific, many of her class were being downgraded and reequipped to serve as minelayers, seaplane tenders, and the like. But the battle fleet farthest from the United States and closest to the potential enemy was the last to receive the newest, most modern destroyers then joining the U.S. Fleet. It claimed no battleships, no aircraft carriers, and only a few relatively modern cruisers.

॰

The onset of the war found the U.S. Navy overextended, spread too thin, as yet too small to undertake all of its wartime missions. There was no remedy for the shortfalls except time. But there was also no time. A line had to be drawn across each of the world's oceans and seas. Delaying actions had to be waged and countermeasures such as hit-and-run strikes by carrier battle groups had to be supported. Many vitally needed surface warships had to be detached from the overworked battle groups so they could be retrofitted with modern weapons and control systems. And tens of thousands of wartime junior officers and junior enlisted men had to be recruited and trained to bring the peacetime complements of active ships to wartime strength as well as to man dozens of new ships just then joining the Fleet.

The men were a mixed bag and the ships were a mixed bag. There was no standard in equipment aboard warships of similar classes. LCdr Butch Parker's *Parrott* was outfitted with four ancient 4.5-inch guns that had to be directed individually by means of optical sights. The main batteries in newer ships were controlled as units by central director stations, but only the very newest ships had gunnery radars aboard to control the gun directors. Very early in the war, all three types of gun direction might be found in a given ad hoc battle force. Though the offensive capabilities derived from the three methods of gunnery control rendered such ships very different, doctrine decreed that all destroyers were interchangeable, and not a few battle-force leaders treated them or were forced to treat them as such—with inevitably bloody consequences. Though the individually directed naval gun was within months of being utterly phased out, it would be a year before all the newer fleet destroyers were equipped with gunnery radars. The newest destroyers were all equipped with the standard dual-purpose 5-inch, .38-caliber (hereafter simply "5-inch") gun for use against both surface and aerial targets, but many older ships could not elevate their main guns sufficiently to take on aircraft.

More than two years after the onset of the German Luftwaffe's antimaritime war against England, the U.S. Navy had not yet standardized its antiaircraft armament. Many ships were equipped with .50-caliber machine guns, and not enough of them, but these were slowly being replaced by Oerlikon 20mm cannon of Swiss design, a thoroughly reliable "light" antiaircraft weapon. A "medium" 1.1-inch gun designed by the U.S. Navy itself had been adopted more than a year before the war, but it was an unmitigated disaster. Arrayed in quadruple mounts, the 1.1-inch guns were extremely complex and extremely prone to failure. The ammunition was crude and prone to detonating in heated gun barrels. As late as mid-1942, the antiaircraft gunnery officer aboard a heavy cruiser, *San Francisco*, refused to conduct live-fire training with the despised 1.1-inch guns because the lives of his gunners were in jeopardy from premature detonations. A new Swedish-designed Bofors 40mm gun was being readied, but it was in such short supply that an entire class of light antiaircraft cruisers launched on the eve of the war was sent to sea with the unreliable 1.1-inchers.

LCdr Butch Parker's *Parrott* again serves as a case in point regarding both equipment and training. While based in Manila Bay in 1940, the ship was retrofitted with four .50-caliber antiaircraft machine guns—a thoroughly inadequate addition a year after the onset of the Luftwaffe's antimaritime blitz in Europe. The four machine guns were mounted on the amidship deck house and crews were assigned from the ship's main battery of 4.5-inch guns. The only training available was some live-fire familiarization, but no targets were provided and no time was set aside for antiaircraft training. Each gun was fitted with a crude ring sight, but the gunners could not be adequately trained to shoot down aircraft because there were no aircraft made available for such training. Indeed, the squadron gunnery officer ignored all the pleas of all the destroyer captains to obtain the cooperation of Army squadrons based near Manila to provide practice targets. The individual captains were given no discretion in the matter; the squadron trained—or did not train—as a unit. Finally, on the day the destroyer squadron left Manila Bay in September 1941, the makeshift antiaircraft machine-gun crews were briefly allowed to fire their weapons as the ships passed Corregidor. On the day the Pacific War erupted, the antiaircraft gunners had yet to fire at actual airborne targets. On the day *Parrott* became embroiled in her first action—January 24, 1942, at Balikpapan—the needed training still had not taken place. (Indeed, several U.S. destroyers went into action at Balikpapan without torpedoes because there were not enough to go around, and several Allied ships were withheld because there had not been enough fuel purchased for them in the fuel-producing region they were charged with defending.)

Finally, the U.S. naval torpedo of the day was an unmitigated disaster. Developed over the years by the Navy, the device simply did not work far more often than it did. Torpedo attacks by destroyer divisions, supported by cruiser-launched torpedoes, constituted a major doctrinal component of U.S. Navy surface-battle tactics. The only reason this lemon lasted as long as it did without being discovered is that the parsimonious tenor of training exercises prevented many from ever being fired before the start of the war. And of the few that were test fired, apparently none was equipped with a live warhead, which would have destroyed the expensive item to which it was attached. In effect, the warhead and the mechanisms that were to detonate it were never tested under "live" conditions—a crucial omission, to put it mildly.

૨૨

The fact is that the start of the Pacific War found the U.S. Navy traversing a cusp.

On the one side were navies and naval leaders operating on the basis of philosophies developed during the days of sail. For them, about all that had changed was the advent of steam engines and the exchange of hulls hewn of wood for those forged of steel. Men reared in the traditions of sail ruled their navies, but their concepts of war could not rule the seas of the early 1940s.

On the near side of the cusp were the men who had somehow acquired and then mastered the vision of modern war fleets, in which electronics, and not steam, provided the basic motive force for changing philosophies. Alas, the age of electronics spawned its two great gifts—voice-radio communications and all-seeing radar—barely in time for the new war. The Imperial Navy embraced voice-radio communications, but it missed out on radar. The U.S. Navy adopted both but had integrated neither into its surface command philosophies by mid-1942. Young men of vision were quick to learn how to use the new technologies, but the old men they served were slow to grasp even the potential of the new electronic marvels, much less the mechanics. Most of the naval surface engagements of 1942 were fought by a U.S. Navy that had the new wonders at its disposal but beyond the grasp of its leaders.

૨૨

If you train for an event in a particular way, you will almost certainly conduct yourself during the actual event in just that way. Today, this is called *behavior modification*, and it is consciously employed in every sort of training, from marksmanship to typing to flying high-performance jets.

In the 1920s and 1930s, the U.S. Navy imbued its officers

with the need to avoid training in ways that might result in accidental damage to their ships. As a result, virtually every officer in command of a U.S. Navy surface warship in early and mid-1942 was emotionally incapable of literally "closing with the enemy." On the night of August 8, 1942, in which three American heavy cruisers were sunk off Savo Island by direct gunfire, all three of their captains ordered their own guns silenced because, in the words of one, "We might be acting hasty and firing at our own ships." Decades of behavior modification won out over what those men actually saw with their own eyes. (Conversely, throughout the 1930s, the Imperial Navy took its lumps and its losses in realistic training exercises.)

The grand model of the U.S. Navy's interwar training was the Battle of Jutland, one of two major night battles in which modern navies had engaged in the previous 150 years. Though the German Grand Fleet was vastly outnumbered and thus was charged with the loss at Jutland, it had in fact out-fought the British fleet. However, losers are ignored and winners are copied. The U.S. Navy's officers of the early 1940s were still being trained specifically to win a victory at Jutland, in which a British battle *column* engaged a German battle *column*. Among the many things the British and their American emulators overlooked was the way the Germans employed the radio as a means for exchanging information and passing tactical orders. The British, who had failed to recognize the radio's potential, made poor use of the new technology in World War I. Between the wars, the U.S. Navy failed to make adequate use of the radio, one oversight among many that was to have dire consequences in its 1942 battles.

The U.S. Navy studied Jutland and came up with the notion that naval warfare would be capped by a major, decisive fleet engagement. Interestingly, so did the Japanese.

Since Jutland had been fought by columns of ships, the U.S. Navy practiced for war with columns of ships. Actually, this formation ideally suited the prime requirement that U.S. Navy warships avoid collisions with other U.S. navy warships. Columns of ships playing "follow the leader" are easier to control than other types of formations, and the potential for accidents is low. Thus, the "battle" exercises, particularly those conducted at night, were little more than cruising or night-cruising exercises. Safety, not innovation or even education, was paramount. Moreover, the only formation in which American commanders felt comfortable—and to which they invariably resorted—was the single battle column, one ship 500 to 1,000 yards behind the other.

Though Morse radios were available, changes in course during daytime exercises were signaled by means of signal flags. At night, the course changes were signaled by means of a blinker tube, a trigger-controlled flashlight that could be aimed and whose light was hooded so it could be narrowly focused, thus concealing both the signal and the position of the ship sending the signal. Brief experiments to supplement the transmission of orders by flag hoist or blinker tube with Morse radio messages came to nothing.

The TBS (Talk Between Ships) voice radio was introduced into the U.S. Fleet from 1940 onward. It opened the possibility of controlling groups of ships during both day and night operations. Unfortunately, several collisions during exercises in which the TBS was employed as a primary control device sent the great minds of the era scuttling for cover. The best that can be said is that the experiments were inconclusive and the ongoing use of voice radio was uneven.

The TBS radio on each ship was usually located on the bridge, where it could be employed directly by the captain or unit commander. Different fleet units worked up different codes for transmitting essential tactical signals relating to course, speed, distance, bearing, and so forth. Some fleet units came up with simple, direct signals requiring no ciphering or deciphering, but in the South Pacific in mid-1942, the system required someone to pore over a code book in a lighted area. Not only was the method time-consuming— it required hard work and careful attention to detail at both ends— it was also prone to errors in ciphering, transmission, and deciphering.

᪶

Radio was a potentially important means for exchanging information and controlling groups of ships, but it was as dependent upon the vantage point of the commander as were other signaling systems. Good radar of all types appeared to be the principal means for permitting tactically innovative day and night battles to be fought with formations other than the single battle column. Mostly, radar opened enormous new vistas in the arena of night actions.

The Japanese had no radar, but they had acquired other means for fighting at night, and indeed preferred doing so. The U.S. Navy wanted no part of night battles if they could be avoided, but their radar—even the earliest, crudest models—did provide the means for undertaking such engagements and, indeed, for winning them. However, very few American officers senior enough to command groups of ships in battle realized radar's potential, and virtually no effort was expended thinking about ways to identify and use all the wonderful and hitherto unavailable information.

Traditionally, tactical control of a battle force was undertaken by the officer in tactical command. He was stationed with his staff on his flagship's bridge, from which he was afforded as good an all-around view as was practical, given the construction of the ship.

Similarly, control of an individual ship was from an open bridge. In the U.S. Navy between the wars, the captain's ability to see from his bridge was informally supplemented by reports from signalmen, the various officers who worked on the bridge, and gun crews. Not until larger wartime crews were permitted by the huge infusion of manpower beginning in 1940 were formal lookout systems manned aboard U.S. Navy warships. However, most of the lookouts spent most of their training time learning to locate and identify incoming airplanes. Little time was spent training the new men to locate and identify other warships, and *no* formal prewar training time was devoted to developing any such skills at night, except as individual commanders demanded. Good binoculars, in sufficient numbers, were also lacking well into the first year of the Pacific War.

As reports of enemy ships and units beyond the commander's vision arrived from aircraft, submarines, or other surface ships and units, relative positions were manually plotted on charts located on the bridge or within a nearby compartment. The system was a bit tedious and prone to error if continuous information was not available. Even where events were occurring much closer in, within sight of the commander, the system of manually plotting locations on paper charts usually ran somewhat behind real time.

The advent of reliable surface-search radars changed everything, but it took place after the opening of hostilities, and it simply overwhelmed the imaginations of most of the U.S. Navy's senior operational commanders. Indeed, radar's full range of gifts were as yet largely unperceived by its most enthusiastic proponents.

SG radar, the most modern type of the surface-search radars, only began reaching the active fleets in very limited numbers in mid-1942. The SG model's potential was simply mind-boggling. The feature that made the SG model such an important technological leap forward was its Plan Position Indicator (PPI) display.

On all the previous radar models in the world, the display had appeared on a so-called A Scope, which indicated targets as V-shaped interruptions along a horizontal line near the bottom of a cathode-ray tube. On the right side of the A Scope was a low, steady level of interference known as *grass*, which was interrupted only when an echo from the target was received. This "return echo" was shown as a *pip* above the height of the grass. The range to the target was estimated as a measure of time, which was converted to distance by means of a scale located below the scope. The target pip appeared only when the antenna was pointed right at the target and the target bearing was read from a separate indicator matching the direction in which the antenna was pointed. Precisely locating a target was a tedious process prone to error.

The PPI scope presents a 360-degree display as a polar plot, on which the source of the outgoing radar pulse—which is to say, one's own ship—appears at the center of the display. (The modern conception of a radar display is a PPI scope.) Special phosphors embedded in the display screen hold the image of a target pip or pips for several seconds after the solid line representing the outgoing echo passed by. The result is a complete picture of return echoes throughout the radar antenna's entire 360-degree field of view. Bearing to the target can be seen right on the screen, and the range to the target can be estimated easily and swiftly from the distance of the target pip to the center of the screen, or it can be precisely measured by means of a cursor that the operator can match up with any pip on the screen.

The PPI scope—and the reliable radar system of which it was a part—was a quantum leap forward, a virtually immeasurable increase in the amount and nature of comprehensibility of information available. Unfortunately, during the SG radar's earliest deployments in mid-1942, neither the designers nor the operators quite realized its full potential. Everyone who was directly involved in the use of SG radar *sensed* that there was much new and better information to be gained from the equipment, but none of them was quite sure what this "better information" was, nor how to exploit it. Because of this early ignorance—in which the human mind had to expand to meet the potential of science—senior officers were unable to tell the SG operators what to look for and what to report beyond the mere recitation of bearings and distances. However, even that slim information would have been of inestimable value, particularly at night, if the senior commanders had only used it.

The main problem was the very environment in which the PPI scope had to be deployed. Since the process was continuous and ongoing, the PPI scope and the operators and communicators who worked with it had to be placed in a lighted compartment designed to totally seal in light emissions. Typically, at night, information was passed from the radar compartment to the darkened bridge, but the more targets the radar located the more difficult it became for the commander to keep things straight in his head. However, if the commander entered the plotting station to look at the PPI scope himself, he would lose his night vision and would not be able to see if he returned to the darkened bridge. So commanders reared under the old traditions not only had to find it in their hearts to use the new system, they had to allow themselves to become totally dependent upon younger, less experienced men for vital information and interpretations.

Alas, the advent of the SG radar and the PPI scope were so late and so slow in coming that no U.S. Navy tactical commander had direct access to the systems throughout late 1942. The arguments for and potential advantages of the system were rendered moot by its unavailability.

On the other hand, however, good fire-control and fire-direction radars in nearly sufficient numbers were reaching the Pacific Fleet by mid-1942. All of the newer warships were equipped with modern models, many older warships were retrofitted with such systems when they reached ports equipped to undertake installations, and most other fleet-type surface warships were under orders to acquire such sets as soon as possible. All gunnery, day or night, was enhanced by any radar guidance systems, old or new, and no commander in his right mind overlooked that singular advantage he thus gained over his adversaries.

彅

Despite the advent of reliable voice radios, good gunnery radars, and a few good surface-search radar sets, it must be said that, in the end, the U.S. Navy lost its race against time. Its leading lights had seen what needed to be done by 1939, and they had begun putting their combined vision into action. Thousands of officers and sailors had emerged from the pipeline by December 7, 1941, and many thousands more were in the pipeline, with hundreds of thousands to follow. New ships of the best design of the age—indeed, of the dawning new age—were being constructed or launched. New and better weapons were being developed, and proven weapons of foreign design were being built under license. But the new war erupted a full year before all the effort could possibly come together. So, in hallowed if uneasy tradition, the U.S. Navy ventured forth to battle pretty much as it always had: simply with what it had on hand. The initial results were humiliating for the institution and mortal for a large number of the participants. Irreplaceable men and ships were lost at a time when no losses were affordable.

All that was gained in the terrible first half year of the Pacific naval war was a little time and a little needed experience. If the U.S. Navy could hold out long enough, the massive influx of new ships and modern technological developments would certainly overwhelm the Japanese. But if too many ships were lost, if too many men died, if morale was defeated, then the U.S. Navy stood to lose its share of the Pacific War. And if that happened, the war itself would be lost.

PART II

Convoy

3

The first convoy sailed from Nouméa on November 8, 1942, and the second convoy left Espiritu Santo on November 9.

All the U.S. Navy ships—transports and cargomen escorted by cruisers and destroyers—were bound for Guadalcanal, where American ground forces awaited sorely needed supplies and reinforcements. All the news available to U.S. Navy intelligence analysts throughout the Pacific Fleet indicated that powerful Japanese surface forces were being gathered to escort a very large Japanese transport flotilla to Guadalcanal within the week. The same information indicated that Japanese battleships, cruisers, destroyers, and land-based air groups—and possibly several Japanese aircraft carriers—were being readied to help sweep American warships and warplanes from the Guadalcanal area, and that Japanese infantry regiments, including oncoming reinforcements, were being poised to drive Guadalcanal's American defenders into the sea.

There had not been one day associated with the first Allied offensive in the Pacific that could not be considered grim. Every tenuous gain made by hard-pressed U.S. forces at Guadalcanal had been at least matched by a Japanese countermove. That the American Guadalcanal bastion had held as long as three months was considered a miracle by many. Each move by either side had invariably raised the ante. Local actions of no real consequence to global strategies had given way to increasingly larger actions that invariably had a more profound impact upon the will and ability of both sides to maintain the struggle.

Now, in the second week of November 1942, the ultimate showdown—the decisive confrontation—seemed about to erupt.

卍

On the immediate agenda of both sides was the delivery of fresh infantry reinforcements and supplies to their forces ashore on Guadalcanal. The American commanders hoped to get the job done with minimum loss before the potential confrontation erupted; they hoped to unload their navy's transports and cargomen and get clear of Guadalcanal before the Japanese even sailed. Likewise, the Japanese admiral commanding his nation's transport convoy hoped to avoid a direct confrontation. However, his hopes were rooted in the possibility that powerful Japanese surface battle forces would have scoured the Guadalcanal area of American warships and warplanes before he sailed.

The Japanese were prepared for a massive battle; they had thoroughly planned every detail. The Americans were not ready for such a fight. The Japanese were the instigators; they wanted a showdown and a decision. The Americans were obliged to react to Japanese moves and potential moves; they desired no showdowns, no decisions just yet. Withal, few knowledgeable observers on either side could doubt that the situation was ripe for a decisive confrontation. The blow-and-counterblow pattern of the first three months at Guadalcanal could not be sustained by either side. That by the second week of November the Japanese were ready for a decision and the Americans were not was a factor of all that had gone before.

卍

The first Allied offensive in the Pacific had been initiated by desperation. The seizure of the fleet anchorage at Tulagi and a nearly completed Japanese airstrip on nearby Guadalcanal had been aimed at nothing more than forestalling a Japanese drive into the New Hebrides, New Caledonia, Fiji, and Samoa. Until August 7, 1942, when the U.S. 1st Marine Division had been thrust into battle at Guadalcanal and Tulagi, the Japanese had had their way in the Pacific. Their will had been challenged repeatedly in the early months of the war—most particularly in the Philippines and the Dutch East Indies—but they had invariably emerged as victors, each time whittling down the odds more in their favor. America and her British, Commonwealth, and Dutch allies stood defeated on land, at sea, and in the air.

The first setback to the Japanese program of expansion had taken place in the Coral Sea, off New Guinea, in early May 1942. Then, U.S. aircraft carriers had first struck a swift, sudden blow against Japanese surface forces arriving to seize Tulagi and had next confronted a force of Japanese carriers escorting a major transport fleet bound for the Australian base at Port Moresby, New Guinea. Though the Japanese suffered losses—including one light carrier— and were turned back from Port Moresby, they indeed secured Tulagi and sank one of America's six fleet aircraft carriers.

The second setback came a month later, in early June, at Midway. There, a major Japanese invasion force was turned back solely by American land- and carrier-based warplanes. Here again, the U.S. Fleet lost one of its precious carriers. And here, Japan's Combined Fleet—the Imperial Navy's operational arm—lost four fleet carriers. For the first time in the Pacific War, an Allied battle force won a clear, unambiguous victory.

For all the importance of Midway, the Japanese were unwilling to admit to more than a tactical defeat. Indeed, though in fact they lost the ability to conduct strategically meaningful offensive operations far out in the Pacific, they did not then perceive the enormity of their strategic defeat. The rigorous program of expansion through violent means would continue following a brief but necessary period of consolidation at the leading edge of the newly conquered territories.

The airfield that was the target of the U.S. invasion of Guadalcanal on August 7 was a product of the first real consolidation attempted by the Japanese in the first eight months of the Pacific War. Built at the operational extremity of fighters based around Japan's main regional base at Rabaul, the new Guadalcanal airfield was to support continued advances into the Santa Cruz and New Hebrides groups, where new airfields were to be built to support yet farther advances. The U.S. invasion was mounted only one week before the Guadalcanal airfield was to receive its first contingent of Japanese land-based bombers and fighters. Likewise, the Marines seized neighboring Tulagi on the eve of its becoming an operational advance base for warships bound for points east and southeast.

The U.S. offensive immediately turned into a shambles, thus pointing up the shallow strategic depth of the sorely pressed U.S. Fleet. On the second day—by which time the Marines had seized all their immediate objectives on land—the three fleet aircraft carriers committed to support the invasion were precipitously withdrawn some days ahead of schedule. This obliged the transport commander to announce that his surface ships would have to leave the next morning, though few of them had by then fully discharged their cargoes of ammunition, food, or vehicles.

That night—after the carriers departed—the local Japanese fleet commander mounted a surprise attack against the American surface fleet off Guadalcanal. Though technically outnumbered, the Japanese achieved a stunning victory through sheer surprise, audacity, and luck. Four first-line Allied heavy cruisers were sunk and several other U.S. warships were damaged against no Japanese losses and only minor damage inflicted upon the Japanese ships. The Battle of Savo Island was a stunning, clear-cut Japanese victory of immense strategic importance.

The lackluster performance of individual American cruiser captains was exacerbated by a profound by-product of their immersion in the careerist principles of their decades in the Navy. Even when fired on by Japanese cruisers, each American cruiser skipper checked his ship's fire in the belief that the opposing warships *might* be friendly. Not one of the American cruiser skippers was capable of shooting first and asking questions later. Fully eight months into a devastating global war, each of the American cruiser captains lacked "battle awareness." Taken together against the backdrop of the worst defeat ever administered to the U.S. Navy, the strikingly similar individual performances of the three American captains pointed up the crippling leadership problem that had been silently building in the Navy's middle-management strata for decades. Most striking is the fact that each of the American captains was considered a "good man" by his superiors. (If not, he would not have been out there commanding a capital warship covering a breathtakingly risky amphibious landing.) There was nothing in each captain's record to indicate that his vital aggressive instincts had been impaired by the lessons of his peacetime service. The potential ramifications of this discovery, once it was made, sent a shock wave through the Navy's highest command echelons. But that was later. The immediate impact of Savo was at least as sobering and initially more crippling.

The loss of immediate access to needed munitions, supplies, and vehicles would in itself have had a sobering effect upon the conduct of operations ashore at Guadalcanal and Tulagi. However, the clear defeat of the fleet on the eve of its precipitous departure thoroughly demoralized all U.S. and Allied forces throughout the vast South Pacific Area and, indeed, throughout the Pacific. The South Pacific offensive—sorely needed by a demoralized nation—was instantly transformed into a defensive nightmare. The nascent offensive spirit embodied in the bold step forward to Guadalcanal and Tulagi was strangled at the outset. Instantly, the mindset of defeat was rekindled within the headquarters responsible for the conduct of the war in the South Pacific.

Simply stated, the American regional commander, VAdm Robert Ghormley, lost his offensive vision. His outlook was overly conservative, and he let it be known by his actions that he was unwilling to commit scarce and dwindling naval assets to keep the Marines at Guadalcanal and Tulagi resupplied. The only Allied infantry forces available to reinforce the Guadalcanal and Tulagi garrisons were committed to holding far-flung island bastions in the rear. When Ghormley's subordinates suggested that these garrisons be reduced so troops could be sent to the forward area, Ghormley balked. He was certain that the Japanese would retake Guadalcanal and Tulagi, in which case, he thought, the rear garrisons would need every man they could muster if they were to stand against a renewed Japanese advance. Ghormley's thinking was utterly self-defeating, and it stood an excellent chance of becoming self-fulfilling.

In the eastern Solomons, Rabaul-based Japanese bombers, fighters, and surface warships—even surfaced Japanese submarines—launched daily raids against the all but defenseless Marine bastions at Tulagi and around Guadalcanal's Lunga Point, site of the former Japanese airfield. They did so with utter impunity. In their way, the incessant, unanswerable pinpricks were the most humiliating and demoralizing aspects of the funk that overcame the local American commands in the wake of Savo. Nevertheless, the captured airfield was completed by Marine engineers within two weeks of the invasion—a startling achievement in view of how much heavy engineering equipment had remained aboard the departing transports. The first two squadrons of Marine warplanes, one each of fighters and dive-bombers, arrived on August 19. On August 20, for the first time since the American carriers departed on August 8, U.S. fighters from newly named Henderson Field rose to challenge the by-then-daily Japanese noon bomber strike.

On August 21, the advance echelon of a newly landed Imperial Army infantry force attacked a portion of the Marines' Lunga Perimeter, the battle line guarding Henderson Field. There, for the first time in the war, Japanese infantry was soundly defeated by American infantry. On August 24, during the Battle of the Eastern Solomons, Japanese carrier and surface battle forces escorting infantry-laden transports toward Guadalcanal were turned back by an American carrier fleet. (The aggressive American carrier-based air groups were thus three for three.) The Japanese lost one light carrier sunk in the action, and one U.S. carrier was moderately damaged. The next day, August 25, the Japanese transport force was attacked by Marine and Navy dive-bombers based at Henderson Field. It was turned back after suffering heavy losses.

The tide seemed to be turning, but that early view proved illusory. Though Henderson Field was reinforced by one fighter squadron and one dive-bomber squadron within the week, the area commander, Ghormley, remained unwilling to risk major fleet units or ground forces to maintain adequately or to reinforce the Guadalcanal garrison. Indeed, Ghormley was steadfast in his unwillingness to commit surface warships to stop the tide of incoming Japanese infantry reinforcements. While Japanese warships pounded Henderson Field almost nightly—while U.S. Navy and U.S. Marine dive-bombers were virtually helpless—a fresh Imperial Army infantry brigade, along with other units, was landed at Guadalcanal in early September. Daily, fresh Japanese air groups flew down from Rabaul to maintain the pressure on Henderson Field. Daylight bombing raids and nightly naval bombardments prevented the Marines arrayed around Lunga Point from making serious headway on the ground or in the air. And the U.S. Navy barely appeared. Morale suffered right along with operational effectiveness.

On those rare occasions when U.S. warships arrived off Guadalcanal—usually there were one or two antiquated destroyers escorting one or two cargomen—the little sunshine afforded the grim defenders usually resulted in tragedy. By ones and twos, precious destroyers were sunk in brief, sharp night engagements, either by Japanese surface forces or lurking submarines. That such stingy offerings proved sacrificial only strengthened Admiral Ghormley's attitude of unwillingness.

The Japanese infantry brigade that was marshaled east of the Lunga Perimeter in early September was resoundingly defeated by Marines on the ground just south of Henderson Field in two nights of hellish combat on September 12 and 13. The Japanese instantly responded by postponing their long-planned New Guinea offensive and transferring an entire crack infantry division to the task of retaking Guadalcanal.

For the remainder of September and through the first half of October, the Japanese moved their fresh infantry division to Guadalcanal aboard an endless stream of destroyers rigged out as fast troop transports. Such runs were made almost nightly on what Americans came to call the Tokyo Express. In addition to landing troops, the destroyer-transports and their escorts pounded Henderson Field with continued nightly shellings that killed pilots, aircrews, ground crews, and Marine infantrymen; they destroyed or damaged precious airplanes; they invariable damaged Henderson Field and a newly leveled grass strip known as Fighter-1; and they played havoc with tenuous morale.

Despite all the drawbacks, the Marines continued to mount highly conservative offensive sweeps. A fresh Marine regiment was landed during the third week of September, and fresh fighter and dive-bomber squadrons—some Marine units and some Navy squadrons off carriers damaged or destroyed by Japanese submarines—always seemed to arrive in the nick of time. The balance was tenuous and the stakes seemed to grow inexorably. Each side seemed to be locked into a battle of wills that had to be fought with grudgingly supplied men and materiel.

By mid-October, the Japanese were looking for a strategic victory; the Americans simply wanted to hang on because there really was no way to back out. As a result, the two sides had cobbled together strangely complimentary agendas and objectives. To the Japanese admiral who really controlled the regional agenda, Guadalcanal became a place where his forces could pin down their American counterparts and defeat them in detail. While ostensibly an operation built around delivering ground reinforcements to the battle area, the Eastern Solomons carrier battle on August 24 had in fact been an effort to draw out and defeat the American carrier fleet. The Marines trapped on Guadalcanal were viewed by the Japanese as staked bait. So long as they—or the Japanese infantry who might replace them as landlords of Henderson Field—were on the board, the U.S. Fleet might eventually sally in strength. If that happened, the Imperial Navy's Combined Fleet would be on hand to fight the desired decisive grand fleet action of the Pacific War.

The Americans were in no mood—and in no shape—for the decisive naval confrontation. Theirs was a waiting game. In time, if outright defeat could be avoided, American shipyards would turn out enough carriers, battleships, cruisers, and destroyers to crush the Combined Fleet. In time, American factories would build enough bombers to blot out the sun. In time, American training camps would turn out enough troops to roll over Japan's ill-gotten empire.

But that was in the future. For the remainder of 1942, at least, and probably for most of 1943, the American forces in the war zone would be able to do little more than keep the Japanese at bay, if that. Admiral Ghormley did not want to undertake his part in the

Japanese master plan. If he had a glimmer of desire to fight the decisive battle, he didn't have the means to do so.

On the night of October 12, an American surface battle force charged with escorting the first U.S. Army infantry regiment to appear at Guadalcanal confronted a Japanese battle force charged with similar responsibilities. That night, off Cape Esperance, Guadalcanal's western tip, a mixed force of American cruisers and destroyers under RAdm Norman Scott soundly defeated the Japanese battle force. It was the first time in the Pacific War that American surface warships emerged as victors from a fight with Japanese surface warships. The Battle of Cape Esperance was a tonic.

Cape Esperance also proved that at least one U.S. Navy surface force had achieved battle awareness. Norman Scott's winning formula was simply unremitting training. For weeks before the battle, he had trained his battle force as those officers and sailors had never been trained before.

The cauldron was immediately brought back to a rolling boil. Beginning the morning of October 13, Japanese air and surface forces mercilessly pounded the American Lunga Perimeter around the clock. A night bombardment by battleships firing special anti-personnel rounds all but shattered the newly bolstered American fighting spirit. Losses in men, airplanes, and materiel were staggering. At the height of the incessant bombardment, Japanese transports arrived and went to work unloading fresh infantrymen, artillery pieces, tanks, and supplies around Cape Esperance. Baled-together American bombers—anything that could fly—made desperate attacks upon the unloading transports, but they barely stemmed the flow. At one point, defense of Henderson Field had to be placed in the hands of a carrier-based air group in order to give the ground crew ashore respite to build up a force of bombers from the scrap of dozens of wrecked machines. So much aviation gasoline was burned off by direct hits that there was barely enough to fuel the Marine, Navy, and Army fighters based at Henderson Field's relatively unscathed satellite fighter strip, Fighter-1.

With the help of the carrier-based air group and new units rushed forward from rear bases, the Americans trapped at Guadalcanal slowly turned the tide in a matter of days. The Japanese lost so many bombers and fighters as they clawed to the brink of victory that they were unable to continue. As American air strength slowly rose, Japanese air strength perceptibly ebbed. In the end, both sides disengaged in exhaustion.

If the Japanese were unable to gain a victory over the so-called Cactus Air Force—a sobriquet coined from Guadalcanal's American code name—they were able to land thousands of fresh troops, guns, and supplies. In the end, they outnumbered the American defenders on the ground, but not by much.

An absolutely decisive event occurred in the midst of the mid-October slugging match. Admiral Ghormley was replaced as South Pacific Area commander by VAdm William Halsey. It was as if a light went on. Certainly, a ray of hope shined through the pall of defeat that was Ghormley's chief legacy. Halsey cleaned house with fervor, and he and his new staff worked tirelessly to turn the prevailing attitude of defeat into a mind-set for victory. But events at the front overtook the well-intentioned changes before they could quite take hold.

The anticipated massive Japanese ground offensive began on October 23 with a botched, unsynchronized attack upon the western flank of the newly expanded Lunga Perimeter. The main ground assault went off two nights later—two nights late. Two Japanese infantry regiments were soundly defeated by two inferior Marine and U.S. Army infantry battalions in two nights of wild, desperate fighting on a ridge just south of Henderson Field.

Once again using the Imperial Army units on Guadalcanal as foils, the Combined Fleet launched another attempt to defeat the U.S. carriers on the high seas. Throughout October 26, two American carriers traded blows with four Japanese carriers. In the end, one of the American carriers was lost, the other was moderately damaged, and two Japanese carriers were moderately damaged. While technically a Japanese victory, the Battle of the Santa Cruz Islands cost Japan the last of her best carrier pilots and aircrew—a disastrous process that had begun at Midway. The cost was so great, in fact, that Japanese carriers were never again called upon to conduct bold, meaningful offensive operations.

However, the Imperial Navy's ardor for the decisive surface battle was not dampened by Santa Cruz. Before the ashes of the

October defeats had quite cooled, the Combined Fleet planners were putting the finishing touches on their master plan for the ultimate surface-fleet confrontation off Guadalcanal. Once again, the dispatch of fat transports laden with fresh Imperial Army infantrymen was the bait. If the Americans came to fight, the planners reasoned, they would be defeated. If the Americans avoided a fight, the reasoning continued, the Imperial Army would have been given the means to achieve their victory on land, to recapture Henderson Field.

Their recent land victories restored the vigor of the institutionally combative Marines on Guadalcanal. Only a week after the great October defensive battles, in the first serious offensive operations since the August 7 landings, American battalions slowly pushed Imperial Army units from the immediate vicinity of the burgeoning Henderson Field air-base complex.

The new spirit that had begun to suffuse the American high command in the region had not quite fully taken hold, but Admiral Halsey was quick to recognize the opportunities and the risks arising from the October Japanese defeats. The first thing he did was shuffle his garrison forces in the rear in order to obtain a fresh, reinforced U.S. Army infantry regiment for dispatch to Guadalcanal. A fresh Marine regiment was also slated for transfer to Guadalcanal from Samoa, and one of its battalions was shipped post haste.

Halsey's reasoning with respect to rear-area combat garrisons was simple. Its sharp contrast to Admiral Ghormley's reasoning points up the chief differences between the two men. Ghormley had been unwilling to weaken his rear garrisons, some of which were quite strong, because he felt they would face battle as soon as the Marines at Guadalcanal had been defeated. Halsey felt that all available combat troops should be rushed to Guadalcanal precisely to make that defeat unlikely.

As to the impending naval confrontation, Halsey's best showing of surface warships could not possibly outnumber the Combined Fleet's best showing. Of the six fleet carriers America had had on December 7, 1941, four had been sunk and both of the survivors were undergoing repairs for battle damage. Only two modern "fast" battleships were available, and about a dozen heavy and light cruisers. Halsey had numerous destroyers, many of them quite modern. The Japanese certainly had at least two fleet carriers at their disposal. They had at least four battleships at the ready, and others within easy reach. They far outnumbered Halsey's forces in heavy and light cruisers, and they had many more modern destroyers than Halsey had. So, though they had been badly defeated in October, the Japanese were in a position to deal the cards in November.

This they chose to do.

4

The timing of the arrival of three groups of U.S. Navy transports and cargomen at Guadalcanal during early November 1942 was in no way providential. U.S. Navy intelligence analysts had been eavesdropping on Japan's most sensitive military radio transmissions since early in the Pacific War, and the current traffic emanating from major Japanese commands ashore and at sea pointed directly to the certainty of yet another major attempt by the Japanese to retake Guadalcanal's American-held Lunga Perimeter and its vital airfield complex. Although all the ground units involved in the transfer had already been earmarked for shipment to Guadalcanal, the hard news concerning Japanese intentions had determined the exact timing. The objective of the move was for the American transports and cargomen to land the reinforcements and supplies and sail safely from the area before a similar, massively supported Japanese reinforcement and resupply effort got underway from Japanese bases in proximity to Guadalcanal.

The Americans sailed in three separate convoys. The first, carrying the fresh U.S. 2nd Marine Raider Battalion and one battalion of the independent 147th Infantry Regiment (Ohio State National Guard) arrived with attached artillery units at Aola Bay, about 40 miles east of Lunga, on November 4. Once the landing force was landed, the Navy began moving a fresh Seabee battalion ashore to carve out a new airbase complex at the bay. (It was immediately determined that the ground around the Aola plantation was too marshy to support the proposed airfield and the bulk of the force eventually decamped westward to Koli Point, about half the distance back to Lunga.) The significance of the establishment of a new airbase and its defensive perimeter was threefold: The American high command was confident enough to route valuable resources—particularly combat troops—away from the focal point at Lunga; the American long-range planners were finally able to see forward to the day when the Henderson Field complex at Lunga could itself support the eventual drive up the Solomons toward the main Japanese base at Rabaul; and the ongoing doubt regarding the survivability of the Lunga Perimeter in the face of incessant Japanese assaults would be requited by the establishment of the back-up perimeter east of Lunga, which is to say farther away from the Japanese, who were mostly west of Lunga.

As soon as the main Aola Bay landing had been completed, three Navy transports escorted by a heavy cruiser and four destroyers departed for Espiritu Santo, the nearest safe U.S.-controlled harbor. Many of the ships just back from Aola Bay would be dispatched back to Guadalcanal within days. Two destroyer-transports—which were capable of lending limited naval gunfire support to the landing force—were temporarily retained at Aola Bay.

On November 8, Task Force 67 was organized at Noumea, the Allied regional main base. Its purpose was to transport two battalions and the headquarters of the U.S. Army's 182nd Infantry Regiment to Lunga along with a battalion of Marine infantry replacements and a naval ground force. Four veteran transports were selected for the troop lift and one cruiser and three destroyers were selected to screen them. The task force fell under the direct command of RAdm Richmond Kelly Turner, the hard-driving chief of the South Pacific Amphibious Force. While it was by no means unusual for Admiral Turner to take a personal role in overseeing the deployment of a key landing force, the importance of this particular mission was signified by its being his first direct command at sea in over two months. Task Force 67 departed Noumea at 1500, November 8.

At the same time Task Force 67 was departing from Noumea, Task Group 62.4 was preparing to leave Espiritu Santo, the closest secure harbor and base to Guadalcanal. The task group comprised three so-called attack cargomen embarking the 1st Marine Aviation Engineer Battalion, an assortment of Marine infantry and aviation replacements, ground-support personnel from the 1st Marine Aircraft Wing, and a variety of ammunition, fuel, and foodstuffs. This reinforcement group was directly screened by a light antiaircraft cruiser and four fleet destroyers commanded by RAdm Norman Scott, who had beaten a Japanese naval surface force at Cape Esperance on the night of October 12. Scott's group left Espiritu Santo at 0830, November 9.

Both reinforcement groups were given out-of-the-way tracks north of San Cristobal Island. Thus, because Scott's force started from closer in, it was expected to arrive off Lunga on November 11, a day ahead of Turner's force from Noumea.

A third U.S. naval force departed from Espiritu Santo on November 10, at 0500. This was Task Group 67.4, commanded by RAdm Daniel Callaghan. He had served as the South Pacific chief of staff until his boss, VAdm Robert Ghormley, had been relieved by VAdm Bill Halsey in October. Callaghan's force consisted of two heavy cruisers, two light cruisers, and six fleet destroyers. Its job, once it reached Guadalcanal, was to screen the unloading operation off Lunga and, eventually, challenge the Japanese surface force that intelligence indicated would be dispatched to massively bombard Henderson Field on the night of November 12.

Finally, a fourth U.S. naval force was to be in position to deflect the Japanese bombardment effort. This force was built around fleet carrier *Enterprise* and her air group of fighters, dive-bombers, and torpedo bombers. The carrier had been badly damaged during the carrier battle off the Santa Cruz Islands in late October and she was laid up at Noumea for repairs. Though the work was far from finished—among many other problems, one of her three aircraft elevators was inoperable—*Enterprise*'s potential punch was considered so vital that she was being readied to go to sea at the last minute, thus providing repair crews with every possible moment in which to advance her readiness. When the last remotely operational fleet carrier in the U.S. Pacific Fleet sailed, she would be escorted by a very large surface force, including two new fast battleships.

The commitment of virtually every fleet surface asset—and the only fleet carrier left in the Pacific Fleet inventory—points up the resolve of the new U.S. commander in the South Pacific. While the U.S. infantry forces ashore had been turning in one impressive victory after another, and though the Lunga Perimeter was more capable than ever before of defending itself against a massive air, land, and naval assault, Admiral Halsey was determined to nip the Japanese plan in the bud. He intended to challenge their warships before Henderson Field could be bombarded, and he intended to destroy their reinforcements at sea before they could be landed. Numerous new air squadrons were on the move toward Henderson Field, thus telegraphing Halsey's intention to stop Japanese aerial bombardments along with naval and land assaults. Of course, Halsey could not have put his resolve into action if agencies far from the scene had not provided him with the warships, warplanes, and soldiers and Marines with which to stand against the Japanese. But it is a hallmark of Halsey's early tenure that he placed his fighting assets in proximity to the enemy—within range of the sound of the guns, in harm's way.

5

The Japanese had other plans.

There was virtually no aspect of the new American resolve or its many manifestations that could have been seriously anticipated by the Japanese. They had always called the shots at Guadalcanal, and their contemplated November "final" offensive was fully in keeping with the pattern long established during the arduous seesaw effort.

The "final" offensive was just that in Japanese eyes. This stance was taken not only because they had been frustrated in every one of their progressively larger, more grandiose efforts to destroy the American Lunga garrison and retake the air-base complex, but because the fragile operational coalition between the Imperial Army and Imperial Navy commands overseeing the Guadalcanal effort was on the verge of self-destructing.

The Japanese Pacific War was in reality two separate efforts by the two rival services. At times, the services' separate agendas merged. If this happened, combined operations might be cobbled together. But the two services invariably maintained distinctly independent agendas overseen by distinctly separate headquarters. Coordination and cooperation, where it took place at all, was the result of temporary personal accommodations between commanders or members of their staffs. The Imperial Army and Imperial Navy had been bitter political rivals for too many years to have established anything remotely like the hallmark unity of command achieved by the U.S. military services in the Pacific Theater. (The U.S. effort was not without its interservice bloodletting, to be sure, but the services were all oriented in the same direction and were institutionally predisposed toward cooperation.)

For Japan's part, the Guadalcanal campaign through late October had been run as an uneasy alliance driven by the mutual needs of the two services. The incursion through the Solomon Islands from Rabaul had been an effort by the Imperial Navy all the way. When light naval landing forces had been challenged and overwhelmed by the U.S. 1st Marine Division in early August, the Navy had been unable to mount a meaningful counterthrust by land forces.

Though surprised and off balance, the Imperial Navy air and surface units then staging into Rabaul for eventual deployment to the not-quite-ready new bases at Tulagi and Guadalcanal had hit back with what they had on hand. The aerial counterthrust launched from Rabaul had been worrisome to the American fleet commander, VAdm Frank Jack Fletcher, but that effort by the shocked Japanese temporarily ran out of steam within two days. The counterthrust by a Rabaul-based naval surface battle force had destroyed four Allied heavy cruisers and, more important, the will of the local American naval leaders. However, the Imperial Navy units at Rabaul had been unable to follow up on that success and soon had to turn to the Imperial Army for help.

The Army had answered the call, but its initial effort was weak, based as it was on faulty and optimistic Navy intelligence analyses. After the weak effort had been disastrously defeated, a larger but still inadequate effort had been mounted by an Imperial Army independent brigade supported by light naval forces based at Rabaul. Though it provided a greater challenge to the survival skills of the isolated Marine division at Lunga, the infantry brigade was also soundly defeated, after which it became painfully obvious to the senior Imperial Army commander in the region, LtGen Harukichi Hyakutake, that he would have to devote the bulk of his attention to pulling the Imperial Navy's chestnuts from the fire at Guadalcanal. Because the Navy was cast in the role of supplicant, Hyakutake was able to demand considerable naval supports for his new effort. An entire fresh infantry division, one of the Imperial Army's very best, was rerouted to Rabaul for eventual transfer to Guadalcanal.

By then, the clear pattern of Japanese preoffensive operations had been established. On a scale that grew with each successive effort, the infantry would be staged into Guadalcanal by transports and destroyer-transports, which with their non-troop-carrying warship escorts would bombard the Lunga Perimeter—particularly Henderson Field—as often and as thoroughly as possible. As the land assault force was built up, naval aviation units from Rabaul's constantly replenished 11th Air Fleet would mount larger, more intense strikes aimed at wearing down the thin American Marine, Army, and Navy squadrons of the Cactus Air Force based at Henderson Field and adjacent Fighter-1. As the day of the assault drew nearer, all the pressure increased in the air and sea over and adjacent to Lunga. During the buildup stages, Imperial Army units already ashore frequently applied pressure in the form of strong probes against the Marine perimeter line.

It had happened thus in August, September, and October. Each effort had been geometrically larger than the one before; each had been a more serious threat to the survival of Lunga Perimeter. And each had been a larger, more humiliating defeat for the Imperial Army and 11th Air Fleet. Only the surface units of the Combined Fleet had come through each showdown with their dignity relatively intact, but even the Combined Fleet was on the ropes by late October, following the last big defeat. Slowly, its valuable warships and troop transports were being lost or damaged, and it was becoming increasingly difficult to make good the steadily mounting losses of experienced fighter pilots and bomber crews. Most important, the Imperial Army headquarters on Guadalcanal—General Hyakutake's 17th Army—had flat-out lied to the Combined Fleet about the early outcome of the late-October offensive. At a crucial moment, Hyakutake's headquarters had radioed the news that Henderson Field had fallen. This had sent a very large part of the Truk-based Combined Fleet into action against two American carrier task forces near the Santa Cruz Islands. While the outcome of the Santa Cruz carrier battle could be counted a Japanese tactical victory (one American carrier, *Hornet*, had been sunk and the other, *Enterprise*, had been seriously damaged—against two Japanese carriers moderately damaged), so many Japanese aircrews were lost that the Japanese naval air arm was rendered seriously handicapped. Moreover, as the November combined planning unfolded, the Combined Fleet staff was still seething over the outright lie that had sent its carriers into action in the first place. Hyakutake's 17th Army saved face by explaining that the false information had resulted from a communications error. Whatever the case, the fragile regional alliance was in jeopardy. But more important than that, the Imperial Army and Imperial Navy were virtually on the ropes as a result of steadily mounting losses in a far-reaching campaign that neither had foreseen and to which neither had devoted its best thinking. It was tacitly understood by both parties that the November offensive was to be the last serious effort to retake Guadalcanal.

卍

The heart of the new Japanese effort was the bulk of the fresh but second-rate 38th Infantry Division. More than a regiment of the division was already ashore at Guadalcanal, and elements of the division had already seen combat in peripheral actions associated with the abortive October offensive. It was 17th Army's desire to land the remainder of the division as soon as possible to mount November's "final" offensive.

The local Imperial Navy headquarters, VAdm Gunichi Mikawa's Rabaul-based 8th Fleet, concurred. If the Army provided the transports, 8th Fleet would provide the escorts. Farther afield, from his Truk headquarters, Adm Isoroku Yamamoto, the Combined Fleet commander, agreed to commit massive bombardment units, including two elderly battleships equipped with hundreds of 14-inch high-capacity bombardment projectiles of a new type.

As always, Combined Fleet had an agenda of its own. In addition to supporting 38th Infantry Division's transfer to Guadalcanal and subsequent assault, Yamamoto's headquarters hoped to draw out the last large reserve of U.S. Navy surface units available in the South Pacific. It was a clear objective of the Combined Fleet planners to suck the American warships into a night surface engagement and defeat them. The strategic implications of such an American defeat could force the U.S. Navy out of an active war role for as much as a year or two. There was an element of risk, of course. A decisive American victory would be catastrophic to an Imperial Navy incapable of producing replacement warships as quickly as American yards could churn out new American warships. But the Imperial Navy's highest operational commander, Yamamoto, was an inveterate gambler. The pot he saw looming before him in late October, when he agreed to support the local Army and Navy commanders, was too tempting; he could not fold until he saw the outcome. Thus, during the same week the Japanese carrier arm was withdrawn to lick its wounds in the wake of Santa Cruz, the surface battle arm was advanced in the certainty it would crush both the American surface fleet in the South Pacific and what it perceived to be the last vestiges of American moral resolve throughout the Pacific and at home.

Following months of carrier-dominated naval actions—four carrier-versus-carrier battles between May and October—the surface forces of both navies were, in the minds of many naval officers, being recalled to their rightful places at the top of their respective strategic hierarchies. Surface battle, particularly action involving battleships, was the one thing for which the high commanders of both navies had trained from their earliest days as cadets and ensigns. It was possible—some thought it probable—that a November showdown near Guadalcanal could yet prove to be *the* decisive action of the war. (The Japanese did not yet recognize their Midway defeat as being in any way decisive, and the Americans knew that ultimate victory was a long way off, if indeed it was attainable.)

For all the hopes of a decisive battle and victory, however, the Combined Fleet nevertheless held its newest and best battleships, along with many cruisers and destroyers, in *reserve* at Truk. So far as the Combined Fleet intelligence analysts could determine, the main strength of the carrier-depleted U.S. Pacific Fleet—its battleships—had not sallied from its West Coast or Hawaiian ports. Though present (and detected) in proximity to the battle arena, no Japanese carriers were committed, in part because the Japanese thought the Americans had no fleet carriers left after Santa Cruz. So far as the Combined Fleet was concerned, the upcoming November action had yet to draw the anticipated all-or-nothing response from the hard-pressed Americans. As soon as the American battleships could be pinpointed—most likely by the screen of submarines patrolling the far reaches of the battle area—the main body of the Combined Fleet would sally from Truk. If the American battleships did not arrive, then the forces in the Solomons would certainly destroy more of America's precious lesser warships and, along with them, more of America's precious and diminishing reserve of fighting spirit. To Japanese thinking, anything short of an outright defeat would be a victory.

꿔

A large part of 38th Infantry Division was lifted to Guadalcanal from Rabaul and the Shortland Islands between November 2 and 10 by sixty-five destroyer-transport sorties and even aboard two cruisers. Japanese troop strength on Guadalcanal thus rose from a high of 22,000 on October 23, the night the October land offensive began, to 30,000 on November 11. While the massive sea lift more than made good October's crushing losses, thousands of the Japanese ashore on Guadalcanal were either noncombatant support personnel or too sick from hunger or a variety of exotic diseases to make a contribution.

The successful sea lift was not without its bruises. On November 7, two Japanese destroyers were damaged by Cactus-based bombers and had to be withdrawn from the arena, and, on the night of November 8, another Japanese destroyer was severely damaged, this time by one of a small squadron of PT boats that had begun operating out of Tulagi in late October. In return, an American merchantman had to be beached after it was torpedoed in the channel near Lunga Point by a Japanese fleet submarine.

The last part of the Japanese sea lift was to be undertaken by twelve Imperial Army high-speed transports heavily escorted by a large component of 8th Fleet. The transports were scheduled to depart from the Shortland anchorages on the evening of November 13. In addition to the rear echelon of the infantry division, which could have been more safely lifted aboard speedy destroyer-transports, the slow Army transports would be carrying large weapons, supplies, and equipment, which could neither be carried by nor landed from warships.

The components of the Combined Fleet were to mount massive bombardments of Henderson Field and its environs on the nights of November 12 and 13. The specific aim of this effort was to destroy the American air-base facilities and destroy bombers and fighters—and their crews—in advance of the vulnerable transports' sally from the Shortlands. Secondarily, at least on the face of it, the bombardment forces hoped to inflict losses upon U.S. surface battle forces.

6

Southard was a 1921-vintage four-stack destroyer. Obsolete by any modern standards, she had been downgraded and refitted as a high-speed destroyer-minesweeper in early 1941. She had lost her torpedo tubes in the refit, but she retained her 4.5-inch guns, depth-charge rails, and an attack speed of 30 knots. In addition to her nominal duties as a minesweeper, Southard had been at work in the South Pacific undertaking antisubmarine screening for warships and transports. She had towed PT boats to Tulagi from Noumea and often lifted loads of 250 55-gallon drums of aviation gasoline to Lunga to replenish the Cactus Air Force. On her trips back to Espiritu Santo, she often carried sick and wounded Marines. Though duty aboard Southard was not in the least glamorous, her crew knew better than most that they formed a vital link in the tenuous chain that kept Guadalcanal anchored to the Allied cause.

Chief among its attributes, Southard's crew was in every way battle ready—and "battle aware." Her sonarmen were among the best in the area, having undertaken hundreds of hours of antisubmarine listening, albeit without results so far. More vulnerable than most warship crews—and clearly more expendable, as evidenced by their frequent solitary trips to Guadalcanal—*Southard's* crewmen kept themselves honed to a fine fighting edge. Like most crews at that time and in that place, *Southard's* invariably took its infrequent rest breaks at its battle stations. This was as much a manifestation of the impossibly long hours the crew worked as it was a sign of how concerned most sailors were that action could erupt at any moment. Typically, crewmen manning topside battle stations stayed topside because it would be easier to abandon ship from there. Sailors working below invariably had exit and escape routes mapped out in their heads in the event their ship was precipitously sunk.

In the earliest morning hours of November 10, 1942, *Southard* was on her way back from Espiritu Santo to Aola Bay, to which she was carrying a mixed load of supplies. As usual, she was making the trip alone.

Just before 0230, November 10, just off Cape Recherche, San Cristobal, *Southard's* highly skilled lookouts spotted an odd silhouette on the calm surface. Guncrews were silently and swiftly called to battle stations and the aging warship's main battery swung out to track the possible target.

Unwittingly coming within *Southard's* gun range was *I-172*, a thoroughly modern Japanese fleet submarine. One of a number of picket boats deployed to monitor the passage of American fleet units, *I-172* was routinely recharging her batteries preparatory to spending the daylight hours of November 10 cruising her search area submerged. No doubt many Japanese crewmen were topside to partake of fresh air carried on the light, cooling breeze.

As the Japanese idled away the minutes, *Southard* crept to within killing range and opened fire at the clear target at 0231. Observers aboard the oncoming minesweeper saw a flash of flame as their shells struck the water close aboard the submarine. As *Southard's* manually directed 4.5-inch guns continued to put out rounds, the skilled Japanese crew—undoubtedly wound as tight as their American counterparts—sprang to the open hatches and immediately commenced to dive their boat. In an amazingly short time, *Southard's* surfaced target fired a pair of torpedoes at its assailant and disappeared.

The minesweeper's practiced sonarmen took over the conning

of the ship and needed only ten minutes to gain a firm fix on the departing submarine. As soon as *I-172* was pinpointed, *Southard's* ready depth charges were armed, and the torpedomen manning them awaited only a depth setting before dropping them on the target.

Cannily employing the steady stream of fixes from his sonarmen, LCdr John Tennent, *Southard's* skipper, skillfully maneuvered his ship against the target. At 0242, Tennent ordered the first depth charges away.

Contact was lost in the turmoil of the multiple underwater detonations, but *Southard's* overpracticed sonarmen had the scent of blood and would not be deterred. They played their enervating cat-and-mouse game for hours, the incessant *pinging* in their ears driving them to all but distraction. After chasing down scores of false or misleading contacts, daybreak found *Southard* no closer to a kill than she had been three hours earlier. Then, at 0607, contact was firmly reestablished. The torpedomen manning the depth charges once again reported themselves ready. Lieutenant Commander Tennent once again skillfully brought his fast ship to attack position.

Over the next hours, *Southard* launched six separate depth-charge attacks against her slower but infinitely wily target. The last attack, launched at about 1000, used up nine of *Southard's* dwindling supply of depth charges. But it was the charm. At 1003, *I-172's* conning tower broached the surface 2,000 yards from the minesweeper.

Southard's gunners, inured to long working hours without sleep, snapped to the moment the submarine heaved out of the water. Instantly, round after round was loosed from the guns. Suddenly, a 4.5-inch salvo crashed into the conning tower and the submarine rolled fiercely under the impact. Then, without further ado, the submarine's stern rose all the way out of the water and stood tall for a moment. As the American gunners continued to fire, the submarine righted itself, then slid back beneath the surface. As *Southard* searched for traces of the submarine, she was joined by her passing sister ship, *Hovey,* and a PBY Catalina patrol bomber out of Espiritu Santo. The ships and patrol bomber scoured the area but found no sign of their quarry. That is because *I-172* was dead.

꿔

Southard's contact with *I-172* had an immediate chilling effect upon RAdm Kelly Turner's travel plans. It had originally been the South Pacific Amphibious Force commander's intention to slip his three surface groups around San Cristobal to buffalo the Japanese picket submarines he knew from long experience would be covering and threatening the direct route. Though the possibility of encountering submarines off the beaten track had gnawed at Turner's mind, the certainty represented by the *Southard–I-172* encounter obliged Turner to stick to the shortest route even if it was certain to be potentially as dangerous. At least the precious transports would be exposed at sea for fewer hours.

RAdm Norman Scott's Task Group 62.4 was already too advanced along the northern San Cristobal route to be rerouted. As it happened, Scott's group was pinpointed and positively identified before noon on November 10 by a Japanese twin-float seaplane based aboard a surface tender in the near vicinity.

Lt Stew Moredock, a blooded veteran of the Cape Esperance battle, where he had served aboard a heavy cruiser subsequently dispatched to the rear after she suffered extensive battle damage, was by no means used to the heady world of Fleet Intelligence in which he had been immersed over the preceding month. Seconded to Admiral Scott's staff as the admiral's operations officer, Moredock had been floored by the admiral's early revelation that Pacific Fleet Intelligence was regularly reading Japan's most sensitive operational fleet message traffic. Lieutenant Moredock had seen many examples of this ability, particularly as he updated his admiral's situation map during the previous weeks, as Japanese fleet units were on the move toward Truk and the Shortlands in preparation for the November offensive. But Moredock's growing familiarity with the ultra-secret code analysis was turned on its ear by a specific example that directly affected Moredock.

As the Japanese reconnaissance plane that spotted Scott's task group shot off a coded message to Truk and Rabaul to report its position and what it had seen, the transmission was monitored by American-manned radios, and the coded message was passed on to Pacific Fleet headquarters at Pearl Harbor. Since it came from a sensitive operational area, the message was decoded immediately. Among the many other recipients of the decoded finding was Admiral Scott's flagship, light antiaircraft cruiser *Atlanta*. The news was in Lt Stew Moredock's hands within brief hours of the original sighting, a startling achievement in Moredock's eyes.

Though the Japanese knew that Scott was on the move, they did not know that he knew they knew, nor could they know that Admiral Turner knew, nor that RAdm Dan Callaghan, the supporting surface battle-force commander, knew. The Japanese subsequently alerted their air and surface forces arrayed against Guadalcanal. They updated their plans in order to interdict the reinforcement as massively as possible. That Turner, Scott, and Callaghan were kept apprised of the developing Japanese plan was key to the potential outcome of the plans of both navies.

For the moment, however, all the Japanese knew was that one of their picket submarines, *I-172*, was out of contact and that a small group of American cargomen was being escorted around San Cristobal by a small force of light American warships.

7

Armistice Day—Wednesday, November 11, 1942—began at Guadalcanal with a predawn launch of eight Marine F4F Wildcat fighters assigned to put in a quick strafing attack at Rekata Bay, on neighboring Malaita. There the Japanese had long operated a base for floatplane fighters and scouts charged with reconnoitering Guadalcanal and the Slot—as New Georgia Sound, the channel through the double chain of the Solomon Islands south of Bougainville, had been dubbed by American sailors and fliers. The fighter sweep was led by Marine Capt Joe Foss, an extraordinarily skilled and successful fighter pilot already approaching legendary stature. The Marine fighters encountered no fire from the ground, quickly sprayed the crude facilities, and turned for home. The purpose of the strike—to confound the ability of the Japanese scouts to monitor the arrival of the first relay of supply ships—was fulfilled.

RAdm Norman Scott's Task Group 62.4 arrived at the head of Lengo Channel at the crack of dawn, right on schedule. While the main body slowed to traverse the narrow passage, destroyer *Fletcher* raced ahead to see who controlled the area around Guadalcanal's Lunga Point that morning. The come-ahead soon reached Scott's flagship, light cruiser *Atlanta,* and the main body arrived off Lunga Point at 0530, November 11. The three cargomen were met offshore by the Lunga Boat Pool, a flotilla of light landing boats that had been cobbled together from offerings from departing transports and cargomen during the initial fleet withdrawal in early August. As the warship escorts—four fleet destroyers and *Atlanta*—wove intricate patterns to seaward, the unloading operation began immediately, its objective to get many men and much materiel ashore before the first anticipated Japanese bomber raid flew into sight. Veterans of numerous harrowing trips to the area, the cargo crewmen were delighted to see what appeared to be normal activity going in and out of nearby Henderson Field, which was itself hidden from view by an intervening grove of coconut palms.

From his flagship at sea that morning, RAdm Kelly Turner sent the following message to the ships of his Task Force 67 and Scott's Task Group 62.4:

> It is expected that Task Force 67 while unloading will be
> subjected to heavy air attack from both carrier-based
> and land-based aircraft. . . . In view of expected air
> attacks on November 12, and since a heavy landing
> attack probably will be made by the enemy on
> November 13, it becomes highly essential to get troops,
> organizational weapons, ammunition, and food ashore at
> the earliest possible moment.

The first Japanese raid of the day was extraordinary. Normally, the first bombers were launched from Rabaul or several new intervening airstrips and timed to strike Lunga roads or Henderson Field around noon. In most cases, the attackers were twin-engine G4M Betty medium bombers equipped with 250-kg general-purpose bombs.

News of the first raid of November 11 arrived at 0905. According to reports from Allied officers, "coastwatchers," concealed in lookout camps along the Slot to the north, the strike was composed of a dozen A6M Zero fighters and nine D3A Val dive-bombers, a carrier type equipped with up to one heavy 250-kg and two light 60-kg bombs. The significance of the timing and the bomber type was that they could very well have been launched by the two carriers that were known to have been in the northern Solomons area the day before. There was no way to tell yet whether the two carriers were advancing on Guadalcanal or if the Vals were temporarily based at one of the intermediate airfields in the Shortlands or Bougainville.

As it turned out, the strike was mounted by squadrons from light carrier *Hiyo* that were temporarily based at an airfield on Bougainville while their ship remained well out of range. But this was the concern of admirals. The concern of the men in the ships was to destroy or evade the incoming dive-bombers.

To make matters worse, one of the vessels manning the antisubmarine screen around the cargomen reported at 0915 that it was searching for a possible submarine a sonarman thought he had heard.

As the landing craft scattered for shore, General Quarters klaxons resounded across the channel and Task Force 62.4 formed up in a column with *Atlanta* leading the three cargomen and the four destroyers deployed to screen either flank in pairs. That *Atlanta* was available was fortuitous. Her whole purpose in life was to provide dense antiaircraft cover for other ships with her sixteen 5-inch twin-mount rapid-fire dual-purpose guns and a formidable array of lighter automatic antiaircraft cannon. The destroyers were each equipped with four or five single-mount 5-inch dual-purpose guns and a more modest array of automatic weapons. The cargomen typically sported four 3-inch dual-purpose guns apiece plus a light array of automatic antiaircraft weapons.

The Japanese Zero-escorted vee-of-vees dive-bomber formation was first observed at 0936 as it swept in over Cape Esperance, Guadalcanal's western tip.

↻

There were at least eight Marine F4F Wildcat fighters over the channel when the first raid alert was sounded, and these maneuvered into position to cut off the bombers as they headed for the maneuvering surface ships. The Marines were under strict orders to get at the bombers no matter what—before they dropped their bombs if possible, or afterward if that was the best they could do. The Marine fighter pilots were specifically enjoined from taking on

Zero fighters unless they could not find the bombers or unless the Zeros attacked them.

Marine 2ndLt Sam Folsom, a veteran but unblooded junior member of Marine Fighting Squadron 121 (VMF-121), was on duty with the group of ready fighters on Fighter-1, Henderson Field's grass satellite—known to the pilots as "the Cow Pasture"— when news of the incoming raid arrived. He scrambled with seven other Wildcat pilots from his own and at least one other Marine squadron and was over the island clawing through 18,000 feet when the radio announced that the Japanese had arrived. By then well inland, the flight immediately turned around toward the channel. As it did, the pilots spotted a squadron of Zeros that would otherwise have caught them from behind and above.

In a matter of seconds, the Marine formation broke up into two-plane elements and individual fighters as the Wildcat pilots sought to defend themselves against the breaking formation of diving Zeros. As Sam Folsom searched in vain for a firm target, a Zero to his immediate right burst into flames and a Wildcat dived away directly in front of him, trailing plumes of oily black smoke. As Folsom briefly looked after the falling Wildcat, he saw the pilot tumble out of the cockpit. A second later, the falling American's parachute blossomed into the clear blue sky.

Then Lieutenant Folsom was in the middle of the swirling dogfight. A Val diving from above and behind overshot Folsom's fighter and was suddenly, briefly, in Folsom's gunsight. Mildly rattled, Folsom could not quite get the pipper of the gunsight reflected on his windscreen to line up on the receding Val, which was going quite a bit faster than the Wildcat. Though the Val clearly had the speed advantage, Folsom saw that its pilot apparently did not seem to know how to exploit it; intent upon his mission of attacking the shipping below, he allowed Folsom to stay on his tail and follow him down out of the main melee. Folsom well knew that the range was too great for accurate shooting from the F4F's six powerful .50-caliber wing-mounted machine guns, but he could not get on enough speed to close the gap with the diving Val, so he decided to shoot anyway. Though the shooting was poor, Folsom was surprised after several bursts to see that the Japanese dive-bomber was starting to smoke. Elated, with the scent of blood and victory keen in his nose and oblivious of the possibility that he might be following his quarry into the friendly antiaircraft umbrella, Folsom poured in all his remaining bullets and sent the Val into a steeper spiraling dive. Unfortunately, the earthward-bound Val flew into sparse cloud cover at 3,000 feet, thus denying Folsom credit for a more-than-probable kill. However, as far as Sam Folsom was concerned, he had finally broken the ice only a week before VMF-121 was scheduled to depart Guadalcanal.

VMF-121's 2ndLt David Allen was the first Wildcat pilot to get a solid piece of one of the Zeros. He made a swift diving run over Savo and shot the Zero right out of the sky. However, he was caught low during his recovery by a second Zero, which dived down on his tail. The Zero wrecked Allen's Wildcat with its pairs of 7.7mm cowl-mounted machine guns and 20mm wing-mounted automatic cannon, and Allen had to bail out 800 feet over the water. The Marine pilot got clear of the cockpit okay, but he had a brief encounter with his fighter's tail assembly before pulling free, opening his parachute, and landing gently in the water. Lieutenant Allen was soon picked up by a crash boat and returned to the beach.

The results of the swirling dogfight were mixed. In all, six Wildcats, almost all of them flown by green pilots from a newly deployed squadron, were knocked down in the fray. One new pilot who was downed, SSgt W. H. Coahran, of VMF-112, was seen bailing out of his disabled Wildcat over Japanese territory on Guadalcanal. Coahran was followed down by 2ndLt Wayne Laird, who was in turn bounced by a Zero as he circled over the spot where Coahran landed. Laird managed to outmaneuver the Zero and shoot it down, but he lost sight of Staff Sergeant Coahran, who was never seen again.

卐

The dive-bombing attack against the shipping commenced at 0940. As the Zeros fought off the oncoming Marine Wildcats high overhead, the Vals tipped their noses over from 8,000 feet and went after the valuable cargomen, which were making 14 knots in the company of *Atlanta* and the destroyers. After diving through streams of tracer from the light automatic weapons and bursting 5-inch and 3-inch rounds, each pilot released his payload at about

1,500 feet and leveled off to rendezvous and race for safety. *Zeilin's* gunners saw many rounds from their guns and possibly from other ships strike the lead Val. Though the damage might already have been inflicted by 2ndLt Sam Folsom, the gunners claimed that their hits started a fire in the port wing, forcing the attack leader to pull up early. Apparently he did not drop his 250-kg centerline bomb.

Betelgeuse, an old warhorse with many resupply trips to Guadalcanal to her credit, was attacked from her port side by a Val that dropped two wing-mounted 60-kg bombs. One of the bombs landed only 20 feet from the side of the ship, and the other detonated only 40 feet away. Numerous fragments from one or both bombs struck the side of the ship and her superstructure. Despite the brief rain of steel, the ship's four 3-inch guns and all her 20mm and .50-caliber automatic weapons immediately traversed to fire on a passing Val as it plowed on toward *Zeilin*, just to port. As the *Betelgeuse* gunners ceased firing to avoid hitting the friendly vessel that suddenly loomed in their gunsights, they saw the Val's bomb strike *Zeilin* a glancing blow.

Zeilin's 3-inch guns put up a steady volume of fire at the Vals approaching from the west and the ship turned through 45 degrees to the right with the rest of the formation. As she did, it appeared to her topside crew that five of the Vals were singling her out for attention. As the Vals came within range, the cargoman's eight 20mm guns commenced firing. Despite the intense, concentrated fire, two of the bombers scored near misses to port at 0942. At 0943, as numerous 7.7mm rounds put out by the pilots and rear gunners of two of the passing Vals struck *Zeilin*, a third bomb glanced off her starboard hull and exploded underwater. The concussion caused a flare-back in the after fire room, and steam pressure was lost to the steering gear.

As *Zeilin* was weathering the shock of the detonation, *Betelguese's* helmsman realized that the near misses beside his ship had jarred his rudder-angle indicator out of alignment. No one knew quite where the moving ship's rudder was, which caused great if temporary consternation on the bridge.

Meantime, *Zeilin's* helmsman lost control of his rudder due to the detonation of the bomb against his ship. When the smoke cleared, she was heading directly toward *Betelgeuse*, whose own helmsman had just regained control of his own rudder. *Betelgeuse's* captain bellowed, "Emergency full speed ahead," and bells and re-peaters clanged and clicked all the way down to the engine room. *Betelgeuse* pulled clear of *Zeilin's* oncoming bow and regained her position in the moving formation. *Zeilin's* quick-acting machinist's mates had the disabled steering gear back on line at 0944, within a minute of the breakdown, and *Zeilin* came to her proper place in the formation.

All in the same minute, as *Betelgeuse* was passing beyond *Zeilin's* runaway reach, yet another Val was descending in a shallow glide-bombing dive from 8,000 feet. The pilot leveled off at about 900 feet and released his bomb off *Betelgeuse's* port quarter. This missile detonated only 20 feet from the cargoman and put the two after 3-inch guns temporarily out of commission. While the Val was pulling away, *Betelgeuse's* 20mm and .50-caliber gunners pierced it with numerous rounds. As the cargoman's excited topside crew looked on, the Val caught fire, veered to port, and crashed in flames about 300 yards to port.

Yet another Val was by then boring in on *Betelgeuse*, this one from the port quarter toward the starboard bow at a height of about 1,200 feet. Cdr Harry Power, *Betelgeuse's* captain, was transfixed as he watched the Val's bomb cross his ship diagonally, barely clear the bow, and plunge sharply into the water only 20 feet off the starboard bow. The gunners had their stride by then, for this Val was struck by numerous 20mm rounds. Observers clearly saw flames leap out from the dive-bomber's lower fuselage directly be-tween her neatly spatted wheels. As flames spread and smoke bil-lowed out behind, the Val flew directly down the side of the ship, acquiring more 20mm and .50-caliber rounds as it went. Then it veered sharply to starboard, completed a large circle to port, and crashed in flames about 2,000 yards off its intended victim's star-board bow.

Libra's gunners commenced firing at 0941 at two Vals by then at low level and heading for her from the port quarter. The first Val dropped a pair of 60-kg bombs at 0943; one landed about 100 feet off *Libra's* port quarter and the other detonated about 20 feet away and forward of the first. As the Val followed through in its dive, the pilot fired his twin cowl-mounted 7.7mm machine guns and stripped *Libra* of her radio antenna and fore truck.

Marine 2ndLt Tom Mann, of VMF-121, had gotten rounds into at least two Vals as they were diving on the ships—he was given credit for both of them—and then followed through to nail a third Val just as it appeared to loft its bomb over one of the destroyers guarding a cargoman's flank. Mann hammered another Val as it departed after dropping its payload, then closed on his fifth solid target of the morning. Intent upon the Val in his sights, Mann did not see another Val to his left as it turned into him and opened fire with its 7.7mm cowl guns. Mann's entire left side was peppered with pieces of shattered bullets and slivers of metal from his own airplane. The Wildcat lurched, shuddered, and skidded into the water well away from the receding surface force. The flight was arrested so abruptly that Lieutenant Mann lost seven teeth when his face smacked into the gunsight. Mann exited the sinking airplane and activated his Mae West life jacket. (He floated in the water until dusk, then swam to one of the islands near Tulagi, where friendly islanders treated his wounds and arranged his evacuation a week later. Mann was eventually credited with four kills.)

Lacking additional targets, *Betelgeuse* ceased fire at 0946, only six minutes after the Vals tipped over to deliver their attacks. For all the near misses, only three members of her crew and three Marine passengers were injured, only one seriously enough to remain on the sick list. *Betelgeuse* turned back toward the anchorage at 1000, secured from General Quarters at 1018, and dropped her anchor at 1020. Unloading was immediately resumed and two submersible pumps and attendants were sent over to help *Zeilin* cope with the effects of the bomb that had sprung her hull plates. Though spread over a wide area, *Betelgeuse*'s damage from at least four near misses was thoroughly manageable, and most of it was repaired by the end of the day.

Zeilin's gunners also ceased firing at 0946, as their ship turned left to come to a northward heading at 14 knots with the rest of the tightly knit task group. Her total damage at the close of the raid consisted of leaks, large and small, in three of her after holds and flooding in both of her shaft alleys. She had just one casualty aboard, a mess attendant who had been struck in the right thigh by a bomb fragment as he helped man one of the antiaircraft guns. *Zeilin* dropped her anchor in the transport area at 1041 and immediately went to work discharging all of her passengers except a handful of Marines who were helping to man her antiaircraft guns.

Altogether, the Marine pilots claimed five Zeros and five Vals definitely destroyed and one Val, Sam Folsom's, probably destroyed. The ships claimed four Vals destroyed. It is known that no Vals returned to their base, so, given the free-wheeling nature of the action and usually excessive claims in such circumstances, nine confirmed kills and one probable kill for nine targets is not far out of line. In all likelihood, Folsom's probable was claimed as a kill by whoever saw it actually strike the water.

8

For forty minutes following the morning's abortive Japanese dive-bombing attack, the three cargomen discharged their passengers and cargoes as quickly as their own small boats and others sent from shore could work the cargo booms and landing nets draped over their sides. However, at 1100, they again received a warning that an indeterminate number of unidentified warplanes was in the area. The landing boats instantly headed for the beach, the ships' crews instantly secured their work, and the three cargomen got underway at 1102. As before, *Atlanta* took the lead while the destroyers moved in pairs to the flanks of the single column of three cargomen. Speed quickly rose to the standard 14 knots.

At 1103, as before, one of the warships on antisubmarine duty in the channel picked up a sonar contact and moved to deliver a depth-charge attack offshore about a mile east of Koli Point. However, no firm contact was made.

Betelgeuse sounded General Quarters at 1107 and all the cargo booms and gear were secured. The big problem was securing a net load of gasoline drums that had been arrested in midair by the precipitous departure from the unloading area. The volatile fuel was lowered to a protected spot and special covers were placed over the fuel drums to absorb the effects of potential bomb blasts. *Zeilin*, which was ahead of *Betelgeuse*, and *Libra*, which was behind, undertook similar housekeeping duties. While all this was going on, the tightly knit group of cargomen and escorts was weaving through the unloading area in a series of tortuous maneuvers designed to throw off the aim of potentially unseen aerial assailants and submarines.

A hard contact report arrived at 1120 as the ships continued to steam on odd courses through the area: Enemy warplanes were definitely in the immediate vicinity of Guadalcanal.

The Japanese bombers were finally spotted by ships' lookouts at 1125. These appeared to be G4M Betty medium bombers operating at great height, a relief of the first magnitude to the men aboard the ships. If they had to bear the brunt of an air strike, a high-level bombing attack was the method least likely to net results for the attackers. The Bettys flying from west to east were over the channel and, it appeared, at the margin of beach verging on Henderson Field. It was initially difficult for the men aboard the ships to determine if they were going to be the target at all; high-level bombers would certainly find more lucrative targets on and around Henderson Field. As always, the twenty-seven Bettys were arranged in a shallow stepped-down vee-of-vees formation.

Although the Bettys were clearly out of range, each cargoman opened fire at 1126 with its four 3-inch guns, arranging a pattern of black antiaircraft puffs in such a way as to—hopefully—deter the pilots from turning directly over the moving formation of ships.

⚛

The bombing raid was indeed directed at the Henderson Field complex.

The combat air patrol circling above the island and channel when the alert was sounded consisted of six Wildcats from VMF-112 under the leadership of the squadron commander, Maj Paul Fontana. The squadron had arrived at Fighter-1 only a few days before, at the end of a long dry spell for the Cactus fighters. Its first combat mission had been a strafing strike against a flotilla of troop-carrying destroyers that Henderson-based scout bombers had located in the Slot. The results of the action had been less than satisfying because the new Wildcats' machine guns had shown a marked tendency to freeze up after firing only a few rounds apiece. This problem, typical of many faced by newly arrived air units, was cleared up after consultation between Fontana's ground crew and more experienced maintenance men and armorers attached to Maj Duke Davis's VMF-121. The misfires were caused by protective cosmoline, which needed to be thoroughly removed from newly installed guns to prevent them from freezing up at high altitudes in the extremely humid air of equatorial Guadalcanal. By November 11, that and numerous other wrinkles had been ironed out, and Major Fontana and his subordinates were ready to get onto the scorecards in a big way. (One of Fontana's lieutenants had scored the squadron's first two kills earlier in the week, and two others had scored one kill apiece against a Zero and a Val during the November 11 morning raid.)

One of the last of seventeen Wildcats aloft that forenoon was flown by 1stLt Roger Haberman. Universally known as "Uncle"—because he was one, an unusual distinction among the young fighter pilots, and because his first name begged confusion on the jargon-filled airwaves—Haberman actually had the day off and was washing his clothing in the Lunga River when the day's second air-raid alert sounded. After tossing his wet clothes in his jeep, Haberman drove up to the VMF-121 flight line to see what was going on. The news was that the second strike in an hour was on its way and that there were still some ready fighters waiting for willing pilots. A respected flight leader in VMF-21, Uncle Haberman had 5.5 kills to his credit, ample evidence that his fighting spirit was holding its own in a squadron known for its aggressive high-scoring ways. He instantly suited up and grabbed the first available fighter.

Haberman's group of five Wildcats was making a flat left turn 19,000 feet over the field, still clawing for altitude, when nearly all the pilots saw the Bettys at exactly their altitude and heading toward them. As Haberman turned to the right, the other four turned to the left to get at the lead nine-plane bomber squadron. The six ready fighters, five pick-up fighters, and six combat-air-patrol fighters all struck the Betty formation at about the same moment.

As the combat air patrol bored through the light Zero escort—

as few as five fighters were along to protect the twenty-seven Bettys—Maj Paul Fontana immediately got his first Betty ever in his sights and easily downed it with a skill born of years of practice. In this regard, he was like all of his contemporaries who had thus far commanded Marine fighter squadrons at Cactus, for they all did well and scored early.

The last of Major Fontana's combat air patrol to get at the Bettys was being flown by 2ndLt Jim Johnson, whose Wildcat had been slowed in its long climb by a faulty engine. By the time Lieutenant Johnson found the Japanese medium bombers, he was still much lower than he would have liked. Nevertheless, he pitched in after a pair of stragglers and fixed the very last Betty in the formation in his sights. The approach was flat and the extremely fast Betty threatened to pull ahead of the sluggish Wildcat, sucking Johnson into a tail chase from which the Betty never deviated. At length, Lieutenant Johnson patiently pulled up within range and fired his first burst, to which the Betty's 20mm tail gunner responded. Throttling his keenly felt desire to flinch away from the approaching 20mm rounds, Johnson saw his Wildcat's six streams of tracer rounds falling directly into the Betty, so he held his ground and fired off burst after burst. Suddenly, another Wildcat, greedy for a kill, hurtled by overhead, all its guns right on Johnson's Betty, which blew up. Jim Johnson was given credit for that kill, his first, but so was the other Wildcat pilot, a VMF-121 veteran who also claimed another Betty.

MSgt Joe Palko, a VMF-121 pilot with 3.5 kills credited, was one of the section leaders in the group of four that turned away from Uncle Haberman. He lost contact with the other section while the four Wildcats were recovering from their initial overhead run on the Bettys. Soon, Palko found himself vying with 2ndLt Edward Pedersen, of the VMF-112 combat air patrol, for a position directly off the tail of one of the Bettys, which their combined shooting soon set afire. Palko and Pedersen attempted to deliver high-side firing runs at high speed, but they were soon drawn flat by the bomber's ongoing shallow dive. As the two section leaders delivered alternate firing runs at the crippled Betty, Palko's wingman, 2ndLt Jeff deBlanc, a green VMF-112 pilot who had become mixed in with the VMF-121 pick-up formation during the last mad scramble, saw large yellow popcorn-ball rounds coming at the two lead Wildcats from the Betty's 20mm stinger. All of a sudden, the two lead Wildcats brushed together and Palko's fell away, out of control. Lieutenant deBlanc could not be certain if the 20mm rounds had struck Palko's airplane and jarred it into Pedersen's, or if Palko himself had been hit and lost control, or if the two Wildcat pilots had simply cut things too fine. Whatever the cause, Palko's fighter staggered away from Pedersen's and began a long dive toward the water. Meantime, Lieutenant Pedersen bored on up the Betty's tail and finished shooting the bomber down in flames. Then he bailed out of his own collision-crippled Wildcat. After seeing Pedersen's parachute blossom, Lieutenant deBlanc followed Palko's Wildcat down and watched it fall into the beach at Tulagi. The extremely talented pilot at its controls perished. Lieutenant Pedersen landed safely in the water, from which he was plucked in due course.

Maj Duke Davis, of VMF-121, had scrambled from Fighter-1 in the lead of his squadron's six ready fighters and the pick-up group of five led by 1stLt Uncle Haberman. Davis, who had five kills to his credit and who was thus an ace, was boring in after a Betty when a 20mm explosive round burst in his Wildcat's cockpit and sent him diving away from the fight with a faceful of tiny shrapnel slivers. He landed safely and turned himself in for treatment, but he shrugged off a suggestion that he be evacuated to the rear for additional treatment.

Lieutenant Uncle Haberman's early turn to the right carried him directly beneath the midsection of the bomber formation. A quick count of the thus far undisturbed bomber vees indicated that there were fourteen Bettys in front and thirteen behind. The continuing turn carried Haberman directly beneath the rear group. He was so close that the gunners manning stingers and waist guns could not bring their 20mm cannon and 7.7mm machine guns to bear. The Marine ace selected a target from among the many and opened fire. The Betty immediately made a left turn to the north, away from the formation, and began angling down toward the water in a shallow dive. Haberman's .50-caliber bullets reached out and pulverized the tail-gun blister, spewing glass splinters all across the sky. Now firmly on the target, Haberman pulled his gunsight pipper slightly to the left and let go another practiced burst at the Betty's left engine nacelle. He saw solid hits going in and then witnessed a thin stream of coolant vapor trailing behind the left wing. Certain he had crippled the Betty, Haberman decided to end the matter. He nudged his gunsight across the belly of the Japanese bomber and settled the pipper directly over the right engine nacelle. Once again, solid hits went in, apparently striking an oil line. Instantly, the Wildcat's windshield was spattered by gooey oil, as was the leading edge of the fighter's wings. At just that moment, an ongoing problem with faulty ammunition reared out of the blue and cut off all six of Uncle Haberman's machine guns.

As Haberman paused to recharge the faulty machine guns, the Japanese bomber cut into one of the few clouds in that part of the sky. Haberman edged around the cloud and, sure enough, the Betty reappeared—right in front of his Wildcat's nose, at the same altitude and making a flat right turn toward Cape Esperance, nearly 40 miles away. Haberman's Wildcat had a 35-knot speed advantage at that moment, which he used to help him turn inside the partially crippled bomber, itself an extremely lithe airplane. A burst from the near waist gun clipped Haberman in the right arm and dug a groove across the top of his right thigh. Haberman had been unable to recharge his own guns, so he could not return the fire.

It was at this juncture that a wild sort of thought popped into Uncle Haberman's head. He had heard that a Catholic priest still lived in the Cape Esperance area (which was actually overrun with Japanese serving the frequent destroyer drops of men, equipment, and supplies). He felt that if the Wildcat were to be disabled by gunfire or, say, in a midair collision, he would be able to find the priest and get himself returned to Lunga. As the thought ran its course, Haberman decided to tear off the Betty's right aileron with his left wing, so he pushed his lingering speed advantage to do exactly that bit of handiwork. At the precise critical instant, the Japanese pilot lifted up his left wing, leaving Haberman to helplessly skid through beneath. As Haberman reflexively looked over at the looming Betty, he saw two airmen in the starboard waist gun position looking back at him with huge, frightened eyes.

The Betty had by then descended to about 15,000 feet, picking up speed all the way. By then, also, the wound in Haberman's right arm—the one he used to control the stick—was causing him extreme pain. He decided to let the Betty go and head back to Fighter-1. There, because of the pain, Lieutenant Haberman opted to make a wrong-way approach, against the traffic pattern. He went straight in from west to east and landed in a cloud of dust. As the dust settled, Haberman was nonplussed to see that 1stLt Greg Loesch, a squadron mate, had had exactly the same thought. The two had unwittingly landed their Wildcats only 25 feet apart at about the same instant, quite a feat on that narrow, uncontrolled dirt strip for fighters that could not always be kept absolutely up to snuff.

❦

The ships in the channel put out their large-caliber antiaircraft rounds for only four minutes, until 1130, and ceased firing without observing any hits on the Japanese warplanes. However, keen-eyed lookouts did spot a bomb as it burst in the area in which the cargo-men had been peacefully unloading thirty minutes earlier, and six burning Bettys or accompanying Zeros were seen crashing into the water. *Libra*'s executive officer distinctly saw a parachute float down into the hills southwest of Henderson Field.

The only American death that forenoon was MSgt Joe Palko. The afternoon death count came to one Zero and seven Bettys, including a confirmed kill for Uncle Haberman. In all, that Armistice Day, Marine pilots officially scored eighteen kills and one probable. The Cactus Air Force lost eight Wildcats destroyed and five pilots killed.

❦

The three cargomen were on their way back to the unloading area by 1140 and were all anchored within minutes of noon, working hard to clear their cargoes and remaining passengers.

The unloading wound down routinely in mid-afternoon and damaged and flooded *Zeilin* made ready to depart the area. In the final minutes, destroyer *McCalla*, which would be staying, transferred four downed Japanese aviators to *Zeilin* for transportation to a prisoner stockade in the rear. As this transfer was taking place, *Zeilin* turned over four of her tank lighters to the Lunga Boat Pool.

These large ramped landing boats had been slung from davits near the fantail. Since there was still extensive flooding aboard *Zeilin*, which was down about ten feet at the stern, it was decided to lighten her by leaving the boats. The sailors and coastguardsmen manning the Lunga Boat Pool were delighted to accept the infusion of well-maintained replacements into their ragtag little navy. *Zeilin* got underway for her return to Espiritu Santo at precisely 1600 in the company of destroyer *Lardner.*

The balance of RAdm Norman Scott's warships—*Atlanta* and three fleet destroyers—escorted *Libra* and *Betelegeuse* through Indispensable Strait and then returned to Sealark Channel to search the waters around Savo Island and await the arrival of RAdm Kelly Turner's larger force of transports and warships. The two cargomen were to mark time through the night, maintaining alternate courses to the north and south in protected waters just beyond the usual range of marauding Japanese night-bombardment forces. No Japanese warships were expected this night, but no one ever really knew; Admiral Scott had won the U.S. Navy's only night surface victory of the war by defeating a Japanese bombardment force that he caught coming on unannounced. As it turned out, no Japanese warships entered Savo Sound this night.

9

Following a relatively uneventful journey to Guadalcanal, during which several of its warships joined the transports of RAdm Kelly Turner's Task Group 67.1, RAdm Dan Callaghan's Task Group 67.4—four cruisers and four destroyers—arrived off Savo at 2300, November 11, and looked in vain for Japanese surface forces.

At 0115, November 12, as RAdm Kelly Turner's Task Group 67.1—four troop-laden transports, plus escorts—continued to close on Guadalcanal, destroyer *O'Bannon* reported a possible submarine contact on the surface off her starboard beam. All the ships immediately executed an emergency turn to port while *O'Bannon* illuminated what was believed to be a midget submarine, a highly doubtful eventuality. In any case, *O'Bannon* fired two 5-inch salvos and destroyer *Shaw* charged in to deliver a partial depth-charge barrage at what she characterized as a "doubtful" contact. Everyone was jumpy.

Turner's enlarged task group arrived at the transport area off Kukum, just west of Lunga Point, without further incident at 0531. All the transports anchored at 0541 and immediately began unloading the troops of the 182nd Infantry Regiment into their own boats and those sent to help by the Lunga Boat Pool. Immediately, heavy cruiser *Pensacola* and destroyers *Gwin* and *Preston* were dispatched to Noumea to join fleet carrier *Enterprise*'s Task Force 16.

As the unloading operation got underway, one of the destroyers screening the transport area made a submarine contact and delivered a depth-charge attack that was rated "ineffective." The contact faded and could not be regained during the course of intensive searches. By then, everyone conceded that there was indeed a Japanese submarine residing in Lengo Channel.

Betelgeuse and *Libra* had joined the transports and anchored 2 miles east of Lunga Point by 0630. And destroyer-minesweepers *Hovey* and *Southard* arrived from Tulagi, where they had spent the night, to begin antisubmarine sweeps around the transport area.

The unloading operation was going smoothly and without incident when, at 0642, Admiral Turner's flagship, transport *McCawley,* was taken under sporadic and inaccurate fire by a Japanese 150mm howitzer emplaced well to the west. Moments after the first rounds landed only 100 yards off *McCawley*'s port bow, a Marine artillery battery located ashore began firing counterbattery. At 0728, light cruiser *Helena* and destroyers *Monssen* and *Shaw* took up positions off the beach west of Kokumbona Village to help silence the imprudent Japanese artillery piece. Soon destroyers *Cushing* and *Buchanan* were temporarily detached from Task Group 67.4 to bombard known Japanese shore installations farther to the west. Their 5-inch fire resulted in numerous sympathetic detonations in the trees, following which the two destroyers closed to within 1,500 yards of the shore to use their 1.1-inch and 20mm antiaircraft guns to spray landing boats the Japanese had pulled up onto the beach. They were soon joined in this satisfying work by *Helena, Monssen,* and *Shaw.* It was estimated that up to thirty of the boats were destroyed by the American warships, an important contribution.

Unidentified aircraft were spotted as they approached the transport area at 1005. All the ships that could bear opened fire with their longer-ranged antiaircraft weapons, but the targets were immediately identified as a friendly Marine transport plane and five fighters on their way to Henderson Field from Espiritu Santo. "Cease fire" was given by flag hoist and the shooting stopped before anyone was hurt. The transport crews were *extremely* jumpy.

卍

The unloading operation proceeded without a hitch until 1315, when the radio station ashore informed the fleet that a large force of Japanese planes would be arriving over Guadalcanal at 1330 from the north-northwest. This news was the product of a report from Paul Mason, an Australian coastwatcher manning a post high in the mountains of southern Bougainville. Though sought by Japanese patrols scouring the area, Mason and Paul Read, another coastwatcher manning a station overlooking Buka Passage, off northern Bougainville, had been providing accurate and timely information about Japanese air strikes and naval surface forces from the day the Guadalcanal action got underway on August 7.

As soon as the news arrived, all the warships that had been dispatched earlier to fire on shore targets were recalled to screen the transports and cargomen, which secured the unloading operation and got underway in two columns of three ships each surrounded by a formidable array of warships, including light antiaircraft cruisers *Atlanta* and *Juneau*.

The appointed moment came and went. Lookouts aboard all ships strained their eyes to locate approaching aircraft, but there was nothing. At 1350, a revised estimate was given: According to the radar station ashore, the Japanese strike group of about thirty warplanes was still 109 miles out and approaching from the northwest. It was expected over the fleet at about 1415.

In fact, there were twenty-one to twenty-five torpedo-laden Betty bombers escorted by eight to twelve Zeros, and they completely buffaloed the Marine ground-control station and, by extension, the combat air patrol, which was at 29,000 feet looking for a high-altitude bombing raid when in fact the Bettys were approaching at low altitude.

卍

No sooner were the low-flying Bettys spotted by lookouts, however, than they disappeared behind Florida Island's eastern cape, the Ass's Ears.

Then they were back! Seconds after destroyer *Fletcher*, the rearmost ship in the American screen, regained a fix on the Bettys by means of her modern radar, her own gunners saw the Bettys as they popped out from behind Florida's concealing bulk to sweep up the wakes of the combined task force in a breathtaking line-abreast formation. As soon as the task force was in sight, the Betty formation split into two groups and commenced the attack literally at wavetop height. One group, the nearer, maneuvered up from the south while the other swung out to find a position to the north. Observers throughout the surface formation were universally awed by the fact that they could see foam streaming back behind propellers beating so close to the water.

Initially concerned with the nearer southern bombers, Admiral Turner first maneuvered his ships so that the fat transports showed their vulnerable sides to the bombardiers. When the southern Bettys were truly committed—moments after the fleet's large-caliber antiaircraft guns opened fire at 1412—the task force commander ordered an emergency turn to port, thus presenting the narrow, receding sterns of all his ships to the oncoming torpedo bombers.

S1 Don Dahlke, a torpedoman striker manning *Fletcher*'s starboard midships 20mm gun, was able to get a clear bead on the nearest gray-green Betty of the southern bomber formation as it came up the starboard side from dead astern only 30 feet above the water. Dahlke had excelled as a gunner during numerous practice drills, but this was his first actual attempt to fire in anger. Everything clicked; all the training he had received in his eleven-month naval career came together as he coolly fixed his gun's ring sight on the glass bombardier's blister in the nose of the cigar-shaped mid-wing bomber. A light burst of tracer—every fourth round—showed Dahlke that he was dead on, and he opened fire in earnest. The swift destroyer, one of the newest in the U.S. Fleet, was making full speed dead ahead, but the bomber was going over 150 miles per hour faster as its pilot sighted a target ahead for the deadly 21--inch aerial torpedo slung in the open bomb bay. After each short burst, Seaman Dahlke had to swivel the gun forward to regain his aiming point. Since Dahlke was firmly cinched into the 20mm gun's harness, sighting was effectively accomplished simply by moving his body to the right in order to carry the gun's barrel to the left. Tracer was clearly entering the target between the bombardier's nose blister and the cockpit, just above and behind. A small, detached portion of Dahlke's mind registered the fact that dark holes were appearing in the side of the passing bomber. Soon, he and others could see that the explosive rounds were literally chewing sections of metal from the airplane's side. Then, after what seemed like hours, Dahlke's gun ran out of space forward. Without hesitating, and with no curiosity whatever regarding his target's fate, the gunner swiveled his sights well astern in the hope of picking up yet another viable target.

The moment Don Dahlke turned away, most of the rest of *Fletcher*'s topside crew saw the first Betty's torpedo tumble end-over-end from the bomb bay. Then the Betty itself staggered and fell into the water, where it was consumed by a large ball of fire. Meantime, Seaman Dahlke found a second target and poured rounds into it much as he had the first Betty. After only one brief burst, however, the second bomber pulled up to evade Dahlke's remarkably accurate fire. Dahlke caught a third airplane out of the corner of his eye as it came nose-on right up *Fletcher*'s wake. Just as Dahlke got his sight on the dangerous intruder, it dawned on him that he was about to open fire on a friendly but out-of-place Marine Wildcat fighter. Several rounds left the gun before Seaman Dahlke could check his reflexes, but the Wildcat streaked by, apparently without ill effect.

TM3 Walter Hogan, who was manning *Fletcher*'s starboard forward 20mm gun, had a great deal of trouble keeping his bead on the second Betty to pass up that side of the ship. Every time the 5-inch gun in Mount-2 fired a round from directly behind Hogan's gun, Hogan was knocked flat on his back. That happened three times, but Hogan resumed his position each time within three or four seconds.

Fletcher's modern dual-40mm gun mount, the very first to arrive in the war zone aboard a destroyer, reached out to hit a Betty about 2,000 yards from the ship, a superb volley by any standards, and the destroyer's five modern director-controlled single-mount 5-inch guns tracked targets from 14,000 yards down to 3,000 yards.

Fletcher certainly made a dent in the intact Betty formation that had to pass her and destroyers *Monssen* and *Sterett* before most of the other ships could reach them.

₹

The two heavy cruisers in the channel attempted a novel experiment aimed at disrupting both of the oncoming bomber formations. Minutes after her 5-inch secondary battery began putting out rounds aimed at directly destroying the Japanese bombers, heavy cruiser *Portland*, a veteran of the Santa Cruz carrier battle three weeks earlier, unleashed a six-gun main-battery salvo. The improperly fused 8-inch rounds were hardly capable of destroying an airplane, except perhaps by scoring an accidental direct hit, but *Portland*'s main-battery officer was not looking for a direct hit. His objective was to put up a solid wall of white water directly in front of the low-flying Bettys. If his aim was true, the 8-inch detonations might throw off the aim of the bombardiers or perhaps even cause a Betty to crash.

The experiment was noble, but getting the large rounds to land just right was more a matter of luck than skill. The first six rounds fired were of the armor-piercing type normally carried in the big guns in these waters. These did not make a big enough splash, so the second salvo was six high-capacity bombardment rounds. These made the desired big splash, but they did not land in quite the right spot at quite the right moment, and all the Japanese bombers breasted the white-water tide without being appreciably jarred from their course. *San Francisco*'s main battery attempted the same ploy, but it had the same results; the battery was fired a bit too early or a bit too short, so the wall of water had receded by the time the Bettys arrived. Moreover, the lighter antiaircraft weapons aboard both heavy cruisers were handicapped by the enormous amount of smoke that was a by-product of the main battery salvos.

₹

The well-practiced gunners aboard *Betelgeuse*, the last ship in the right transport column, picked up a Betty as it bored in from the port quarter. While the 3-inch guns continued to fire, the cargo-man's 20mm gunners had to watch and wait until the attacker flew within range. As soon as the 20mm guns opened, the Betty staggered in its course only 300 yards from the ship and precipitously veered to the left. It crashed into the water only 1,000 yards from *Betelgeuse.*

Within two minutes, two more Bettys were observed as they closed on *Betelgeuse* from directly astern. Both targets were coming steady on at only 60 feet—easy, stable no-deflection targets for the cargoman's stern 3-inch gun. One proximity-fused round burst beside both planes and sent both Japanese pilots careering from their course. Both planes dropped their torpedoes from 1,500 yards. The starboard Betty's torpedo was clearly visible to Cdr Harry Power, *Betelgeuse's* captain, as it momentarily hung by its tail and plunged into the water at an angle of about 60 degrees. As soon as the torpedo nosed into the water, it was bounced clear off the surface by the force of its momentum, then it nosed back into the water and disappeared. As soon as both torpedoes were away, the Bettys diverged to pass up each side of what had until then been a relatively silent ship. As they came even with the cargoman at a height of about 50 feet, their wingtips were no more than 75 feet out. In addition to fire from the five hitherto silent 20mm cannon mounted on each side of the ship, the Bettys were both suddenly subjected to gunfire put out by scores of infantry weapons in the hands of the Marine aviation engineers still embarked.

The starboard Betty had begun burning as it came even with one of the midships hatches, and it was a mass of flames by the time Cdr Harry Power saw it come even with his flying bridge. Nevertheless, it was still able to put up a fight.

When the air-raid alert had first sounded, AS Robert Dombrow, who had been in trouble with authority time and again during his service aboard *Betelgeuse,* had been released from confinement in one of the crew's heads *(Betelgeuse* had no brig), where he had been dining on bread and water as a condition of his latest ten-day sentence. As Dombrow was servicing the 20mm gun on the starboard side of the flying bridge, the Japanese manning the waist 7.7mm machine gun returned *Betelgeuse's* fire and bullets struck the gunner, loader, and Dombrow. Though staggered by the blow, Dombrow refused relief; he told Commander Power to "Go to hell, sir" at the mere suggestion that he seek treatment before the shooting stopped.

Meantime, the starboard Betty crashed into the water about 100 yards off the starboard bow, thus obliging Commander Power to order the rudder put over hard left and then hard right to keep the ship from running over flames that were higher than her masts. At the same time, massive gunfire ignited a fire beneath the starboard wing of the Betty passing up *Betelgeuse*'s port side. Tracer could be plainly seen as it entered the cockpit area, and the plane soon appeared to be out of control, either due to damage to the controls or injury to the pilot. The Betty swerved across the bow from port to starboard and pancaked into the water, where it sank to the top of its fuselage. It was still afloat when last seen from the passing cargoman, which ceased fire altogether at 1418. In addition to causing minor material damage, the Betty gunners had wounded six *Betelgeuse* crewmen and seven Marines.

〰

Only three Bettys came within machine-gun range of transport *Crescent City*, the center ship of the left transport column, and all of them passed close aboard the port side of the ship. The transport's topside crew saw only one of the Bettys drop its torpedo, which struck the water tail first before skidding and diving from view. The transport's guns clearly struck all three Bettys, as did those of numerous other ships on the far side of the formation. The lead Betty burst into flames as it passed *Crescent City*'s fantail and fell into the channel moments later. The second Betty plunged into the sea off the transport's port beam, and the third Betty overtook the formation before veering toward a beach near the Japanese-occupied western end of Guadalcanal. However, it crashed into the water well short of its objective.

〰

It is more than likely that transport *President Adams*, in the center of the right column, contributed to the destruction of the three Bettys struck by rounds from *Crescent City*, directly across the way. Many of *President Adams*'s coxswains and boatswain's mates, who regularly served as members of many of the antiaircraft guns, were off the ship, manning the landing craft, so the hits were scored largely by less well-trained crewmen pressed into temporary service. Contributing to the volume of fire were numerous soldiers who had unslung their rifles and automatic weapons, and boat crewmen who opened fire with the .30- and .50-caliber machine guns aboard landing craft swinging from *President Adams*'s boat davits. Indeed, the landing-craft gunners were credited with destroying one of the Bettys.

Cox William Lindner, a 20mm gunner, was firing solid bursts into the noses of two of the passing Bettys when he instinctively saw that his line of fire was about to cross one of the ships across the way. He instantly checked fire but followed the Bettys in his ring sight until they were in the clear again. Then he resumed firing until both bombers, which were by then enveloped in flames, crashed into the water.

Finally, GM1 Wesley Walker, the temporary captain of the makeshift four-man crew manning *President Adams*'s only 5-inch gun, came up with an innovative method for hitting one of the passing Bettys. After learning early on that the fantail-mounted gun could not traverse quickly enough to follow the speeding Bettys, Walker selected a point in space he felt the bombers would eventually pass. He was rewarded for his foresight when, indeed, a Betty filled his trainer's sight. However, the fuse of the single round the 5-inch crew was able to get away was set for too great a distance and thus did no damage. Undaunted, Walker selected a new, still-secret proximity-fused round and reset the trap for another oncoming Betty. Once again, a Betty flew into the sight of the waiting 5-inch gun—and it fell under the impact of the single proximity-fused round, which detonated within feet of its fuselage, a clean kill.

☙

Destroyer *Laffey* was approached by a lone Betty from the direction of her starboard quarter. Immediately, all four of the destroyer's 5-inch mounts trained out and locked on as the director trainer found the target. As the 5-inchers opened fire, the 1.1-inch and 20mm guns followed suit, tracking the torpedo bomber from aft to forward as it attempted to retire to safety. Soon, the two after 5-inch mounts had swung all the way forward into their fixed stops, which had been placed to prevent the guns from firing into fixed structures. Unfortunately, the designers of the stops had failed to take other factors into account. As Mount-3 fired its last round after the departing Betty, the fireball of burning powder expelled through the barrel completely enveloped the 1.1-inch mount trainer, who was seriously burned through his skivvy shirt from shoulder to waist.

卍

Destroyer-minesweeper *Southard*'s 4.5-inch guns were able to bear on the dozen Bettys attacking from astern, but there were only five bombers remaining aloft by the time her guns could get a clear shot. When the bombers approached to within 2,000 yards, LCdr John Tennent ordered the rudder placed hard to port to give the guns on both sides of his ship an opportunity to fire. The move was hardly required since three of the Bettys swerved astern of *Southard* and passed directly over her fantail, thereby providing the ship's unmasked 20mm and .50-caliber guns with superb targets. All three of these Bettys were struck by so many rounds from *Southard* and nearby vessels that they fell burning into the channel within 1,000 yards of *Southard*.

Of the two remaining Bettys, one was struck by fire from *Southard*'s machine guns as well as rounds from other ships. It was observed crashing off one of Guadalcanal's Marine-held beaches. *Southard* had the last Betty in the group under fire when a Marine F4F roared in from above, obliging the quick-witted gunners to cease firing. The Betty, which cartwheeled into the water 2,000 yards beyond *Southard*, was credited to the Marine pilot.

卍

Destroyer-minesweeper *Hovey*'s 4.5-inch main battery was incapable of training skyward, but the ancient warship nonetheless weighed into the fray with her 20mm and .50-caliber antiaircraft guns. Moments after a Betty approaching from dead astern disappeared in a tremendous burst of exploding gasoline, one of *Hovey*'s .50-caliber guns put numerous rounds into the right engine and wing of another passing Betty. As the engine erupted in smoke and flame, the Betty sideslipped and crashed astern of the minesweeper.

꩜

The Marine combat air patrol—eight VMF-121 Wildcats led by Capt Joe Foss—was late getting into the fray because it lost sight of the Bettys as they passed around a large cloud that hung 20,000 feet over Florida Island. The Bettys were still high enough to make Foss believe they would be launching a high-altitude bombing attack, so he kept his Wildcats tethered at 29,000 feet until the Bettys reappeared and he saw that they were low and splitting into two attack groups. Because so much precious time had been lost, Foss had no choice but to put everything he had on the nearer northern formation. By then, the Bettys were passing below 500 feet.

"Put your engines on low blower," the flight leader yelled into his mike. "They're coming in low. Let's go get 'em, boys!" Then he pointed his Wildcat's nose straight down at the far-distant Japanese flight leader's bomber. The descent from the freezing upper atmosphere was so rapid that the insides of many of the Wildcats' windscreens frosted over. Captain Foss, among others, had to scratch off the rime in front of his face so he could see through the windscreen again.

Capt Frank Clark, an Army Air Forces pilot at the controls of one of the eight 67th Pursuit Squadron P-39 Airacobra fighters scrambled in response to news of the raid, also apparently had a problem with frost on his canopy. However, unlike the Marine pilots, Clark was unable to clear his windscreen or, for some reason, control his dive. His P-39 was seen knifing straight into the water without ever making a move to pull up.

꩜

In the meantime, Maj Paul Fontana's ready group of eight VMF-112 Wildcats had been suckered by the high approach of the incoming strike group into a long, fruitless climb from Fighter-1. While climbing leftward at 20,000 feet and about 10 miles north of Henderson Field to come on station as ordered by the ground fighter-control officer, Major Fontana was informed that the Japanese formation had disappeared from radar and might be at low altitude to the south. Fontana obligingly dived to lower altitude on a southerly heading and thus spotted the Japanese northern formation.

Following through on his long dive, Major Fontana racked up his second kill of the tour when he flew up to within about 50 yards of one of the bombers in the lead vee and opened fire. The Betty instantly burned and crashed into the water.

Careful to avoid the bursts of friendly antiaircraft fire that were by then reaching out toward the bombers, Fontana was just shifting his attention to a second Betty when his Wildcat was scoured from wingtip to wingtip by an unseen Zero. Though full of holes, the sturdy Wildcat barely staggered under the impact. Fontana put on full throttle as the faster-diving Zero screamed by and initiated a climbing turn to the left. Fontana nimbly moved inside the Zero's turn and opened fire. The squadron commander's six .50-caliber machine guns set the Japanese fighter ablaze, providing Fontana with his second kill in as many minutes.

⚛

Major Fontana's wingman, SSgt Tom Hurst, became separated from the squadron commander in the wild action that saw him triumph over both a Zero and a Betty. During the action, however, Hurst's F4F was disabled and he was obliged to ditch off Guadalcanal. After exiting the sinking fighter, Hurst saw several soldierly looking men on the nearby beach, but he could not easily identify them until he swam close inshore. It turned out that they were Japanese, so he turned back toward the channel. One of the screen destroyers had by then been attracted by the commotion on the beach, but it was driven off by Japanese artillery fire as it moved to pick up the downed aviator. (It was nearly dark before Staff Sergeant Hurst, who had sustained no injuries, was finally rescued by a landing boat commandeered from the Lunga Boat Pool by the VMF-112 intelligence officer.)

⚛

When Major Fontana's second-element leader, 2ndLt Bill Wamel, first saw the Japanese bombers glide beneath his Wildcat's left wing, he sang out "Tallyho!" on his radio and commenced a diving left turn to get on their tails. As Wamel steadied up in a shallow full-power dive right up the tails of the group of Bettys, he saw another gaggle of the Japanese medium bombers setting up a torpedo run at right angles to the shipping in the channel. As Wamel slowly came to within a half-mile of the nearest destroyer, all the ships in the channel seemed to open fire right at him. Fearful of having to break away before getting his licks in, Wamel armed all six of his wing guns and fired a three-second burst, but he was far out of range. Suddenly, one of the Bettys blew up from an apparent direct hit scored by one of the ships, and seconds after that Wamel's fighter was rocked by a near miss that propelled several large slivers of shrapnel through his cockpit.

Shaken by the near miss, Lieutenant Wamel nevertheless ignored the output of the Betty's 20mm stinger and bored on up the bomber's wake. He opened fire again when he knew he was well within range, but only one of the six wing guns worked as the Wildcat overran the target. Wamel pulled out to the right and dumped speed so he could reacquire the Betty, but his subsequent efforts to regain the speed he had lost came to nothing. The throttle would not respond, so Wamel pulled away and headed back toward Guadalcanal. His only hope was to get over friendly territory before the Wildcat's engine died.

The Wildcat carried Bill Wamel almost to the friendly beach, but he felt it give its last gasp well short of land so he turned into the light offshore breeze. Though Wamel's Wildcat was one of the first to arrive at Guadalcanal equipped with a shoulder harness, Wamel had neglected to secure his. Now it was too late. He also forgot to lower his landing flaps to slow the fighter. The combination of oversights was potentially mortal. Wamel's dying Wildcat sliced into the surface at great speed, and the sudden braking action of the water pitched the pilot's forehead right into the gun sight. Wamel, who was on full automatic, unfastened his seat belt and climbed out of the cockpit in one motion. He pivoted to the rear, took one step, and walked right into the water off the trailing edge of the wing. When he looked up, a landing boat was already bearing down on him. Bill Wamel reached shore safely and had the cut over his eye sutured almost before his squadron mates returned. However, within several days, he had to be evacuated when an undisclosed concussion proved to be the source of some temporary but mighty erratic mood swings.

↻

VMF-112's 2ndLt Jeff deBlanc, who was flying wing on 2ndLt Bill Wamel, got right on the tail of a Betty and smoked it with a solid burst. As the Betty burned, however, deBlanc came under the influence of target fixation. Staring through the gunsight reflected on his windscreen and then through the spinning strobelike orb of the propeller, Lieutenant deBlanc was unable to tear his eyes away from the Betty. By the time he was able to yank free of the stunning vision, deBlanc was far beyond the fleet. He executed a hasty wing-over and raced back toward the action in the hope of meeting another Betty head on as it tried to escape the mayhem over the channel. He saw one Betty emerge from the wall of antiaircraft fire surrounding the transports and their escorts, and it was heading straight for him.

Endowed with uncanny 20/10 eyesight, deBlanc was able to select an aiming point and open fire while at the maximum effective range of his machine guns. Suddenly, the Betty's left engine flared. Within seconds, the amazingly fast closing rate carried the Wildcat over the top of the Betty. At the last instant, deBlanc's attention was fixed by motion in the cockpit. He saw three people crowded into the tiny compartment, where the pilot seemed to be slumped forward and the standing man seemed to be struggling to pull him from the control yoke before the bomber nosed downward. An instant after streaking by, deBlanc pulled a hasty wingover and came up astern the bomber. He felt like a sitting duck for the 20mm tail gunner, but no fire came his way because, as he saw, the gun blister was empty. Somehow, the bomber disappeared from view. Jeff deBlanc was certain it crashed, but he did not see it go in and thus accepted credit for a probable.

↻

Destroyer *Buchanan*, which had rejoined the flotilla in the channel after taking part of the destruction of Japanese landing barges on a Guadalcanal beach, was sailing between *San Francisco* and *Atlanta*, when her 5-inch guns opened fire on the northern formation of Bettys approaching from the starboard bow at a range of about 12,000 yards. The guns held the targets while the destroyer undertook a tortuous turn in company with the flanking cruisers. At 1416, one of the Bettys crossed ahead of *Buchanan* only 100 yards away and 50 feet off the water. It curved back and dropped its torpedo at a point about 300 yards off the destroyer's starboard bow. The torpedo was seen to fall cleanly into the water, but its wake was not observed as it passed ahead of *Buchanan* because the entire topside crew was diverted by the burst of a misguided friendly 5-inch shell in the after side of the after stack. The friendly round holed the starboard side of the stack, severely damaged the torpedo mount, and obliterated a 20mm machine gun and its crew of three. In all, the round killed five and wounded seven. Seconds, later, five 20mm explosive rounds fired from port struck the base of the torpedo mount and the Mount-2 5-inch gun shield.

At 1419, *Buchanan's* port machine-gun battery locked onto a Betty that was passing close aboard at an altitude of 50 feet. As the Betty drew ahead, its 20mm stinger opened fire. Damage was nil, but a signalman on the port wing of the bridge was slightly injured by shrapnel. The main battery fired at this and other retiring Bettys as they flew on ahead, and one of the 5-inch guns got a kill or an assist at long range.

�

Light antiaircraft cruisers *Atlanta* and *Juneau* should have been in their element that afternoon. They had been built specifically to take out bombers intent upon wreaking havoc upon other ships. Each was armed with sixteen 5-inch guns mounted in eight dual mounts, up to seven of which could be trained to one side or the other at any time. Each ship's main battery was augmented by four quad-1.1-inch mounts and eight single 20mm antiaircraft guns. Altogether, *Atlanta* and *Juneau* were capable of putting an immense cloud of fused rounds in the path of the oncoming Bettys.

Unfortunately, *Atlanta* was placed nearly in the center of the formation, and not on a flank, where her rapid-fire guns would have been given freer rein. As soon as the broad line-abreast Japanese bomber formation drew inside the outer ring of destroyers, BM1 Leighton Spadone, a seven-year Navy veteran commanding the starboard midships 1.1-inch mount, constantly had to check fire and reacquire targets when the friendly ships he was trying to protect kept appearing in his sights. Other mount captains and the cruiser's main-battery director were experiencing the same difficulty, which cut into *Atlanta's* effective output of rounds.

Busy as he was guiding his mount onto enemy bombers while avoiding friendly ships, BM1 Spadone was consciously struck by the resolute bravery of the oncoming Japanese airmen, who he felt knew they were facing certain annihilation.

Cox Ted Blahnik, the director pointer controlling light cruiser *Helena's* starboard quad-40mm mount, had been waiting for months to lay his sight on a hostile target. Though *Helena* had been well blooded in the night battle off Cape Esperance on October 12, the defense against the Bettys was her first antiaircraft action. Blahnik got the word from Sky Control, the position high over the bridge from which the antiaircraft gunnery officer held forth, and had the nearest approaching Betty firmly in his sight within minutes. Once Blahnik was locked on target, the 40mm gun pointer matched bearings with his own sight and locked his control apparatus to the director; he would resume local control only if the director was disabled.

Coxswain Blahnik received "Open fire!" from Sky Control when the Bettys were 3,500 yards out. He coolly squeezed the trigger and watched the 40mm tracer rounds streak out toward the Betty he was holding in his sight. The well-practiced loaders in the gun tub beneath Blahnik's position never missed a beat. Suddenly, however, the stream of tracer stopped altogether. Nonplussed, Blahnik looked around from his sight to see what was the matter. Wordlessly, the mount captain pointed toward one of the transports. Blahnik had not seen the friendly vessel enter his cone of fire as he traversed the director and the mount locked in its train to fire on the Betty in his sight.

In addition to the 40mm guns, *Helena* fired her four dual 5-inch mounts and all the 20mm guns that could bear from positions along the main deck and throughout her superstructure. For all that, the light cruiser claimed only one sure kill and several assists or probables. Unfortunately, it was probably *Helena's* guns that fired the rounds that struck destroyer *Buchanan*, killing five Americans.

Even *Helena's* main battery of fifteen rapid-fire 6-inch guns mounted in five three-gun turrets were brought into the fray. At first used to try to knock down the Bettys, the guns were eventually ordered by the cruiser's gunnery officer, LCdr Rodman Smith, to fire at the downed torpedo bombers floating in the water. The order offended the sensibilities of Lt Warren Boles, the main-battery assistant, who responded over the open gunnery circuit, "But they're down and burning!" To which the gun boss rejoined, "Shoot the bastards."

卍

For some reason, destroyer *Laffey*, which was accompanying *San Francisco* in the defense against the northern bomber force, was the target of two of the very few aerial torpedoes that were successfully dropped. One of the two was heading directly amidships and the destroyer was unable to evade, but the fish exploded prematurely short of the mark. The second torpedo could be clearly seen from topside structures as it carved a bubbly path through the calm water, passed directly beneath the keel, and emerged just ahead of the destroyer's bow.

卍

Capt Joe Foss pulled out of his screaming dive within 100 yards of a retiring Betty and fired a full burst into its starboard engine, which began smoking. The Betty pilot immediately moved to pancake his laden bomber in the water, but the right wing got low and the Betty cartwheeled and fell apart.

Foss's momentum carried him through the formation of smoking Bettys and on toward the furiously firing warships, dead ahead. As the ace lined up on a fresh Betty, one of the Zero escorts streaked out of nowhere and delivered a high-side firing pass on Foss's F4F. Extremely annoyed by the interruption, Foss reflexively pulled his sight up onto the passing intruder and downed him with a short burst. The bomber was still a possibility, so Foss pulled back onto its tail, careful to remain clear of the 20mm stinger's cone of fire. Still somewhat shaken by the close encounter with the Zero, Foss did not pay careful enough attention to his shooting, so missed the Betty. He next crossed over from right to left and fired a short burst into the left wing root, where one of the bomber's volatile and unprotected main fuel tanks lay. Immediately, flames spread from the breached tank to the left engine. The doomed Betty eased into the water for a perfect flame-quenching landing. As Foss streaked by overhead, the bilged bomber's dorsal-turret gunner put a burst into the Wildcat's engine housing, but with no apparent effect.

The triple kill brought Capt Joe Foss's score to twenty-two, making him the Cactus Air Force's highest-scoring ace and the second-highest-scoring American ace in history.

Foss next went after yet another Betty, but he could not get in a killing shot before he was jumped by a pair of Zeros. He flew as low as he dared and streaked toward Savo—still on the bomber's tail—as bullets from the Zeros' guns foamed the water around him. Suddenly, an Army P-39 cut in front of Foss and poured fire from its two .50-caliber and four .30-caliber wing guns and single 20mm nose cannon into the bomber. The Zeros chasing Foss turned their attention to the overeager Army airman, who nevertheless clung to the Betty's tail as it flew up into a cloud. By some miracle, the P-39 not only evaded the Zeros but destroyed the Betty as well.

Foss willingly dropped out of the fight when his .50-caliber ammunition boxes registered empty and he had to switch to his reserve fuel tank. As luck would have it, he came across an un-engaged Betty. Almost tearfully, he tried to locate a friendly fighter on the tactical radio, but could not talk anyone into going after the Betty. On the way back to Fighter-1, Joe Foss counted the remains of a dozen Bettys in the water.

※

Foss's two-division formation came unglued long before it reached the Bettys as each Wildcat pilot selected a target and followed it through the dive. Three bombers emerged within sight of 2ndLt Sam Folsom, who pulled into a high-side firing run in such a way as to get rounds into all three. As Folsom was about to touch his trigger, one of the Bettys staggered away in flames, the victim of another Wildcat pilot who had swooped in from astern. Still lacking even one confirmed kill, Folsom became desperate for a score. He found another Betty only 10 feet off the water, pulled up on its tail, and parked there, blazing away without giving any consideration to the bomber's 20mm stinger. After absorbing several long bursts, but without ever catching fire, the Betty simply skidded into the water. Folsom's fighter was shaken by the cloud of spray put up by the fallen Betty, but flew on toward another Betty further on.

The fresh Betty was piloted by a cannier airman than Folsom's first kill. As the bomber skidded from side to side to throw off the Wildcat pilot's aim, the 20mm gunner in the tail churned out burst after burst of deadly explosive rounds. Intent upon the kill, Folsom ignored the return fire and poured bullets into the bomber's right engine. All at once, the engine belched a great gout of white smoke and the Betty's tail smacked the waves. There was a huge comb of spray, and Folsom was sure he had downed another bomber, but the Betty remained unsteadily airborne after recovering from the jolt. Moments after Folsom loosed the last of his ammunition, the Betty's right wing dropped and the bomber cartwheeled to destruction.

As Folsom banked up and away to return to Fighter-1, with heady cries of self-congratulation filling his head, streams of 7.7mm tracer passed his wings. He had been picked up by five Zeros intent upon avenging the two downed Bettys. Sam Folsom was 300 feet above open water and had no ammunition left. All he could do was fly for his life. As the Zeros came on firing, Folsom skidded and sideslipped, chopped the throttle, and generally did his best to keep his Wildcat's armored seat back between himself and the Japanese bullets. The sturdy Wildcat absorbed the punishment, but Folsom was despairing of survival when the firing abruptly stopped. The Zeros had left him.

While making his final approach on Fighter-1, Folsom discovered that a 20mm round had carried away the flap-control rods in the Wildcat's left wing. When he lowered the flaps to land, only the right one responded, very nearly flipping the Wildcat over on its back. Withal, 2ndLt Sam Folsom got down in one piece with two firm kills to his credit.

꿦

Another VMF-121 pilot who finally made the charts was 2ndLt Jack Schuler. Schuler had been in plenty of dogfights during VMF-121's tour, but he had never quite gotten a solid piece of any of the many Zeros with which he had tangled. In fact, the only perfect attack he had ever launched had come against a Betty at the very start of his combat tour. Despite the perfect firing run, however, he had drawn a blank; his new Wildcat's new machine guns had balked because the thin layer of cosmoline that coated them had frozen solid at altitude.

When Joe Foss peeled out over on the low-flying Bettys, Jack Schuler had picked one out of the crowd and had kept right on top of it during the long descent. Like his good friend, Sam Folsom, Schuler was determined to score a kill or go out in a blaze of glory.

Following the long vertical dive, in which his air-speed indicator showed over 400 knots, Schuler's big fear was that he was going to overrun the Betty he had been tracking. He had plenty of time to ease out of the dive, but matching speeds was tricky business under the circumstances. Schuler could see smoke-shrouded ships flashing past from the corners of his eyes, but it never quite registered that he was following the Betty through the middle of the fleet and its antiaircraft umbrella. His only concern beyond lining up on the Betty was keeping himself from running into a ship, for he was by then at only 50 feet. It never entered his head then that he might be downed by friendly fire put out by overexcited shipborne gunners.

Schuler got perfectly lined up behind the as-yet unwary Betty and came up very close on its tail. His mind's eye clearly saw a human form in the Betty's tail blister, but his thinking was lagging just a hair behind reality because of his adrenaline-induced high; he was acting and reacting faster than he knew what was going on. So, when the 20mm cannon ahead began winking out bullets, Lieutenant Schuler wasted a precious split second trying to decipher what appeared to him to be a signal-lantern message. Instantly abashed by his error, Schuler peered through the gunsight reflected on his windscreen and set the pipper on the bomber. It vividly occurred to Schuler that he had remained scoreless to this point partly because he had wasted ammunition on tricky snap shots. This time he was determined; he would emerge from the fight with enough bullets left over to scythe a wide path of destruction through the Japanese formation.

The pilot's trigger finger closed slowly on the trigger, and the guns burped out a brief burst, perhaps only six rounds per gun. The tracer converged perfectly on the 20mm gun blister, and tiny slivers of glass ballooned into the slipstream. As Schuler's fighter slowly overtook the speeding bomber, and with the immediate danger overcome, he nudged the pipper a hair to the right, directly over the right wing root. Again he nudged the trigger and watched his tracer go in at just the right spot. Almost immediately, a thin wisp of flame shot out of the shredded wing root. Schuler instinctively eased back the throttle a hair, just in time to give him an extra margin of safety when the bomber blew up right in front of his propeller spinner. The large main section of the shattered fuselage plummeted into the water and broke into numerous smaller pieces, each trailing its own plume of smoke. From the main point of impact streamed a long smear of burning gasoline.

With the smell of blood in his nostrils, Schuler became a hunter as he had never been before. His head swiveled to cover the entire sky, questing after another potential kill. But the only Bettys he could see were strewn across the surface of the water. Many of them were whole, but none of them was airborne. Schuler chased back and forth across the channel in response to several radio reports pinpointing Zeros, but he kept finding empty sky.

卐

The incredible bravery of the Japanese aviators persisted even after the bombers were downed. Destroyer *Cushing* came alongside one floating Betty to rescue a Japanese airman who was standing in the ankle-deep water on its wing. As the destroyer slowed, the Japanese man pulled out a small pistol and fired at the destroyer. Instantly, the gunner on one of the high deckhouse 20mm guns requested and received permission to return the fire. The gun had to be depressed almost vertically to bear on the Japanese, and there was a misfire. Shrapnel from the exploding 20mm round severed an artery in the arm of the loader, S1 Ed Shively. Immediately, a cook manning the single 20mm gun near the destroyer's bow blew the shooter in half with a short burst.

In all, fifty-nine kills were credited for the twenty-one to twenty-five Bettys and eight to twelve Zeros thought to have participated in the attack. It is believed that one Betty and several Zeros returned to their base.

Though the American victory over the Bettys was virtually complete, it was not without a heavy price. In addition to sailors and Marines killed and wounded by hostile and friendly rounds, heavy cruiser *San Francisco* sustained numerous casualties in a gruesome by-product of the turkey shoot.

10

At 1408, the instant the survivors of the lead vee of Bettys passed beyond destroyer *Fletcher*'s obscuring bulk, heavy cruiser *San Francisco* got into the fight with her 5-inch secondary battery, which succeeded in downing one bomber with one of its first salvos. Next, as the 5-inch guns took on additional bombers, the main battery swung out and fired a salvo of the 8-inch armor-piercing rounds normally carried in the breeches when the ship was in potentially hostile waters. The first salvo caromed off the waves and caused no damage. Unlike *Portland*, however, *San Francisco* did not switch over to explosive rounds for the second salvo, which was fired too low or too early. By the time the Bettys arrived at the spot where the 8-inch rounds had splashed, there was nothing left of the wall of water except a filmy rainbow mist. The effort was then abandoned as futile.

San Francisco's after pair of quadruple 1.1-inch mounts was fired only with the greatest reluctance by gunners who had ample cause to fear the consequences of bringing their erratic and dangerous weapons into action. During gunnery practice months earlier, the poorly manufactured 1.1-inch rounds had shown a marked propensity for detonating within or just beyond the gun barrels.

Casualties had included a new ensign who had taken shrapnel in the shoulder and a gunner's mate who had been blinded in one eye. Following that incident, the 1.1-inch battery undertook no more live practice firing, merely practice gun-handling drills. The battery was fully manned, of course, but employed against the oncoming Bettys only with understandable reluctance.

One torpedo appears to have been aimed directly at *San Francisco*, and only precipitous maneuvering avoided a collision with the lethal cylinder, which passed forward along the starboard side. Another torpedo was seen bounding upward at a 45-degree angle as soon as it struck the water; it nearly rebounded into the Betty that had dropped it before splashing harmlessly back into the water.

At 1416, gunners aboard Admiral Turner's flagship, *McCawley*, which was leading the left transport column, managed to disable one of the last of the passing Bettys. As hundreds of amazed spectators looked on in helpless dismay, the Betty lurched from its course and flew straight up *San Francisco*'s wake. As the Betty wobbled toward RAdm Dan Callaghan's flagship, it dropped its torpedo alongside the heavy cruiser's starboard quarter and then pivoted inboard.

S1 George Murphy, a gunner's mate striker serving as first loader on the starboard after 1.1-inch mount, could not see the oncoming Betty, but he thought the ship might be in trouble because of the mount's angle of deflection and point of aim. But Murphy had no idea how grave the situation was about to become only 80 feet forward of his position. The Betty's starboard wing passed directly over the head of Lt Howard Westin, who was manning the after 1.1-inch director.

As a member of the cruiser's aviation division, S1 Willie Boyce, a plane captain, had the run of the ship during General Quarters. For this action, he had selected a vantage point amidships, near the airplane hangar. Boyce was one of many to spot the burning Betty as it curved toward his ship. He was certain it would overfly Battle-2, the emergency after battle station manned by the cruiser's executive officer and a staff identical to the one manning the fighting bridge. If the Betty indeed overflew Battle-2, Boyce reasoned, it would come down in the vicinity of the volatile hangar. With that thought firmly in mind, Seaman Boyce began running aft to be as far from the hangar as possible when the Betty hit in a few seconds.

As the bomber's starboard wingtip angled in over the cruiser's after superstructure, it clipped Lt(jg) Jack Bennett in the elbow and passed forward without inflicting more harm to him. In another second, however, the wing collided with the cruiser's after control station.

The Betty's momentum carried it all the way around into the structure, where the force of the impact caused its laden fuel tanks to rupture. The impact alone demolished Control Aft and the flames gutted Battle-2 as well as the after 5-inch antiaircraft battery director and the after radar-control station. The crews of the three 20mm guns positioned on a platform surrounding the 5-inch director were also incinerated as they continued to fire on the Betty during the last instant of its plunge into their ship.

The sailors manning the starboard after 1.1-inch mounts instinctively jumped away from their guns at the moment of impact. The consensus, discussed much later, was that the ship had been struck by a torpedo just forward of the rear-facing mount. The gun trainer, who remained at his station, commanded the rest of the crew to reman the weapon, but there were by then no more targets. By the time the crew had settled in, the mount captain, BM1 Reinhardt Keppler, was long on his way forward to help pull wounded and dead shipmates from the flaming structures.

S1 Willie Boyce was still running aft when the Betty struck. Fortunately, his momentum had just carried him beneath an overhang as the flaming aviation gasoline poured down from above. He stopped on a dime, hemmed in on all sides by walls of flame. As the gasoline continued to pour down from above, Boyce saw the bomber's fuselage fall directly over the port side, where it finally came to rest in the water. One of the many topside crewmen who hated to wear confining antiflash clothing in the tropical heat, Boyce was thankful to his toes, which were sloshing in sweaty boots, that he had heeded the standing order this day. After taking as much heat as he could, Boyce dashed through the diminishing wall of flame and made a beeline for the starboard side of the ship, as far as he could get in the least amount of time.

After taking a quick look around the horizon to see if any more

Bettys were coming at him, Lt Howard Westin, the after 1.1-inch battery commander, grabbed a sailor manning a damage-control telephone and together they ran out the fire hose located beneath Turret-3, the after triple 8-inch turret. As soon as the hose was deployed, Westin signaled another sailor to turn on the water, but there was not enough pressure to reach the burning 20mm gun platform, about 20 feet over Westin's head. Westin immediately signaled for the water to be turned off, then led the hose up the ladder that climbed the face of Turret-3. The added height did the trick and the fire on the gun platform was quenched less than a minute after the water was turned on again. Other quick-thinking hosemen doused all the fires within minutes of impact, though rescuers such as BM1 Reinhardt Keppler had already moved right through the flames to pull their shipmates from the conflagration.

As soon as S1 Willie Boyce was clear of the flames, he began throwing off the heavy antiflash clothing that had saved his life. He was just a little addled by the heat and excitement when he pushed back the hood of his flash jacket and pulled off his sweat-fogged sunglasses. He spoke aloud to himself, "What the hell'd you do that for?" even as he was in the act of tossing the sunglasses over the side while thinking that he should be putting them down in the scupper a foot from his hand.

⁂

Fifteen men were killed outright by the impact of the Betty or its flaming fuel, and twenty-nine who were dragged from the inferno suffered from a wide range of injuries.

RM3 Robert Coates, who left his station in Radio-2, an unscathed compartment directly beneath the incinerated 20mm gun platform, pulled one grievously burned victim from the smoldering ruins. While awaiting corpsmen and a litter, the terribly burned and somewhat delirious sailor alternately called for his mother and begged Coates to "put me out of my misery."

Cdr Mark Crouter, *San Francisco*'s exec and the senior man in the impact area, emerged from Battle-2 with extensive burns. On reporting to the midships dressing station, however, Commander Crouter refused preferential treatment. In fact, he perched himself on a mess bench and drove the young doctor on duty there to distraction by refusing any treatment whatsoever until everyone else, even men with far lesser injuries, had been treated. The doctor did not put up an argument he knew he was destined to lose, but he did detail a corpsman to wrap a blanket around the exec's shoulders and give him a sedative to help ease the pain until the other casualties had been treated. Later, when all the injured were transferred to transport *President Jackson* for treatment and evacuation to Noumea, Commander Crouter refused to leave his ship.

After fully recovering from the shock of nearly burning to death, S1 Willie Boyce ventured down to the crew's mess hall to visit with a buddy who had come a lot closer. After chiding the burned man for going on duty near the crash site dressed only in a skivvy shirt and dungarees, Boyce asked if there was anything the burned man needed. "Willie," the shipmate explained, "after the plane crash and during the scuffle I lost my crucifix. I want one. Would you find me another?" Boyce ran topside and asked another Catholic member of the aviation division if he would be willing to give up his crucifix for the burned man. The sailor complied without a word, and Boyce returned to the mess hall to deliver the article. After placing the crucifix on the burned man's incongruously unburned chest, Boyce again returned topside. Days later, he heard that his severely injured buddy was among seven *San Francisco* sailors who succumbed to their injuries aboard *President Jackson*.

卍

As soon as the shooting over the fleet stopped, destroyer *Laffey* was dispatched to rescue Japanese airmen from the water or the floating wrecks of their bombers. Several minutes later, a lookout reported seeing a swimmer several hundred yards off the starboard beam, so the ship turned and slowed to investigate as all light weapons were trained outboard as a precaution. The swimmer, who was unidentifiable beneath a thick coat of fuel oil, suddenly called out, "Don't shoot. I'm American." Still exercising great caution, deck hands threw out a line and hauled the swimmer aboard. He was indeed an American, S1 Ralph Boncoskey, a *San Francisco* crewman who had jumped overboard to avoid being incinerated by the Betty that had crashed into his ship. Boncoskey was taken below to have his superficial burns treated by the destroyer's doctor.

II

At 1527, long after it was determined that there were no more Japanese aircraft in the area or on the way, RAdm Kelly Turner's transports and cargomen returned to their anchorages off Kukum and Lunga Point, where they were joined by the landing craft they had cast off earlier as well as others from the Lunga Boat Pool. The few hours remaining were filled with furious activity, for the news was that all the transports and cargomen would be sailing for Espiritu Santo. News from scouts and observers operating far up the Slot confirmed rumors that a power-ful—perhaps overwhelming—Japanese surface battle group was on the way to Guadalcanal.

The airwaves had been filled with sighting reports from all along the Solomons chain. A message arriving at 1035 indicated that two battleships or heavy cruisers, one cruiser, and six destroy-ers had been sighted 335 miles from Guadalcanal. A message at 1045 stated that five destroyers had been sighted 195 miles from Guadalcanal. At 1450, Admiral Turner was warned that two Jap-anese aircraft carriers and two destroyers had been sighted in ex-tremely heavy weather 265 miles east of Henderson Field. This report turned out to be erroneous, but it had an immediate impact on Turner's thinking. Adding to the general concern, Turner's grim experience had taught him that scout aircraft frequently missed much of what there was to find. Further, since no Japanese transports had been sighted on the move toward Guadalcanal, Turner was obliged to reason that the Japanese warships were specifically charged with destroying his transports and cargomen or, secondarily, bombarding Henderson Field. Knowing what he knew from radio-intelligence intercepts and the scouting reports and after factoring in potential omissions and surprises, it was clear to Turner that he had to be gone before sunset.

༆

Far to the north, from a high hill overlooking the Shortlands anchorages, coastwatcher Paul Mason had reported on November 6 that thirty-three Japanese vessels of all types were in sight of his lookout. Coastwatcher Jack Read, in northern Bougainville, had been under severe pressure from Japanese scouting parties late in October, so had been ordered off the air until things cooled down. However, on November 8, Read broke radio silence to report that a dozen transports were steaming southeastward past his vantage point overlooking Buka Passage. On November 10, Mason reported seeing sixty-one vessels of all types anchored in the Shortlands, including six cruisers and thirty-three destroyers.

The Allied intelligence-analysis agencies were being overwhelmed by sightings, warnings, alerts, and surmises. It was extremely difficult to piece together a cogent picture, but it was evident that the Japanese had another big push in the works. Radio intelligence strongly indicated that a very large surface battle group had left the Truk anchorage for a journey toward the Solomons. Radio intercepts also revealed that a large surface bombardment force would be dispatched to clear the way for a large force of troop transports charged with delivering infantry reinforcements to Guadalcanal. At least two battleships appeared to be involved in the Japanese order of battle.

When Admiral Turner added up what he knew from aircraft sightings on November 12, he came up far short with respect to the numbers and types of warships—and transports—previously sighted or whose presence had been divined by radio intelligence. Chiefly, he had no fresh news as to the whereabouts of the two battleships.

Facing the unknown with Turner's four transports and two cargomen were two heavy cruisers, one light cruiser, two light anti-aircraft cruisers, eleven fleet destroyers, and two fast destroyer-minesweepers. Turner was willing to leave all the warships except the minesweepers at Guadalcanal under RAdm Dan Callaghan's command, but experience had shown that there was an upper limit of ships that could be effectively controlled during a night surface action. In the end, it was decided to leave Callaghan all five cruisers and eight of the eleven available destroyers. In any event, two of the three destroyers that would be accompanying Turner were low on fuel and the third, *Buchanan*, was damaged.

Other large American fleet units were converging on Guadalcanal, but there was no way they could arrive in time to participate in an action this night. These included Task Force 16, a battle force built around fleet carrier *Enterprise*, which had pulled out of Noumea on November 11 with most of a Seabee battalion embarked to complete as much repair work as possible before the Pacific Fleet's last partially operational fleet carrier was recalled to battle. Also sailing northward from Noumea as part of Task Force 16 were *Washington* and *South Dakota*, the only operational fast battleships in the U.S. Pacific Fleet.

By late afternoon, at Guadalcanal, it was estimated that all the troops and 90 percent of the materiel aboard the transports could be landed by nightfall. The two remaining cargomen, *Libra* and *Betelguese*, would require several additional days to unload their cargoes, but Turner decided that they should sail for the rear with him.

Dan Callaghan's reconstituted and enlarged Task Group 67.4 would accompany Turner's Task Group 67.1 out of the immediate area and then return to engage the oncoming Japanese in Indispensable Strait or off Savo, wherever they could be found. All the details that could be set in advance were discussed in a three-way conversation between Turner, Callaghan, and RAdm Norman Scott, who would be Callaghan's second in command aboard *Atlanta*.

卍

The Japanese plan was fully in motion.

As Turner's Task Group 67.1 sailed from Lengo Channel on the evening of November 12, RAdm Raizo Tanaka, embarked in fleet destroyer *Hayashio*, led a dozen heavily escorted Imperial Army transports out of the Shortlands anchorage. Tanaka, who had formed the Tokyo Express in August in response to the Imperial Army's need to ferry its soldiers to Guadalcanal, was one of Japan's best and most experienced commanders at sea. That he was unenthusiastic about leading a dozen slow, fat transports into waters dominated by the Cactus Air Force was a crucial sign that the Japanese plan was flawed. After all, Tanaka had personally devised the system of delivering troops and supplies by means of fast destroyers. Under Tanaka's proven and successful method, the troops were invariably landed during the night of the same day they left the Shortlands. Every time Tanaka had employed standard transports, he had run afoul of the Cactus Air Force. The transports could not possibly reach Guadalcanal before the night of November 13. Thus, they would be exposed to Cactus bombers and fighters for most of the daylight hours of November 13—longer if their progress was in any way delayed.

Still, Tanaka's superiors had a point in favor of risking the Army transports. Cactus bombers had grown increasingly numerous, aggressive, and effective, and far too many of Tanaka's precious destroyers had been damaged or lost. Two had been taken out of service by crippling bomb hits on November 7, and these losses had been severely compounded the next night when Tulagi-based PT boats went into action against a group of Japanese destroyers. The speedy plywood boats had damaged one destroyer, and their unexpected presence had severely shaken the Japanese.

The senior commanders who were counting on Tanaka's getting through had assembled two powerful surface battle forces to clear the way for the vulnerable transports. Preceding Tanaka from the Shortlands was a bombardment force, commanded by VAdm Hiroaki Abe, which was due to arrive at Guadalcanal in the early-morning hours of November 12. A second, somewhat lighter force, commanded by VAdm Gunichi Mikawa, was charged with similar responsibilities; it was to leave the Shortlands after sunrise on November 13 and proceed to Guadalcanal by a circuitous northern route far from the regularly patrolled Allied aerial search sectors and bombard Henderson Field that night. If the two bombardments were successful, Cactus Air would not be able to interdict Tanaka while he was making his final daylight dash to Cape Esperance, where the vulnerable transports were to be unloaded and on their way well before dawn on November 14.

Tanaka was frankly skeptical.

卍

VAdm Hiroaki Abe, commander of the bombardment force due to arrive off Guadalcanal on the night of November 12–13, was a blooded destroyer specialist. The knowledge that his actions might decide the fate of 12,000 soldiers, many tons of precious supplies, and the outcome of the Guadalcanal campaign weighed heavily upon Abe, who felt that the monthly cycles of buildup, attack, and defeat were draining Japan of her best ships and men. In fact, Abe, who was widely known as an extremely cautious man, left his briefing aboard Adm Isoroku Yamamoto's flagship with the firm conviction that his bombardment force would be challenged in the restricted waters off Guadalcanal. Abe was exremely unhappy with that prospect, and he frankly transmitted his concerns to at least several of his captains.

Eight fleet destroyers and a light cruiser left Truk on November 9 and joined two battleships and three destroyers in the Shortlands early on November 12. The combined force was located by an American B-17 heavy bomber out of New Guinea at about 0830. The B-17, which radioed several sighting reports to Admiral Turner via its New Guinea base, was eventually chased away by several Zero fighters launched from carrier *Junyo*, which was already in the area but which remained undetected. News of the B-17 contact went a long way toward heightening Admiral Abe's deep concerns over his prospects when he reached Guadalcanal.

卍

RAdm Dan Callaghan did not like his assignment. Though extremely well thought of in high places and the senior of the two rear admirals to be left behind with the battle force, Callaghan was not the logical choice for command. He had no direct combat experience; all his time in the South Pacific until a few weeks earlier had been as chief of staff to VAdm Robert Ghormley, the overcautious area commander who had been relieved by VAdm Bill Halsey. Though available to stay on as Halsey's staff chief, Callaghan had been let go in a virtually clean sweep of the area headquarters; Halsey had the pick of all his favorites from the carrier fleet he had commanded early in the war, and he barely knew Callaghan. In the end, Kelly Turner had taken in Callaghan, but that had meant moving RAdm Norman Scott to a lesser command.

No one could know it, but Scott's obligatory subordination to Callaghan was crucial. Scott was a winner, an authentic tiger who knew how to train his subordinates and lead them in battle. He had won the U.S. Navy's only surface victory of the war at Cape Esperance in mid-October. Though his leadership had shown several flawed tendencies, Scott was not above self-criticism, and he was working tirelessly on correcting himself and his captains when he was replaced by Dan Callaghan.

Neither admiral had yet had an opportunity to make a mark on their respective new commands, though Scott's hand was by far the surer in view of his experience and fully developed command philosophy. Callaghan had never been to war as anything except a subordinate, and the departed Ghormley, a vacillating worrier whose instinctive focus upon details invariably caused him to lose sight of the big picture, had hardly been a strong role model.

RM3 Bill Potwin, who stood his watch on *San Francisco*'s flag bridge until relieved at 1730, was struck by the handsome, silver-thatched Callaghan's demeanor. A highly regarded and extremely hard-working officer who had served as President Franklin Roosevelt's naval aide before the war and as *San Francisco*'s first wartime skipper, Callaghan endlessly paced the flag bridge, muttering that he was reluctant to carry out his orders, expressing his desire to talk things over directly with Halsey, admitting that there was no time to do so, and revealing to the rattled officers and sailors on duty around him that they were in for a rough night.

BM2 Vance Carter was taking an early evening breather beside his battle station, *San Francisco*'s Turret-2, when he glanced up at the flag bridge. There he saw Callaghan's familiar visage as the admiral stared out to sea. Carter was struck by the look of absolute somber concentration that marred the admiral's youthfully handsome features.

⚛

All the American ships entered Lengo Channel at 1915 and proceeded eastward at 14 knots. The readiness level was immediately reduced to Condition-II, which allowed many tired and tense sailors and officers to leave their battle stations for a quick meal or even a shower and a change of clothes. However, most of the crewmen dropped off to sleep at or near their battle stations after washing down a quick sandwich with a scalding cup of coffee.

The ships cleared Lengo Channel at 2030. At 2200, as soon as the transports and cargomen and their escorts—*Shaw, Buchanan, McCalla, Southard,* and *Hovey*—were safely away, Task Force 67.1 turned back in the hope it would meet the Japanese force off Savo at about midnight.

Emulating a plan devised by Admiral Scott for the Cape Esperance Battle, Admiral Callaghan arranged his entire thirteen-ship force in an easy-to-handle single column: Destroyers *Cushing, Laffey, Sterett,* and *O'Bannon* were in the vanguard; cruisers *Atlanta, San Francisco, Portland, Helena,* and *Juneau* were in the center; and destroyers *Aaron Ward, Barton, Monssen,* and *Fletcher* were in the rear.

As the return trip began, in the strange way that sailors have of sharing solid information and rumors, word went out about a number of disquieting factors: There were thirteen ships in the line and the numerals of Task Force 67 add up to 13. The sailors aboard *Fletcher,* the thirteenth ship in the column, had two more numbers to add: The destroyer's bow number was 445, which adds up to 13, and she had a total of thirteen 5-inch, 40mm, and 20mm guns aboard.

After midnight it would be Friday, November 13.

PART III

The Ships

12

Each of the navies contesting the outcome of the maritime portion of the Guadalcanal campaign employed five basic "fleet" warship types in the Eastern Solomons: battleships, aircraft carriers, cruisers, destroyers, and submarines. These standard types were in many cases augmented by a yet-emerging array of specialized auxiliaries such as various types of transports, tenders, minesweepers, and tugs, to name a few.

Within the five major warship categories were numerous subdivisions, such as light and heavy cruisers, old and "fast" battleships, fleet and coastal submarines, emerging classes of antiaircraft cruisers and destroyers, and a dizzying array of separate and special destroyer types and sizes. Except for the "old" battleships of both nations—World War I–era constructions upgraded for use in the new war—nearly all the fleet-type warships employed in the Solomons had been built following Japan's abrogation of the 1930 naval disarmament accord. However, there were ships of the earlier and later eras in use by both sides, along with other ships designed in the late 1930s and launched in the year before, or even in the months after, Pearl Harbor.

Launched in 1932, the oldest warship under RAdm Dan Callaghan's command on the evening of November 12, 1942, was heavy cruiser *Portland*, which had been designed with her one sister ship especially to counter a type of German commerce raider that had plagued all the world's seas during World War I. *Portland*'s chief characteristic was her huge fuel tanks and, by extension, her extremely long range. She was an extremely thin-skinned vessel, which helped her maintain her range and speed advantages, but which rendered her especially vulnerable to torpedoes. Indeed, *Portland* had been struck by three Japanese submarine-launched torpedoes while serving in the antiaircraft screen at the Santa Cruz carrier battle, but she had been spared a cataclysmic demise by the failure of all the torpedoes to detonate. Weighing in at 9,800 tons, she was well within the standard size of American heavy cruisers of her vintage. (U.S. cruisers were rated "light" or "heavy" according to the size of their main guns, and not by virtue of displacement; light cruiser *Helena* boasted a marginally greater displacement than heavy cruisers *San Francisco* and *Portland*, but she carried smaller main guns.) *Portland* was armed with nine 8-inch main guns mounted in two triple turrets forward and one triple turret aft, and eight 5-inch dual-purpose guns deployed four to a side in single mounts. She had been modernized over the years, and particularly around the outbreak of the war. Her fire-control radars were well within the U.S. Navy standard of the day, but she had no surface-search radar.

Heavy cruiser *San Francisco*, which was launched in early 1934, was armed with nine 8-inch main guns in two triple turrets forward and one triple turret aft, and eight 5-inch dual-purpose guns in four single mounts to a side. She also boasted two quadruple 1.1-inch antiaircraft mounts amidships and two on the fantail, and an uneven array of nineteen 20mm antiaircraft guns. Like *Portland*, she was well within the U.S. Navy standard of the day, for heavy cruisers. However, also like *Portland*, *San Francisco* lacked modern search radars. Moreover, the *San Francisco* returning to Savo Sound on the evening of November 12 was a wounded ship: Her after gunnery-control radar had been demolished and her secondary command center had been severely damaged. In addition, she had undergone a change of command only days earlier, and there were still a number of internal organizational pressures to be mitigated.

Light cruiser *Helena* was far and away the most modern and best equipped of Dan Callaghan's three gun cruisers. Her communications array was the best to be found in the battle force, and she had the *only* modern SG surface-search radar set among the three gun cruisers. Moreover, she was the only American cruiser commanded by a blooded, successful, and proven aggressive veteran of an American surface victory. Equipped with fifteen 6-inch main guns mounted in five triple turrets, *Helena*'s firepower was superior to that of either of the heavy cruisers.

Light antiaircraft cruisers *Atlanta* and *Juneau* were nearly identical twins. They had been designed specifically to escort aircraft carriers, but their sixteen-gun batteries of rapid-fire 5-inch guns had been proven effective in a shore-bombardment role when a sister ship had supported the initial landings near Guadalcanal. With the shrinkage in U.S. Navy carrier assets, the two had been relegated to a surface-escort role during the preceding weeks, but, until the evening of November 12, neither had been considered for a surface-battle role. The *Atlanta*-class cruisers were little more than high-speed ordnance magazines surmounted by a superstructure and eight dual-5-inch antiaircraft mounts. Each also carried a pair of quadruple 21-inch torpedo mounts, one on each side. It is doubtful if either ship carried any armor-piercing rounds, and their radars and associated gun-direction installations were set to locate and track airplanes. Each of the small 6,000-ton cruisers was extremely thin-skinned and therefore particularly vulnerable to both gunfire and torpedo damage. That one, *Atlanta*, was the flagship of a battle-wise commander like RAdm Norman Scott merely points up the paucity of alternatives to their being anywhere near the potential arena of a serious night surface engagement. *Juneau* boasted one of the four modern SG surface-search radars available that night.

The eight American destroyers accompanying the mixed bag of cruisers were yet more of a mixed bag. The oldest by far was *Cushing*, which had been launched on the last day of 1935. At 1,465 tons, she was also the smallest, and she was serviced by the smallest crew, 172 officers and men. It is worth noting that *Cushing* alone among the eight U.S. destroyers sailing back toward Savo required a 21-man "fire brigade" to pass 5-inch rounds from her ready service ammunition compartment to her forward gun mount. During an action, every one of those 21 sailors (and 1 officer, who had been placed in the line to gain seasoning) was fully exposed to enemy fire. *Cushing* was also equipped with twelve 21-inch torpedo tubes in three quadruple midships mounts—one on the centerline and one at each waist.

Sailing behind *Cushing* was *Laffey*, one of four 1,630-ton *Benson*-class destroyers in the American line that night. Commissioned less than two months before Pearl Harbor, *Laffey* still lacked surface-search radar, but her gunnery radar was on par with the best sets available anywhere at that time. Because of numerous, concurrent, and ongoing fleet modernization programs, the U.S. warships of a particular class were not necessarily identical. Depending upon the major port in which a particular ship happened to find itself at a particular time, *Benson*-class destroyers might or might not be fitted out with a 1.1-inch antiaircraft mount or a specific number of 20mm antiaircraft guns. In addition to her four modern dual-purpose 5-inch mounts, *Laffey* mounted one quadruple 1.1-inch antiaircraft mount and five single 20mm cannon. She also carried five 21-inch torpedoes in her single quintuple midships mount. *Laffey* and her sisters were among the newest and most reliable destroyers in the U.S. Fleet.

The third vanguard destroyer was *Sterett*, a 1,500-ton *Craven*-class destroyer commissioned at the end of 1938. In addition to her four 5-inch gun mounts and six 20mm antiaircraft guns, *Sterett* was outfitted with eight 21-inch torpedoes mounted in two quadruple mounts, one mount to a side.

The fourth and last of the vanguard destroyers was *O'Bannon*, a thoroughly modern example of the new *Fletcher*-class ships that were just beginning to reach the Fleet. *O'Bannon*, which had been launched in mid-March 1942, displaced 2,050 tons, and was crewed by 300 officers and men. She mounted five 5-inch guns—two forward, one amidships, and two aft—controlled by the best gun-direction system available to any navy's destroyers. Her antiaircraft groupment consisted of eight 20mm guns, and her armaments were rounded out by ten 21-inch torpedoes in two quintuple centerline mounts forward and aft of her after stack. *O'Bannon* was also equipped with one of four SG surface-search radar sets available in the American column.

Aaron Ward was the first of the four rear-guard destroyers. Another *Benson*-class ship, she was configured somewhat differently from *Laffey* in that she had not been outfitted with 1.1-inch antiaircraft guns. She mounted four 5-inch guns, eight 20mm guns, and five 21-inch torpedoes. The second rear-guard destroyer was *Barton*, a *Benson*-class ship identically configured to *Aaron Ward*.

Monssen, the last and oldest of the *Benson*-class destroyers in Callaghan's line, was somewhat more powerful than her three sisters. In addition to her four 5-inch and eight 20mm guns, she mounted ten 21-inch torpedoes in two quintuple centerline mounts. She was also far and away the most blooded ship of her class. She had provided shore bombardment on numerous occasions beginning on D-Day at Guadalcanal and she had participated in the antiaircraft screen around one of the carriers at the Eastern Solomons battle.

Though the first of her class to be laid down, *Fletcher* had been launched in May 1942, about six weeks after her sister ship, *O'Bannon*. Her later departure for the war zone had resulted in her being diverted for several last-minute upgrades, including the replacement of several 20mm guns with the first dual 40mm antiaircraft mount to find its way to the South Pacific aboard a destroyer. The most important upgrade of all was the installation of her new SG surface-search radar.

※

The largest, oldest, and slowest warships in Solomons waters the evening of November 12 were *Hiei* and *Kirishima*, two of four modernized *Kongo*-class "battlecruisers" built in 1912 and 1913. Though upgraded and redesignated as battleships in the late 1930s, the *Kongo*-class warships were not meant to participate in a modern surface engagement. Rather, like their sister ships, *Kongo* and *Haruna*, had done about a month earlier, *Hiei* and *Kirishima* were sailing to Guadalcanal to deliver a magazine-load of 14-inch high-capacity bombardment projectiles to Henderson Field—the hard

way. Each battleship mounted eight 14-inch guns in four dual turrets, fourteen single-mount 6-inch guns, eight 5-inch antiaircraft
guns in four dual mounts, and twenty 25mm antiaircraft guns.
This was a formidable array by any standard. Neither ship had
radar and their automated gunnery control system was cruder than
systems aboard American warships. For purposes of fulfilling their
bombardment mission, the battleships would rely upon their superior illumination rounds, the best night-vision binoculars in the
world, and observers specially selected for their superior eyesight.

The Japanese force incorporated only one cruiser that night,
light cruiser *Nagara*, the flagship of RAdm Susumu Kimura's
Destroyer Squadron 10. (It was common practice for Japanese
destroyer squadrons to incorporate a light cruiser as flagship.)
Launched in 1921, the 5,170-ton cruiser was moderately upgraded
in the mid-1930s, following the abrogation of the 1930 naval accord. By late 1942, she mounted seven 5.5-inch single-mount main
guns, a pair of 3-inch single-mount antiaircraft guns, and eight
24-inch torpedo tubes arrayed in four dual mounts. It is important
to underscore the presence of the torpedo tubes aboard *Nagara*
and most other Japanese cruisers, for no U.S. cruisers of the
period, except the *Atlanta*-class light antiaircraft cruisers, were so
equipped.

Three of the five destroyers comprising Destroyer Squadron
10—*Akatsuki*, *Ikazuchi*, and *Inazuma*—were *Akatsuki*-class vessels
of 1931–1932 vintage. These were 2,090-ton ships rated at 38
knots. When commissioned, this class had been equipped with six
5-inch single-purpose guns arrayed in three dual mounts. Between
late 1941 and early 1942, however, one of the two after dual mounts
had been removed to make room for additional antiaircraft guns
and the remaining mounts, one forward and one aft, had been modernized to carry dual-purpose guns. In all, these destroyers carried
four 5-inch guns, fourteen 25mm dual-mount antiaircraft guns,
four 13mm antiaircraft machine guns, and nine 24-inch torpedo
tubes in three triple mounts.

Two of the three remaining Destroyer Squadron 10 ships were
Amatsukaze and *Yukikaze*, veteran *Kagero*-class destroyers of 2,033
tons rated at 35.5 knots of speed. Each of these vessels, launched in
1939, mounted six 5-inch dual-purpose guns arrayed in three dual

mounts, one forward and two aft, plus four 25mm and three 13mm antiaircraft guns, and eight 24-inch torpedo tubes in two quadruple centerline mounts.

The remaining Destroyer Squadron 10 destroyer was *Teruzuki*, an *Akitsuki*-class antiaircraft destroyer designed to fill roughly the same niche intended for the American *Atlanta*-class cruisers. Commissioned in November 1941, *Teruzuki* displaced 2,701 tons and was rated at 33 knots. She mounted eight 3.9-inch antiaircraft guns in four dual mounts, two forward and two aft, as well as two dual 25mm mounts. She carried only one quadruple 24-inch torpedo mount. Beyond a doubt, she had been attached to Destroyer Squadron 10 to fend off Cactus-based bombers and fighters in the event the battleships were caught in the open during daylight hours; her bombardment and surface-action capabilities were considered negligible.

The balance of the Japanese force on its way to Guadalcanal was Destroyer Squadron 4, five reasonably modern fleet destroyers commanded by RAdm Tamotsu Takama, who was embarked in *Asagumo*, a 1,961-ton *Asashio*-class destroyer launched in late 1937. Rated at 35 knots, *Asagumo* mounted six 5-inch dual-purpose guns in one forward and two after mounts, four 25mm antiaircraft cannon in two dual mounts, and eight 24-inch torpedo tubes arrayed in two quadruple mounts.

Destroyer Division 4's remaining destroyers—*Harusame, Murasame, Samidare,* and *Yudachi*—were all 1,580-ton *Shiratsuyu*-class vessels launched in 1935 and 1936. Rated at 34 knots, they each mounted five 5-inch dual-purpose guns, two in a forward mount, one in an after mount, and two in a mount farthest aft. Antiaircraft guns included four 25mm cannon and two 13mm machine guns, and each carried eight 24-inch torpedo tubes in a pair of quadruple mounts.

In many ways, the Japanese destroyers were of the same general type as the American destroyers built before 1939. There were differences, to be sure. Except for *Teruzuki*, they and the older American destroyers all shared the same basic technologies insofar as general design and types of guns were concerned.

Overall, the Japanese warships had about ten percent more torpedo tubes than the American warships: ninety-five Japanese torpedo tubes versus eighty-six American torpedo tubes. In addition, the Japanese had two important qualitative advantages: Their 24-inch Long Lance torpedoes were faster, larger, longer ranged, and more reliable than the American 21-inchers, and their destroyers carried enough reloads for at least partial second torpedo salvos.

The Japanese warships had no gunnery radars, as did all the American warships. This last was of potentially dubious advantage to the Americans inasmuch as Japanese captains and gunnery officers invariably believed and relied upon the observations of their highly skilled and highly trained observers while their American counterparts did not always believe the reports emanating from less well-trained, less experienced operators of sometimes balky equipment still considered "newfangled" or, at best, "experimental" by many American senior officers.

Other American technological advantages were in many ways offset by several Japanese technological advantages. Greatly enhancing the results of eyeball observations was a special Japanese flashless powder, which was particularly useful at night. The Japanese had also developed a superior starshell, which burned brighter and hung over its targets far longer than its American counterpart.

In most measurable ways, the thirteen American warships and fourteen Japanese warships were about evenly matched. However, the critical differences were not measurable: The Japanese were more experienced and perhaps better trained while the Americans knew they had to win the impending battle so, perhaps, had the greater will to win.

Among the unmeasurable and imponderable factors were the expectations and plans of the opposing groups of commanders and leaders.

13

In many ways, the composition of Dan Callaghan's makeshift battle force was a sobering reflection of the vagaries of the Pacific War to that date. In better times, ships of a particular class were grouped together in standing squadrons and divisions. In that manner, similar ships with similar fighting characteristics could be sent into action together under senior commanders and captains who had worked together to forge the various vessels and their crews into an integrated fighting force. But the U.S. Fleet was spread thin fighting a two-ocean war it was close to losing, and the incredible losses from sinkings and battle damage had gutted all but a few of the old standing squadrons and divisions. Formations of cruisers and destroyers had been formed and reformed, closing ranks as they sustained their own losses, accepting orphans and early arrivals from destroyed or not-yet-formed squadrons and divisions.

The odds Dan Callaghan and his sailors thought they were facing that night had made a harried, worried man of the commander and would have done the same for the commanded had they known as much—and as little—as he knew. The ongoing and unremitting war had proven time and again to survivor and tyro

alike that, when you go, you go with what you have. On the evening of November 12, 1942, Dan Callaghan's makeshift battle
force, an uneven amalgam of two uneven amalgams, was all the
U.S. Fleet had to offer up to the gods of this vast and undecided
war.

Callaghan was sailing into his first battle without a plan
and without a realistic means for controlling the ships under his
command.

San Francisco was Admiral Callaghan's flagship mainly because
she had been his first wartime command and, significantly, because
she was the namesake of his hometown. While a good ship by most
standards of the day, *San Francisco* had proven to be only a marginally efficient surface-force flagship in her single earlier surface
engagement—at Cape Esperance in mid-October, when she had
embarked RAdm Norman Scott and his staff. Her array of radios,
while impressive, was not really up to the pressures of controlling a
diffused surface battle at night. She did not have SG surface-search
radar, so Admiral Callaghan could not benefit from the clear real-
time picture that modern marvel might have afforded him during a
night battle that would certainly degenerate into a confusing melee,
as was the nature of such actions. While it was necessary for *San
Francisco* to accompany Callaghan's battle force, there was at least
one superior candidate for the role of flagship. That ship was
Helena, a proven veteran of Cape Esperance that did have one of the
four new SG radar sets available to Callaghan's battle force.

That the new SG surface-search radar was a winner in a night
surface action had been effectively demonstrated at Cape Esperance
a month earlier. There, *Helena* had been the first American ship to
locate the Japanese battle force and the only U.S. warship involved
in the action to have a clear picture of the battle from start to finish.
RAdm Norman Scott, who had discounted many of *Helena*'s real-
time sighting reports at Cape Esperance, had vowed to mend his
ways after the conclusion of the battle, and he had been hard at
work developing the SG system's battle potential when he had been
relieved by Dan Callaghan and obliged to transfer his flag to *Atlanta*, a cruiser that did not have the system. Light cruiser *Juneau*
and destroyers *Fletcher* and *O'Bannon* also had SG surface-search
radar systems, but *Juneau* was the last of five cruisers and *O'Bannon*

and *Fletcher* had each been placed at the rear of their destroyer groups. Respectively, the three were 8,000, 3,000, and 12,000 yards behind *Cushing*, the column's vanguard (and least modern) destroyer. Indeed, *Fletcher* was the last ship in the 7-mile American column. *Helena*'s SG radar, the only one of the four that was manned by watchstanders who had proven themselves in battle, was 7,000 yards behind *Cushing* and 2,000 yards behind the flagship. Of the four SG sets, *Helena*'s had the broadest reach because it was mounted higher than the other three sets.

In sum, the placement of the four SG sets reflects no evidence of any thought having been devoted to the potential benefits of the modern marvel. Quite the opposite is true. Dan Callaghan had had no prior experience with surface-search radar and probably had not even been adequately briefed about its potential. He promulgated no plans for utilizing the many advantages it might have afforded him and his battle force.

In addition, it is extremely difficult at this far remove in time to conjure up a *good* reason for dispatching heavy cruiser *Pensacola* for duty with carrier *Enterprise*'s Task Force 16 when *Juneau*, if not RAdm Norman Scott's flagship, *Atlanta*, could certainly have been spared. Both antiaircraft cruisers had been miserably employed during the daytime action against the torpedo-laden Bettys and thus need not have been there. Moreover, Admirals Turner, Callaghan, and Scott had for days had ample reason to believe that there might be a surface battle on the night of November 12 or 13, which renders the dispatch of *Pensacola* and her 8-inch main battery all the more puzzling.

卍

All the main guns of all the American participants were controlled by battery directors employing FC and FD gunnery radars. Since radar was a fairly modern marvel, the presence of radar-directed guns was a fairly new wrinkle in the conduct of surface gunnery action. LCdr Butch Parker, who had been blooded aboard old four-stack destroyers in the East Indies, had not had modern directors aboard any of the ships he had commanded. Until the introduction of battery directors, gunnery officers had stood upon an exposed platform over the bridge and had selected targets by sight and guided their guns by means of a crude sighting apparatus. The only difference between the method employed in late 1941 and early 1942 with the method employed in 1898, 1918, and 1938 was that the gunnery officer used sound-powered battle phones rather than an array of voice tubes to communicate firing information to his gunners.

Going into an action or potential action, the sight-setter in each mount or turret aligned his sights with the director sight and gave up control to the director officer, who was often the ship's gunnery officer in the case of the destroyers. (The cruisers were equipped to split control between separate directors overseeing their forward and after batteries, and each of the gun cruisers employed separate directors for their starboard and port secondary 5-inch mounts.)

Once the mounts and turrets were locked in train with the director, each turn of the director caused the guns to traverse in unison. Likewise, the guns were automatically raised and lowered by the director, thus providing range settings. If director control was lost for any reason or for any length of time, each mount or turret was fully capable of instantly going to local control. Each mount or turret was fully equipped with the optical gear necessary to bring the gun to bear on its target and the mechanical gear required to fire the shell.

Shells and powder were moved upward toward the mounts and turrets by means of hoists from magazines at the lowest level of each ship devoted to a particular mount or turret. Each shell and each powder bag arrived in an upper handling room, which was usually but not always located beneath the mount or turret being serviced. In the case of about half the guns aboard each destroyer, mounts resting atop a deck structure were serviced by upper handling rooms just below the level of the main deck. Generally, the same rule applied to guns in raised cruiser turrets. In *Cushing's* case, the mounts farthest forward and farthest aft, Mount-1 and Mount-4, were serviced, respectively, from the same handling rooms that serviced Mount-2 and Mount-3. In this case, rounds and powder were handed through a scuttle at the level of the main deck to bucket-brigade-type lines manned by exposed sailors.

Powder bags were stored in separate metal canisters usually

referred to as "powder cans." Each can was unloaded in the magazine and usually returned to its rack as soon as it was empty. Armor-piercing rounds, starshells, or point-detonation rounds (for use against shore targets or aircraft) were selected on the basis of orders from the mount captain or turret captain overseeing the operations of a particular gun. Several ships had new variable-time-fused shells to replace the less-desirable point-detonation rounds, but they were just entering the logistical system and were thus in short supply.

Most ships had a gun or guns specially designated to fire starshells, though it or they could fire other types of rounds if required to do so. Where large formations were involved, specific destroyers were often designated to fire all the starshells for the groups of ships to which they were assigned. (For example, all of *Sterett*'s guns were loaded with starshells to aid the forward group of U.S. warships returning to Sealark Channel.) In general, the main guns aboard the gun cruisers were all loaded with armor-piercing rounds while the 5-inch secondary batteries were set to provide a mix of starshells and variable-time or point-detonation rounds.

Each round had a safety device that had to be overridden at or before the time it was fired so that it would detonate only as desired. In all cases, the safety had to be deactivated and the shell had to spin a specific number of times before a detonation could take place. The newer ships moved shells from the handling room to the mount by means of a contraption that both deactivated the safety by mechanical means (5-inch rounds had little "ears" near the point that had to be clipped) and spun it a few times on the way up to the mount. *Cushing*'s fuse-setters, as they were called, were located within the crew shelter of each mount and were activated by a crank in the control of a sailor somewhat misleadingly called a "shell loader." Once the safety was deactivated—once the fuse was set—the shell was potentially lethal to the mount crew. It was thus a standard procedure to unload guns "through the muzzle" rather than try to remove an activated shell from the breech once the breech was closed.

In the event of a misfire, where the shell and the powder remained in the breech and could not be fired by normal means, extraordinary and often heroic split-second decisions had to be made.

If rapping the breech with a rawhide mallet did not get the desired result, the breech had to be opened and the shell and powder had to be removed by hand. It was well within the realm of possibility that the act of opening the breech would set off the powder. If that happened, men were sure to die. Safety precautions that could be imposed during training could not be imposed in the heat of battle and, as a matter of course, no one left a mount when a misfire was being cleared, unless by his own volition.

The size and composition of gun crews and the specific duties of the gunners varied from ship to ship. Such variations were usually factors of the vintage of the ship and its guns.

While all the guns aboard any American warship were controlled by the gunnery department, relatively few of the men manning them were rated as gunner's mates, that is, sailors specially trained to both fire and maintain the guns. On most ships, the deck division—boatswain's mates, coxswains, and their seaman strikers—provided numerous bodies to man the guns in action, including mount captains overseeing junior gunner's mates. Often as not, sailors holding a wide variety of ratings—cooks and storekeepers, and even engineering specialists such as firemen, watertenders, machinist's mates, and electrician's mates—manned guns in action. The difference was that the gunner's mates and their strikers were generally in charge of maintaining the guns during work hours while the deck force kept the ship clean and the cooks cooked, or whatever. Gunnery, then, was a secondary trade for most of the men employed in firing the guns in battle. This is not to say, however, that the paramount importance of such duty was not underscored by unremitting training.

⚛

The torpedo tubes aboard the destroyers and the *Atlanta*-class light cruisers were maintained, controlled, and fired by torpedo specialists, the least knowledgeable of whom was usually the junior officer in charge. Sailors with other ratings rarely had anything to do with the torpedoes, which were part of a system far more complex than the various parts of the gunnery system. All the torpedomen aboard a ship were not needed to man the directors and tubes during an action, so the juniors were usually doled out to the other divisions for secondary jobs. (*Fletcher*'s S1 Don Dahlke, who shot down a Betty as a 20mm gunner, was a torpedoman striker.) The torpedo department also maintained and operated a ship's depth-charge system.

As with gun mounts and turrets, the torpedoman manning a seat atop and at the rear of each mount aligned his sights with those of the dominant director; typically, there was one director located on each wing of the bridge. The mounts were trained by keeping the local control aligned with the director, and firing was undertaken by the director operator, usually a first-class torpedoman. If the fish were not expelled from the tubes on command of the director, or if the director was disabled, the torpedoes could be fired under local control. If both means failed, the mount captain's assistant was also on hand to activate the compressed-air firing system by means of a sharp rap with a mallet.

The 21-inch torpedo of the day was a remarkably unreliable contraption, though its shortcomings had not yet been perceived in November 1942, nearly a full year into the war. This is partly because torpedoes had not been employed in all of the few surface actions that had thus far occurred and partly because, where they had been relied on, dead men told no tales.

It is a matter of record that LCdr Butch Parker's first order upon assuming command of *Cushing* following his adventurous return from the East Indies was that all of her twelve torpedoes be immediately replaced. Parker did not then know the precise reasons for the failures, but he knew the system was a bad one.

Each torpedo was a miniature ship equipped with two miniature steam-turbine engines. If properly maintained, each torpedo's propulsion system was a good one. The crux of the problem lay in three separate devices—the depth mechanism and both exploders.

The depth was generally set manually before or during an action or by means of controls associated with the torpedo director. In fact, the torpedoes generally ran quite a bit deeper than set, a condition that had not been observable during peacetime tests and training because the fish were fired into nets and then recovered in order to conserve them. There was no way for a net to reveal where the torpedo struck, and observers on the surface could not determine the depth of a hit, only its lateral position.

The magnetic exploder carried in each torpedo warhead had been developed years before the war but was not adequately tested for fear that it might fall into the hands of potential enemies. It turned out to be oversensitive at very short range and not sensitive enough at longer ranges. (In the case of its use in torpedoes fired by submarines, it was liable to go off near the friendly hull and, at least, give away the position of the ship that fired it.) Combined with the defective depth control, the magnetic exploder was prone to failure because it was generally guided too far below the target to be effective—even if it did go off.

This left the mechanical contact exploder, which was carried by all torpedoes. The firing pin that activated the detonator moved at right angles to the force line on contact between the warhead and the hull of the target vessel—were it to hit at all. A hit at a high angle of incidence—say 90 degrees—usually jammed the pin.

14

The men under RAdm Dan Callaghan's command were affected in many different ways by the prospect of battle. Here and there aboard the ships, sailors gathered to trade gossip, tell stale jokes, even to sing songs. Chaplains aboard the bigger ships and lay religious leaders in all the ships did a thriving business. Throughout all the ships, sailors visited with their particular friends to buck up flagging spirits and, in numerous cases, to bid farewell after revealing premonitions of death. By far the great majority of sailors undertook mundane tasks to pass the anxious hours and, perhaps, come out marginally better prepared for the impending battle. At the practical level, there was little anyone could do to be better prepared. Training over the past weeks had been intense. The guns had been cleaned and oiled the moment the cease fire had been given at the conclusion of the afternoon's torpedo raid. Medical supplies were laid out in wardrooms, crew mess halls, and other designated battle-dressing stations, but that was about all anyone could do especially to honor the upcoming action. Gunners and their numerous assistants were at their stations or resting within a step or two away. Mess attendants and cooks who had no particular battle chores or had not yet been called to General Quarters were scuttling to and fro delivering hot coffee, the real life's blood of the U.S. Navy. If there was a universal wish, it was that the battle would get underway or the ships would sail from danger; anything to relieve the strange tense boredom that suffused all the ships. Not surprisingly, there was very little bluster to be heard in the strangely whispered conversations among crewmen. Above all, everyone was dog tired from having stood continuous General-Quarters or Condition-II watches for two full days.

The night air was dead still, and where any voices could be heard through the stillness, they conveyed routine instructions aimed at running the ships. The air also was balmy, about the temperature of a warm bath. There was an offshore breeze from the southeast that carried with it the heady, pungent perfume of tropical flowers, an odor that soon became cloying and ended up being rather sickening. In later years, the worst memories of many of the survivors would be triggered by the sweet odor of tropical flowers.

࿔

At about 2230, when Cdr Turk Wirth arrived on heavy cruiser *Portland*'s bridge from Battle-2 to receive a situation update, the skipper, Capt Laurence DuBose, handed him a dispatch formalizing the flag conference Admirals Turner and Callaghan had earlier held over the open voice channel. The essence of the report was that the Japanese were sending in "big fellows," which everyone took to mean battleships. As Wirth read the report, the captain offered him coffee.

"This is suicide, you know," the captain blurted out as he handed his exec the steaming cup.

"Oh, I don't know," Wirth responded in an affable tone as he accepted the stimulant.

"You're an incorrigible optimist," DuBose chided as the two ducked into the blind charthouse to have a final smoke. After lighting their cigarettes, they stared blankly around the compartment, not exchanging a word. At last, Captain DuBose muttered, "But you know the date. If we can get across midnight into tomorrow, we may make it."

Commander Wirth chuckled inwardly; he knew that the cap-

Transport *President Jackson* and other U.S. Navy ships take on Japanese Betty torpedo bombers on the afternoon of November 12, 1942. The smoke cloud in the center is a Betty bomber that has just crashed. *(Official U.S.N. Photo)*

S1 Don Dahlke, of destroyer *Fletcher*, receives Silver Star medal from Adm Bill Halsey. *(Compliments of D. H. Dahlke)*

Destroyer *Cushing* in July 1942. *(Official U.S.N. Photo)*

Destroyer *Laffey* in September 1942. *(Official U.S.N. Photo)*

LCdr Butch Parker, of *Cushing*. *(Compliments of E. N. Parker)*

Lt(jg) Tom Evins, *Laffey's* torpedo officer. *(Compliments of T. A. Evins)*

Destroyer *Sterett* in early 1943. *(Official U.S.N. Photo)*

Destroyer *O'Bannon*. Note square SC radar antenna at the top of her mainmast. *(Official U.S.N. Photo)*

Light antiaircraft cruiser *Atlanta* in September 1942. *(Official U.S.N. Photo)*

MM1 Ross Hilton, of *Atlanta*.
(Compliments of J. R. Hilton)

RAdm Norman Scott.
(Official U.S.N. Photo)

Heavy cruiser *San Francisco* returns to Pearl Harbor, December 4, 1942. Note armored conning tower just behind Turret-2. *(Official U.S.N. Photo)*

Right, above

RAdm Dan Callaghan on *San Francisco*'s bridge while he was serving as her captain in 1941. *(Official U.S.N. Photo)*

Right, below

Broadside view of *San Francisco* in San Francisco Bay, December 11, 1942. *(Official U.S.N. Photo)*

BM1 Reinhardt Keppler, recipient of a posthumous Congressional Medal of Honor for his lifesaving efforts aboard *San Francisco. (Official U.S.N. Photo)*

Adm Chester Nimitz flanked by *(right)* LCdr Herbert Schonland and *(left)* LCdr Bruce McCandless, both of whom earned Congressional Medals of Honor for their parts in saving *San Francisco. (Official U.S.N. Photo)*

tain had been president of the Naval Academy class of 1913 and thus considered the number thirteen to be especially lucky.

The two finished their cigarettes in silence and Commander Wirth departed for Battle-2.

While Commander Wirth was with the captain, his bugler, seventeen-year-old S2 Jim Mathews, was using the exec's battle phones to shoot the breeze with a buddy manning a station in the after steering compartment. The man below decks joked that he was glad he wasn't a sitting duck topside, like Mathews. The young bugler replied that the quartermaster had no room to talk since he was located at a spot just below the waterline the sailors called "torpedo junction" with ample justification. The two laughed and continued their banter.

As he stood at his station beside *Atlanta*'s after port 20mm guns, GM2 Frank Roling was approached by a mess attendant who was on duty filling 20mm magazines in the clipping room right behind the gun. The youngster told Roling that he had $100 he had won in a crap game in a change purse in his pocket. After showing Roling the cash, the mess attendant asked him to get the money to his mother in Alabama if Roling survived and he did not. Though a little taken aback, Roling nonetheless agreed.

Roling's gun crew was also visited by a chief gunner's mate, who was routinely checking on all the stations in his care. "Boys," the old chief loudly proclaimed, "this is it, and I've got one year to go to retire." This was followed by a chorus of raucous laughter, which is undoubtedly what the departing chief had in mind as a way to calm the tense gunners.

BM1 Leighton Spadone, the captain of *Atlanta*'s starboard midships 1.1-inch mount, had eaten a full meal late in the afternoon and felt pretty good about the future. Before going to his battle station at 2200, he had visited with his brother, Phil, and they had talked about the probable impending action. As always, the brothers were filled with confidence; Leighton felt no particular anxiety and Phil expressed no special concerns. When it was time to go, Leighton said, "Hang in there, Red. I'll see you later." He went straight to his battle station, where he tested the firing circuits, ready ammunition, and the state of readiness of his crew. Then he settled in for the long wait.

Lookouts could not see a thing, it was that dark. S1 Walt Brandt, a lookout manning *Helena*'s bridge, played around at holding one hand out in front of his face and trying to find it with the other hand. He could not see a thing, not even the wake of the ship dead ahead.

GM2 Jim Tooker, assistant captain and rammer operator of *Cushing*'s Mount-1, strained his eyes into the blackness throughout the evening hours but saw absolutely nothing. So far as Tooker knew, the ships were landlocked between the islands defining the channel, and there was nothing out there to see that would stand out against the obscured night sky.

When S1 John Jenkins, a loader serving destroyer *Laffey*'s starboard after 20mm gun, returned to his battle station after taking a shower and changing into clean clothes, someone showed up with a gallon can of peaches. The gun crew and several sailors from surrounding stations dug in with a special glee, recalling similar parties during the time *Laffey* had been sailing up and down the California coast escorting tankers. As they ate and reminisced, the gunners were constantly interrupted by anxious firemen and machinist's mates who stuck their heads through hatches leading up from the after engine room to ask if anyone topside had seen anything yet.

There was furious activity erupting throughout all the ships as officers and sailors prepared to train out their guns and torpedo tubes, run their ships' engineering plants, treat the wounded, or fight fires and contain other battle damage. Many hundreds of men were on duty below decks, unable to see what was going on, unable to follow events except as they were related by considerate phone talkers manning topside stations. In some cases, the men in the ships had to rely mainly upon their innate senses to figure out what was going on.

EM3 Bill McKinney and S2 Dan Curtin were the only sailors left in the midships berthing compartment aboard *Atlanta* in which both of them bunked. Their job was to man a damage-control substation in the compartment, to be ready to fight fires with their 2½-inch hose and a plethora of other equipment stored in a damage-control locker. As they had many times during surprise drills and in action, McKinney and Curtin faced an uncertain future and relied upon their senses to tell them to do the right thing. When the light cruiser suddenly put on speed after hours of routine sailing, the two quickly donned their antiflash clothing, tested the battle phones by reporting their station "manned and ready," and closed and tightly dogged down all the hatches. As McKinney completed a brief prayer, two ammunition hoists that ran through the compartment erupted in brief furious activity as the 5-inch mount captain overhead requested his ready ammunition supply. At the same time, excess blowers shut down, bringing an eerie, unwholesome silence to the ship's usually throbbing internal spaces.

SM3 Jack Pease, of destroyer *Monssen*, had nothing to do. He had spent the entire evening on the signal bridge, sacked out on a mattress he had secreted in one of the flag bags, a deep, light metal bin containing the destroyer's signal flags. However, Pease had been awakened by a first-class signalman at about 2300 and ordered to the after emergency control station. Since the night was so black, there was really no contribution Pease could make. However, he was on hand to take over the emergency helm in case something happened to the quartermaster manning the station. About all Jack Pease *really* had to do was what he already was doing: standing around wondering what was going on.

卐

Lt(jg) Jack Bennett was normally *San Francisco*'s officer of the deck during night General-Quarters watches, but he had been relieved this night by order of the cruiser's new skipper, Capt Cassin Young. Bennett had just been going off duty to grab a few hours' sleep in the nearby radio-direction-finder shack when Admiral Callaghan had called him over to shake hands; Bennett had been player-coach of the flagship's basketball team when Callaghan had been the captain. As Bennett extended his hand, Captain Young had spied a spot of blood at the younger officer's right elbow and had asked what it was from. When Bennett explained that he had been clipped in his right wing by the right wing of the Betty bomber that had struck the flagship in the afternoon, the captain ordered him to get treatment and rest. Bennett had no intention of sitting this one out, so he went straight to the fantail to resume his usual battle duties, overseeing the two after 1.1-inch mounts.

Earlier in the evening, S1 Willie Boyce had been on his way to the airplane hangar for a rest when his division chief had waylaid him to ask if he had seen the man who was supposed to stand the early watch as a phone talker in the shambles of Battle-2. When Boyce said he did not know where the man was, the chief assigned him, Boyce, to stand the early watch rather than the midwatch to which he had been assigned earlier. Thoroughly put out by the switch, which kept him from hours of planned sleep in a private spot on the well deck, Boyce nonetheless complied and stood the four-hour watch. It was just coming up on midnight when he was relieved and made his way straight for the well deck to sleep.

S1 Gene Oliver, the sight setter in destroyer *Monssen's* Mount-3, was responsible for assuming manual control of the gun in the event something happened to his ship's main-battery director. He had just completed all his prebattle checks and trained the gun to starboard when his sound-powered battle phones crackled to life. Someone in the director was taking it upon himself to inform everyone on the gunnery circuit that it was Friday the Thirteenth, that there were thirteen ships in the column, and that *Monssen's* bow numbers, 436, added up to thirteen. As he listened, Seaman Oliver thought the bearer of the glad tidings was a "dumb bastard" for mentioning it.

PART IV

Friday the Thirteenth

15

While RAdm Dan Callaghan positively *knew* that there was to be a surface action off Savo, RAdm Hiroaki Abe merely felt it—but he did not know. In truth, he had been specifically enjoined from engaging American warships; all Japanese naval commanders in the region had. The no-combat decree worked for Callaghan in at least one other very important respect: The new 14-inch high-capacity incendiary bombardment shells that had been fired by battleships *Kongo* and *Haruna* against Henderson Field in mid-October had been so highly rated by senior Japanese officers that *Hiei*'s and *Kirishima*'s magazines were choked with them; neither ship was capable of engaging in a protracted hot surface action because neither had many armor-piercing shells aboard.

At 1530, November 12, hours after sighting the B-17 that had sighted and reported his advancing column at 1030, Abe acted upon his fears by placing his lesser ships in an unwieldy battle formation comprising two protective half-arcs around a column composed of light cruiser *Nagara* in the van 2,000 yards ahead of flagship *Hiei*, and *Kirishima* in the rear, 2,000 yards behind *Hiei*. The five destroyers of RAdm Tamotsu Takama's Destroyer Squadron 4 were echeloned in an arc 8,000 yards ahead of *Nagara* and RAdm Susumu Kimura's Destroyer Squadron 10 was arrayed in two groups of three off each of *Nagara's* flanks.

At 1600, by which time the formation had been completed, Abe's force was 200 miles from Savo and advancing at a steady 18 knots. As the Japanese ships approached a darkening sky filled with storm clouds, *Hiei* catapulted one of her scouts to fly ahead and reconnoiter Lengo Channel as far as Lunga Point. Soon after the scout was airborne, the Japanese entered the storm front.

The storm, which happened to be heading in the same direction at the same speed as Abe's bombardment force, both helped and hampered the Japanese. The squall rendered absolute protection against feared submarine attacks or aerial sightings, but many captains feared that the complex deployment of the double screen would be impossible to maintain in the heavy weather and low visibility. All except Admiral Abe seemed to realize that the risk of misadventure would increase as they sailed into the restricted waters leading to Lunga Point. When a senior staff officer suggested that Abe cut back on the force's speed, the admiral responded, "We must maintain this speed to reach the target area in good time." As the spirits of his subordinates fell, those of the cautious battle-group commander rose.

A short time before Admiral Turner's transports departed from Guadalcanal, Abe received his first and only news from the *Hiei* scout: "More than a dozen enemy warships seen off Lunga." To which Abe added with a laugh, "If heaven continues to side with us like this, we may not even have to do business with them."

This last was the crux of Abe's deepest desire: He did not want to engage in a surface battle that night. All he wanted to do was grind Henderson Field to dust and get out of there.

The Japanese bored on through the unremitting storm. Though his captains were ever more fearful of a collision, Abe had supreme confidence in their abilities and particularly in Admiral Kimura's as the navigator responsible for arriving off Cape Esperance on time and without mishap.

At midnight, an Imperial Army radio station on Guadalcanal reported a major storm in progress. (Admiral Callaghan's ships remained in clear weather as they closed on Cape Esperance from the opposite direction.) By then, Abe's complex deployment had slowly frayed until none of the captains knew quite where he was in relation to other ships. It was obvious to all that if Abe continued on as he was, the moving squall that had screened his warships from American eyes would also screen potential targets from Japanese eyes. Abe decided to get out of the rain so that he could see enemy ships, if there were any, or his targets ashore. It was simply a matter of letting the squall get ahead of his ships.

Abe ordered all his ships to prepare to execute a simultaneous 180-degree turn, then left them standing by for many minutes while his staff communicators attempted to reach destroyers *Yudachi* and *Harusame*, which appeared to have gone astray. It turned out that, at the moment of transmission, the two right-flank destroyers had precipitously veered away from the main body to keep from running aground. In the rush, the two had missed Abe's order and had to be reapprised of the admiral's intentions. The turn, when it came, was as orderly as the broken formation could manage. At least there were no collisions. As soon as the turn was executed, Abe slowed his force to 12 knots to allow his skewed formation to re-form.

The Japanese sailed north, away from Cape Esperance, for over 30 minutes before escaping the rain at 0040. Abe ordered another turnabout and directed his warships back toward Guadalcanal, still at 12 knots. Despite all the effort expended in getting the original protective formation re-formed, the outer port arc of three destroyers—*Asagumo*, *Murasame*, and *Samidare*—had fallen behind the inner port arc and was even trailing behind *Kirishima*, the rear ship of the central column.

At length, Savo's volcanic outline was spotted 60 degrees to port. Moments later, keen-eyed lookouts reported seeing the shape of mountains dead ahead. Cdr Tameichi Hara, destroyer *Amatsukaze*'s veteran skipper, was instantly fearful of an attack from out of the shadows, so he ordered all his guns and torpedo tubes trained out to starboard. But there was nothing there.

The army radio station ashore reported that the storm had passed it by, the weather was clearing, and no American ships could be seen off Lunga Point in the brightening moonlight. By then, 0130, the Japanese bombardment force was about 12 miles off

Guadalcanal, on course 105 degrees, and speeding ahead at 23 knots. Hundreds of sailors aboard *Hiei* and *Kirishima* were hard at work stacking 1-ton 14-inch incendiary shells in and around the main turrets of both battleships, all ready to be fired at Henderson Field.

Still wary of a possible seaborne American threat, Abe had nonetheless committed his ships to the bombardment action. He sailed straight on toward Lunga Point, watchful and hopeful.

16

Friday, November 13, 1942, 0124.
   "Radar contact. Bearing 312 [degrees] True. Distance 27,100 yards."
The word was passed from the lips of *Helena*'s SG radar operator to the ears of her skipper, Capt Gib Hoover. As at Cape Esperance a month earlier, *Helena* was the first American ship to get a solid fix on an oncoming Japanese surface force. As at Cape Esperance, Captain Hoover instantly passed the news to his battle-force flagship, *San Francisco*. And, as at Cape Esperance, the officer in tactical command hesitated.

As soon as the news of the first radar contact flashed through the American column, a weird pall of silence enveloped each of the ships. Ens Bin Cochran, who was on *Helena*'s open fighting bridge, heard only the normal sailing sounds: blowers forcing air into the below-decks compartments, the usual gentle roar of the engines that almost no one ever really heard anymore, and the gentle whisper of the light breeze coming up from the southeast.

At 0125, *Helena*'s SG operator flashed another sighting report to the bridge: "Radar contact. Bearing 310 True. Distance, 31,900 yards." This was clearly a second group.

At 0128, four minutes after news of the first contact had rippled through the air waves, Admiral Callaghan delivered his first order: All ships were to change course two points to starboard, to course 310, directly toward the radar contact. Since the move was to be executed in column, only one ship at a time undertook it, starting with the lead destroyer, LCdr Butch Parker's *Cushing*. It would be many minutes before all thirteen ships, which were now running at 500-yard intervals, could complete the maneuver.

When the data was in, many of the men in the know throughout the column felt some consternation over Callaghan's apparent plan. Quite clearly, he was looking for a head-on clash where many thought a sweep around the Japanese force would put all the American ships in a better position to launch torpedoes. At Cape Esperance, Norman Scott had achieved his victory largely by completing a maneuver known as "Crossing the T"—where the American column had swept across the front of the Japanese column more or less at right angles. This had allowed most of the American guns to be fired into the Japanese ships while many of the Japanese guns were masked and thus prevented from returning the fire.

That's what it looked like at 0128. In fact, Admiral Callaghan *was* trying to figure out a way to cross the T, but he was apparently having a difficult time visualizing the positions of the two Japanese forces located thus far, his own position relative to them, and the relative positions they would occupy once they had closed to gunfire and torpedo range. Since he had direct access to no reliable radar, he could not see what was going on, but could only compute estimates in his head.

꩜

At 0131, *Helena* reported via TBS, "Now three targets. Bearing 312 [degrees]. Distance 26,000 [yards]." And moments later she followed with, "Their course 107. Speed possibly 23 [knots]."

Admiral Callaghan reacted to the new sighting report by ordering *Cushing* to turn right to course 000 degrees, due north. This placed one Japanese group dead ahead of *Cushing* and two to port. Speed was raised from 18 to 20 knots.

By then, Admiral Callaghan's control had begun breaking down. There was only one open TBS voice-radio frequency, and all the urgent business of the task force had to be conducted on it. Not only did Admiral Callaghan have to transmit and receive, all the ships had to provide information or request clarifications or repeats of garbled sentences. It became increasingly difficult to maintain order as radio discipline unraveled for a variety of good reasons.

Course was changed again to 310 degrees, but Callaghan shifted *Cushing* back to 000 degrees at 0137.

↻

At 0139, *Helena's* SG operator reported four solid targets in line off *Helena's* port bow. However, he did not give a bearing or range. Admiral Callaghan was in the process of requesting an amplification on this report when he was crowded off the TBS frequency by two urgent sighting reports. The first was from destroyer *O'Bannon*, the fourth ship in column, which reported at 0140 that her SG radar had picked up three distinct targets. One Japanese group was at 11,000 yards bearing 287 degrees; the second was at 8,500 yards bearing 318 degrees; and the third was at 6,000 yards bearing 042 degrees.

Next, at 0141, Cdr Murray Stokes, the Destroyer Division 10 commander, embarked in *Cushing*, reported that he could *see* two Japanese destroyers (which turned out to be *Yudachi* and *Harusame*) crossing ahead of *Cushing* from port to starboard and only 3,000 yards out.

Cushing was one of the most ably commanded ships in action that night; her captain, LCdr Butch Parker, had already won two Navy Crosses in the East Indies and was known as one of the most aggressive fighting skippers in the entire U.S. Fleet. It was perhaps because of Parker's outstanding experience and leadership traits that *Cushing* was placed at the point of Callaghan's destroyer vanguard; certainly, it was not because *Cushing* boasted the best radar or gunnery systems. If *Cushing* had one thing going for her this night, it was the rigorous training and performance standards imposed by Butch Parker, a leader most *Cushing* crewmen would gladly have died trying to impress. The faith of the task force commander and *Cushing's* crew immediately paid off. At 0141, as Commander Stokes was passing the news of his sighting over the TBS,

Butch Parker ordered *Cushing* into an abrupt left turn to 330 degrees, both to avoid colliding with the Japanese destroyers and to bring his torpedo tubes to bear.

Five hundred yards behind *Cushing*, destroyer *Laffey*'s torpedo officer, Lt(jg) Tom Evins, saw *Yudachi* and *Harusame* race by the lead ship. "Looks like two bright wakes going from port to starboard," Evins described to his torpedo-circuit talker. "They seem to be about 3,000 yards out." Right on top of us, he ruefully thought as he turned to the torpedo-director operator to tell him to train out the tubes. But the experienced senior torpedoman had anticipated the order and was already at work.

卍

The TBS circuit became filled with queries from nearly all the American warships: Where are the targets; what is the correct course and speed; can we open fire? Commander Stokes, who wanted to get permission to fire the four torpedoes in *Cushing*'s centerline mount at *Yudachi* and *Harusame*, had to bully his way onto the overloaded circuit to put in his request.

As the destroyer division commander was trying to get through to the task force commander, there was a furious burst of activity on *Cushing*'s bridge and around her centerline torpedo mount. *Cushing* was all set to fire four torpedoes within the minute, but by the time Admiral Callaghan heard Commander Stokes and gave the affirmative, the torpedoes had to be withheld because the Japanese destroyers had turned away from *Cushing*.

卍

Meanwhile, Y2 Tom Foreman, the Destroyer Division 10 yeoman, was standing his watch as fire control radarman in *Cushing*'s gun director. Foreman was not privy to the running conversations on the TBS and knew nothing of events outside the tiny director compartment except what he could feel by the seat of his pants. Suddenly, the radarscope in front of Foreman lighted up with what looked like numerous targets. It was Foreman's guess that the radar was malfunctioning, perhaps picking up incomplete readings on the land masses all around. After all, he was getting what appeared to be targets no matter which way he turned the radar antenna, and that surely was not correct. Nevertheless, Foreman reported the targets to the gunnery officer along with his assessment that there was a malfunction occurring. The gunnery officer reported the possible malfunction to the captain and tried to lock onto a target with his optical sights. Meantime, to be absolutely sure the radar was indeed down, Y2 Foreman stood up to look over the edge of the open-topped director. As dark as the night was, he could easily see warships everywhere in front of him.

Below decks, in the after fireroom, the ship's oil king arrived to start a fuel-oil booster pump. He calmly gave out the news that there were many ships topside "and they aren't all American." The engineers had been expecting something to happen for so long that the news seemed almost routine.

The Japanese main body was about 12 miles offshore at 0140, clearly prepared to bombard Henderson Field, but strangely unprepared to engage in a surface action. The routine operation of all the Japanese ships was shattered when destroyer *Yudachi* reported at 0142, "Enemy sighted," as she and *Harusame* swept past *Cushing*. Immediately, Admiral Abe roared at his flag signal officer, "What is the range and bearing? And where is *Yudachi?*"

Cdr Kiyoshi Kiikawa, *Yudachi* 's veteran skipper, was still somewhat shaken by the thoroughly unexpected encounter with *Cushing* and was unable to determine precisely where he was. He knew that *Yudachi*, which had gone astray from the leading screen during the first 180-degree turn in the rain, was ahead of *Harusame* and heading roughly from west to east, away from Guadalcanal. But that was about all he knew; Commander Kiikawa even had no idea where Abe's main body might be.

Suddenly, *Hiei* 's masthead lookout shouted, "Four black objects ahead. Looks like warships. Five degrees to starboard; eight thousand meters. Unsure yet; visibility bad."

Admiral Abe was totally frustrated with *Yudachi* 's performance, and thoroughly preoccupied with it. He took no part in the shouting of questions and answers between his staff officers and the lookout in the masthead. At long last, however, he directed *Hiei* 's and *Kirishima's* gunners to unload the bombardment projectiles in the 14-inch gun breeches and ordered armor-piercing rounds from deep within the bowels of the main-battery magazines. Hundreds of seamen jumped to comply, for a single hit among the unsheltered stacks of incendiary rounds in passageways leading from the magazines to the turrets would doom the great battleships and all who sailed in them.

The Japanese could not understand why the Americans did not open fire. The range was closing rapidly as the two battle forces careened toward one another at a combined rate of over 40 knots. As ammunition handlers exchanged the stacked bombardment rounds for armor-piercing rounds stored deep in the magazines—as safety measures were hurriedly reimposed aboard the two vulnerable battleships—Abe and all his officers tried to decipher the intentions of their seemingly somnolent opposite numbers. No solution came to them, and neither did any gunfire. It took eight minutes to clear the turrets and passageways of the volatile bombardment shells and load armor-piercing rounds in all of the 14-inch guns. As soon as Abe heard that the moment of greatest danger had passed, he got to work planning his part in the inevitable clash.

By sheer luck, the confusion of the two 180-degree turns to evade the storm front had left *Hiei* and *Kirishima* screened by a seven-ship arc centered on light cruiser *Nagara*, dead ahead of *Hiei*. The advance screen of five destroyers had been broken up into two groups, which were now ahead and to starboard, screening the flank at some distance. It would be impossible for the single American column to engage—or even pinpoint—all of the dispersed Japanese warships.

৬

Admiral Callaghan was not precisely somnolent, but he was strangely slow to act. After keeping his commanders waiting three long minutes for a definitive order, Callaghan passed half an order at 0145: "Stand by to open fire." Then he fell silent again as each of the vanguard captains followed his instincts and trained out his ship's guns and torpedo tubes to track targets that had long since been fixed on gunnery radars.

It is likely that Callaghan was delayed in ordering his ships to commence firing by a distraction that had been set in motion minutes earlier, when *Cushing* had abruptly and aggressively turned left to engage the only enemy ships in sight at 0141. The turn had had a ripple effect right down the American column coming along in her wake. Each of the three following destroyers had swung out in turn to follow *Cushing*. *Laffey* had had no difficulties keeping station on *Cushing*, and neither, apparently, had *Sterett*. However, *O'Bannon* was obliged to veer sharply inside *Sterett*'s turn as the van destroyers bunched up, and this caused *Atlanta* to make a yet more radical turn. When Admiral Callaghan saw *Atlanta*, dead ahead of his flagship, abruptly swing away from the desired course, he dropped everything to query her skipper, Capt Samuel Jenkins, "What are you doing?"

"Avoiding our own destroyers," Jenkins matter-of-factly responded.

Though *Sterett* and *O'Bannon* separated, *Atlanta* came on too fast and had to ease up on *O'Bannon*'s port quarter. This obliged at least two captains to direct their attention away from the closing Japanese ships ahead and toward one another and the friendly warships ahead and behind.

Most of *Cushing*'s topside crewmen who were facing forward also plainly saw the oncoming targets with their own eyes. As LCdr Butch Parker moved to comply with Cdr Murray Stokes's suggestion that *Cushing* return to her assigned course, 000 degrees, several lookouts yelled, "Ships to port!" Butch Parker swiveled his head to the left and saw several large vessels—including a huge ship, quite obviously a battleship—heading straight for him from an angle of only 20 degrees from the port bow. Lookouts also spotted another large ship off the starboard bow, heading more or less eastward.

GM2 Jim Tooker, Mount-1's assistant captain and rammer operator, was behind the gun shield and could not see the Japanese ships, but a number of his ammunition handlers all shouted at once that a huge warship was bearing down on *Cushing* from the port bow and looked like it might be intent upon ramming.

At Jim Tooker's left hand, S2 Felton Maillot, *Cushing*'s Mount-1 shell loader, was busily preparing shells to be fired when someone yelled, "Dead ahead!" When Maillot reflexively looked up, the vista was filled with a huge shadow even blacker than the black, black night. The shadow soon resolved itself into the oncoming bows of a huge ship, by far the biggest ship the twenty-two-year-old had ever seen. Then he directed his attention back down at the ready shells in his care and went back to work.

With no thought to the incongruity, GM2 Tooker trained the mount to port and awaited the order to fire on the oncoming target—*Hiei*.

But no such order arrived.

卍

Immediately after *Yudachi* and *Harusame* sailed from danger, sharp-eyed Lt(jg) Tom Evins, *Laffey's* torpedo officer, spotted a larger target. He turned again to his director operator and asked, "Have you got the third ship? The one with the big silhouette? She looks like a cruiser." But he hardly heard the torepdoman's response as he worked to get his torpedo battery lined up on the target.

"I have an enemy cruiser to starboard," Evins sang out to *Laffey's* captain, LCdr Bill Hank, who was only a few feet away. "I request permission to fire torpedoes."

Hank immediately replied, "Permission *not* granted." He had received no authority from the flagship and apparently felt he could not yet take matters into his own hands.

Crestfallen, Lieutenant (jg) Evins nevertheless ordered his director operator to keep his sights on the target; he knew he would receive the desired order in moments.

But no such order arrived.

卍

Though *Sterett's* gunnery officer, Lt Cal Calhoun, was standing with his head and shoulders through the hatch of his ship's gun director, he was unable to see the passage of *Yudachi* and *Harusame*. However, Calhouns' fire-control radarman was able to find huge *Hiei* by the size of the image she painted on his radarscope. *Sterett's* four 5-inch guns and eight torpedo tubes had been tracking the Japanese flagship since the first fire-direction radar contact, but to no avail without orders to open fire. Lieutenant Calhoun was straining his eyes for a direct glimpse of the Japanese behemoth when she finally loomed into view. Surely *Sterett* would break her rigorous silence now that the best target in the ocean was in plain sight.

But no such order arrived.

卍

BM1 Leighton Spadone, the captain of *Atlanta*'s starboard midships 1.1-inch mount, was on the wrong side of his ship to see the oncoming Japanese, but *Hiei*'s progress was amply described by Spadone's division officer, Lt(jg) David Hall. "I can see them now," Hall matter-of-factly informed all four of his 1.1-inch mount captains on the battle phones, "Just off the port beam, range three-oh-double-oh [3,000 yards]."

BM1 Spadone, who had served in a 5-inch battery aboard a battleship before the war, thought to himself, "Boy, that's close."

Then the battle phones sounded a head's up from the division officer: "Stand by. Action to port." A moment later, this was followed by: "Range two-three-double-oh." It was Spadone's experience that it would be impossible for the fourteen 5-inch guns *Atlanta* could train to port to miss any target only 2,000 yards away.

Everyone in the U.S. column—and particularly everyone aboard the five leading warships, which all held ample targets in their sights—was awaiting Admiral Callaghan's order to commence firing.

But no such order arrived.

17

The battle-aware admiral and admiral's staff sharing *Atlanta*'s bridge with Capt Samuel Jenkins and his staff were wondering when Admiral Callaghan was going to release his ships to fire at the numerous closing and passing targets all the American vanguard warships had boresighted. There was nothing for Norman Scott to do except wait and wonder what his superior had in mind. But that issue was never decided; events overtook Dan Callaghan's thought processes and Norman Scott's deep concerns. At 0150, precisely, Japanese ships snapped on their searchlights.

The battle was underway.

Only a beat behind the illumination of the first searchlight—by destroyer *Akatsuki*—Cdr Murray Stokes calmly ordered *Cushing*'s LCdr Butch Parker to commence firing; it was clearly foolhardy for the vanguard destroyer to remain silent and on its assigned course while a Japanese battleship and its numerous consorts were bearing down on her, gaining a greater position advantage with every passing millisecond.

As many members of the topside crew looked on in disbelief,

Hiei passed within 500 feet of *Cushing's* port side. Butch Parker instinctively ordered torpedoes fired at her, but immediately realized that the Japanese flagship would be long gone before the torpedo director could get settled on her. Rather than waste the effort in a sea full of dangerous targets, Parker countermanded his own order with a loud, curt, "Do not fire torpedoes!" This was followed by an order to his helmsman to put the rudder over hard to the right.

Y2 Tom Foreman, who had looked over the top of the gun director to check on the amazing scene painted on his radarscope, was back in his seat. He selected the nearest target, a small ship about 2,000 yards off the starboard bow, and began firing the guns as soon as he received permission. The guns opened fire just as the ship responded to Butch Parker's order to turn to the left, thus shifting the emerging group of Japanese destroyers from the starboard bow to nearly dead ahead. This masked the after 5-inch mounts, which momentarily checked fire. However, gunners forward and the men on the bridge were certain of hits on the destroyer Y2 Foreman had selected as his primary target.

卍

Foreman was a little off in his aim and his estimate. All sorts of shells and tracer rounds—undoubtedly they were from several American ships—fell about *Amatsukaze*, which was well to *Hiei's* far side but coming on rapidly. The Japanese destroyer's skipper, Cdr Tameichi Hara, was certain he had sailed into a zone filled with overs meant for *Hiei*, but he was, at best, partially correct. The bright flashes from the bursting rounds and passing tracer ruined Commander Hara's night vision and it appeared to him that his ship would be struck by the next salvo. As Hara cast about for a quick solution, he noticed the dark black silhouette of Florida ahead to port. He was immediately fearful of falling afoul the many reefs known to be in that direction.

"Gain speed," Hara commanded. "Let's get the hell out of here to starboard." Followed by *Yukikaze*, *Amatsukaze* raced behind the larger bulk of *Nagara* and outran *Cushing's* aimed fire.

卍

It was only after the 5-inch guns opened fire ahead and to starboard, at *Amatsukaze*, that Cdr Murray Stokes turned to see that *Hiei* was bathed in light from several searchlights and was already taking hits in her foremast and superstructure from at least one of the vanguard destroyers behind *Cushing*. The only gun aboard *Cushing* that trained out on *Hiei* was a topside 20mm, whose gunner cut loose without being told. LCdr Butch Parker also saw that *Hiei* was well lighted as she cut astern of *Laffey* and came right to pass down the starboard side of the rest of the American column. As his own vessel came far enough to the right, Parker commanded, "Torpedo action! Starboard!" and ordered his torpedo officer to fire six torpedoes at the Japanese flagship, two from the centerline mount and all four from the starboard waist mount.

As the torpedoes were being fired, a Japanese destroyer to port began scoring hits on *Cushing*. Within seconds, the gunfire from port was bolstered by rounds fired from the starboard side—a veritable cascade of incoming fire. No one aboard *Cushing* paid the slightest attention to *Hiei* from that moment on.

As soon as Lieutenant Commander Parker saw that the after mounts had been masked by the swing to the right to fire torpedoes at *Hiei*, he ordered the helmsman to come back to the left. The two after guns were thus able to bear on the target and resume firing. Y2 Tom Foreman had a perfect fix on the target and simply kept his sight aligned on it as the ship moved about underneath him.

Suddenly, the gun director took a direct hit on its face. The assistant director officer and rangekeeper operator were killed instantly and the gunnery officer was seriously wounded and thrown over the top of the director; he landed on the bridge at the feet of Butch Parker, who had him carried straight to the wardroom, which doubled as a surgery during a battle. However, the gunnery officer died on the way. Y2 Tom Foreman was badly shaken but unhurt, as were two others. The sixth man, a fire controlman striker, emerged with a broken leg. The gun director itself was disabled, so Y2 Foreman decided to leave. The fire controlman striker asked for some help, and Foreman complied by climbing a few rungs down the ladder and easing the man down onto his back. Inasmuch as the incoming was still falling all around the bridge,

Foreman climbed all the way down to the deck below the bridge and gently eased the injured man off his back.

卍

Mount-1 was putting out rounds with ruthless efficiency when a Japanese shell detonated in the forward upper handling room, right behind the open forward mount, and killed the entire handling-room crew. GM2 Jim Tooker, the Mount-1 rammerman, was blown clear of the gun and landed near a fire hose. He shook off the effects of the blast and grabbed the hose as he yelled orders for someone to turn on the water. Joined by GM1 Tom Osuna, the mount captain, Tooker ran the hose straight back to the burning handling room. There were bodies and parts of bodies everywhere, but the smoke was too thick for Tooker to see where they were; squeamish about stepping on the body of someone he knew—and he knew them all—he inched forward, gingerly reconnoitering with the toes of his shoes. He and Osuna fought the advancing flames until the hose pressure suddenly failed. This was because *Cushing's* engineering plant had been badly damaged and was no longer operating.

卍

One of the incoming rounds detonated at the base of *Cushing's* after stack. The damage caused the forced draft blowers to suck the soot from the stack into the after fire room, which hampered the engineers, who were certain the Japanese had fired poison-gas shells at their ship. All hands donned their gas masks, which hampered them even more.

The problem in the after fire room was compounded when the steam pressure in one of the boilers went to zero. There was some frantic movement aimed at finding the cause of the failure, but the matter was arrested when the loudspeaker blared, "Abandon the fire rooms, but not the ship."

WT1 Dennis Behl could not imagine why the order had been passed; his after fire room was not in any way damaged and he thought he had figured out why the steam pressure had dropped in the errant boiler. But he also felt that other men had a firmer sense of what shape the rest of the ship was in, so he reluctantly complied and ordered his firemen and watertenders to secure the boilers and get topside.

In fact, the order to abandon the after fire room was given on the basis of erroneous information. Butch Parker had been told that the fire room had been breached and was flooding. He ordered the crew out to save their lives.

On the other hand, the forward fire room really had suffered a calamitous breakdown. It was struck by a round that put both forced draft blowers out of commission, ruptured the auxiliary steam line, and started a fire. Soon, any possible later efforts to reoccupy the after fire room to at least get up power to fight the fires were rendered moot when the feed water in one of the boilers evaporated and the boiler burned up. Thus, with both fire rooms out of commission—one because of shell damage and the other because of bad information—*Cushing* had no power, no engines, no water pressure, no electrical energy, no means of keeping up with the fight or running away.

For emphasis, shrapnel from a round that wiped out the after repair party near the machine shop punctured the lubricating oil storage tank in the engine room. The engines continued to run for some minutes, but the bearings were undoubtedly wiped by the friction and the ship would have been stopped in any event.

18

The second ship in the American vanguard, *Laffey*, had targets aplenty for her guns and torpedoes, but her captain, LCdr Bill Hank, obediently withheld fire until told to commence. The order did not arrive until 0152, long minutes after it might have done the most good. As it was, the order posed more problems than it solved. Specifically, Admiral Callaghan's voice on the open TBS ordered, "Odd-numbered ships fire to starboard; even-numbered ships fire to port."

Laffey was the second ship in the column, an even-numbered ship. Admiral Callaghan's order obliged *Laffey*'s gunners and torpedomen to shift their rapt attention from targets to starboard—including *Nagara*—to relatively unmonitored targets to port. The shift wasted several precious seconds.

As everyone on the bridge and manning the gun and torpedo mounts turned to the left, a vessel later described as a "light cruiser" with a searchlight aimed at vessels astern of *Laffey* was immediately seen bearing down on *Laffey*'s port bow. Range was about 1,800 yards and closing fast. The target was certainly *Akatsuki*, whose two dual 5-inch mounts apparently made her seem cruiserlike in the dark and at a distance. In any event, *Laffey*'s guns were right on her in a trice and she was seen to suffer several direct hits from the first and second salvos.

The intense gunfire at the target to port had an immediate negative impact upon Lt(jg) Tom Evins's efforts to get his port torpedo director aligned. When Mount-2 was trained to either beam and fired, the gun's muzzle flash erupted only a few feet in front of the torpedo director on that side of the ship. As the target moved from the port bow to the port beam, Mount-2 was going off practically in Evins's face, and he knew that his director operator, TM1 Frederick Sanderson, must have been rendered deaf and blind also. The main thing keeping Evins and Sanderson at their virtually untenable post was the certain knowledge that they would soon be given an opportunity to fire the five torpedoes in *Laffey*'s single quintuple centerline mount. But it was not to be quite yet.

Most of the crew failed to notice that *Laffey*'s three vertical white battle recognition lights were left on during the entire exchange with *Akatsuki*. One who did, and who prayed that the signalman in charge would wake up and turn them off, was S1 John Jenkins, the loader on the after 20mm gun whose crew had earlier shared the gallon can of peaches. Jenkins was glancing nervously between the recognition lights and *Akatsuki* when *Laffey* was harassed by fire from another passing Japanese ship he felt had been attracted by the recognition lights. *Laffey* was sprayed with the fallout from one or two near misses, which caused several casualties and left the strong smell of cordite in the air. By the time the smoke from the near misses cleared, *Akatsuki* and the unseen assailant were gone and *Laffey*'s main guns abruptly ceased firing.

The very brief eruption was followed by several minutes of haunting quiet. During the lull, the captain of Mount-1 emerged on the main deck holding both hands over his abdomen and complaining of pain in the abdominal area. He was checked over and found to be in a semidazed state but otherwise uninjured. As a precaution, he was replaced on the spot and sent to be looked after at a nearby dressing station manned by the ship's chief corpsman. Four other sailors reported in with minor shrapnel wounds and all were given first aid by the chief doc.

Suddenly, the brief calm was broken by shouted news that a huge ship—*Hiei*—was bearing down directly on *Laffey* from port. As soon as the word was passed, all of *Laffey*'s 5-inch guns, most of her five 20mm guns, and her 1.1-inch mount opened fire.

Lt(jg) Tom Evins heard his talker, whose unblinking eyes were the size of silver dollars, sing out, "Fire torpedoes to port!" The torpedo mount was still trained out to starboard, and it took one interminable minute for it to be retrained to port. The torpedoes had already been preset for a high-speed run at a depth of 10 feet. The need was too urgent and events were shaping up too fast to change any of those or other settings; the moment the ready light came on at the port bridge director, TM1 Frederick Sanderson, the director operator, sent the first fish on its way. As the first tube expelled the torpedo in a surge of compressed air, the captain ordered Evins to cease firing. But he changed his mind a second later and ordered Evins to proceed. The four remaining torpedoes of *Laffey*'s total battery of five were hurled into the water at three-second intervals. Tom Evins looked after them for the moment it took their luminescent wakes to disappear into the blackness. Then his attention was wrenched upward, where he saw *Hiei*'s giant bows coming right at him, edge on.

During the time the 5-inch mounts were able to bear upon *Hiei*'s huge pagoda-shaped bridge structure, they fired into it with merciless precision. Since all his torpedoes were in the water, Lt(jg) Tom Evins had nothing to do except watch the show from his vantage point on the bridge. He was particularly struck by the flare of bursting shells behind the battleship's numerous portholes.

Moments after the gunfire erupted, S1 John Jenkins's 20mm gun went silent—long before it might have run out of ammunition. Jenkins looked up in surprise and saw the gunner hanging lifeless from the straps binding him into the shoulder harness. Jenkins leaped behind the gunner's body and swiveled the dead man and the gun through a swirl of Japanese 25mm rounds that were striking the area around him. Then, using the dead gunner as a shield, Jenkins fired the remainder of the magazine in the breech directly into a large square porthole at what he judged to be extremely close range. As the gun fired the last round in the magazine, Jenkins watched in awed amazement as *Hiei*'s pagoda-shaped bridge structure slowly collapsed like a house of cards and fell forward over the battleship's number-two 14-inch turret.

Hiei 's communications were thoroughly disrupted by *Laffey*'s shells, and many Japanese officers and sailors manning the flagship's bridge were killed or seriously injured by gunfire or in the collapse. Among the dead was Admiral Abe's chief of staff. Abe was only slightly injured in the conflagration, but he was so dazed that he was unable to exert any influence upon the course of the battle from that moment onward.

Hiei was so close to *Laffey* that her giant 14-inch guns could not be adequately depressed to fire on the destroyer at her feet. A number of the 6-inch guns in her secondary battery did fire, but they all missed. The only hits registered on *Laffey* by *Hiei* were from bursts fired by her 25mm antiaircraft guns. These killed or wounded several exposed 20mm gunners and torpedomen, but inflicted no material damage.

༰

LCdr Bill Hank, a 1925 Annapolis graduate, could well have been the worst ship-handler in command of a U.S. ship off Guadalcanal that night. Indeed, he had a marked propensity for running *Laffey* into solid objects, particularly when trying to dock her. The ship, which was been commissioned under Hank's command at the end of March 1942, had had a gash torn in her side near the bow during one memorable collision. (The crew ruefully referred to the patch as an "armored belt" because it was ⅜-inch steel while the rest of the hull was ¼-inch steel.) As Ens David Sterrett, the machine-gun officer, looked on in helpless dismay at the impending collision with *Hiei*, he could not suppress the thought that the maneuver was at least one with which the captain had had ample experience.

But Bill Hank had already proven himself a competent battle commander at Cape Esperance in mid-October. Many members of the topside crew had seen a miraculous change come over the normally excitable skipper that night, when he went dead calm in action. The change had already occurred this night as well. Bill Hank was fully in command of himself and his vessel. With a cool precision that would have changed Ensign Sterrett's opinion on the spot,

Hank barked two precise, measured commands to his helmsman: "Emergency back." followed seconds later by "Emergency full ahead." There was not a trace of anxiety in his voice, though everyone around him was anxiously staring up at the stories-high bows of the battleship as they threatened to slice *Laffey* in two.

News of the impending—some said inevitable—collision reached the engineering officer, Lt Eugene Barham, in the forward engine room, by way of his phone talker. Bill Hank's "Emergency back" order arrived by way of the engine-order telegraph. No sooner had Barham relayed the order to his throttlemen, however, than the telegraph rang up "Emergency full ahead." Barham personally grabbed the ahead throttle and spun it while the throttleman closed the astern throttle. At the same instant, in the adjacent fire rooms, all burners and feed pumps were opened fully, and steam pressure was holding. *Laffey* seemed to leap ahead.

From Ensign Sterrett's vantage point, *Laffey* seemed to clear *Hiei*'s bows by less than 20 feet. Then she surged ahead at full power as *Hiei* knifed through the American vanguard directly astern of the departing destroyer.

꙰

As soon as *Hiei* had passed astern and drawn away to about 2,000 yards off *Laffey*'s starboard quarter, Lieutenant Commander Hank ordered his gunnery officer, Lt William Ratcliff, to cease firing all the ship's guns. A quick tally revealed that *Laffey* had expended 100 5-inch rounds, 1,000 20mm rounds, and 700 1.1-inch rounds. It is difficult to conceive that many of them missed *Hiei*.

Lt(jg) Tom Evins was certain that at least two or three of his torpedoes scored hits—he could hardly have missed so large a target at so near a range—but apparently none of them actually detonated. It was later deduced that the range was so short that the torpedoes had not had a sufficient run—500 yards—in which to arm. That is possible, but it is also possible that the impact detonators failed. Whatever the cause, *Hiei* received no torpedo damage from *Laffey*'s five fish. Many observers felt that the last two torpedoes passed astern of *Hiei*.

19

Sterett, the third destroyer in the American vanguard, had been monitoring radar reports from the other ships and found distant targets with her own FD fire-direction radar at about 0134. Moments before any of the American ships opened fire, officers on *Sterett*'s bridge had visual contact with three ships off the starboard bow—*Nagara* for sure, and possibly *Amatsukaze* and *Yukikaze*—and two ships to port—*Hiei* and what everyone took to be a light cruiser but which was, in fact, *Akatsuki*.

Adding appreciably to *Sterett*'s woes in the seconds before the action commenced was the ignition of a bank of searchlights—some observers aboard *Sterett* felt there were at least nine lights—by *Hiei*, to port. The intensely bright lights instantly destroyed the night vision of and dazzled most of *Sterett*'s topside crew. Already keyed up as he faced his first surface action, Ens Perry Hall, *Sterett*'s assistant damage control officer, who was standing his watch on the bridge, felt like he was trapped at the end of a blind alley, unarmed and facing a man with a gun, as if there were no escape. Withal, the key man—the fire controlman manning the gunnery radar—was safely within the enclosed gun director and was unaffected by the light.

As with *Laffey*'s LCdr Bill Hank, *Sterett*'s Cdr Jesse Coward awaited Admiral Callaghan's specific order to open fire. Since *Sterett* was the third ship in the column, she was obliged by the 0152 order to train out her guns and torpedo tubes to starboard.

As luck would have it, *Sterett* had her guns and tubes aligned on *Hiei,* the most lucrative target to port. Nevertheless, Commander Coward ordered his weapons systems to retrain to the opposite side both to comply with the flag's order and to avoid undue concentration of the task force's fire power to one side. Thus, *Sterett* opened fire a minute or two behind *Cushing* and within the same minute as *Laffey.* High up in the gun director, Lt Cal Calhoun, the gunnery officer, ordered his fire controlman to align on the nearest target showing on the gunnery radarscope and open fire immediately.

Sterett's target was *Nagara,* the largest vessel in the Japanese starboard column, then 4,000 yards off the starboard bow. Though all of *Sterett*'s eight starboard torpedo tubes were trained out, the target's silhouette was initially too vague for a torpedo attack and the abrupt changes in course by the two American destroyers ahead prevented the starboard torpedo-director operator from finding an easy solution at that moment.

Sterett's guns were all loaded with starshells in anticipation that other ships, which would do the actual damage to the oncoming Japanese force, would need their assistance. Without any hesitation, Lieutenant Calhoun ordered the guns trained directly on *Nagara* and fired. The result was an awesome display of pyrotechnics. The guns were right on target, and the starshells erupted on the light cruiser's forecastle and around her forward 5.5-inch mounts. Many observers thought the light cruiser was aflame while others thought *Nagara* fired off flares of her own. Lieutenant Calhoun, high in the director, thought the effect was caused by *Sterett*'s starshells breaking up on impact.

Without missing a beat, all of *Sterett*'s guns were reloaded with standard armor-piercing rounds and automatically refired by the director. A total of twelve such four-gun salvos were fired in rapid succession. Throughout, all the guns were swung increasingly aftward as *Nagara* swiftly passed by on an opposite course.

In the middle of the close-range shoot-out, at 0154, *Sterett* was struck by a shell fired from off her port quarter that parted the starboard cable controlling her steering gear. Without skipping a beat, Commander Coward began issuing what amounted to an avalanche of orders to his helmsman and engineering officer and steered his ship on her engines, a tricky maneuver in the best of circumstances and a display of consummate seamanship under night-battle conditions. Through it all, the destroyer's guns maintained their fire at *Nagara;* indeed, Lt Cal Calhoun, in the gun director, was unaware that his ship had suffered a steering breakdown.

At length, Lieutenant Calhoun had to order the guns to check fire. It had been inevitable from the start that the constant shifts aftward would eventually bring *O'Bannon*, the next ship aft, into *Sterett*'s line of fire. However, the process was accelerated as the fourth vanguard destroyer swung out of line to starboard and came on fast. Calhoun checked fire just as *O'Bannon* arrived off the starboard quarter, between *Sterett* and *Nagara.*

Having lost *Nagara* behind *O'Bannon*, Lieutenant Calhoun ordered the director retrained on *Hiei*, which had just passed astern of *Laffey*. At that moment, the Japanese flagship was concentrating her fire on *San Francisco.*

At 0158, moments after *Sterett*'s guns opened on *Hiei*, Commander Coward received what, to him, was an inexplicable order from Admiral Callaghan, who blurted out "Cease fire!" over the open TBS circuit. Coward's ship was hotly engaged at that moment, but he obediently ordered his guns silenced.

After but a brief pause to consider the sanity of the order against the backdrop of objective reality—the sea was full of burning warships and lucrative targets, and shells were burning hotly through the night sky in all directions as far as the eye could see—*Sterett* resumed firing. During the moments-long lull in her own firing, *Sterett* was beset with the fallout from numerous near misses. Shortly after *Sterett* checked fire to avoid hitting *O'Bannon*, her foremast took a direct hit, which disabled the SC radar antenna and knocked out the emergency identification lights and the TBS transmitting antenna. Numerous chunks of shrapnel also struck the gun director, which was within 8 feet of the detonation. The director trainer was wounded in the neck, the assistant gunnery officer was wounded in the back, and the rangefinder operator was wounded in the back. Lt Cal Calhoun, who was standing exposed in the director's rear hatchway, was struck in the head by several fragments and a piece of the mast, but his well-padded talker's helmet absorbed the debris and Calhoun emerged unscathed. Another steel sliver carried away the transmission button for Calhoun's sound-powered telephone from beneath the gunnery officer's right index finger, and Calhoun later counted twenty-three other pieces of shrapnel that were absorbed by the loosely stuffed collar of his kapok life jacket. For all that, however, the director crew did not falter and maintained full control of the guns.

Just as quickly as the guns began firing again, *Sterett* got four torpedoes away toward *Hiei*. The guns were on target. To be sure, many of the men topside aboard the American destroyer thought they saw at least two large red incandescent flashes beneath the passing behemoth. The timing was right (the torpedoes were being clocked to the target) so these were taken to be torpedo hits. Many Americans saw a half-dozen Japanese sailors jump from the battleship's deck to the water in the vicinity of the two red flashes. It is certain that *Hiei* was hit by *someone's* torpedoes at this moment, but more hits were claimed in the course of the melee than actually occurred and there is no certainty that these particular hits were caused by *Sterett's* own fish.

In the meantime, as *Hiei* advanced at about 5 knots, *Sterett* closed to within 500 yards and fired eight four-gun salvos directly at the battleship's superstructure. At that range, all of the 5-inch rounds struck in the vicinity of *Hiei*'s already severely damaged bridge. When it seemed that the battleship might crush the destroyer, *Sterett* dashed ahead of the giant's bows, so close that *Hiei*'s guns could not depress far enough to hit her.

With that, *Sterett* emerged into a lull and took the opportunity to lick her wounds.

20

Destroyer *O'Bannon*'s first contact with the oncoming Japanese battle force was at 0130, when her modern SG surface-search radar picked up targets directly ahead and on her starboard bow. In the following minutes, SoM3 Roy Conn, the lead radarman, maintained steady contacts and reported his findings to the captain, Cdr Edwin Wilkinson. As SoM3 Conn looked on, the image of a ragged V of ships emerged on his PPI scope.

At 0144, after *O'Bannon* had followed the three destroyers ahead through several turns ordered by Admiral Callaghan, Commander Wilkinson ordered all five 5-inch mounts and both quintuple torpedo mounts to train out on radar-acquired targets to starboard, notably *Nagara*. One minute later, at 0145, lookouts reported sighting five ships off the port beam at a distance of 4,000 yards. These targets were on a parallel opposite course and approaching at slow speed. It was at this moment that Admiral Callaghan ordered all ships to "stand by to open fire."

Within the same minute he heard Admiral Callaghan's truncated command, Commander Wilkinson reacted instinctively to the jam-up of the destroyers ahead by ordering numerous course and speed changes to keep from hitting *Sterett*. This was the ripple caused by *Cushing's* hard turn at 0141 to avoid *Yudachi* and *Haru-same*. When the ship settled back on course, Commander Wilkinson ordered *O'Bannon's* main guns and all her torpedo tubes to be shifted to port. He had at least two good reasons for ordering the shift: A huge ship—*Hiei*—was looming well ahead of the port bow, and it was feared that *Sterett*, which wound up close ahead to starboard, might become entangled with *O'Bannon's* guns if they were opened on targets in that direction. By then, the image on SoM3 Roy Conn's PPI scope was changing so rapidly that Conn's ability to describe events actually fell behind what the men on the destroyer's open bridge could see with their own eyes.

When *Akatsuki* turned on her powerful searchlight against *Cushing* at 0150, *O'Bannon's* guns were already aimed almost directly at her. As soon as the lights went on, Commander Wilkinson bellowed, "Action port! Get that searchlight!" Immediately, Lt George Philip, the gunnery officer, ordered the guns to "Commence firing!" *O'Bannon* was thus among the first American warships to open fire. Almost as soon as the guns threw out their first salvo, something behind *Hiei* flared up and perfectly silhouetted the Japanese flagship.

The radar-directed guns appeared to be dead on target with the first salvo, for lookouts and officers all noted that the 5-inch tracer rounds struck the Japanese vessel near the light, which went out and was replaced by what appeared to be several fires. It was also noted that *Akatsuki's* own gunfire became sporadic as *O'Bannon* and other American vessels continued to score numerous hits.

As most of *O'Bannon's* topside crew followed the action to port, a diligent lookout on the starboard side sang out that the ship was about to collide with *Sterett*. The near confrontation between the friendly destroyers arose as a result of *Sterett's* parted steering cable. To *O'Bannon's* exec, LCdr Donald MacDonald, who was conning his ship, *Sterett* seemed to go momentarily dead in the water. This obliged him to veer sharply to starboard and add speed. The result was that *O'Bannon* began passing *Sterett's* starboard quarter, thus obliging *Sterett* to cease firing on *Nagara*, her target to starboard, while *O'Bannon's* guns had to cease firing at *Akatsuki*, her target to port. Moments later, *Sterett* was falling away astern and *O'Bannon* was trying to rejoin the column behind *Laffey*.

From his position in the center of the bridge, Lieutenant Commander MacDonald saw that each of the lead destroyers was bathed in light, which he thought was from air-dropped flares, but was, in fact, from the superior Japanese starshells. Each of them was also the focal point of lines of large-caliber tracer, most of it deliberately fired by unseen warships on all sides. *Cushing*, which was still ahead of *Laffey*, appeared to be bearing the brunt of numerous hits from port and starboard.

As soon as *O'Bannon*'s guns were clear of friendly targets, they resumed firing, this time at *Hiei* 's lumbering bulk. The guns were again dead on target. As the action was heating up and Lieutenant Commander MacDonald was thinking about remaining at full speed to pass directly in front of *Hiei*, the TBS crackled to life. It was Admiral Callaghan's voice: "Cease firing." *O'Bannon* obediently checked fire, but within seconds Commander Wilkinson ordered the guns back into action.

Just as the firing resumed, Commander Wilkinson looked ahead to try to locate *Cushing* and *Laffey*, but both friendly vessels had disappeared. He feared that one or both had been sunk. In fact, *O'Bannon* had probably passed *Cushing*, which by then had lost way, and *Laffey* had probably begun her full-speed run to clear the area of the growing melee. For all practical purposes, then, *O'Bannon* was the lead American warship.

While the exec conned the ship and the captain looked around for the missing friendly destroyers, Lieutenant Philip, the gunnery officer, repeatedly called down to the plotting room, at bridge level just below the director, to order the range to *Hiei* decreased. At length, the gunnery computer operator shouted back rather hotly that he was already at minimum range and could no longer decrease. From that point, the gunnery solution was simple: All the fire controlman in the director had to do was hold the director sights on the huge, slowly oncoming battleship while the loaders reloaded. Then, as soon as he heard "Ready!" five times over the gunnery circuit, he simply had to close the firing key, steady the sight, and wait for the next chorus from the loaders. Load, point, fire . . . load, point fire; it was that easy. Observers reported that numerous hits were carving pieces out of *Hiei* like "a knife cutting through a block of butter."

O'Bannon's guns remained on *Hiei* as the battleship closed to within 1,800 yards. Then, without warning, *O'Bannon* was targeted by heavy gunfire from starboard. The captain and others on the bridge were unable to locate the source of the flurry of near misses, but observers elsewhere reported that it was emanating from a three-funnel cruiser astern and to starboard—busy *Nagara*. *O'Bannon*'s five guns were retrained to starboard and *Nagara*'s fire was returned. Several hits and fires were observed around the Japanese light cruiser's after gun mounts.

While *O'Bannon*'s guns were dueling *Nagara* to starboard, her torpedo tubes remained trained to port, from which direction *Hiei* was still slowing advancing. The behemoth was contending with many visible fires topside and her output of gunfire was visibly falling off. Nevertheless, portions of her main and secondary batteries remained active and attempted to reach out to *O'Bannon*. MM1 Horace Mabry, a member of *O'Bannon*'s after repair party, found himself staring straight down the barrels of a pair of *Hiei*'s 14-inch guns just as those huge guns fired. As nearly as Mabry could estimate, the 1-ton rounds passed only 10 feet over his head and nearly sucked his shirt off his back. Fortunately, they missed the ship entirely and plunged into the water to starboard. Other 14-inch rounds, and 6-inch shells as well, passed directly over the on-coming destroyer.

When the range to *Hiei* fell below 1,200 yards, Commander Wilkinson ordered his torpedo officer to fire two torpedoes directly at the battleship. At first, Wilkinson intended to withhold the remainder of his torpedoes until the first two had completed their runs, but he thought better of that after a few moments and ordered more torpedoes into the water. As soon as the third fish was away, however, *Hiei* shuddered under the impact of a tremendous explosion that enveloped her in flames from bow to stern and showered *O'Bannon*'s forecastle with burning debris. Commander Wilkinson decided to save the remaining seven fish and ordered the torpedomen to check fire.

Moments after the third torpedo was away, LCdr Donald MacDonald turned *O'Bannon* hard right and rang up "Ahead, full." He almost instantly regretted the maneuver, for it seemed that *O'Bannon* was about to rip straight into *Hiei*, which had reflexively turned to avoid more torpedo hits and had thus shaped a course directly across *O'Bannon*'s projected track.

"Hard right," Lieutenant Commander MacDonald bellowed at his helmsman. "Emergency full astern!" The speeding destroyer's forward progress was arrested at virtually the last instant and she pivoted clear of the turning battleship's great bows. As soon as MacDonald saw that he had avoided the collision, he ordered "Engines ahead, full," and conned *O'Bannon* due east, away from the dreadnought.

As their ship twisted away from *Hiei*, *O'Bannon*'s gunners lost track of *Nagara*. Then the ship emerged from the melee.

21

At 0150, one sharp searchlight beam from destroyer *Akat-suki* penetrated the blackness toward the highest near sil-houette in the American column. The light from off her port bow struck *Atlanta* on the port wing of her bridge, startling all who stood in its sharp luminescence. The source of the light was so close and the light itself so intense that Lt Stew Moredock, RAdm Norman Scott's operations officer, could just about feel the heat it was throwing off.

Instantaneously, *Atlanta*'s gunnery officer shifted his attention from a solid radar target crossing from port to starboard due north and 3,000 yards ahead and yelled, "Commence firing! Counter-illuminate!"

As all four of her 36-inch searchlights snapped on, *Atlanta* became the first ship on either side to open fire. Immediately, her after group of four dual 5-inch mounts put out rounds straight up the cone of light, right at the searchlights themselves, right at *Akatsuki*. The target was only 1,600 yards to port, too close to miss.

At the same time *Atlanta*'s after gun group opened on *Akatsuki*, her forward group of three dual 5-inch mounts was shifted to a destroyer—possibly *Inazuma*—which was about 300 yards behind

Akatsuki. All the guns of both groups appeared to be dead on their targets. At least twenty rounds were observed striking all parts of the rear destroyer's hull and upper works, and numerous hits were scored on *Akatsuki*. But not soon enough.

Especially concerned with his crew of engineers who were sealed below decks in the fire rooms and engine rooms, *Atlanta's* chief engineer, LCdr Arthur Loeser, had arranged for topside talkers to keep him abreast of what was going on outside while he relayed a running commentary via loudspeakers from his station in the forward engine room. Thus the engineering staff throughout the cruiser was listening as Lieutenant Commander Loeser described the first seconds of the gunnery exchange—"We're really putting rounds into them!"

Even as at least one of *Atlanta's* two targets disappeared from view, the American light cruiser's forward superstructure was raked by a dozen 5.5-inch rounds fired by light cruiser *Nagara*, which had by then turned back the way she had come and was at that moment swiftly steaming down the starboard side of and on the same general heading as the American column. Among other areas that were struck were *Atlanta's* charthouse and forward 5-inch gun director. But the worst blows—several of them—fell upon the bridge area and the men occupying it.

Lt Stew Moredock, who was observing the action from the port wing of the bridge, just ahead of the charthouse, was struck in the right arm by a piece of shrapnel, but he felt no pain and did not yet know he had been wounded. However, as soon as Moredock tried to use the injured limb, he was gripped by intense pain. Instinctively, he glanced back at Admiral Scott, who was standing right outside the charthouse. At that moment, the admiral was in the process of taking a step forward. Then he collapsed to the steel deck, dead as he was caving in. Three of Admiral Scott's staffers died with him; only Stew Moredock survived. Only three of the thirteen enlisted sailors on the bridge survived along with Lieutenant Moredock and two or three other officers. One of the survivors was Capt Samuel Jenkins, who had made a fortuitous trip to the port wing of the bridge to find targets for his ship's port torpedo mount. Though the captain had turned back to starboard by the time *Nagara*'s 5.5-inch shells struck the bridge, he was shielded from the effects of the blast and suffered no injuries.

At nearly the instant *Atlanta*'s bridge was devastated, the Japanese destroyers to port put at least eight rounds into that side of the ship, from up near *Atlanta*'s bows to just beneath Mount-2. One of these rounds detonated directly on the face of Mount-1, killing every member but one of the right-hand gun crew. Another round struck the mount's upper handling room, killing and injuring everyone there and cutting the flow of ammunition to the viable left gun.

As soon as Mount-1's right gun was disabled, GM3 Ed Huddleston, the left gun's first shellman, took command from the wounded chief turret captain. Though Huddleston's ears were still ringing from the effects of the direct hit on the mount, he called Lt Lloyd Mustin, the assistant gunnery officer, to request permission to secure. Mustin agreed, but cautioned Huddleston to be careful since the ship was still taking hits. As soon as Huddleston stepped through the hatch to the main deck, a Japanese shell ignited the ammunition and powder in Mount-2's upper handling room. Though a cloud of shrapnel and debris erupted from the struck space, Huddleston was not touched, so he turned to help the next man out of his own mount. All the wounded from Mount-1 were laid out on the main deck beside the mount and given rudimentary first aid. Then, as Japanese shells continued to strike the ship, Huddleston was confronted by a panicked lieutenant who was yelling, "Abandon ship!" Huddleston was not so easily rattled, but other sailors who were immediately released several life rafts and followed them straight over the side.

One of *Nagara*'s 5.5-inch rounds killed a pair of mess attendants who were passing one another as each ran to the opposite side of the ship from his battle station in each of the midships 20mm ammunition clipping rooms. Neither of those places was damaged and no one inside them was injured.

A 5-inch round fired from port struck the mast, toppling it and spreading shrapnel into the adjacent after stack and across the after searchlight platform. Another Japanese round penetrated the unoccupied flag cabin, and two more 5-inch rounds struck the after superstructure; one of them went all the way through Mount-4, the port waist mount, and then bored all the way through the ship. In fact, this armor-piercing round did not detonate until it had penetrated Mount-5, the starboard waist mount. All but one member of the gun crew was killed; the survivor was blown into the water after being forcibly ejected from the mount when its roof was blown open. Finally, three lighter rounds, probably 3-inch antiaircraft rounds fired from starboard by *Nagara*, struck Mount-6.

卍

The Mount-5 handling-room crew evacuated the compartment in good order after the mount directly overhead was hit. However, as soon as the ammunition handlers were outside on the unengaged starboard deck, someone mentioned that at least several live 5-inch rounds were rolling around in the handling room. S2 Don McKay volunteered to go back in to retrieve them. The room was filled with stagnant smoke, so someone tied a rope around McKay's waist and promised to reel him in if he ran into trouble. With that, McKay held his breath and groped his way into the darkened compartment. He found several shells on the deck, picked them up, and passed them outside one at a time. Then he took a breather. As McKay was completing his second trip into the smoke-filled compartment, an officer appeared and asked what was going on. He put a stop to McKay's trips when he learned that McKay did not have a gas mask, much less a more sophisticated device known as an RBA (Rescue Breathing Apparatus). The officer felt the compartment was probably filled with poisonous gas in addition to the stagnant smoke. A runner was sent to find someone with an RBA.

卍

The vanguard Japanese destroyer captains, drilled to perfection in their navy's highly aggressive torpedo tactics, exploited their initial immediate advantage and supplemented the gunfire with several salvos of their deadly 24-inch Long Lance torpedoes.

Crewmen in blind engineering spaces throughout the ship heard LCdr Arthur Loeser's mike open once again. Loeser said, "Ah . . ." and the entire world fell in. Loeser's voice was stilled in mid-sentence—and forever.

The first Japanese torpedo to find any target struck *Atlanta* on the port side, nearly amidships and exactly in the center of her forward engine room. In addition to killing virtually everyone in the forward engine room, the detonation blasted a hole in the overhead and killed nearly everyone manning a damage-control station in the crew's mess hall. The shock of the massive detonation lifted the light cruiser right out of the water.

When she landed, *Atlanta* came down with a jolt that sent shudders and shivers up the spines of every member of her crew who was still vertical. BM1 Leighton Spadone, whose 1.1-inch mount was on the starboard side of the ship and well aft of the blast, was severely jostled as the entire ship flexed and strained as steel decks and bulkheads resonated the force of the detonation in all directions from the point of impact. Spadone and many others throughout the stricken cruiser distinctly heard and felt another massive explosion, right on the heels of the first. Many thought this was caused by a second torpedo, but it was almost certainly a sympathetic detonation in the engineering spaces.

EM3 Bill McKinney and S2 Dan Curtin, who were manning a damage-control substation in a large crew's quarters on the fourth deck, two compartments forward of the forward fire room, were knocked off their feet by the force of the blast. Immediately, the two jumped up and examined the area, but they could find no damage. A quick check also revealed that the battle phones and ship's service phones were dead, and their only light was provided by a battery-powered battle lantern. McKinney was aware that *Atlanta's* guns were no longer firing and that the ship was slowing down. He could clearly hear rending and tearing noises from above, as if the ammunition hoists running through the compartment to Mount-3 were buckling off their tracks.

Most of the firemen, machinist's mates, and watertenders who were working in the forward engine room were killed or wounded in the torpedo blast, which knocked out all the cruiser's power except an emergency diesel generator. The Navy's first anitaircraft cruiser had been rendered powerless and set adrift within minutes of opening fire.

⚛

In the immediate wake of the torpedo hit, the survivors among her engine-room and fire-room watches had to fend for themselves. The inhabitants of the after fire room were immediately beset by an enormous in-rush of water through the breached double forward bulkhead. Fortunately, all hands managed to scramble up ladders leading to escape trunks overhead. Those who went up the port ladder made it to safety without much of a struggle, but three who opted for the starboard ladder were unknowingly beset by rigidly enforced rules pertaining to the watertight integrity of the ship.

MM1 Ross Hilton, the machine-shop supervisor, and another machinist's mate were only just recovering from the effects of the blast directly beneath their station when they saw that someone below was undogging the clips securing the heavy counterweighted starboard escape hatch in the midships passageway. However, as soon as Hilton began releasing the clips from his side of the hatch, an overexcited lieutenant appeared and bellowed, "Dog that hatch back down, Hilton!"

"But, sir," Hilton protested, "there's someone alive down there."

"I don't give a damn! Dog it down!"

"Sir, they're trying to get out. They're alive!"

The officer reached for his .45-caliber pistol, fixed a murderous stare at Hilton, and piped in his by-then shrill voice, "Dog it down or I'll blow your brains out!"

Hilton was thinking about what to do or say next when a sailor arrived behind the officer and told him of an urgent matter requiring his presence elsewhere. As soon as the officer was distracted and gone, Hilton and his companion bent over to undog the hatch. By then, the man beneath the hatch had virtually completed the job, so Hilton and his companion jerked the hatch open. Immediately, a fuel-covered machinist's mate and two fuel-covered firemen cannonballed onto the deck. Behind them, the water had risen to within 2 feet of the overhead; the three would have drowned in a matter of moments. Hilton and his companion immediately re-sealed the hatch while the rescued machinist's mate explained that everyone else from the after fire room had escaped up the port ladder.

⌁

After helping to clear volatile ammunition from the Mount-5 handling room, S2 Don McKay tagged along with an officer and several other sailors who were on their way forward to look for topside damage caused from the torpedo detonation. As the small group passed an escape hatch leading up from the damaged engineering spaces, the officer ordered McKay to redog several clips that someone had left open. McKay said that he thought someone might be trying to get out, but the officer remained firm; he had direct orders from his superiors to batten down all hatches. As they spoke, a thin gout of water burbled up from the edge of the hatchway. The officer left McKay and several others to redog that hatch and check others in the vicinity. He said he would be back for them. By then, the forward engine room and after fire room were both flooded to the overheads, and all the men remaining in the former were dead.

⌁

S2 Dave Driscoll, the Mount-8 shell-hoist loader, worked himself to a smooth, continuous flow while the action was hot, but a distinct shudder Driscoll felt early in the action was followed by an order to cease firing. Mindful for the first time of the intense physical ordeal of continuously throwing heavy 5-inch shells onto the moving hoist, Driscoll and the other shellmen reacted to the cease-fire order by dropping to the deck or reeling back against the support of the bulkheads of the gray steel compartment in which they had been sealed. After a minute or two, the babble of many confused voices making its way down the hoist from the gun chamber overhead was suddenly overwhelmed by an unwelcome command: "Abandon ship!" S2 Driscoll reacted by repeating the order down the powder hoist to the men who had been sealed into the Mount-8 magazine. Then, as others climbed up to Mount-8, Driscoll undogged the handling-room hatch to gain access to an adjacent berthing compartment. There being no one in the berthing compartment, Driscoll next defied rigid regulations and undogged the hatch leading to the magazine. He was immediately confronted by sailors from the lower handling room crew, all of whom displayed expressions of pure animal fear mixed with pure human relief. S2 Dave Driscoll fell in with the thundering herd and began climbing the nearest ladder of the main deck.

⇄

Despite all the obvious hits and the jolt he had received from the torpedo blast, BM1 Leighton Spadone was not overly concerned until he realized that his ship was no longer firing her guns. As Spadone's confidence reached its low ebb, he found himself muttering, "Please, God, stop them from firing, stop them from firing, stop them from firing. . . ." However, his prayers were answered by hits that seemed to be coming in from somewhere aft of the ship.

Atlanta had been in the last stages of speeding up and completing a right turn to regain her position in the column when she was struck by the torpedo. She was pointed south and sliding powerlessly to the end of that maneuver when *San Francisco's* main battery fired a full nine-gun salvo at what must have been *Hiei*. *Atlanta's* unchecked forward momentum carried her directly into *San Francisco's* line of fire.

Every one of the flagship's nine 8-inch rounds—and every one from the next full salvo—struck *Atlanta* from a relative angle of 240 degrees, aft of the port beam, at a range estimated to be about 3,600 yards. Captain Jenkins, who had not yet had an opportunity to assess the damage or extent of casualties on his shattered bridge, was game to take the assailing vessel under fire with the remaining 5-inch mounts that could be brought to bear, but he recognized the familiarly American outline of the flagship in the flare of her own main battery and so countermanded the order as soon as he uttered it. It is doubtful in any case that the order could have been relayed to the guns because all power and communications throughout the stricken vessel were out.

Mount-3 received two direct 8-inch hits, as did Mount-6 and Mount-5. The rest of the 8-inch hits were scattered in two large groupings throughout the forward and after superstructures. By no means fatal to the stricken ship, the incoming friendly rounds nevertheless cut down many *Atlanta* crewmen.

One of the mess attendants assigned to the crew running the ammunition hoist to the two midships 1.1-inch mounts was in mortal fear of being hit on the head and killed. When F1 Chuck Dodd, who was in charge of the crew, had enough of standing around with nothing to do in the vulnerable little compartment, he gave the order to head to the starboard side of the ship. One of *San Francisco's* 8-inch rounds detonated nearby as Dodd opened the hatch. Its blast jarred the steel ladder running through the compartment from the bulkhead. The heavy ladder fell on the fearful mess attendant, crushing his helmet and his skull.

↻

RM3 Ray Duke, a member of a repair party stationed topside in a passageway just forward of the radio transmission room, was in the act of cutting loose a fire extinguisher from an outside bulkhead when he was struck by shrapnel in the right knee. The force of the impact, which shattered the knee, threw Duke and the heavy TBS transceiver he was backpacking headfirst down an 11-foot ladder. Duke landed on his head and shoulders but was saved by his steel helmet, which took most of the impact when he landed. The nearby 1.1-inch ammunition handling room was on fire, and the area was filled with smoke. Slightly dazed and in need of fresh air, RM3 Duke staggered into the open on the unengaged starboard side and breathed deeply to regain his composure. His ordeal had only just begun.

His lungs filled with fresh air, Duke hobbled into the burning and smoking 1.1-inch handling room to see if he could help there. He immediately found a friend who was lying in the middle of the ruin with his right leg shot off at the knee. Duke offered to fetch the other man some morphine and staggered down to the next deck to find a boatswain's mate he knew was authorized to carry the narcotic. However, as soon as Duke asked for morphine, the boatswain's mate jabbed *him* with a full syrette and made him lie down on the deck. Duke tried to protest, but he was groggy from shock and smoke inhalation and never quite got the words out. No sooner was Duke on the deck than the adjacent pay office took a direct hit. The beam from the large flashlight he still carried revealed a hole in the bulkhead about half the size of a basketball. Shrapnel from the blast went right between Duke's legs, ripping off a large chunk of flesh from his left thigh right above the knee and severing the femoral artery. Blood was pulsing from the wound in spurts that appeared as thick as his wrist. Another piece of shrapnel slid between Duke and the steel deck and sliced open the back of his right thigh from knee to buttocks. At the same time, shrapnel punctured the 1.1-inch coolant tank right overhead and Duke was bathed in hot salt water. As soon as Duke recovered his senses, he and a sailor right beside him helped one another up a nearby ladder and crawled out onto the port quarterdeck. At that point, Duke stood up and walked all of 10 feet before his damaged right knee gave way. He fell heavily to the deck and lay there until someone came by and administered a second shot of morphine. Soon after that, a supply officer held Duke's head in his lap while a corpsman laved the wounds, applied bandages, and administered yet another dose of morphine. With that, RM3 Ray Duke lost track of his surroundings.

❧

The electrician's mates manning the after searchlights were in danger of being roasted alive by fires reaching nearly as high as the platform on which they were trapped. Not only was there no evident way off the platform, dense smoke and shooting flames from shrapnel holes in the after stack, to which the searchlight platform was affixed, totally obscured the vista and blocked all possible escape routes. Indeed, there was so much acrid smoke billowing up around the after searchlights that the operators were not certain if they would die from roasting or smoke inhalation.

Suddenly, when their plight seemed hopeless, the searchlight operators were graced by a sudden rise in their fortunes, a wind change that both blew the smoke away and revealed the silent passage of *Hiei* only 100 yards from the ship. Though the searchlight operators were certain they were dead meat as they stared up at the battleship's searchlights, which were 20 feet over their heads, *Hiei* went on her way without firing at burning *Atlanta*. Meantime, the wind held the smoke and diverted the flames away from the search-light platform, so all hands scrambled down to the relative safety of the main deck, where they went to work fighting fires.

Atlanta's emergency diesel generator got the lights back on at 0156. By then, thankfully, *Atlanta* was out of the line of fire, and the fury of the widening battle had passed her by.

22

From his place on *San Francisco*'s navigation bridge, LCdr Bruce McCandless, the ship's communicator, now standing his second consecutive watch as officer of the deck, saw *Atlanta* twist away from the column's base course. Uncertain if he was to follow the turn or remain on course, McCandless shouted down the voice tube to Admiral Callaghan, who was on the flag bridge, one deck below, "The *Atlanta*'s turned left! Shall I follow?"

The reply was immediate: "No! Hold your course!" But only a few seconds later the admiral ordered, "Follow the *Atlanta!*" To comply, Lieutenant Commander McCandless directed the flagship slightly to the right to clear *Atlanta*'s oncoming stern.

S1 Willie Boyce had come off watch at midnight and had flaked out in a private spot on the well deck. As *San Francisco* swung into the right turn, Boyce came instantly awake, certain because of a particular queasiness in the pit of his stomach that the ship was turning. He sat bolt upright, instinctively certain that something "big" was about to happen.

Lieutenant Commander McCandless next ordered left full rudder in order to parallel *Atlanta*'s course, which had shifted to the northwest. As the ship began swinging hard to port, LCdr Willie Wilbourne, her gunnery officer, ordered the main battery, which was already swinging out to starboard, to train on the nearest enemy vessel and open fire at his order. The nearest target to starboard was a destroyer that was being followed by at least one other destroyer. It is probable that the two were *Akatsuki* and *Inazuma*. (It is true that the two were generally on the port side of the American vanguard, but the sharp left turn would have placed them temporarily off *San Francisco*'s starboard bow.)

Next, at 0150, the one thing S1 Willie Boyce feared the most about serving topside overtook him. Arriving from a dark void, the piercing shaft of *Akatsuki*'s searchlight swung through the blackness and came to rest on the ship dead ahead. Boyce saw *Atlanta*'s own searchlights open, followed by a double line of glowing 5-inch tracer rounds. In the same moment, *San Francisco* was captured by *Hiei*'s sweeping searchlight battery, in the fallout from searchlights momentarily opened by friendly warships astern, and along her starboard side as *Akatsuki*'s searchlight brushed past twisting *Atlanta*. Immediately, as the first of *Atlanta*'s 5-inch rounds struck *Akatsuki*'s intrusive light, Seaman Boyce watched it go from bright white to dull red before it faded altogether.

As the American flagship's main battery loosed its first nine-gun salvo, her starboard forward 5-inch gun—Mount-1—began filling the sky over the Japanese destroyers with starshells. No sooner were *San Francisco*'s starshells away than Lieutenant Commander McCandless swung the ship far back to the right to follow *Atlanta*'s next abrupt turn in that direction. However, as *Atlanta* swung even further to the right, McCandless steadied up on Course 000, due north.

On the well deck, standing alone in the dark, S1 Willie Boyce was nearly thrown from his feet by the swift series of tight turns. At the same time, Boyce could tell from the changing noise from two forced-air blowers nearby that the ship was undergoing numerous continuous speed changes. For a few moments every few moments, the overlapping reports of 8-inch and 5-inch guns seemed to abate as the gun directors fell behind the swift maneuvering. After only a minute of savoring the multitude of sensations, however,

Boyce decided to find some cover. He made his way directly to a gear locker, undogged the door, moved aside a collection of swabs, brooms, and buckets, and stepped inside to evade any possible flying debris. Then he sheepishly peered around the corner of the open doorway and requited his insatiable curiosity by looking at the fight shaping up to starboard.

⇄

At 0152, a few seconds after *Atlanta* was struck by a torpedo, Admiral Callaghan's universally confusing order—"Odd-numbered ships fire to starboard; even-numbered ships fire to port."—was given. *San Francisco* was an even-numbered ship and thus should have retrained her guns to port. However, Capt Cassin Young simply ignored the order and allowed his main battery to remain trained on the firm target to starboard.

A total of nine full 8-inch salvos were fired at *Akatsuki* before Captain Young spotted a "small cruiser or large destroyer" just forward of the starboard beam at a range estimated to be 3,300 yards. All three three-gun main-battery turrets were shifted to the new target from *Akatsuki*, which they had undoubtedly hit and which appeared to be turning away. Suddenly, a huge pillar of fire flared behind the new target. This was probably *Akatsuki* blowing up and sinking with her entire crew. *San Francisco's* next salvo was dead on the new, beautifully backlit target—*Atlanta*. So was the next salvo.

⇄

Even before the second salvo was fired at the near target, LCdr Willie Wilbourne saw *Hiei* loom into sight 30 degrees and 2,200 yards off *San Francisco's* starboard bow. The main battery was instantly shifted from the now-burning near target to the battleship.

Inasmuch as the forward turrets were being trained by the forward main-battery director, BM2 Vance Carter, the Turret-2 trainer, had nothing better to do than take quick peeks at the outside world through his sight port. Already nearly overcome by the noise and shuddering movement within the turret, Carter was totally transfixed by his first view of *Hiei*. Cold shivers climbed up and down Carter's spine as the mountainous silhouette appeared at what seemed to be absolute point-blank range. After months afloat in the hostile South Pacific, the turret trainer had adjusted his thinking to include confrontations with other cruisers, but he felt there was no way to beat a battleship. Though Carter was a veteran of Cape Esperance and every one of *San Francisco's* air actions, the fleeting vision of *Hiei* shook his confidence. He involuntarily pulled his head away from the sight port and determined to look outside no more.

San Francisco got in the first shot, a full-battery salvo at 2,200 yards. All the 8-inch rounds except one fell short of the target. Unable to bring her after battery to bear, *Hiei* got off a four-gun salvo from her two forward 14-inch turrets. This salvo was short, as was the next, which seemed to arrive after a very long interval. It was noted that all the short rounds gave off a vivid greenish light upon impact, indicating that they were the thin-wall antipersonnel incendiary rounds meant for shore bombardment.

Undeterred by the Japanese fire, Lieutenant Commander Wilbourne coolly corrected the aim of his turrets and ordered the main battery to commence rapid firing on full automatic. Only the two forward turrets could go on automatic; the after director had been demolished in the Betty crash that afternoon and Turret-3 had to be trained and fired under local control.

The next two main-battery salvos were quickly pumped directly into the slow-moving Japanese flagship, and all shots were seen to fall directly amidships at the water line. Lookouts and gunnery personnel saw steel hull plates and other wreckage fly from the side of the battleship, which had intense fires burning topside in the vicinity of her main mast. They also saw many of the 5-inch hits scored by friendly destroyers as *Hiei* was beset by the American vanguard.

As soon as *San Francisco's* second salvo, her thirteenth overall, was fired at the huge target to starboard, it apparently belatedly dawned on Admiral Callaghan that his flagship had fired its tenth and eleventh 8-inch salvos into *Atlanta*. At 0158, he reflexively yelled, "Cease firing!"—right into the open TBS microphone. Undoubtedly, the order was meant only for Captain Young or Lieutenant Commander Wilbourne, aboard *San Francisco*, but it was nonetheless broadcast to all of the American warships, sowing an incredible confusion at a crucial moment. Among other vessels, *San Francisco* instantly ceased firing.

⇄

It is uncertain how long *San Francisco*'s guns remained silent. However long the lull was—it could not have been more than two minutes and was probably not much more than one minute—speed was reduced to 17 knots and the navigator lost track of his course. The main guns remained trained on *Hiei* through several course changes; when they resumed firing, the Japanese battleship was still off *San Francisco*'s starboard bow. By now, however, *Hiei* had switched on one grouping of three searchlights and a smaller Japanese ship—probably *Inazuma*—on *San Francisco*'s starboard quarter was illuminating from that direction.

Lt(jg) Jack Bennett was at his battle station near the after 1.1-inch mounts when the guns were targeted by the destroyer that illuminated *San Francisco* from the starboard quarter. The antiaircraft guns would not normally have been trained out during a surface engagement, but there was so much happening so close in that their imminent use appeared likely. However, the starboard mount was hit by 5-inch rounds right off the bat. Bennett happened to be looking right at the port mount when it was struck a second later. The detonation looked like a pair of grindstones shooting off sparks in all directions. The gun barrels were twisted, totally useless, and personnel casualties were very heavy. Before the destroyer to starboard could get off more than the two salvos, it was engaged by an American warship farther back in the column and was thus obliged to run.

No sooner had that small victory registered than very large projectiles began falling short from what appeared to be an entirely new direction. Though no one aboard *San Francisco* could see another large ship to port, it is apparent that *Kirishima* had crept into the fray and was trying to get the range on the large American ship that was the center of so much attention. Potentially, a total of sixteen 14-inch guns and up to twenty-eight 6-inch guns from the two battleships alone could be devoted to destroying *San Francisco*.

As *San Francisco*'s starboard 5-inch battery and after 8-inch turret engaged *Inazuma* to starboard, Admiral Callaghan blurted out, "We want the big ones! Get the big ones!"

Indeed, *San Francisco*'s two forward 8-inch turrets maintained a steady volume of fire at *Hiei*, which seemed to be swinging to the left to evade them. Just before *San Francisco* had to cease firing her forward main guns at *Hiei* because they could no longer bear, she was struck along her starboard side by many 6-inch shells fired by *Hiei*'s secondary battery.

At that moment, Admiral Callaghan and his entire staff were on the starboard side of the flag bridge, watching the mushrooming exchange with *Hiei*. RM3 Bill Potwin, who was manning a radio deep within the ship, distinctly heard Admiral Callaghan's voice on the intercom: "Tell the navigator to get us out of here." Then at least one of *Hiei*'s 14-inch rounds fell directly upon the navigation bridge and erupted. At the same time, many 6-inch shells put three of *San Francisco*'s four starboard 5-inch guns out of action and killed or wounded many of the men manning the vulnerable open 5-inch mounts. One shell, which struck high above the bridge, demolished the Marine-manned starboard forward 1.1-inch antiaircraft mount. In addition to killing or maiming virtually all the Marines manning the mount, steel shards holed the water jackets around the twisted gun barrels, and that sent hot water cascading directly down upon the navigation and flag bridges. A piece of shrapnel also touched off loose 1.1-inch ammunition in the adjacent clipping room, thus marking *San Francisco*'s position with a towering perpetual fountain of bursting 1.1-inch tracer.

In addition to his regular duties as the flagship's navigator, Cdr Rae Arison had been pressed into service as Admiral Callaghan's operations officer because the admiral's staff was composed mostly of communicators, none of whom qualified for the important operations job. As a result of the double duty, Arison literally had to be in two places at the same time—on the flag bridge with the admiral and in the charthouse, one deck above, overseeing several young and inexperienced ensigns who had been foisted off on him.

After running back and forth and up and down between the two locations for hours before and after midnight, Commander Arison happened to be on the navigation bridge when the first radar contacts were reported by other ships. This obliged him to go to the charthouse to plot the targets while keeping both Captain Young and Admiral Callaghan apprised by means of a voice tube and a telephone. A minute or so before the shooting started, Arison ventured out to the navigation bridge to eyeball the situation he had been following thus far by means of reports from other men. He found that Captain Young had left the armored conning tower because it afforded poor visibility at night. With Young was LCdr Bruce McCandless and three ensigns, one of whom was the junior watch stander and two of whom were onlookers who had just reported out of school and who were being indoctrinated as junior watch standers.

Following his look around, Arison returned to the charthouse, but he was there for only a few moments when the compartment was struck by a 14-inch shell and demolished. The radioman sitting on Arison's right side was killed instantly and the commander was struck in the right arm by a large fragment that fractured the elbow and knocked out about two inches of both the radius and the ulna. Since the charthouse was a shambles, Commander Arison decided to return to the bridge to report to Captain Young. He only got as far as the curtained doorway before another 14-inch round burst behind him and catapulted him headfirst between the wheel stanchion and the engine-room telegraph and out onto the navigation bridge. The same blast felled Captain Young, the junior watchstander, the two officer trainees, and several enlisted talkers. Miraculously, QM3 Harry Higdon, the steersman, was not touched at all. LCdr Bruce McCandless, who was standing beside Higdon, was struck in the chest by several fragments, but none penetrated the kapok life vest he was wearing; he emerged with nothing more than a few superficial scratches.

McCandless had by no means recovered from the shock of the blast when QM3 Higdon announced, "I've lost steering control!" and spun the useless wheel for emphasis. As it turned out, the engine-control repeater was also down. Thus, *San Francisco* was swinging out of control to the left at a speed of 18 knots.

៕

Cdr Joseph Hubbard, the acting exec, now running a partially restored Battle-2, must have clearly seen the red flashes of the 6-inch and 14-inch sheels striking all around the bridge, and he might have sensed that the ship was sliding out of control in the aftermath of the fatal blasts. He immediately contacted Central Station—the main damage-control nerve center he had overseen until fleeting up to exec that afternoon—and ordered LCdr Rocky Schonland, his replacement as first lieutenant, to shift steering and engine control to Battle-2.

Only a moment after the shift was completed, Lt Howard Westin, who was manning an emergency spotting station directly over Commander Hubbard's head, saw a large red tracer round coming right at him. Westin instinctively yelled, "Look out! Here comes one!" as he ducked behind a steel column. But the warning was too late; Commander Hubbard and his entire staff in Battle-2 were killed instantly when the shell struck their compartment dead on.

In Radio-2, a blind compartment beneath Battle-2 which contained radios and the repeaters for *San Francisco*'s gunnery radars, the large-caliber hit knocked a large bank of lead-acid storage batteries from the starboard bulkhead and showered the armored deck overhead with what sounded to the radiomen like an avalanche of stones. Immediately, one radioman's eyes got as large as they could and the man blandly announced, "They're hitting us."

FC1 Gene McGuire, who was alone in the after 5-inch antiaircraft director, directly over Lieutenant Westin's head, simultaneously felt his battle phones go dead and glimpsed the carnage below. McGuire immediately leaped before he looked and fell most of the way into Battle-2 when he reached the end of a ladder that had been partially shot away by the Japanese shell. There were only dead men in the compartment, but McGuire could hear moaning over his head. He boosted himself back out of the charnal house and found Lieutenant Westin lying in a pool of his own blood. The shell had struck before Westin was quite under cover and shrapnel had torn away the two middle fingers of his left hand and collapsed his left knee. Using a phone cord he found wrapped around the officer's body, McGuire tied off the pulsing wounds in Westin's arm and leg. Then he boosted the unconscious officer across his shoulder and climbed down a nearby ladder. This ladder had also been severed above the deck, and McGuire stepped off the end into thin air. The two finally came to rest on the well deck.

❧

Near the spot where Lieutenant Westin and FC1 McGuire came to rest, S1 Willie Boyce had become a passive participant in a strange minuet of survival. As the battle had gotten underway, Boyce had stepped into a gear locker, which seemed to afford at least minimal protection against flying shrapnel. As soon as the first Japanese shells fell short of *San Francisco*, a dark form had appeared out of the blackness and Boyce found himself being wordlessly shouldered further back into the locker. As the minutes passed—as Japanese shells found their mark—the first intruder had been muscled out of the way by another, and that one by another, and he by another. Each time another sailor seeking cover arrived, the men already in the locker took a step back in wordless unison.

Though Seaman Boyce had never been claustrophobic, he soon found sympathy with those who were. He craved the protection of the locker, but he did not want to be boxed in. At length, he called, "Out, please. I want out. Step aside, please." The crowd did not budge until someone near the front observed, "We got a brave one back there. Let him out; there'll be more room for me." When Boyce reached the front of the crowd, he could go no further. Instead, he peered around the edge of the hatchway. There was a brief lull in the firing just then; he heard one of the men at his back mutter the Lord's Prayer.

❧

Immediately after Battle-2 was demolished, LCdr Bruce Mc-Candless heard the voice tube from the armored conning tower, directly below the pilothouse, announce, "I have control." The speaker was QM3 Floyd Rogers, who was alone in the conning tower and who had sensed that the ship was again out of control.

From his place on the navigation bridge, Lieutenant Commander McCandless acknowledged Rogers's assumption of control and told Rogers that he and QM3 Harry Higdon would be right down to help.

As soon as McCandless left the navigation bridge, Cdr Rae Arison, the wounded navigator, who was crumpled up in a distant corner, managed to regain his feet. Just as he did, however, he was engulfed by another huge blast, his third within the previous minute or two. The force of the explosion lifted him over the rail. A detached part of Arison's mind noted that he did two complete turns in the air before he came down feet-first on the elevated barrel of the starboard forward 5-inch gun—Mount-1, three decks below the bridge. The impact broke both of the navigator's legs and he tumbled off right into the arms of the gun captain. The gunner was too caught up in the fight to help Arison. Rather, he pushed the officer to the side to get him out of the way. The push carried Arison directly to a break in the deck and he fell down a ladder to the main deck and came to rest beside a corner of the deckhouse. When he looked back the way he had come, everything above him seemed to be engulfed in flames.

As soon as LCdr Bruce McCandless arrived in the conning tower, he peered through a slit in the armored bulkhead and gave QM3 Floyd Rogers a new course aimed at taking the ship out of the fight between Savo and Cape Esperance. Then he placed QM3 Harry Higdon at the slit to act as Rogers's eyes while he went back up to the navigation bridge to see if any of the fallen men there were alive. Most important, McCandless wanted to see if Captain Young was still alive and in shape to command the ship.

卍

Within the same minute that Lieutenant Commander McCandless returned to the navigation bridge—he could not identify Captain Young in the grisly pile of bodies there—*San Francisco* was suddenly beset by yet another Japanese destroyer, probably *Ikazuchi*. This one cut across the heavy cruiser's starboard bow and sailed down her port side on a reverse heading. Her first shots struck the forward part of the bridge while McCandless was searching through the bodies a few yards aft. McCandless was not hurt, but he fell into a hole in the deck as he flinched away from the incoming shells.

The American flagship's port 5-inch battery engaged *Ikazuchi*, which shifted fire from the bridge to counter the counterbattery fire. In a matter of seconds, three of the four virtually unprotected guns were struck and put out of action.

As Lieutenant Commander McCandless climbed out of the hole in the deck, he happened to peer through a tear in the sheet-metal port bridge screen. He was thus just in time to see the remaining port 5-inch gun—Mount-8, the aftmost, which was firing under local control—get its last ready round in among what appeared to be the Japanese destroyer's depth charge racks. Many observers declared the resulting explosion sank *Ikazuchi* outright, and others thought they saw her go dead in the water with her stern awash. However, no such thing occurred.

⛩

Working straight through his almost total fear in the wake of at least two direct 5-inch hits on the after 1.1-inch mounts, Lt(jg) Jack Bennett tried to pull a sailor out of the twisted starboard mount. He grabbed the man's legs and heaved. And that was all he came away with—the man's severed legs. He saw the head of another victim, its crown severed like half of a ripe cantaloupe.

Within a minute, all the living survivors appeared to have been pulled from the wreckage of the gun mounts. Lieutenant (jg) Bennett drew out the pack of six morphine syrettes with which each officer had been outfitted and went to work administering the narcotic to the injured men who were yelling the loudest. When all six syrettes were used up, he took a second pack from the belt of a dead officer and used them up on six more screaming sailors.

⛩

As *San Francisco* limped clear of the close-in fight with the destroyer, LCdr Bruce McCandless made his way to the flag bridge in the vague hope of finding Admiral Callaghan alive. No one had heard a peep out of the admiral since RM3 Bill Potwin had overheard his call to retire. McCandless found the admiral and his entire staff crumpled together in a pile on the starboard side of the flag bridge. A cursory check of the bodies in the dark convinced McCandless that every one of them was dead. However, the admiral's air staff officer, LCdr Emmet O'Beirne, was at the bottom of the pile, severely wounded but alive. McCandless overlooked him, and he would not be rescued for many hours.

There was nothing left for McCandless to do except return to the conning tower and navigate the ship. Once there, he called LCdr Rocky Schonland, who was running the expanding damage-control effort from Central Station. A quick tally of dead and wounded senior officers had revealed to McCandless that Schonland was the ship's most senior officer still on his feet. The news from McCandlesss placed Rocky Schonland in a dilemma. Though new to the title of first lieutenant, Schonland was well versed in damage-control techniques and, furthermore, was fully immersed in the incredibly complex job at hand. Without any hesitation, Schonland sent word to McCandless to carry on where he was, that they would sort out the command question at a more opportune time.

With that, LCdr Bruce McCandless reaffirmed his earlier instruction to the steersman to shape a course that would take the grievously wounded former flagship away from the ongoing battle. No sooner had he given the order than a 14-inch shell—the last such from *Hiei* to *San Francisco*—burst against the top of the conning tower, only 2 feet over the heads of its three inmates. McCandless, who was staring out through the view port, received a shrapnel wound in the forehead, but his eyes were saved by his binoculars, which were shattered by another piece of shrapnel. McCandless was knocked unconscious for a few moments and, when he came to, he heard QM3 Floyd Rogers repeat a by-now familiar litany: "We've lost steering and engine control!"

As it turned out, shrapnel from a recent hit had struck a diesel oil storage tank located just beneath the well deck and directly above the after engine room. The same shell, or one right behind it, also shattered the ventilator shaft carrying fresh, cool air to the after engine room. Diesel oil from the breached tank cascaded down the breached ventilator shaft and fell directly onto the after generators. A great deal of smoke instantly issued from the oil-soaked generators, which were in danger of catching fire at any second. The officer in charge of the after engine room, Lt(jg) Herschel Chipp, had no time to seek advice or permission from the chief engineer, who was in the forward engine room; Chipp simply ordered the generators tripped off, knowing full well that power to the after turret and the steering- and engine-control systems would be lost. But there was no choice; a fire would do the same, and worse, for fire damage could not be repaired any time soon.

As soon as Lieutenant (jg) Chipp told the chief engineer what he had done, electrician's mates in both engine rooms went right to work to restore power to the steering system by cross-connecting the entire electrical load through the forward generators. This meant peremptorily cutting out selected services and creating temporary blackouts in nonessential spaces to keep the instantly overloaded electrical grid from completely breaking down.

Meantime, Central Station contacted Lieutenant Commander McCandless with an offer to relay steering and engine changes dictated from the conning tower by means of the last remaining phone wire still open between the two places. As McCandless stated the desired changes, a talker in Central Station repeated them to the forward engine room, which still controlled the ship's speed, and the after steering control station, a hot little compartment in which only one machinist's mate was on hand to take direct control of the rudder.

The tenuous system worked as long as it needed to. However, the decision to close the steering- and engine-control circuits in the conning tower also shut off the ventilators supplying fresh air to the enclosed armored compartment. It soon became necessary for McCandless, Higdon, and Rogers to step outside in relays to cool off and breathe fresh air. Moreover, the three soon noticed that the ship had a tendency to steer well to the left of a desired course. There was no time or means as yet to locate the source of this disturbing effect; all the three could do was compensate by dead reckoning.

In time, *San Francisco* limped clear of the central melee. But she was not yet out of danger.

23

Portland, affectionately dubbed "Sweet Pea" by her adoring crew, was going into action with a list of minor ailments that might have affected her performance in a night action. Though the condition of the ship's armament was considered excellent by her gunnery officer, LCdr Elliott Shanklin, the FC radar on the forward main-battery director was down with numerous short circuits, the FD radar on the starboard antiaircraft director was so balky that it had never been really considered operational, the director controlling one 1.1-inch mount had been damaged during the carrier battle at Santa Cruz three weeks earlier, and the automatic transmission controlling the starboard searchlights had been jarred out of alignment during the afternoon antiair engagement. None of the damage was individually or cumulatively critical; the gunners were at the top of their form.

Portland's first direct contact with Japanese vessels came at 0142, when her main-battery radar picked up three separate blips covering a 15-degree arc to the northwest at 11,000 to 14,000 yards. Shortly thereafter, the FC radar on the after main-battery came up with a solid target 30 degrees off the port bow. This was a firm enough fix for Lieutenant Commander Shanklin to get the plotting room involved in tracking it as a probable gunnery target.

Portland was the seventh ship in the American column and was thus totally unaffected by the confusion in the van attending *Cushing*'s several precipitous turns beginning with her near collision with *Yudachi* and *Harusame*. Indeed, officers and men manning topside battle stations aboard the heavy cruiser had a distant, detached view of the proceedings.

The first action ahead that involved *Portland* occurred just as she was coming up on the point at which she would have to execute a left turn to follow the ships ahead. That was at 0150, the precise instant *Akatsuki* and *Hiei* first turned on their searchlights. The first shaft of light to find *Portland* was *Akatsuki* 's; it struck from broad on the cruiser's port bow to about 30 degrees on the starboard bow as it quickly swept along the entire line of American destroyers and cruisers.

As the heavy cruiser proceeded through her turn, and as the Japanese lights and starshells were countered by *Atlanta*'s searchlights and numerous American starshells, Capt Laurance DuBose ordered, "Action starboard," but he changed his mind before the big guns could be brought to bear and yelled, "Commence firing on vessels in the left group." The completion of the left turn unmasked the starboard 5-inch battery, and starshell illumination was opened as the main battery finished its swing under radar control.

The plotting room estimated that the range to the first target was 6,200 yards, a gunnery solution that was confirmed by the gunnery officer's aides in Spot-1, the main-battery director. Lieutenant Commander Shanklin ordered, "Commence firing." However, only Turret-1 and Turret-2 obeyed; Turret-3, which had to retrain all the way around the fantail, had not yet matched aiming points with the director.

Despite the sluggish and incomplete start, *Portland* apparently drew blood with her first salvo. At any rate—as bursting shells from every vessel in range competed for attention—Lieutenant Commander Shanklin clearly saw four bursts of flame leap from his target. It is impossible to guess whose shells Shanklin saw, but it is certain that the object of the attention was *Akatsuki*. She had drawn attention to herself by flicking on her searchlight at 0150 and leaving it on long enough to sweep the light over at least half of the American column.

Captain DuBose, Lieutenant Commander Shanklin, and many other *Portland* men reported seeing numerous hits from their ship's second salvo, a full nine-gun broadside this time. Once again, the likelihood of at least several hits was great, but many ships had found the range to *Akatsuki* by then. What is certain is that *Akatsuki* exploded and sank moments after this cluster of hits on her was seen. A minute later, as *Portland* raced after *San Francisco*, Lt Ken West, *Portland's* antiaircraft machine-gun officer, clearly saw the rounded bottom of a destroyer awash on the surface close by his ship.

⚛

On the down side, *Portland* was struck by a large-caliber shell in the starboard aircraft hangar at 0152, as soon as she got her first partial salvo away. The two after starboard 5-inch guns—Mount-5 and Mount-7—were knocked out of commission when their power cables were ruptured in the blast. The sight setter in the starboard 1.1-inch director was struck in the right leg by shrapnel, which also wounded a warrant gunner and the exec, Cdr Turk Wirth, as they watched the action erupt from their station in Battle-2. Also, a large piece of the shell's base plate fell directly on the helmet of a loader manning one of the 5-inch guns. Though the loader's helmet was creased down the middle and he was knocked down by the impact, the man was not injured.

In addition to the damage caused by the aimed fire, *Portland* fell prey to a nearly expended starshell, which fell burning to her forecastle. Several crewmen from the forward port 1.1-inch mount left their station and surged forward to help douse the light, which was as liable to start a fire as it was to draw enemy fire. The gunners beat the forward repair party to the nearest fire hose, but events overtook them as they raced to turn the hose on.

⚛

As soon as *Portland* received Admiral Callaghan's cease-fire order at 0158, Captain DuBose shot back an unceremonious, "What's the dope? Did you want a ceasefire?" Amazingly, he received a verbal "Affirmative" via TBS from the flagship. As *Port-land*'s captain ordered, "Check fire," the TBS crackled with "All ships take course zero-zero-zero." This obliged Captain DuBose to guide his now-silent heavy cruiser to a due northerly heading while her main battery locked onto a new target about 7,000 yards out.

By then, smoke from gunfire, flares, and fires aboard numerous ships ahead had clouded the air throughout the moving center of the central melee. Though observers topside could discern the vague outlines of the target held firmly in the after main-battery director's FC radar image, members of the bridge watch could not agree on what the target was—a small light cruiser or a large destroyer. Although the cease-fire order was still in effect, the radar lock on the target was too good to ignore or risk losing. The captain ordered the main guns back into action, and LCdr Elliott Shanklin immediately complied with a full-battery salvo. The forward turrets came to rest directly over the starshell burning away on the cruiser's forecastle. The muzzle blast not only flattened the 1.1-inch gunners who had rushed to douse the incendiary device, it hurled the starshell over the side, into the water, where it sizzled briefly and died.

Before observers topside could do much more than note several bursts from apparent hits on the smoke-obscured target, *Portland* fired yet another full main-battery salvo. And, again, several apparent hits were observed and flames could be seen breaking out along the target's main deck.

卍

At about 0200, as the turret crews were reloading the 8-inch guns, lookouts yelled a warning that unidentified destroyers were passing close aboard *Portland*'s starboard quarter on an opposite heading. These must have been *Inazuma* and *Ikazuchi*. The two forward starboard 5-inch guns—Mount-1 and Mount-3—trained out and fired a spread of starshells, but the space around the ship appeared to be empty.

Just as the main-battery turret crews were completing the reloading operation—before anyone on the bridge could react to a lookout's shouted warning that he saw a torpedo wake coming from the starboard quarter—the entire ship shuddered under the impact of a torpedo hit. A tremendous volume of seawater thrown up by the blast cascaded down on *Portland* for what seemed like several minutes, and the sheer weight of it caused further damage, as did objects large and small that had been ripped loose and thrown aloft by the blast.

S2 Jim Mathews, the exec's talker, was outside Battle-2, on the starboard catwalk, when the torpedo hit. Mathews at first assumed the terrific jolt was some sort of output from the main battery, but then he realized that the big guns had not fired at the moment of impact.

The exec, Cdr Turk Wirth, had been wounded early in the action and was prone on the deck inside Battle-2 when the force of the blast lifted him from the deck plates. Wirth had not yet settled down or quite realized what had happened when he heard his quartermaster exclaim, "Jeez! Here come three more!" Wirth and a wounded warrant officer beside him braced for more detonations, but there were none. The quartermaster blandly explained that he had been referring to three large-caliber tracer rounds he had seen coming at him.

The center of the detonation was on the starboard side less than 30 feet from the stern. Both inboard propellers were blown off, the rudder was jammed 5 degrees to the right, the steering engine rooms were flooded, and all hands in them were killed, and the after main deck around the blast site was blown up and over the port quarter. Worst of all, side plating around the blast site was blown inboard 45 degrees to the centerline, forcing the ship around as if the rudder had been set hard to starboard.

Among several miraculous escapes was that of a sailor who was standing on the armored deck beneath the main deck and right above the blast. He was thrown from his feet and rolled up in a curl of 4-inch armored decking. He sustained only a few cuts and scrapes, but many men in compartments beneath him—throughout "Torpedo Junction"—were killed instantly or mortally wounded in the blast. In gun mounts and directors all around the blast site, gunners and fire controlmen shrugged off sometimes grievous injuries and stayed at their posts. The starboard director trainer was bleeding copiously onto the deck from serious leg injuries, but it took a direct inquiry from his officer to get him to admit to his injuries. Even then, the young sailor refused to relinquish his duties.

One large chunk of deck plating struck a Marine 5-inch shell-man in the face, hit another 5-inch gun crewman in the back of the head, glanced off a ready box door, and struck a third gunner between the eyes. The first two men the fragment struck were killed in their tracks, but the third man, who was knocked unconscious, did not suffer even a broken nose. His face was swollen and his eye was blackened, but he emerged without serious injury.

Cox John Reimer, captain of a 20mm gun group located on the starboard side of the after signal bridge, right over Turret-3, was lifted off his feet by the force of the blast and thrown in a heap to the deck. As soon as Reimer regained his stance, he called each member of his crew to ask if anyone was hit. All hands reported that they were okay, so Coxswain Reimer reported by battle phone to the machine-gun control station that the guns were manned and ready. Then he lifted his hands to put them to his ears to blot out the ongoing noise of the battle. Reimer's left arm would not go up. He stepped inside the ammunition locker and stared at his arm in the eerie red glow of a battle lantern. There was a hole all the way through the upper arm, and much blood. A fellow gunner applied a tourniquet and Reimer, who still felt no pain, went forward to Battle-2 to lie down beside Commander Wirth.

For all her travail, *Portland* deserved her reputation as a lucky ship. She had been struck at Santa Cruz by three submarine-fired torpedoes that had failed to detonate and, though she was hit this night, she was not mortally hurt. The torpedo went in at a point just 10 feet aft of the compartment in which bombs for her scout planes were stored. A blast there would certainly have set off the bombs, and they in turn would certainly have touched off a sympathetic detonation in the adjacent magazine servicing Turret-3.

⟳

Before the shrapnel and spray had quite settled, the ship began a hard swing to the right and the helmsman told Captain DuBose that he had lost steering control. Over the next half-minute, the captain tried to regain steering control by means of several alternative methods, which included steering on his ship's engines, but nothing worked.

The damage reports sounded awesome, and indeed the damage looked awesome: Turret-3 was jammed in train and elevation, its traversing gear locked by the force of the blast; a huge horseshoe-shaped section of the deck had been blown away from Turret-3's barbette aft to a small island stern post and from the starboard side nearly as far as the port railing; and, of course, there was a huge hole in the starboard side. The first lieutenant, who was manning Central Station, the main damage-control nerve center, reported that his inclinometer showed a 4-degree list to starboard.

As soon as Captain DuBose gave up on trying to steer on the engines—he did not yet know that two screws had been blown away—he took immediate steps to correct the fractional list by shifting fuel and water.

↻

Above the bridge in Plot-1, LCdr Elliott Shanklin polled his subordinates and learned that, though his after main turret could not traverse or elevate, the two forward main turrets and six of eight 5-inch mounts were still operational. By the time the ship had completed one full turn, the two starboard 5-inch directors and many lookouts had picked out a large, slow-moving target to starboard.

The one functioning main-battery director was located aft, and its performance had declined since the torpedo detonation due to excessive vibration. Nevertheless, the director fire controlman got a firm radar fix and announced that the range to the large target was 4,200 yards. The target itself—*Hiei*—was clearly visible due to fires raging along her main deck and throughout her superstructure. Despite his ship's dilemma, Captain DuBose was too feisty a commander to pass up an easy shot at a Japanese battleship. "Commence firing when on the target," he told his gun boss.

The two forward turrets were fixed on *Hiei* and trained around as *Portland* began her second involuntary turn to starboard. Lieutenant Commander Shanklin gave the order to fire when the Japanese flagship was dead ahead.

From his vantage point high in Sky Control, Lt Ken West, the antiaircraft machine-gun officer, followed the trail of 8-inch tracer rounds from Turret-2 and was stunned to see the outline of a Japanese destroyer—*Yudachi*—appear in the eerie light. In the momentary passage of the 8-inch rounds, West could see that the Japanese ship was heading the same way as *Portland* and that the 8-inch rounds bound for *Hiei* passed as close as 10 feet from her bridge. When West regained his night vision a moment later, however, it was too dark to see the destroyer again. She had simply vanished.

Over the next few minutes, as *Portland* continued to circle away from *Hiei*, but before her forward turrets were masked, she was able to fire a total of four six-gun salvos. Many hits were observed and many new fires were started aboard *Hiei*.

The Japanese flagship did not take the beating without lashing back. While her after main guns continued to fire at *San Francisco*, she shifted her forward guns to *Portland* and cut loose with a salvo. Lt Ken West and the antiaircraft officer were crouched behind the thin sheet-metal screen surrounding Sky Control and could plainly see oncoming red dots expand as they thundered in *Portland*'s direction. Wordlessly, the two stared at one another, grinned sheepishly, shrugged a silent "What the hell," and stood up to watch the show.

The first 14-inch salvo passed harmlessly over *Portland*. Then the huge Japanese guns were realigned and fired again. Two 14-inch bombardment rounds from the second salvo struck *Portland*'s side, but they caused minimal damage and inflicted minimal casualties. Then *Hiei* left the circling, vulnerable heavy cruiser to herself.

Heartened by his ship's proven ability to inflict damage despite her own damaged and precarious state, Captain DuBose cast about for fresh targets. But he had lost his fix on friendly ships and was by then unable to distinguish them from enemy warships. Fearful of engaging friendlies, he ordered all guns to cease firing while remaining vigilant.

By then, the battle had passed slowly circling *Portland*.

24

Helena was among the first U.S. warships to open fire. Unlike *Atlanta*, which was directly threatened, *Helena* fired so
soon because her captain by then felt he had waited long
enough. Not for the first time in these waters, Capt Gib Hoover
took matters into his own hands while the admiral in command
pondered the alternatives and dithered over a decision. Hoover,
whose ship had weathered the Japanese attack at Pearl Harbor, was
a hard-charging shoot-first-and-ask-questions-later warrior who
was apparently incapable of allowing an enemy ship to gain anything resembling the upper hand or to slip from his sights. It had
been so at Cape Esperance, where he had avoided dire consequences
for ignoring orders and going it alone because doing so had turned
out to be right.

As at Cape Esperance, Gib Hoover's instincts were abetted by
the acuity of his SG radar-assisted night vision. The first of all the
American ships to find targets, *Helena* had been tracking the oncoming Japanese the longest. In fact, it was a source of considerable
irritation to Captain Hoover that he both had to track the Japanese
and take the time to report to Admiral Callaghan over the deterio-
rating TBS voice-radio net. He would rather have hosted the admi-

ral aboard his amply appointed modern cruiser so the admiral could see for himself.

As *Helena* sailed due north at 0149, Captain Hoover learned that the SG operator had several firm targets averaging 4,300 yards out. The forward main-battery director, which mounted a reliable FC radar set, concurred. When he heard how short the range was, *Helena's* plotting-room officer blurted out to her air-defense officer, "For Christ's sake, what are we going to do? Throw potatoes at them? We're so close!"

Altogether, *Helena* had five radar sets devoted to tracking the numerous targets ahead. The SG radar was doing area sweeps, clarifying the picture each time its antenna revolved atop the foremast. The FC radar in Director-1, the highest main-battery director, was locked onto a particular target well ahead to port, and it was controlling the train and elevation of all the main guns—fifteen 6-inch tubes deployed in five triple turrets. Director-2, the forward 6-inch director, had a lock on the same target and was backing Director-1 in control of train. Director-3, the after main-battery director, was also locked on and backing Director-1 in control of elevation. The forward 5-inch director, which mounted a new FD radar set, had not yet locked onto a particular target, but it had a firm picture of the oncoming Japanese battle force. Altogether, it was a set-up right out of the gunnery textbooks.

Capt Gib Hoover had been waiting eight interminable minutes for Admiral Callaghan to unleash him. He had had enough waiting by 0150. The target, selected solely by means of the search and gunnery radars, was the farthest to the left of many possible targets. It was *Akatsuki*, and the matter was about to be settled by Captain Hoover's decision to open fire without hearing from Admiral Callaghan. However, the moment was ruined when the Japanese destroyer's searchlight went on.

Every officer and crewman topside aboard *Helena* was certain that *Akatsuki's* searchlight was aimed directly at him. (So was every member of every topside crew ahead of *Helena*, so pervasive is the effect of being in the limelight.) Despite the gravity of the situation, Ens Bin Cochran, a junior navigator, was unable to suppress a reflexive chuckle when he saw that every senior officer on the open fighting bridge had instinctively crouched or leaned into a shadow.

After he ducked, LCdr Rodman Smith, the gunnery officer, duck-walked toward the captain behind the meager protection of the thin sheet-metal bridge screen. Before he got there, however, Smith shouted, "Permission to fire, Captain?"

Though Gib Hoover had reached his decision to fire before he knew there would be a searchlight to pin his ship against the black night background, his mission in life had instantly become the destruction of the searchlight—if not of the ship that wielded it. From his own place behind the bridge screen, Captain Hoover nodded emphatically and shouted back at Lieutenant Commander Smith, "Open fire!" Before anyone really had time to brace himself, the entire ship shuddered as all fifteen 6-inch guns erupted in a crescendo of smoke and flame.

Then, as *Helena*'s turret crews stooped to begin the reloading process, the ship was struck by two medium-caliber shells; one fell in the vicinity of the after stack and the other struck the searchlight tower, mortally wounding one electrician's mate. A third shell, which struck the airplane crane unnoticed, might also have arrived at this juncture. The fact that *Helena* was hit so soon after the light came on lends credence to Captain Hoover's surmise that his ship was the searchlight's main target. The damage was minor, but it caused Gib Hoover's blood to boil. Interestingly, recovered fragments from these shells imply that the lighter Japanese warships initially had bombardment rounds in the breeches of their guns.

Helena's own first salvo struck home at a range of 4,000 yards. Fires were immediately noted as they burst to life along the target's main deck. As the flames rose, *Helena*'s bridge watch and lookouts saw several other Japanese ships in the glare, thus visually confirming the findings of the SG radar. Later, Captain Hoover tartly noted that a fire aboard an enemy vessel "is the ideal method of night illumination."

The main battery maintained continuous rapid fire for two minutes. This was brutal work for the loaders, particularly the shellmen—rugged youngsters who had the strength and stamina to throw one 105-pound projectile after the other into the breeches. After the shell was in the breech, the second powderman rolled the brass powder case to the first powderman across a table onto which it had been deposited by the powder hoist. As soon as the first powderman dropped the case into the breech behind the shell, the gun captain rammed the loaded tray home and closed the hydraulic breech block. As soon as the breech closed, the individual gun was fired by means of a continuous electric current running through the firing pin. The recoil automatically popped the breech open and the hot empty brass case was automatically ejected through a scuttle in the bottom rear of the turret. Then the entire process was repeated. Long practice and the thrill of the moment kept the guns more or less in tune, but observers outside the turrets and on other ships heard and saw the rounds going out as a continuous flow rather than in solid fifteen- or even three-gun salvos. One way or another, all the onlookers—Japanese as well as Americans—found the display to be breathtaking.

The gunnery technique *Helena* employed was known as a "rocking ladder," a favorite of the main-battery assistant, Lt Warren Boles. First the guns fired a bit over, then a bit under, then a bit over, then a bit under—all within a 200-yard range variation. That Lieutenant Boles employed this sophisticated method and went directly to rapid continuous fire before visually confirming that the guns were on target belies his absolute faith in the solutions pieced together by his ship's well-tuned radar equipment.

Less than a minute after opening fire, *Helena* came up to the spot at which she had to follow *Portland* through the left turn that had been completed by the entire column ahead. The move was made with practiced agility; the gunners hardly knew it occurred, so firm was the radar's control of the turrets. For that matter, a momentary stop followed by a burst of power all the way up to full speed, and several other adjustments in speed and bearing, were all absorbed without effect by the gun directors.

As had many men aboard several of the ships ahead, Ens Bin Cochran noticed that *Akatsuki*'s searchlight dimmed rather than cut off—as if the shutters were voluntarily closed over it. The gunnery officer, LCdr Rodman Smith, was certain that virtually every round *Helena* fired connected with the target. Here, as with claims by ships ahead, it is likely that Smith did see his own rounds going in, but it is certain that he also counted hits by other ships in his tally. Whatever the case, Lieutenant Commander Smith soon reported that the target had sunk, as indeed she had.

As the main battery concentrated on *Akatsuki*, the FD radar set in *Helena's* forward 5-inch director locked onto a second target slightly to the left and about 6,200 yards from *Helena*. The two port dual 5-inch mounts went to rapid continuous fire instants behind the main battery and remained locked on their target for as long as the main guns fired at *Akatsuki*. Hits were seen, but the extent of the damage they caused was not evident to any observers. In all likelihood, the target was either *Inazuma* or *Ikazuchi*; there were no Japanese ships farther to the left than those two. Though both of these destroyers were damaged in the course of the fight, they were also the targets of numerous other U.S. warships ahead of *Helena*. At any rate, *Inazuma* and *Ikazuchi* both remained active, as evidenced by passing exchanges with *San Francisco* and *Portland* minutes after this initial encounter with *Helena*.

The incredibly violent demise of *Akatsuki* was followed by a long lull for *Helena's* gunners as topside observers tried to sort friend from foe in the shifting tableau of incredible confusion that raged on ahead. Before *Helena* could find a new target, the lull was formalized at 0158 by Admiral Callaghan's order to cease firing. In all, during the first five or six minutes of the action, *Helena's* main battery expended 175 6-inch rounds and the two port 5-inch mounts got off a total of 20 rounds.

Helena was in a fortunate position. She had opened fire on *Akatsuki* while far enough back in the pack to avoid many of the consequences of being one of the first two U.S. ships off the mark; all the U.S. ships ahead had borne the brunt of the early Japanese firing, and the onslaughts of several Japanese destroyers had been dissipated by the actions of the U.S. ships ahead.

Minutes after *Helena* fired her last salvos at *Akatsuki* and one of the two left-hand Japanese destroyers, she passed up *Portland* 's port side as the latter abruptly swung to starboard following the torpedo hit. This inadvertent passage prevented *Helena* from tangling with the Japanese destroyers passing along *Portland* 's engaged starboard side. Thus, *Helena* was not beset by any Japanese warships during a lull that lasted, for her, at least ten minutes; the attention of the Japanese was almost wholly absorbed by the American warships ahead and behind. About all *Helena* had to do during those long minutes after she helped destroy *Akatsuki* was avoid damaged ships ahead and try to separate friend from foe.

25

T

he first phase of the action petered out as *Helena* passed up *Portland*'s port side into a void through which the central melee had raged only moments earlier. The forward elements of the two opposing forces had quite literally passed one another. In those minutes, several of the Japanese leaders turned and retraced their tracks and several of the followers diverted to courses aimed at taking them around the central conflagration.

During the lull that overtook the advance elements, the two American vanguard destroyers—*Cushing* and *Laffey*—met their separate and solitary fates.

Moments after *Cushing* became powerless as a result of hits in her engineering spaces, the battle passed her by—or, at any rate, none of the gunners aboard the many warships passing in the opposite direction thought to send any more rounds her way. The lull lasted perhaps as long as five minutes, and it gave *Cushing*'s crew time to beat down many fires, collect many of the wounded, and assess much of the damage. During the lull, *Cushing* took the opportunity to fire at warships that could be positively identified as Japanese. In some cases, dubious identifications were confirmed by flashes of recognition signals, but in no case was a proper countersign received.

Earlier, a Japanese shell had detonated near the port torpedo mount just as it got its first torpedo away. The two torpedomen manning the mount were seriously injured and its power was cut. After several confused minutes during the lull, relief torpedomen led by TM1 Allen Eads, the ship's senior torpedo rating, converged on the port mount, which they trained by hand. Eads got two of the three remaining fish away at a passing target 4,000 yards out before he was ordered to secure. There was still one torpedo remaining in the port mount, but someone in authority thought the ships passing to port might be friendly.

Thus far, *Cushing* had fired nine of her twelve torpedoes. LCdr Butch Parker claimed two hits on *Hiei* and the torpedomen themselves thought they also hit another target. However, it is uncertain if any of the torpedoes connected, or if they detonated in the event they did find targets.

卍

After the hose pressure failed as he was fighting the fire in Mount-1's ammunition handling room, GM2 Jim Tooker returned to the mount because he could not think of any other place to be. When he got there, Tooker was approached by the junior ensign who had been assigned to the gun as an ammunition passer in order to gain some seasoning. The young officer had had some rough moments during his first action three weeks earlier, against Japanese carrier bombers at Santa Cruz, but he had been very collected during the torpedo-bomber attack that afternoon. As Tooker entered the mount, the ensign asked if the gun could still be fired even though the power was out. Tooker said that it could and was immediately caught up in the rush to put together a makeshift crew from among the surviving gunners and ammunition passers. The ready service ammunition locker, forward of the mount, was opened and rounds and powder bags were quickly passed into the mount and loaded by hand.

Jim Tooker, who was filling in as first powderman, had lost count of the rounds going out when he was pulled back to full awareness by a misfire stuck in the breech. The first solution to this dangerous situation was to strike the breech with a rawhide mallet usually stored on the rammer mechanism that was Tooker's domain. He turned to retrieve the mallet and noticed that his former station had been blown away. The mallet was gone and there was no ready solution. A moment later, as Tooker and the others were trying to work things out in their heads, a Japanese round detonated against the ready service ammunition locker.

Mount-1 was clearly out of the fight.

卍

When WT1 Dennis Behl exited the air lock on the after main deck from the after fire room, he saw for the first time that *Cushing* had taken many more hits than he had been able to perceive while below decks. The ship was dead in the water, and there seemed to be numerous fires from the bridge forward. Uncertain of what to do, Behl went straight to Mount-3 to see if he could help there. Before Behl could find work, however, a large vessel with three stacks approached the stern from the starboard quarter and opened fire. The intruder was *Nagara*, which had been midway along in a passage beside *Atlanta* when her captain had obeyed a weak signal, apparently dispatched by Admiral Abe, to turn her back the way she had come.

Cushing's powerless ammunition and powder hoists were unable to resupply the three remaining 5-inch guns. Mount-2 fired at *Nagara* until the ready ammunition stored in the gun shelter caught fire. There was no way to fight the fire without water pressure. The forward repair party, located near the galley, had been virtually wiped out by earlier hits, so there were no trained personnel to fight the fire in any case. Someone tried to start the nearest handy-billy portable pump, but it had been damaged. That put Mount-2 permanently out of action. Within a minute of that setback, Mount-4 used up the last of its ready ammunition and powder and thus fell silent.

As *Nagara* pumped salvo after salvo into his ship, LCdr Butch Parker leaned over the after bridge railing and, in the light of *Nagara*'s newly illuminated searchlight, ordered the torpedomen manning the centerline mount to fire the two remaining torpedoes to starboard. However, the two torpedoes could not be expended because the mount could not be trained even by hand; apparently it had been jammed by a near miss.

By the time *Nagara* had approached to within about 2,000 yards and illuminated *Cushing*, only one of the destroyer's mounts had ammunition of any sort on hand, and that was Mount-3, *Cushing*'s designated starshell gun.

Though there were many wounded and dead men around Mount-3, the gun was putting a starshell round out about every four seconds as the surviving gunners and a clutch of volunteers worked feverishly in precise, mindless rhythm. As the sight setter traversed by hand, the gun captain, Cox John Bilyeau, pumped round after round into the circling cruiser's superstructure. WT1 Dennis Behl, who had gone through boot camp with Bilyeau in 1937, saw one of the Mount-3 rounds strike the cruiser dead center on her bridge. However, the Japanese light cruiser appeared unfazed; her captain was content with circling 2,000-4,000 yards out and returning the fire with his ship's seven-gun 5.5-inch main battery. The damage *Nagara* inflicted throughout the American destroyer was massive. Then even Mount-3 stopped firing.

⌖

When the night's action had first gotten underway, there had been a furious burst of activity in the magazine supplying powder and shells to Mount-3—calls for armor-piercing rounds followed by a quick call for starshells—but the hoist, which was controlled from above, soon stopped and no more shells were requested. S1 Hugh O'Fallon, the senior of the three men in the magazine, waited for one minute before calling the mount on the sound-powered battle phone, but there was no response. He tried shouting up the hoist shaft, but again there was no response. He had no idea that there was no longer any power to the phone or to run the silent hoist.

O'Fallon's perfect quandary was interrupted when the powder passer from the adjacent powder room started pushing himself through the open powder scuttle, which was too small in any case. The man was extremely distraught and it took long moments of smooth talk before O'Fallon got him calmed down. With great difficulty, the thoroughly fearful powder passer spluttered out the news that a round had passed through the powder room. O'Fallon pushed the man back out of the scuttle and put his own head through to see what damage the Japanese round had caused. There was smoke and some obvious damage to the overhead. Unable to see more, O'Fallon opened the hatch to the adjacent chamber and entered. What he saw left him utterly shaken. Apparently one of *Nagara's* 5.5-inch armor-piercing rounds had entered the chamber through the port side of the ship, ripped a long gash right along the overhead, and exited the starboard side of the ship. It passed only a foot above the highest row of powder cans.

As S1 O'Fallon stared in disbelief, he sensed for the first time that the ship's engines had stopped; there was an eerie, unusual silence at the core of the vessel, though the sounds of battle were still resonating through the steel bulkheads and deck plates. It was time to leave.

O'Fallon opened the magazine hatch and led his helpers and the powder passer toward the machine shop, from which he expected to get outside. However, the hatch would not open and could not be forced, so O'Fallon and the others went aft to the crew's quarters, then up a ladder leading to the main deck. As O'Fallon looked around outside, he could see other ships burning in the near distance. He turned and went forward to the hatch he had been unable to open a minute earlier. It proved to be jammed shut by a stack of bodies—the after repair party, all of whom were dead. As O'Fallon was checking the last body, *Nagara* fired several rounds through the tops of *Cushing's* stacks.

卍

S1 Ed Shively, who had been wounded in the arm by his own 20mm gun in the afternoon, was in the sick bay trying to shake off the effects of a large dose of morphine. He was still somewhere in the nether world when the charthouse, directly over his head, was struck by a Japanese shell. As Shively came instantly awake, the bulkhead split open and a tongue of flame and smoke spilled into the medical compartment. Shively, the only patient there, was saved because there was a bunk above his that absorbed and deflected the worst effects of the flame.

Clad only in a pair of skivvy shorts he had borrowed earlier from the ship's surgeon, Shively bolted from his bunk and ran straight out of the compartment. He did not have a clue about where he was going until he found himself standing at his 20mm gun station. As the shocked man focused, he saw that all three of the 20mm guns had been knocked out and only two of the six gun crewmen were apparently still alive.

Shively's dazed attention was arrested by a glowing red spot that appeared to be heading directly at him. The Japanese round detonated in the stack right over his head and showered him with shrapnel. Shively was amazed to find himself still on his feet.

⚛

It was at that juncture that LCdr Butch Parker made an inevitable decision. *Cushing* was dead in the water and was thoroughly unable to defend herself against *Nagara*, which was simply circling a few thousand yards away, pumping out rounds with total impunity. There were at least fifty dead crewmen aboard *Cushing*, several of whom had been killed by a detonation in the wardroom while awaiting treatment for wounds acquired in other parts of the ship. There was only one way to prevent further serious loss of life, only one decision to be made by *Cushing*'s captain. With great reluctance but with no shred of hesitation, Butch Parker ordered, "Abandon ship."

⚛

When WT1 Dennis Behl heard the abandon-ship order, he had immediate second thoughts about obeying; he felt that leaving the ship would be unnatural. But as scores of the men around him jumped and dived over the side, Behl felt his resolve fade, and he soon followed. As soon as Behl hit the water, all his attention and energy were given over to getting as far away as he could before the raging fires reached *Cushing*'s magazines.

Y2 Tom Foreman did not hear the order to abandon *Cushing* because he was unconscious when it was passed. Foreman had escaped injury earlier when the gun director had taken a direct hit, and he had carried a fire controlman with a broken leg from the director to the deck beneath the bridge. Foreman was bending over the injured fire controlman when *Nagara* opened fire, and he was apparently engulfed in the detonation of the light cruiser's very first salvo. A small piece of shrapnel behind his left ear knocked him unconscious and other steel slivers hit him in the left leg and sprayed his kapok life jacket without penetrating to his body. When Foreman revived, he found that the fire controlman had sustained additional injuries and was in need of medical attention. However, Foreman's spirit flagged and he told the fire controlman he could not help. The fire controlman became justifiably upset and ranted at Foreman that if he died he was going to come back and haunt him. Thoroughly engulfed by his own needs, Foreman did not even think about the seriocomic aspects of the exchange as he pulled a rubber tourniquet from his aid pouch and tied it around his own copiously bleeding left thigh. When Foreman tried to stand, his left leg would not support his weight; he thought the femur was broken, but, in fact the tendon had been severed by the shrapnel. Next, Foreman crawled to the front of the charthouse and headed down the ladder head first. He fell most of the way to the main deck when he came to the end of the shell-severed ladder. The loss of a shoe on the way down bothered Foreman more than the exploding ammunition ready boxes nearby. Finally, as things became fuzzier and fuzzier, a mess attendant who stopped to help told Foreman about the abandon-ship order. Foreman asked the mess attendant to go into the water with him, but the man refused because he could not swim. Foreman pulled himself across the hot deck and slid over the side. Despite his useless left leg, he started swimming. However, he immediately entered a large pool of fuel oil that was pouring out of a gash in *Cushing*'s hull. He was immediately blinded by the oil, but he never stopped swimming until he reached fresher water.

After leaving the Mount-3 magazine, S1 Hugh O'Fallon took cover from *Nagara*'s continuing fire behind the port side of the after deckhouse. He stayed there until he heard the order to abandon ship, then began throwing sealed empty powder tanks into the water from a neat stack of them he found outside the Mount-3 upper handling room. When most of the tanks were gone, O'Fallon inflated his life belt and jumped straight over the side. He immediately placed a powder tank under each arm and kicked for his life.

S1 Ed Shively, who was clad only in the skivvy drawers and T-shirt he had been wearing when he left the sick bay, thought twice about jumping from the 20mm gun platform between the stacks because he had no life jacket. However, on climbing down to the main deck, Shively found a powder can, which he closed with a lid he found, and jumped overboard along with a large group of other sailors. He narrowly escaped death once again when one of *Nagara*'s dual 25mm antiaircraft guns fired a burst into the water next to him.

GM2 Jim Tooker and several other men from Mount-1 went straight to their abandon-ship station on the starboard side of the wardroom in order to launch a life raft stowed there. However, before anyone could act, one of *Nagara*'s 5.5-inch rounds struck the outside of the wardroom and blew away part of the raft. All hands immediately ran around to the port side, pulled down the raft stowed there, and quickly manhandled it into the water. Just then, shrapnel from another hit on the starboard side of the wardroom flew out of a new hole in the port bulkhead and wounded nearly everyone standing over the freshly launched raft. Jim Tooker, who had already been injured, emerged with three new shrapnel wounds in his left leg. The raft had gone into the water upside down, but several men dived in after it and helped those remaining on deck to ease their most seriously wounded companion onto the relatively dry bottom. Then they pushed away from the side of the ship and everyone who was physically able furiously paddled or kicked to get all the speed on that they could.

Nagara's captain eventually tired of the easy game and sailed from sight. *Cushing* burned fiercely, but she was not quite ready to go down, and all the swimmers had ample time to put adequate distance between themselves and her expected fiery demise.

26

Immediately at the conclusion of *Laffey's* close encounter with *Hiei*, LCdr Bill Hank decided to put some distance between his ship and what looked to be a general melee forming astern. When *Laffey* had gone on emergency power to pass *Hiei*, she had become separated from the rest of the American column. When she passed *Cushing* was not noted, but she certainly did. She was pointed directly at Savo, and she continued straight for its concealing bulk. During the journey, which was made through another lull, *Kirishima* was spotted 10,000 yards off the port beam. All guns were trained out on her, but fire was prudently withheld. Many of the topside crewmen also saw several destroyers around *Kirishima*, but the Japanese apparently did not see *Laffey*. These sleeping dogs were allowed to lie.

As *Laffey* approached Savo, two dark shapes loomed out of the blackness with appalling suddenness. These were quickly perceived as two large Japanese destroyers, *Asagumo* followed by *Murasame*. They and *Samidare* had formed the left flank of the broken outer Japanese destroyer screen during the long run down the Slot to Guadalcanal. The three had maintained their position on the battleships' left flank, but they had fallen far behind the rest of the formation in the storm and were now racing to catch up.

The two large destroyers were passing across *Laffey's* bows from port to starboard 3,000 yards out and at a speed of about 25 knots. The fire controlman manning the director sights fixed the 5-inch guns on the leading destroyer as it crossed ahead, but Lt William Ratliff, *Laffey's* gunnery officer, decided to withhold fire. As the lead Japanese destroyer surged on to the right, the gun director's point of aim was shifted to the second destroyer. Without her even being seen, a third destroyer approaching the port bow— *Samidare*—snapped on her searchlight, which caught *Laffey* full in its beam. This was followed by the glare of bursting starshells directly over *Laffey.*

A minute or two earlier, *Laffey's* torpedo officer, Lt(jg) Tom Evins, had climbed from the bridge to the main deck to collect observations of the earlier action against *Hiei* from his torpedomen. He was just about to climb back to the bridge—and was unaware of the approach of the Japanese destroyers—when the lights went on. In the brief silent second before anyone could react, Evins heard someone nearby mutter a fatalistic, "Oh-oh." In the next second, Evins was hanging from a stanchion trying to keep himself from being thrown to the deck or over the side.

All three Japanese warships opened fire at *Laffey,* and apparently all of them were dead on target with their combined total of sixteen 5-inch guns. For all practical purposes, a dozen hits were virtually simultaneous.

❀

As *Laffey* shifted targets and counter-illuminated *Samidare,* Lieutenant Ratliff saw at least one of his first 5-inch rounds strike *Samidare* in the vicinity of her port bow at a range of only 1,000 yards. The Japanese searchlight went dark just as *Laffey* was struck in the fantail by one torpedo. It is marginally possible that this was an American torpedo that had been launched at a Japanese target farther back. If so, it is one of a very few American torpedoes that detonated on contact that night. However, destroyer *Teruzuki's* claim of hitting *Laffey* with a going-away shot is more credible.

The force of the blast blew off both of *Laffey's* screws and ripped away the rudder and underplating in its vicinity. By one estimate, the entire fantail section was lifted 15 feet out of the water in a progressive whipping motion. A solid sheet of water mixed with many large pieces of steel then poured down on the stern of the ship. The stern then settled back into the water with a sharp starboard list that brought the level of the sea to about the top of the after deckhouse. As many observers were deciding that the ship was about to sink, *Laffey* came back to an even keel with what appeared to be her normal freeboard. A fire had broken out in a ruptured fuel tank aft of Mount-4, but it was virtually inaccessible because the rear deck plating had been thrown up and over Mount-4, which became jammed and therefore ceased firing. A powder can in the after control station burst open and the scattered powder fueled a brief flash fire.

The fire from Mount-1, the gun farthest from the blast, was briefly disrupted when, among many others, the entire crew in the upper handling room reflexively hit the deck. S1 Rod Lambert, one of two sixteen-year-olds in the crew—and a veteran of a full year in the Navy—braved a brief look up from his prone position and saw a steel cable support part and unravel like a strand of wrapping twine. The entire deck beneath Lambert's torso shimmied and swayed. At that point, he just got up and headed for the main deck. When he got there, he stood in the open to exchange a few words with another sailor. He was barely able to understand what the other man was saying when the other man simply vanished. Lambert looked down and saw only one of the man's shoes on the deck. In another moment, Lambert passed out from shock and fear.

꙰

Below decks, in the forward engine room, Lt Eugene Barham, the engineering officer, felt that the ship had nearly broken in two. It was immediately noted that the turbines were speeding up despite the face that the ship was losing way. This was a certain indication to Barham and his machinist's mates that the propellers had been blown off the ship.

In the after engine room, after seeing that the throttleman closed down the throttle controlling the port propeller shaft, MM1 Jim Moore was ordered by his division chief to check on the men manning the lower level. The two pumpmen below were okay, though still rattled by the nearby blast. Moore got down to check the after bulkhead where the propeller shaft penetrated into the water. The seal had been breached and water was pouring in. The starboard shaft was bouncing up and down, which was ample proof that *Laffey* had no way to propel herself. Before Moore could report, however, the lights went out, which meant that the power was gone.

As the throttlemen closed off the throttle valves to prevent a runaway, Lieutenant Barham realized that pressure was building in the boilers and that the steam and water lines had ruptured or, at best, were about to rupture. He unhesitatingly passed orders to evacuate all the engineering spaces. It was none too soon. Boiling water cascading to the steel deck plates drove the temperature in the confined spaces to levels higher than human beings could tolerate. Superheated steam escaping from the breached steam lines at about 600 pounds pressure could flash-cook anyone it touched.

When the chief machinist's mate ordered all hands out of the after engine room, the man farthest from the escape hatch, and thus the last to leave, was MM1 Jim Moore. When he got to the spot where he had stowed his life jacket, he found that the garment was missing. Though Moore had a flashlight and was momentarily tempted to look for a replacement life jacket, he got hold of himself and decided that there was no time for that. Indeed, the heat from the escaping stem was growing unbearable. Moore sucked in his breath to avoid breathing superheated fumes and climbed the ladder to the main deck as fast as he could. His waning strength barely carried him through the hatch. As soon as Moore hit the cool outside air in clothing dripping from sweat and condensing steam, he flopped down in a sitting position and breathed deeply, gratefully. He had barely recovered when he responded to a call to help man a bucket brigade aft.

As soon as Lieutenant Barham emerged on the main deck and checked with his supervisors to see that all hands had gotten out safely, he walked aft down the starboard side of the ship to inspect the torpedo damage and adjacent fire, which seeping fuel oil had carried to the mattresses in the large after crew's berthing compartment. As Barham returned up the starboard side, he evaluated the damage caused by the shock of the blast to the ship's deck and strength members. He found a two-foot bulge in the main deck forward of the torpedo damage. At the least, this indicated that the ship had indeed broken in two and that the two parts were joined only by *Laffey's* thin outer skin.

⚛

Through it all, *Laffey's* three remaining 5-inch mounts were held on *Samidare* by the director, and they continued to pour rounds in her direction. Lieutenant Ratliff, the gunnery officer, reported that a fire broke out well forward on the target. Meanwhile, however, the Japanese destroyers now to starboard—*Asagumo* and *Murasame*—were still scoring numerous hits on *Laffey*. One round detonated in the pilot house, killing the communications officer and wounding others. Countless rounds fell into the amidships workshops, and one wrecked Mount-3.

One Japanese round penetrated Mount-2 and detonated a ready powder charge. All but two members of the gun crew were killed in the contained blast. The only thing that saved the ship from blowing up then and there was the quick action of GM3 Roy Myers, who instantly flooded the upper handling room.

Another round struck the base of the gun director, severing its control over Mount-1, the last remaining operational gun. When director control was lost, the Mount-1 gun captain, BM2 Robert Rider, assumed local control without skipping a beat. Thus, Mount-1 continued to fire at its original target, *Samidare*. Though Lieutenant Ratliff believed he saw the target dead in the water and burning, *Samidare* was still underway. Indeed, none of the three Japanese destroyers in this group—the only group that could have been in that place at that time—was seriously damaged, and none was stopped, even momentarily, during the entire battle. (Yet more inexplicable is Ratliff's later assertion that the target blew up as *Laffey* drifted by on the last of her momentum.)

As *Laffey* drifted clear of the melee—as the Japanese swept on out of range—Mount-1 ceased firing. Several parting 5-inch rounds fell upon *Laffey* in the vicinity of the bridge just as the hapless destroyer was straddled by a salvo of 14-inch rounds. These had been fired by *Kirishima*, which had crossed astern of *Laffey* and was running between Savo and Florida from what, to her captain, appeared to be an American ambush. One 14-inch round from a follow-up salvo passed all the way through the amidships deckhouse from starboard to port. It emerged almost in front of Lt(jg) Tom Evins's nose and trailed a shower of sparks from an electrical junction box it carried away. Evins braced for a massive detonation, but none occurred.

Apparently the eight-minute bonus allowed the Japanese by Dan Callaghan's long wait to open fire had at least spared *Laffey* this one cruel blow. The 14-inch round that did not explode must have been one of the armor-piercing shells brought up from the depths of the main-battery magazine to replace the hurriedly stowed thin-skinned bombardment projectiles. If one of those point-contact rounds had detonated against *Laffey*, personnel casualties topside would have been massive. As it was, seawater thrown up by several of the 14-inch near misses practically swamped the American destroyer; at moments, the water was knee-deep on the bridge.

❦

Laffey was thoroughly adrift; she had no power at all. Three of her four 5-inch mounts were wrecked, as was the gun director and several 20mm guns. The Mount-4 upper handling room, and possibly the after magazine, was ablaze, as was the after crew's berthing compartment and the amidships workshop area. The Japanese were all gone, so the attention of every living man in command of his senses was turned to putting out the fires and saving the ship.

Lt(jg) Tom Evins crawled up the slanting deck to Mount-4 to help a small group of sailors trying to free the gun crew from the smashed enclosure. Several of the gunners had sustained horrible injuries in the torpedo detonation; some of them were alive and conscious. One was a youngster who, in addition to having both of his legs smashed, was pinned to the deck by massive wreckage. It soon developed that the youngster's back was being scorched by the fires raging in the compartment beneath him, and there was little hope of freeing him before he was cooked alive. As Evins and others fought the visible fire just aft of the mount, TM1 Frederick Sanderson and TM1 James Geer devoted themselves to the seemingly impossible task of freeing the trapped gunner.

The firefighting effort would have been ludicrous under less trying circumstances. Ens David Sterrett, who, as the ship's machine-gun officer, had not been seriously employed in the fight, was on the scene of the fire early. As soon as he realized that the ship was totally lacking in power to run the fire mains, he rallied bystanders by grabbing a 5-inch powder can, filling it with water, and throwing the water at the roaring inferno aft of Mount-4. The fire fighters were reduced to dipping 5-inch shell casings, powder cans, and a few buckets into the water and pouring or throwing their contents on the flames, which were obviously gaining on the effort. A portable gasoline-powered handy-billy pump was in operation, but it was slightly damaged and giving its operators no end of problems. Someone broke out a supply of sand from the after repair stores, but there was not nearly enough of it to smother so large a fire. The wreckage of the fantail deck, which was curled 6 feet above Mount-4, even prevented more than two or three crewmen at a time from handling the meager offerings of water passed back by the others.

After helping to get the firefighting effort underway, Ensign Sterrett went to work throwing filled powder cans overboard. However, it soon became obvious that lifting and tossing all the heavy aluminum tanks could not be accomplished quickly enough to beat the advancing fire. Sterrett was certain that *Laffey* would eventually blow up, but he kept grimly to the task he had laid out for himself.

Though all hands worked relentlessly to save their ship, there was not much to save. Lt Eugene Barham completed his inspection and climbed to the bridge by means of a rope ladder—the steel ladder had been shot away—to report to the captain. He told LCdr Bill Hank everything he knew and added advice that *Laffey* be abandoned. Hank took the grim news with equanimity, but he was still unable to reconcile himself to the notion of leaving the ship. "I am not going to abandon my ship. You get us underway and I will get us out of here."

"Captain," Barham told the skipper, "we don't have any propellers. We just can't get this ship underway. May I have permission to put the boats and rafts in the water in case?"

Hank told Barham to go ahead, but he could not yet bring himself to accept the full impact of Barham's report. However, Lieutenant Barham had only just reached the main deck and was climbing through piles of debris on his way to getting the rafts and boats into the water when the captain ordered everyone to abandon ship.

Barham went to his abandon-ship station on the starboard main deck amidships to assemble the swimming party—randomly selected swimmers and nonswimmers for whom there was not enough room even in *Laffey*'s full complement of life rafts and boats. As the swimmers were gathering, Bill Hank called down from the level just below the bridge to tell Barham to get over the side. Barham called back, "You are coming, aren't you?"

"I'll be right behind you, Chief, as soon as everyone has abandoned."

As Barham turned away from the captain he saw the outline of a large ship with three stacks slow to a crawl only about 2,000 yards off *Laffey*'s starboard beam. *Nagara*, which by then had finished shooting up *Cushing*, stood quietly where she was and trained out her seven 5.5-inch main guns. There was a collective intake of breath as every man aboard *Laffey* who saw her froze and thought about eternity. But the Japanese ship got underway again without firing a shot. Clearly, *Laffey* was a dead loss requiring no additional expenditure of ammunition.

卐

Only when Lt(jg) Tom Evins and scores of other men around Mount-4 heard the order to abandon ship did they altogether abandon hope of beating the fire. At that moment, one of the two torpedomen working to free the young gunner pinned to the hot deck muttered triumphantly, "We got him!" That single cry of good news served as a tonic for the majority. A wire litter was passed to the torpedomen, who lifted the uncomplaining lad from the deck on which he had been slowly cooking and strapped him in.

As the fire fighters dispersed to climb into rafts alongside the ship, Tom Evins sat down to remove his shoes and socks. As he dangled his feet over the side preparatory to slipping into the water, Evins looked back briefly and saw TM1 Frederick Sanderson and TM1 James Geer manhandling the litter over the opposite side.

※

SC1 Sam Weitzel was the last man out of the Mount-3 magazine. He had remained behind to try to cajole a shipmate, who had become catatonic with fear, into leaving. The shipmate, a first-class fireman, had lost control when the torpedo had hit the ship; since then, no one had been able to break his grip on the stanchion to which he had affixed himself. As the man in charge of the magazine, Weitzel felt obliged to remain as long as possible to get the shocked man moving, but his entreaties and displays of brute strength had been to no avail. After one last try following the abandon-ship order, Weitzel reluctantly departed.

※

S1 John Jenkins and a fellow 20mm gunner rushed all the way from the stern, where they had been fighting the fire, to the bow—to get as far away from the fire as they could. Just before diving into the water, Jenkins removed his life jacket; the front had been completely torn away and he was afraid that it would become waterlogged and drag him under. For some reason, Jenkins wanted to keep the ship in sight for as long as he could, so he rolled over onto his back and stroked for his life.

S1 Rod Lambert, the sixteen-year-old who had bolted from the forward ammunition handling room, came to on the main deck near the bows after having earlier fainted from fright. He had no idea how long he had been out. As Lambert was regaining his senses and a bit of his composure, he heard a faint call for help. It took a minute to track the feeble plaints. Lambert found a ship's cook flat on the deck. A closer inspection revealed that at least several of the cook's limbs were missing. Barely recovered from his earlier fright, Lambert was unable even to look at the fatally wounded shipmate and just left. He was wandering about in a daze when a sailor he knew passed him in a headlong rush straight off the bow. "Rod," the sailor called as he leaped into the water, "she's going to blow!" Lambert collected his wits and followed the swimming sailor into the water.

S1 Ward Casey, a pharmacist's mate striker, one of three medical corpsmen aboard the ship, had been rubbernecking topside during *Laffey*'s brush with *Hiei*, and had thus nearly been hit in the shower of 25mm rounds that fell on *Laffey*'s main deck. He had returned to the wardroom posthaste to help with the inflow of wounded and had been tirelessly assisting the ship's surgeon, Lt(jg) Aaron Michelson, with the growing crowd of casualties ever since. When news arrived that the captain had ordered the ship abandoned, Casey volunteered to assist two badly wounded shipmates to the main deck. After assuring Dr. Michelson that he would be right back, the corpsman striker selected two men with broken legs and half-carried them to the side of the ship, where he assisted them into a life raft. As he was leaving the two to return to the wardroom, one said, "Doc, why don't you get off with us? You're here already." Casey was nearing the wardroom hatch when he decided to take the advice. Without further thought, he jumped right over the port side of the ship.

🔁

Ens David Sterrett was reluctant to leave *Laffey*, even after he heard the order to abandon ship. He knew of several cases where warships had been prematurely abandoned in the confusion of battle and he was not yet ready to go to such extreme effort if he would only have to reclaim her in the morning. To be useful, Sterrett made several trips to the officers' staterooms to retrieve mattresses, which he had heard would provide excellent flotation until they became waterlogged. He shoved three of them over the side while most of the crew took to the water. As the last bobbed away from the ship, Sterrett turned aft to survey the progress of the fire. There was no question that it was about the reach the powder magazine he had worked so hard to empty of its volatile contents. Alas, Sterrett's frantic effort had barely made a dent in the magazine's vast supply of powder and shells.

As Ensign Sterrett was deciding it was time to go, LCdr Bill Hank stalked around the forecastle deck. The captain, who wanted to be the last man off and who had insisted upon making one last tour of the main deck, shined a large flashlight in the machine-gun officer's face and blurted out, "Who's that? Oh, Sterrett." Without another word, Hank disappeared around the corner. An instant later, the after magazine blew up.

Ensign Sterrett wound up wedged in a corner as steel shards of every size flew in all directions away from the point of detonation. Next, the ship rolled violently to starboard and Sterrett slid uncontrollably to the side, where he regained his footing and, in one motion, leaped forward to the forecastle, climbed the life lines, and fell a foot or two into the water.

⇌

Lt Eugene Barham and his party of swimmers were only 50 yards from *Laffey* when there was a shocking explosion at their backs. Barham swiveled around and saw that the entire after portion of the ship had disappeared. Huge hunks of steel were still rising into the firelit night sky. Barham thought of diving deep as meager protection against their eventual impact but was kept afloat by his life jacket, so he fatalistically elected to watch the entire show.

Lieutenant Barham was not injured, but Lt(jg) Tom Evins was. Caught totally by surprise by the explosion—it had never occurred to him that *Laffey* might blow up—the torpedo officer had no time to think of anything before he was overtaken by high-velocity debris. He felt as if his right arm had been torn out at the shoulder, he could not catch his breath, and he was unable to offer any resistance to the relentless cascade of hot water that drove him beneath the surface. Only his life jacket worked to save him and he was unaware of even that until he bobbed to the surface.

The two torpedomen and the wounded gunner they had freed in the nick of time from Mount-4 were engulfed in the violent demise of the ship. TM1 James Geer and the injured man were apparently killed outright and TM1 Frederick Sanderson was mortally wounded.

S1 Ward Casey, then only a few yards from the port side of the ship, was sucked beneath the waves. He was unable to reach the surface despite his best efforts until he was on the verge of reflexively breathing in water in mindless pursuit of air.

Even closer to the ship than Casey when it blew up was S1 Rod Lambert. When the bow section stood straight up and backed into the water Lambert was trapped in the whirlpool of suction. He went uncontrollably around and around until suddenly the water closed right over him. He had his life jacket on, but he was so out of his mind with fear that he forgot all about it. When the life jacket carried him back to the surface, Lambert screamed his head off until he simply ran out of steam and bobbed passively in the light chop.

Ens David Sterrett was only twenty strokes from the forecastle when he turned to watch *Laffey's* bows lift out of the water and began their backward dive to the bottom of the channel. Perhaps the last living man to leave the ship, he had come through his ordeal unscathed.

S1 John Jenkins was about 200 yards from the ship, swimming on his back, when she exploded. In the lingering light, Jenkins saw a long, thin object that appeared about to hit him. He thrashed with all his might and moved a few feet just in time to avoid being hit by what he took to be a 5-inch gun barrel.

As soon as *Laffey's* bow slid backward beneath the surface, it became pitch dark. The only sound was the babble of voices.

27

The wild central melee that characterized the first ten minutes of the battle quickly diffused as the leading vessels of both battle forces either recoiled or passed through one another.

On the American side, both admirals were dead, *Cushing* was being abandoned, *Laffey* was in mortal danger of blowing up, *O'Bannon* and *Sterett* had entered void spaces beyond the central melee, *Atlanta* was dead in the water and burning, and *San Francisco* was burning and running for her life. Of the five rear American warships—*Juneau, Aaron Ward, Barton, Monssen,* and *Fletcher*—only *Aaron Ward* was able to engage the Japanese vanguard elements, albeit at long range and with inconclusive results. The other four rear American warships were able to follow the action ahead visually and by means of radar for the first five minutes. Then they were forced into blind meeting engagements with several Japanese ships that had passed around and through the central melee. For all practical purposes, the American rear guard was locked in a separate fight.

On the Japanese side, *Akatsuki* had blown up and sunk with all hands, *Nagara* had been lightly damaged and was in the process of withdrawing, *Hiei* had been struck by at least two torpedoes and countless medium-caliber shells and was finally turning away from the fight, *Kirishima* was virtually unscathed but was also turning to avoid what her captain thought was a clever American trap, *Inazuma* and *Ikazuchi* were still advancing down the track of the American column, and *Teruzuki* was lost somewhere in the void, as were *Yukikaze* and *Harusame*. *Asagumo* was leading *Murasame* and *Samidare* further into the fight, *Amatsukaze* was alone and looking for targets, and *Yudachi* was surging back toward the sound of the guns after her early reflexive and humiliating retreat from the American vanguard.

The only intact elements left to either side were the five-ship American rearguard and the three-ship Japanese rearguard. Every other ship—whether damaged or still able to carry on the fight—was alone, looking for targets or withdrawing. Neither side was operating under the control of senior officers. The central melee was becoming diffused and widening into a particularly hazardous blind free-for-all.

⇄

Cdr Tameichi Hara, captain of destroyer *Amatsukaze*, was reaching a certain level of frustration. He had been more than game to push his ship into the central melee, but had been prevented from doing so by a number of little events: Overs meant for *Hiei* had exploded near *Amatsukaze* and temporarily dazzled Commander Hara and his bridge watch, and, brief minutes later, *Amatsukaze* had to pull up short during her next attempt to close with the Americans because other Japanese destroyers had sailed across her bows.

Amatsukaze was just recovering from her near collision with the friendly ships when Commander Hara saw them turn in such a way as to allow him to join up behind. *Amatsukaze* was just coming to a new heading when the light from Japanese starshells outlined five American warships in column; the nearest, destroyer *Barton*, was estimated to be only 5,000 yards off the starboard bow.

Commander Hara was acknowledged as Japan's leading torpedo-action theorist. As a young lieutenant, he had diligently experimented with a radical new torpedo-attack technique, had ironed out the bugs, and had gotten it accepted as the Imperial

Navy's standard. Ironically, though he had been blooded in night surface actions in the East Indies early in the war, Hara personally had never been able to fire his torpedoes. The theory had been amply proven by others, but Hara himself had never employed it in anger. He was absolutely determined to do so this night.

As the wraithlike American warship approached *Amatsukaze* on a roughly parallel opposite heading, Hara's torpedo officer, Lt Masatoshi Miyoshi, impatiently yelled, "Commander, let's fire the fish!"

By what he reckoned as being 0154, Commander Hara was more than willing. "Ready the fishermen! The target is 30 degrees to starboard and approaching." To achieve success, Commander Hara needed to determine a point at which the tracks of the target and torpedoes would intersect. Given all the possible variables that might occur after the fish were in the water, it was virtually mandatory to fire a spread—literally a pattern in which the torpedoes fanned out from a common firing point to cover areas ahead of and behind the projected impact point. Thus, after calling out the target's current position, Hara added, "Adjusted fire angle, fifteen degrees." The key to Commander Hara's technique was firing the torpedoes at the top of a speeding hyperbolic turn. Even if the target vessel saw Hara's approach, it would not be able to respond. Therefore, Hara completed his string of orders with, "Navigator, turn right close in and follow a hyperbola."

As the Japanese torpedomen rushed to comply with their captain's order, *Amatsukaze* raced directly toward *Barton*, which remained eerily quiet, oblivious. (Two minutes earlier, *Barton* had fired five of her ten torpedoes at a target to port and she was then firing her four 5-inch guns in the same direction; a lot of people— her gunners and torpedomen, at least—should have been staring in *Amatsukaze*'s general direction.) As soon as the range closed to 3,000 yards, Commander Hara barked, "Ready torpedoes! Fire!"

At about 0157, all eight of *Amatsukaze*'s ready torpedoes *shushed* out of their tubes in a rush of compressed air and expelled breaths. Immediately, *Amatsukaze* came right and cut her speed. As the torpedomen struggled to reload all eight tubes in record time, the rest of the topside watch remained vigilant for new targets, new opportunities, or new dangers.

⇄

Cdr Kiyoshi Kiikawa was humiliated; *Yudachi's* blooded captain had run from the fight before the fight quite got started. In doing so, Kiikawa had reacted to the lessons of a bad night he had had as commander of a smaller, more vulnerable destroyer early in the war, off Bali, in the East Indies. At that time, Kiikawa had paid too much attention to approaching enemy warships on one side and had very nearly fallen prey to enemy warships approaching from the other side. When Kiikawa had seen *Cushing* loom out of the darkness just before the start of the action, his instincts had aroused him to avoid a possible trap. So he had run, dragging *Harusame* in his wake. In so doing, he had both upset the American battle plan and prematurely alerted the Americans. The fact that he was out of position—in reality, lost—only added to Kiikawa's paranoia at the crucial moment.

After turning away from *Cushing* at 0142, *Yudachi* frantically radioed a warning to *Hiei*, which did not need the warning. Then she tried to get clear of the opposing forces and get a fix on who was who before engaging. As Commander Kiikawa looked over his shoulder from the bridge of his retreating destroyer, he saw the first flashes of gunfire erupt in the waters he had vacated eight minutes earlier. Shamed and still a bit confused, Kiikawa ordered his helmsman to bring the ship about. Somewhere along the line, *Harusame* went astray, so *Yudachi* charged back into the fray alone at her top speed of 35 knots.

⇄

As *Amatsukaze's* Commander Hara cast about for a target for his eight remaining torpedoes—which were not yet loaded—he saw the outline of a friendly destroyer picked out of the blackness in the waning glare of a starshell. Instantly, Hara identified the ship as *Yudachi*, which was in the act of cutting through the American rearguard directly between the two leading American warships. So intent was Commander Kiikawa upon engaging the Americans that he nervelessly held his course despite the imminent danger of plowing into the second ship's bows at 35 of his own knots and about 20 knots of the American's speed. It was left to the American skipper to collide or evade.

꩜

When *Akatsuki*'s searchlight went on at 0150, *Aaron Ward* had already been tracking *Hiei* for several minutes by means of her finely tuned FD gunnery radar. At 0150, the Japanese flagship was 7,000 yards from *Aaron Ward*, whose guns were trained out to port and locked on. When the searchlights were illuminated, *Aaron Ward*'s captain, Cdr Orville Gregor, was one of the first American skippers to order his guns into action. Over the next four minutes, *Aaron Ward*'s four 5-inch guns put out a total of ten salvos at *Hiei*. Many detonations and small fires were observed all along the target, but Commander Gregor and his gunners were not certain whose hits they were; many other American ships were clearly firing at the battleship.

Aaron Ward checked fire at 0158 in compliance with Admiral Callaghan's order. At that moment, the sky and sea were illuminated by a stunningly bright Japanese starshell that revealed for the first time to the men on the destroyer's bridge that the cruisers ahead had turned or were turning what appeared to be 90 degrees to port. The sky overhead and the sea all around remained bathed in the light of freshly fired Japanese starshells. In the glaring light, many of *Aaron Ward*'s lookouts saw a dark form emerge from the void to starboard. It looked as though another ship was out of control and about to collide with *Aaron Ward* at full speed. At 0159, when the FD radar operator gave out the news that the range to the mystery ship had closed to 1,200 yards, Commander Gregor ordered *Aaron Ward* stopped and then backed with both engines at full emergency power.

꩜

Looking on in the light of a fresh Japanese starshell from the bridge of his own radically turning destroyer, Cdr Tameichi Hara kept his attention riveted on *Barton*, which was rapidly coming up on *Aaron Ward*'s stern and which would have to turn to avoid piling up on the friendly destroyer ahead. If that happened, *Amatsukaze*'s eight-torpedo spread was less likely to connect. Instead of turning, however, *Barton*'s skipper, LCdr Douglas Fox, ordered all engines stopped. Fox's would have been a reasonable response in less hostile circumstances, but it provided just the opportunity Commander Hara's prescient firing pattern needed.

At 0200, as *Aaron Ward* was picking up speed following Commander Gregor's earlier order to back the engines, *Aaron Ward*'s torpedomen saw two torpedo wakes worm into the starshell light and pass beneath the ship from port to starboard. Within the minute and 1,000 yards off *Aaron Ward*'s starboard quarter, two of *Amatsukaze*'s eight torpedoes narrowly missed *Monssen*'s bows and struck *Barton*, one in the forward fire room and one in the forward engine room. With that, the six-month-old American destroyer blew up—just blew up—in an awesome incandescence. Only a second later, the great double-pillar of light waned. *Barton* broke in two and sank. Her entire combat career had lasted about six minutes, during which she had fired five torpedoes and about forty rounds of 5-inch ammunition.

So rapid was the loss of the ship that M1 Wayne Clark, a member of the after repair party, had no time to see or feel anything before the water was already up around his chest. Clark instinctively sucked in his breath at the last possible millisecond and was carried beneath the waves. As Clark reached out to pull himself up the ladder by which he had been standing, he realized that his feet were caught in the netting strung between the railing and the deck to catch expended shell casings. As the after part of the ship plunged downward at an astonishing rate, Clark coolly reached into his pocket and extracted his hunting knife, which many sailors aboard the vulnerable tincans carried. With this, he quickly cut through the hobbling rope and pulled for the surface. On the way up, he unbuckled his steel helmet and flipped it out of the way. When M1 Clark surfaced, debris was still falling into the water.

RM2 Jack Slack, a veteran of numerous early-war raids aboard another destroyer, was manning a 20mm gun on *Barton*'s after deck house. Though gunnery was not a typical job for a radioman, Slack had insisted on a battle station at which he could do something besides copy down message traffic, something he had been doing too much of since being caught at Pearl Harbor on December 7,

1941. Slack's boredom saved his life. *Barton's* severed after section disappeared into the water so fast that Slack never had a chance to jump into the water; he simply found himself in it. For several of the calmest moments of his life, Slack was absolutely certain that he was going to drown as the suction carried him inexorably beneath the waves. As he was about to give in and breathe water, however, his life jacket counteracted the suction and popped him to the surface. All he saw when he cleared his eyes was *Barton's* bow section, standing straight up, the numeral 599 showing clearly in the light of a freshly ignited starshell.

Lt(jg) Wilbur Quint, *Barton's* assistant gunnery officer, was standing near RM2 Slack's 20mm cannon, atop the deckhouse, when he saw the entire forward portion of the ship rear up as a huge gout of flame erupted clear from the bows to amidships. Quint instinctively called out to several men nearby and led them to the nearest life raft. However, before Lieutenant(jg) Quint and the sailors could begin undoing the toggles securing the raft, they were all swept into the water. The next thing Quint knew, he was fighting his way toward the surface with all his might. He was one of two officers to get off the ship.

The only survivor known to have emerged from an internal compartment was RM3 Albert Arcand. One of two radiomen manning the after emergency radio shack, Arcand had felt *Barton's* wrenching last-minute maneuvering and had reacted instantly to the detonation of the two torpedoes in her flank. Hearing bulkheads rip apart all around him, Arcand reached for the dogs on his compartment's hatch. He opened the hatch just as *Barton* slid beneath the surface and was nearly knocked from his feet by a solid wall of water. Somehow, Arcand made it out of the compartment, but the other radioman, who was right behind him, did not. As it was, Arcand was momentarily trapped beneath an overhanging platform. As he concentrated on keeping his mouth closed, he felt himself rising to the surface. He was about to give into an instinctive gasp for air when his head emerged from the water.

All the survivors were from the after section of the ship, and all except RM3 Arcand were manning topside battle stations in the open when the torpedo struck.

After taking a moment to clear fuel oil from his eyes, M1

Wayne Clark saw in the light of the starshells and burning debris that *Barton's* bows were sticking straight up and that the severed after part of the ship had turned turtle with the screws exposed above the water. Seconds later, the after section of the ship disappeared.

🜺

O'Bannon had come unstuck in the dark void at the edges of the battle area after passing *Sterett* and *Cushing* and losing track of *Laffey* after she had surged off on her own. Following her running duel with *Nagara* and her close encounter with *Hiei* near the center of the conflagration, *O'Bannon* had unwittingly shaped a course back around the far edge of the diffusing central melee. As the lone destroyer sailed unmolested during the minutes leading up to 0200, all hands topside could plainly see five burning vessels spread across the starboard quarter and one burning vessel a long way off the port quarter. Gunnery control could find no firm Japanese targets during the interval.

At about 0202, lookouts urgently reported that the bows of a destroyer were sticking straight up out of the water directly in *O'Bannon's* path. At practically the same moment, two torpedoes were spotted heading right at *O'Bannon*. From his position beside the helmsman, where he had his head poked through a porthole in the pilothouse bulkhead, *O'Bannon's* exec, LCdr Donald MacDonald, immediately ordered the ship to swing hard to the left—both to evade the torpedoes and to avoid the obstruction. Though lookouts bellowed the news that the vertical bows belonged to an American ship, it was impossible for Lieutenant Commander MacDonald to turn the speeding destroyer in time to prevent her from overrunning survivors in the water. Nevertheless, a number of quick-thinking and compassionate *O'Bannon* sailors stripped off their kapok life jackets and threw them into the midst of the survivors. The torpedoes passed ahead of *O'Bannon* just as the ship struck the tiny knot of survivors dead on.

From his position low in the water, RM2 Jack Slack turned just in time to see the numeral 450 etched in starshell light on the bow of the ship that was about to run him down. He felt the shock of contact and rode the turbulent bow wave away from the speeding warship. Then he was pulled back toward the side of the passing destroyer and severely buffeted by what might have been a quick turn through *O'Bannon*'s speeding screws. RM3 Albert Arcand was pulling floating debris in around his body when he saw *O'Bannon* bearing straight down on him, so close he could almost touch her flank. Arcand screamed at the top of his lungs, "The screws! The screws!" and then he was rolled over and over in the boiling wake. When he resurfaced, his kapok life jacket was wrapped around his neck. He started to yell in the hope of attracting other survivors and was immediately answered by RM2 Jack Slack. Arcand and Slack were not hurt, but several other swimmers were. At least one of the keel-hauled swimmers, S2 Harold Bone, suffered severe injuries while entangled with *O'Bannon*'s propellers; he emerged with a severely lacerated right calf and a broken and lacerated right foot. It is possible that other *Barton* survivors were killed during *O'Bannon*'s passage.

As if they had not suffered enough, the *Barton* survivors were overwhelmed by a new disaster immediately after *O'Bannon* ran over them. Before the terrorized survivors had an opportunity to regroup, their own dead ship's depth charges detonated directly beneath them. The apparently simultaneous multiple detonation was so forceful that *O'Bannon*'s stern was lifted right out of the water and she temporarily lost all light and power. No doubt, *Barton* survivors were killed or mortally injured by the gut-knotting pressure.

卍

As Cdr Tameichi Hara stood shakily upon *Amatsukaze*'s deck, his theory proven to *his own* satisfaction and gratification, he heard the spontaneous ovation of his crew over the rising crescendo of battle noises in the near distance. By then, *Amatsukaze* was heading west, safely cocooned in darkness.

As the excitement topside died down, Commander Hara went back to work trying to find targets for his eight remaining torpedoes. After several visual sweeps, he saw a sleek, fairly large warship—*Juneau*—in the eerie light of dying starshells.

"Torpedoes ready," Hara bellowed to bring his crew back to earth. "Target seventy degrees to port."

From his place by the torpedo tubes, Lt Masotoshi Miyoshi responded with a bellow of his own, "Torpedoes ready, sir!" There was perhaps a new trace of respect in the younger officer's voice.

"Miyoshi, use only four torpedoes this time, not eight." This was followed with the firing and evasion solutions, a final "Steady," and an emphatic, "Fire!" With that, *Amatsukaze* turned away from *Juneau*, whose topside lookouts had failed to spot her. As the four torpedoes were expelled in a rush of compressed air, Commander Hara began counting off the minutes; it would take at least three and no more than four minutes for any of the torpedoes to connect.

卐

After her breathtaking crossing directly in front of *Aaron Ward*, *Yudachi* had come hard right to rattle the aim of American gunners and to bring her own guns to bear. But Commander Kiikawa had withheld fire, preferring to engage when he was in the best possible position. The right turn at top speed soon left the confused American rearguard behind and brought receding *Juneau* into direct sight. From Kiikawa's vantage point, the rearmost American cruiser was directly to starboard on a parallel course, a perfect setup for torpedoes. Without further ado, Commander Kiikawa ordered his gunners to open fire and his torpedomen to put all eight of the ready torpedoes into the water.

As soon as *Yudachi*'s torpedos were away, but before Kiikawa could order a belated turn, *Juneau*'s forward and after gun directors locked onto *Yudachi*, and seven of her eight dual 5-inch mounts turned and opened fire. Much farther back in the column, topside crewmen aboard *Fletcher*, the thus far unengaged American rear destroyer, saw what appeared to be fourteen solid lines of 5-inch tracer ammunition penetrate the darkness as though fourteen hoses were spraying fireworks through the night sky. Topside and aft of *Juneau*'s bridge, SM2 Joseph Hartney distinctly saw several of his ship's 5-inch tracer rounds strike *Yudachi*'s upper works while, at the same moment, one and possibly two of *Yudachi*'s 5-inch rounds struck *Juneau*'s upper works aft of the fighting bridge. The crewmen manning *Juneau*'s fantail 1.1-inch mounts all undertook a mad dive for cover as shell splinters or, perhaps, 25mm automatic cannon rounds fell all around them.

Then, just seconds after the spectacle opened, *Fletcher's* topside crewmen saw *Juneau* lighted by a powerful momentary red and yellow flash. When the big light went out, the multiple streams of tracer were also gone.

One of *Yudachi*'s four torpedoes had struck *Juneau* low on the port side, just in the nick of time to save the Japanese destroyer from being overwhelmed by *Juneau's* powerful array of automatic 5-inch guns. The force of the blast buckled the main deck just aft of Mount-8, threw three depth charges overboard, and smashed the port motor whaleboat to kindling. To the captain and others topside, the damage seemed minor. But there was clearly more to it, for the helmsman lost control and the ship lost most of her speed.

In fact, *Yudachi*'s torpedo struck the thin-skinned antiaircraft cruiser on her port side below the armor belt and entered the forward fire room. All hands in the fire room, seventeen in all, were killed instantly. The inner surface of the double bulkhead sealing the forward end of the huge compartment was breached by the force of the detonation, but the outer layer of steel remained secure. All hands in the plotting room, just ahead, were thus saved, though all were thrown to the deck and several were injured. At the same time the plotting room went down, the bridge lost control of the ship. The gap was immediately filled by the exec, in Battle-2.

The worst effect of the detonation was that *Juneau's* keel was broken directly beneath the center of the blast. After rising somewhat in the wake of the explosion, the ship settled deeper than she had been sailing and took on a slight list to port. Loss of the forward fire room resulted in total loss of electrical power in the forward part of the ship and to all the gun mounts. An emergency diesel generator was powered up almost immediately after things died down. Next, the entire load was shifted to the generators in the after engine room, but it soon became apparent that they could not carry the entire burden and the emergency diesel generators were brought back on line. Even then, numerous compartments were selectively darkened to conserve power.

Moments after his ship was struck, Capt Lyman Swenson ordered *Juneau's* helmsman to evade all other ships and shape a slow course back through Sealark Channel. If *Juneau's* keel had indeed been severed, Swenson feared that she might literally fall apart at any moment or as a result of any rough handling. Adding considerably to everyone's concerns were several large-caliber near misses—presumably 14-inch rounds fired by *Hiei* or *Kirishima*—that arrived in the minutes it took *Juneau* to lurch from range.

In her brief encounter with *Yudachi*, her only target of the action, *Juneau* fired all of about thirty 5-inch and a few 1.1-inch and 20mm rounds.

卍

From *Yudachi* 's perspective, the American antiaircraft cruiser shuddered to a painful, wounded halt and fell rapidly behind. Commander Kiikawa breathed an immense sigh of relief and ordered his engine rooms to get on all the speed they could muster. The course remained dead ahead, parallel with and in the same direction as the American center and vanguard elements. So intent was Commander Kiikawa upon escape that he totally missed seeing *Helena*, which was still silent and dark in the wake of Admiral Callaghan's cease-fire order. At length *Yudachi* overtook another large American cruiser Commander Kiikawa could see. Without further ado, the excitable Kiikawa reined himself in and coolly coached his torpedomen to exploit what appeared to be a perfect setup on an unsuspecting victim to port. (Apparently, *Yudachi* had again crossed the American track.) At the shortest possible range, *Yudachi* fired all eight of her torpedo reloads at what must have been *Portland*. Then she ran from the scene. None of the torpedoes fired by *Yudachi* struck *Portland*, which had been hit minutes earlier, probably by a torpedo fired by *Inazuma* or *Ikazuchi*.

28

Of all the U.S. warships in action that night, *Monssen* was the one with the longest and closest association with the Marine-manned Lunga Perimeter. On August 7, the day Guadalcanal was invaded by 1st Marine Division, *Monssen* had supported Marines with direct fire from her 5-inch guns, often right over the heads of the attacking troops. On August 24, she had helped keep Japanese dive-bombers from destroying carrier *Enterprise* at the Eastern Solomons Battle. And over the tense weeks of September and October, she had participated in the earliest direct gunfire missions supporting Marine attacks along Guadalcanal's northern shore. Other ships in action that night had undertaken similar missions, but none other had done them all or for so long.

Monssen was in the throes of a somewhat ambivalent command situation. Her senior and long-time captain had just been detached without relief and her exec, LCdr Charlie McCombs, had not been officially fleeted up to full command. Rather, McCombs was named "acting" captain by virtue of his relative youth and inexperience. A thirty-three-year-old 1930 Annapolis graduate, he was as old as and had held commissioned rank for as long as most of the destroyer execs and was indeed the youngest officer in command of any of the

U.S. warships in action that night. Withal, his long service aboard *Monssen* had provided him with more battle experience than most of his more senior colleagues. And, in the end, his "acting" status was moot; Charlie McCombs commanded *Monssen*, period.

卍

By the time their ship's turn finally came, *Monssen*'s crew was more than ready to become directly involved in the fight. That it took so long was both a matter of position—*Monssen* was next to last in the American column—and the result of an inoperable FD gunnery radar; the radar set's transformer had burned out during the air action in the afternoon and no spare was available. Indeed, other than *Cushing*'s initial warning that *Yudachi* was passing ahead of the column at 0142, *Monssen* had no clues from any source about where the Japanese were, or how far away, until the first flashes of gunfire erupted at 0150 an estimated 10,000 yards ahead of *Monssen*'s port bow.

From his place on the main deck aft, Lt(jg) George Hamm, *Monssen*'s after repair officer, clearly saw *Akatsuki*'s searchlight go on at 0150, then enjoyed a ringside seat as the battle erupted between numerous ships ahead. Fires and explosions broke out far ahead as *Monssen* sailed silently toward the central melee, and streams of heavy- and medium-caliber tracer flowed back and forth between distant ships surrealistically lighted by muzzle flashes and detonations. After eight minutes of heavy action ahead, most of the tracer was shut off; the only light to be seen was from several burning warships. As the blanket of quiet and dark descended, Hamm dared to hope that the action had ended altogether.

As soon as it became obvious that there was action ahead, Lieutenant Commander McCombs ordered all ten of *Monssen*'s torpedo tubes trained out to starboard. They were to be fired at the discretion of the torpedo officer, Ens Robert Lassen, at "any good enemy target to starboard," most particularly a cruiser or battleship, "if any should be sighted."

Soon, all eyes were peering across the starboard beam, where Ensign Lassen claimed he spotted a large target. A 20mm gunner with keener eyesight than most claimed to see the distinct and distinctive silhouette of a Japanese battleship from his perch among the forward antiaircraft guns. Between him and Ensign Lassen, *Monssen*'s position was estimated to be 4,000 yards off the battleship's port bow. At about 0157, immediately upon completing the fix, Ensign Lassen ordered all five torpedoes from the after quintuple mount to be fired in a standard spread. Run time to the target was estimated at about three minutes. The after mount was swung out and the torpedoes were fired so precipitously that no one warned the after repair party, on the main deck just beneath the mount. The repairmen were showered with tailings of burning black powder. The after engine room crew also learned that the ship was in action by a plume of burning black smoke that found its way into the air intakes.

Just as the last of the after torpedo tubes had been fired, Japanese starshells from an undetermined source began lighting *Monssen* from well to port. Two minutes later, Lieutenant Commander McCombs saw *Barton*, the next ship ahead, precipitously slow down directly in *Monssen*'s path. After a momentary hesitation to determine the cause of the friendly destroyer's strange behavior, McCombs ordered his helmsman to pull out to starboard and pass *Barton*. It was coming up 0200 when *Monssen*'s bows drew even with *Barton* and a topside lookout saw one of *Amatsukaze*'s inbound torpedoes pass beneath the after control station from starboard to port. Everyone braced as the shouted warning passed all along and through the ship, but nothing happened. Two more torpedoes were spotted coming right at *Monssen*'s bows. Charlie McCombs ordered the rudder to be put over hard right while he rang up flank speed on the port engine and stopped the starboard engine. *Monssen*'s bows swung clear of the projected point of impact and both torpedoes passed ahead with only about 15 yards to spare. Seconds later, the first torpedo struck *Barton*, followed in four seconds by the other.

S1 Gene Oliver, *Monssen*'s Mount-3 sight setter, did not hear the torpedoes strike *Barton*, and was not immediately aware of the huge explosion that instantly engulfed her. Intent upon potential targets to starboard, Oliver heard nothing he considered out of the ordinary until someone else in the mount yelped, "Look at the S.O.B. go up." Oliver turned and looked over his left shoulder, through the open mount doors, just in time to catch the full fury of the expanding ball of incandescent light. He was sure the fireball rose at least 300 feet and as high as 500 feet—an estimate shared by many other observers, including LCdr Charlie McCombs, on *Monssen*'s bridge.

卍

It had been about three minutes since the after torpedoes had been expended in *Hiei*'s direction. Sure enough, at about the moment the torpedoes were scheduled to connect, many topside observers who had just turned away from the painful flash of light that marked *Barton*'s demise saw what they believed to be two torpedo hits on the battleship. (Strangely, every U.S. ship that fired torpedoes at *Hiei* claimed two hits.)

As soon as the hits from the first torpedo salvo were observed, lookouts shouted directions to a second target 4,000 yards out and broad on the starboard beam. Size estimates ranged between cruiser and destroyer; it was certainly the latter, probably *Inazuma* or *Ikazuchi*. As Japanese starshells maintained continuous lighting well to port, the forward torpedo mount was brought to bear and *Monssen*'s five remaining torpedoes were fired singly in another standard spread. As the last of the torpedoes was discharged, the continuous illumination to port petered out. At that juncture, *Monssen*'s four 5-inch guns opened fire for the first time that night. However, before the radarless gun director could get a firm optical fix on the near target, the guns were abruptly shifted to a new target that was observed firing point blank into a U.S. ship about 6,000 yards ahead. Over the next thirty to forty-five seconds, *Monssen*'s four 5-inch mounts fired salvo after salvo at the distant target, and lookouts reported many hits. As soon as the target stopped firing at the friendly warship ahead, *Monssen* lost her fix on the muzzle flashes and was obliged to cease firing also.

Lieutenant Commander McCombs ordered course shifted from due north to 40 degrees, roughly to the northeast. As the helmsman swung the wheel in compliance, McCombs saw what he took to be a Japanese destroyer heading past him on a southwesterly course. The Japanese ship—*Inazuma* or *Ikazuchi*—appeared to be barely underway only 500 to 1,000 yards to starboard. Immediately, all five of *Monssen*'s starboard 20mm guns opened fire on their own and quickly brought streams of tracer to bear on the

Japanese warship's upper works. Only a beat behind the 20mm guns, Mount-4 went to local control, trained out on the Japanese ship, and fired six rounds at what was considered point-blank range. The Japanese ship passed like a wraith, taking the 20mm and 5-inch hits but never returning the fire or deviating from her course.

From his position beneath the after torpedo mount, Lt(jg) George Hamm, the after repair officer, was suddenly overcome by a sharp sinking sensation in the pit of his stomach. It was, he knew, a sense of doom. He was sure he saw or sensed Japanese ships to port and starboard, and he was sure that it was only a matter of time before they reached optimal positions and opened fire. Burdened with a bad case of nothing to do—nothing to keep his mind occupied unless or until there was damage to repair—Hamm's thoughts turned to mortality. The image of his mother's face appeared before him, as if she had just opened a telegram that began, "The Secretary of the Navy regrets to inform you . . ."

卐

Thus far, except for *Amatsukaze*'s passing torpedoes, no one had fired at *Monssen*. No sooner had this happy thought registered on the bridge watch than starshells from a fresh source off the port quarter began bursting overhead and slightly ahead. Lieutenant Commander McCombs was certain that the starshells were being fired by a friendly ship, so he ordered his signalmen to flash the emergency recognition lights. In all likelihood, the ship firing the starshells was one of the trio of destroyers that had finished their brutal bombardment of *Laffey* a minute or two earlier—*Asagumo*, *Murasame*, and *Samidare*.

The instant *Monssen* flashed her recognition lights, she was bathed in the stark beams of two searchlights directed from an estimated 2,500 yards off her starboard beam. Instantly, the starboard 20mm gunners took matters into their own hands again and converged the fire of their five guns at the two light sources. Before hits could be registered, however, *Monssen* took the first hostile hit of her life through the gun shield fronting Mount-1. The entire gun crew was instantly killed.

The impact of the round on Mount-1 had not even registered

on LCdr Charlie McCombs when a lookout shouted news of two torpedoes approaching close to the starboard bow. McCombs applied hard right rudder and attempted to reuse his engine trick for evading the fish, but by then another incoming 5-inch round—one of a veritable shower—had severed the steam line in the forward fire room and another had ruptured the throttle manifold in the after engine room. In addition to cooking many firemen, watertenders, and machinist's mates in high-pressure steam, the hits rendered *Monssen* instantly powerless. As if this was not enough, several of the after lookouts saw two more torpedoes surging in toward their part of the ship. Luckily, the first two torpedoes passed ahead of the slowing bows and the other two torpedoes passed beneath the fantail without detonating. But that was the extent of *Monssen*'s good fortune.

As rounds from the three remaining 5-inch guns struck and doused the aftermost of the two searchlights, *Monssen* was herself struck by several shells from port and many shells from starboard—an indication that she was the target of three Japanese ships. One early hit in the chief petty officers' quarters spread flames into the Mount-2 handling room, and that obliged Mount-2 to cease firing while everyone in the handling room stopped passing ammunition and started battling the life-threatening flames.

Next, the bridge and gun director were struck simultaneously and the after mounts were forced to go to local control. At that point, the hits became too numerous to catalog in the order in which they were received.

卍

MM1 M. F. Wilson and F1 Joe Hughes were the only two men—of nine—who emerged alive from the after engine room. All the others perished when a high-pressure steam line was severed by a shell that actually passed completely through the ship without detonating. As it was, the two survivors hit the top of the ladder together and barely untangled themselves to escape just as the live steam hit the soles of their shoes. From there, they passed through the crew's head and out to the main deck via the Mount-3 handling room. They had not quite closed the hatch to the main deck when a huge tongue of flame erupted from the handling room. The crew's head had taken a direct hit and hot slivers of steel passing through the bulkhead had set off vulnerable ready powder bags on their way up to the mount.

Mount-3 and Mount-4 were firing as fast as they could at a shadowy target to starboard—and apparently getting good hits—when the incoming round exploding in the after crew's head killed all hands in the Mount-3 handling room and destroyed the mount's training mechanism. S1 Gene Oliver, the Mount-3 sight setter, was so intent upon his work that he did not feel the hit that took out the handling room crew and was surprised when someone told him the gun was inoperable.

Mount-4 got only a few more rounds away before its train control was lost. By then, most of *Monssen's* eight 20mm guns had ceased firing due to direct damage or fatalities among the gunners.

卍

Lt(jg) George Hamm, the after repair officer, smelled hot steam vapors from the after engine room, felt the ship slow, and saw and heard numerous Japanese rounds striking the ship. He told his talker to contact the bridge, but when the sailor told him that the circuit was dead, Hamm decided to make his way forward to speak with the captain. He started forward up the starboard side of the main deck and found a spot where live steam was hissing through a crack in the deck. Engineers—those who were alive—were streaming out of nearby hatches. Hamm got as far as the hatch from the forward engine room before he was stopped by billows of live superheated steam. As he focused on the scene in search of holes he might fall through, he saw that the bulkheads all around the hatch had been riddled by shrapnel and that many sailors had been cut down on the exposed deck, including the engine-room chief, who was lying dead, half in and half out of the open hatchway. Lieutenant (jg) Hamm decided to return to the after repair station.

卍

One of numerous hits on the bridge disrupted steering control, but it was quickly picked up by the after emergency steering-control station, which was located aft of the deckhouse. When that station was also disrupted by a hit, an electrician's mate tried to get the primary system going again, but the damaged control board shorted out and an electrical fire erupted. Next, steering control was briefly regained by means of a hand pump in the after steering-control station. When this position was rendered inoperable by yet more hits, the rudder was jammed 26 degrees to starboard.

SM3 Jack Pease, the signalman on duty at the after control station, was struck by numerous matchhead-size fragments from the shell that took out after control. One piece of shrapnel broke the skin over his left chest and cut its way along his rib cage before exiting his back; two others grazed his right arm. Pease did not even feel these wounds, but he knew it when he was blown out of his shoes a few seconds later by a round detonating within the after deckhouse, right beneath his feet. The blast broke Pease's right foot and left blood blisters the size of silver dollars on the soles of both feet. So aggrieved did Pease become over this treatment that he hobbled straight to the nearest 20mm gun and asked the gunner, a boot-camp classmate, for a chance to hit back at the Japanese. The gunner complied and helped Pease get strapped in. Thus, the injured signalman was transformed from hunted to hunter.

Hits in officers' country set the captain's and exec's cabins aflame, and these fires spread to the 20mm clipping room, where ammunition soon began cooking off. The jury-rigged power system between the after fire room and forward engine room was short-lived; the hull around both compartments was holed in numerous places and the system was blown apart. At that point, the numerous fires throughout the ship went out of control, for power to the water mains was instantly lost. Even the portable handy-billy pump, which could be used to power one fire hose, was rendered inoperable by shrapnel damage. Both battle dressing stations took direct hits, thus leaving the countless wounded without hope of receiving adequate medical treatment.

卍

Lt(jg) George Hamm returned to the after repair station following his aborted trip to the bridge. The moment he arrived, a round struck the after torpedo mount, right over his head, and

244

killed its two-man crew. Thoroughly demoralized by the un-counted scenes of terror he had seen, Hamm decided to chuck the whole thing and crawl behind the reel on which the ship's manila lines were stowed. He was already squeezing behind the cover when he found that a sailor who had beaten him there had been cut nearly in half by an incoming round. With that, Hamm pulled him-self together and decided to try to reach the bridge by going up the port side of the main deck.

As far as Lieutenant (jg) Hamm could see in front of him, the entire area around the base of *Monssen*'s superstructure was burning fiercely. Nevertheless, Hamm decided to see how far he could get. He was halfway to his goal when a 5-inch round struck the deck a few feet in front of him. The concussion staggered him to his knees and momentarily blinded him. Hamm felt tiny stings all over his body and wondered if he had been riddled by shrapnel. It eventu-ally dawned on him that he had been blasted by sand that had been glued to the deck to aid footing in rough seas. He also took several tiny slivers of shrapnel in the face.

Certain he had picked the wrong side of the ship, Hamm crossed over to starboard, right into the glare of a searchlight thrown out by a ship off *Monssen*'s starboard bow. Shells were fall-ing in from that direction, too. As Hamm pondered the wisdom of retreating to the fantail, a signalman he knew worked on the bridge was just climbing down to the main deck. Hamm collared the man, who was bleeding copiously from a head wound, and asked him what he knew. The signalman, who was thoroughly panicked, said that all hands on the bridge were dead. But he was not quite right.

卐

As *Monssen* acquired punishing blows from port and starboard, LCdr Charlie McCombs took the only reasonable action open to him: as had LCdr Butch Parker in starkly similar circumstances, McCombs ordered the survivors among his crew to abandon the drifting and powerless ship. Unfortunately, the order got only as far as McCombs's voice reached; communications throughout the ship were out and the bridge was completely isolated by numerous raging fires.

When Charlie McCombs ordered the burning bridge cleared, the helmsman unwittingly stepped off the severed end of a ladder, and the navigator, right behind him, did the same. As the two fell in a heap on the torpedo deck, one of the incoming shells killed the navigator, who had landed on top of the helmsman, but it did not hurt the helmsman.

The torpedo officer, Ens Robert Lassen, and the assistant navigator, Ens R. W. Kittredge, decided to try their luck by leaping from the rail of the fire-engulfed bridge directly to the water. Lassen, who had sustained a shrapnel wound in the leg, hit the water without difficulty, but Kittredge struck the boat davit on the way down and suffered what would be mortal internal injuries.

The two ensigns were followed seconds later by LCdr Charlie McCombs. Before taking the plunge, however, McCombs made certain that at least he was the last man to leave the bridge, if not the ship. Though personally unscathed, McCombs had already stared death down amidst the numerous hits around the bridge. One close call had seen the collar ripped from his life jacket by passing shrapnel, and the chain holding his dog tags had been neatly clipped a half inch left of center at the back of his neck. Thoroughly unfazed, McCombs coolly removed his binoculars and set them down carefully in a safe place—so they would not be broken. Then he kicked off his shoes, climbed up on the bridge rail, and jumped away from the flames. As soon as McCombs surfaced, he jettisoned his heavy .45-caliber pistol and began pulling away from *Monssen*'s expected last big bang on what would turn out to be two shoulders broken on impact with the water.

❀

Certain that he was the most senior officer left alive aboard the ship—he was—Lt(jg) George Hamm was thinking about what to do next when the plotting-room officer, Lt(jg) F. A. Lewis, approached him on the main deck from the direction of the burning bridge. Lewis, who had been wounded in the leg, told Hamm that he thought it was about time to get off the ship. Hamm agreed.

As Lewis hobbled aft to help get the life rafts over the side, Hamm heard someone call his name. It took a minute to locate the source of the call, a fireman who was lying beneath Mount-3. The fireman asked Hamm to help him, and Hamm reflexively moved to comply, but his charitable instincts were arrested when he saw that both of the sailor's legs were badly mangled. Uncertain about what he could do to help the grievously wounded man, Lieutenant (jg) Hamm told the fireman he would find a corpsman and send him to help. Then he left.

Monssen survivors eventually catalogued the following damage:

Hit at the starboard water line 3 feet aft of the stem;

Hit in starboard bow above the after line at Mount-1;

Hit from port at the top of the Mount-1 gun shield, killing the entire gun crew;

Two hits from port in the chief petty officers' quarters, starting a fire in the Mount-2 handling room;

Hit from port through the Mount-2 gun shield, which did not detonate;

Hit from port in the after mess hall;

At least five hits from port and starboard on the bridge and gun director;

Hit in the vicinity of the captain's cabin, starting huge fires in the vicinity of the main radio room that spread rapidly to engulf the entire superstructure;

Ten or more hits from starboard above the water line in the vicinity of the plotting room and the galley;

Hit in the wardroom, killing the ship's doctor and a corpsman;

Hit from port near the laundry;

Four hits from port in the forward fire room;

Two hits from starboard and one hit from port in the forward engine room;

Hit from port in the after uptake;

Two hits from starboard in the after engine room, one of which ruptured the throttle manifold;

Numerous uncounted hits from port and starboard in the vicinity of the after stack and torpedo tubes;

Hit in the crew's head, killing many personnel manning the after casualty dressing station and the entire crew of the Mount-3 upper handling room;

Hit from port in the after depth charge projector;

Hit on the after deckhouse just aft of the searchlight.

⇄

Though Mount-3's training mechanism was inoperable and no rounds were available from the handling room, the entire gun crew had clung determinedly to its post. However, as soon as news of the abandon-ship order reached Mount-3 by word of mouth, the gun captain, BM2 Clyde Storey, delivered the order all the others had been awaiting: "Let's get the fuck outa here!" Immediately, one of the men exiting the left side of the mount was struck by shrapnel and killed as he tried to climb down to the main deck.

SM3 Jack Pease, the wounded after-control signalman, continued to fire a borrowed 20mm gun until all the 20mm gunners on the after deckhouse were obliged to give ground amid the bursting incoming rounds, which were detonating ready ammunition stored in lockers nearby. While most of the gunners climbed down to the main deck, Pease stayed to help another sailor cut loose a life raft lashed to the upper level. The two got the raft overboard without difficulty and then climbed down to the main deck. Just as Pease was about to jump into the water beside his life raft, he decided to inflate his life belt. He squeezed the device that would release carbon dioxide from a cylinder in the belt. There was the expected steady hiss of pressurized gas, but the belt stayed flaccid. A quick inspection revealed for the first time that the belt—and Pease—had been riddled by tiny slivers of shrapnel. Pease, whose right foot was broken, hopped straight to the nearest bulkhead and tore off a life ring. Then he left the ship.

As one large group of survivors gathered on the fantail, S1 Bert Doughty, a 20mm gunner who had escaped a portside gun with his life, was cutting away a balsa raft when there was a terrific *bang* and the lights went out. A hit on the adjacent after depth-charge projector spread shrapnel through the midst of the group around Doughty, who was not only knocked out but also suffered sixteen shrapnel wounds in the jaw and nose, and sustained a ruptured ear drum and fractured skull. Many of the sailors around him were killed and nearly all the rest were wounded.

₹

As Lt(jg) George Hamm made his way to the fantail to see how the evacuation was going, the Japanese searchlights went out and the shelling abruptly ceased. Apparently, *Monssen* was not worth the price of any more 5-inch rounds; she had been reduced to scrap. After seeing to the evacuation on the port side of the fantail, Hamm went over to starboard just in time to see a darkened Japanese destroyer steam by at a high rate of speed. As the destroyer moved abreast of *Monssen*, a pair of 20mm guns topside opened fire and began bouncing rounds off the Japanese warship's side. By then, Hamm only wished that the overeager gunners would stop shooting before they got the Japanese mad enough to return the fire. But the Japanese ship took no notice of *Monssen*'s last defiant cry.

When the Japanese ship had sailed from sight, Lieutenant (jg) Hamm began trying to decide if he wanted to leave the ship. For all the damage and fires, the vessel seemed to be on an even keel and seaworthy. At the least, Hamm wanted to search the main deck for survivors, as well as to get a corpsman to help the wounded fireman he had left beneath Mount-3. Before Hamm could reach a decision, he was joined by Ens John Little, the machine-gun officer who, as it turned out, was the only other officer still aboard *Monssen* who had not been killed or wounded. Before Hamm could speak, Little, who had overseen the last fusillade of 20mm fire and who was still full of fight, asked the seemingly aged twenty-three-year old Hamm if he would like to get the last of the wounded off the starboard fantail in the last of the life rafts. Hamm shrugged and said he would. By the time Hamm reached the starboard abandon-ship station, sailors were towing the last raft away from the ship, though it was only half full and despite the fact that more wounded men were still on deck. Before Hamm could act, however, several sailors jumped into the water and talked the men in the raft into letting them tow it back to the ship.

After leaving his battle station, S1 Gene Oliver, the Mount-3 sight setter, had made his way through the carnage to one of the nests of life rafts stowed on the fantail. There, he used his belt knife to cut the rafts loose, then helped lower them into the water. Next, he went to work helping wounded shipmates don life jackets and lowering them over the side into the rafts. When there was no one left to help, Oliver briefly thought of staying aboard; he did not want to leave, but he did not want to stay, either. Finally, he climbed overboard and joined a group of about a dozen other swimmers gathered around a life raft. Among the wounded in the raft was an engine-room survivor whose feet had been amputated by a flying deck plate. Despite the company, Oliver had never felt so alone in his life.

Lt(jg) George Hamm still did not want to leave the ship. He found three men he knew—BM2 Clyde Storey, F1 Joe Hughes, and GM2 Leo Spurgeon—and asked them if they wanted to try to save the ship. The three agreed, and they helped Hamm break out a fire hose, but there was no water pressure. By then, *Monssen* had acquired a slight list to starboard, but the fires did not seem to be gaining or spreading. Withal, Hamm was afraid to go below decks to fight fires or search for survivors. At length, the petty officers made noises about wanting to leave the ship, but Hamm talked them into staying. As the four men stood on the otherwise abandoned fantail and discussed their options, a burning ship over a mile away— *Laffey*—suddenly blew up. With that pointed example firmly in mind, Lieutenant (jg) Hamm handed BM2 Storey a morphine syrette and sent him to find the fireman he had earlier left beneath Mount-3. Hamm made a quick trip up the port side for a last look and returned to the fantail. By then, Storey, Spurgeon, and Hughes had gone over the side.

By now willing to leave the ship, George Hamm decided to take a 5-inch powder can to help him stay afloat in his flimsy inflatable life belt. He found one of the shiny aluminum cans readily enough, but not a lid, so he ducked into the Mount-3 handling room, at main-deck level, to find one. The confined compartment was filled with the noxious fumes of burned gunpowder, there were several little electrical fires smoldering away, and the five-man handling-room crew was on the deck, killed by the heat and smoke of a flash fire that had spread from the adjacent crew's head. Hamm gingerly picked up a lid for his powder can and retreated to the main deck. He put the lid on the can as he paced to the aftermost portion of the main deck, climbed down onto the starboard propeller guard, removed his pants and shoes, inflated his life belt, and jumped off into the mild Pacific water. Lt(jg) George Hamm was thus the last able-bodied survivor to leave *Monssen*, but at least eight living men, all unconscious or seriously wounded, remained on the burning ship.

29

The last ship in the American column was *Fletcher*, a thoroughly modern fleet destroyer, the namesake of her class. Earlier in the year, the newly commissioned ship had been in just the right place at just the right time and had thus been outfitted with a new SG surface-search radar set.

Unlike the other captains whose warships were fitted out with SG radar, *Fletcher's* Cdr William Cole took a serious and direct view of the modern contrivance's unrealized potential. While *Fletcher's* small contingent of enlisted radarmen had been trained to the peak of knowledge—as had the SG operators on other ships—Commander Cole felt that they required the best, most knowledgeable supervision. It was then a doctrinal imperative that destroyer execs languish as supervisors of their ships' after control stations during General Quarters. Early on, Cole had decided that he wanted *Fletcher's* primary effort devoted to offense, and not salvage. Therefore, he placed his exec, LCdr Joe Wylie, in the charthouse, overseeing the SG radar display. Cole's theory was that Wylie's long years of training and superb knowledge could be best used interpreting the gleanings of the PPI display. While no one quite knew what was the best information that could be obtained from the SG's

PPI display, Cole was convinced that Wylie would be better able to ask the right questions than the operator would be able to offer the right information. A lot depended upon Wylie's insight and intuition. At the least, however, if Wylie was unable to add a thing to the state of the art, *Fletcher* would be no worse off than the SG-equipped ships ahead of her in the column.

The PPI scope was mounted in the charthouse, just abaft the bridge. From there, Lieutenant Commander Wylie spoke with Commander Cole, who was on the bridge, through a louvered light screen in a porthole. Wylie wore a split sound-powered phone connected to the torpedo officer on the bridge and the gunnery officer in the gun director over the bridge. He also had a hand-held microphone patched into the TBS radio. (Thus, Wylie was himself the U.S. Navy's first Combat Information Center, or CIC, a concept and term that had yet to be invented.)

Fletcher's radar picked up and began tracking the oncoming Japanese at about 0130. Sometime later, by means of matching the FD fire-direction radar to a bearing provided by the longer-ranged SG radar, *Fletcher*'s guns were trained on what must have been *Akatsuki*. However, at 0150, as the Japanese destroyer illuminated the American column and thereby drew down the wrath of many of the American ships ahead, *Fletcher* shifted her guns to a target farther to starboard. The new target, which was described by lookouts as a large three-stack cruiser, might have been *Nagara*. The lookouts spotted several "minor" hits on the target—no one could say whose shells they were—and then reported that the cruiser rolled over and sank, which of course did not occur. *Fletcher* dutifully checked fire at 0158 in compliance with Admiral Callaghan's unfortunate order.

At 0159, observers on *Fletcher*'s bridge clearly saw *Monssen*, just ahead, skid out of line to avoid *Barton*. Then, within a minute, as *Fletcher*'s 5-inch guns resumed firing on a new target far in the distance, *Barton* blew up. That was Commander Cole's signal to take matters into his own hands. Until then, *Fletcher* was part of the team, dutifully following the ships ahead and blindly obeying the commands of the unseen commander. However, as soon as Commander Cole realized that Japanese ships were in among the American rearguard destroyers, his obligation to Admiral Callaghan ended; he would fight with *Fletcher* his own way, which is to say with boundless aggression.

Before the huge incandescent brightness of *Barton's* death faded, Cole ordered the engine rooms to "make all speed possible." MM1 Millard Blevins, the forward engine-room throttleman—who controlled the port engine—had anticipated just such an order from a prebattle discussion with the captain and therefore had arranged matters with the chief watertender controlling the boilers tied to Blevins's throttle. As soon as the order to go to full speed was rung up on the engine-room repeater, Blevins yelled "Whirlaway!"—the name of the fastest racehorse in America—and opened the throttle all the way. The code word galvanized the throttleman in the after engine room to do the same. As the full load of steam, which was showing at 615 pounds on the pressure gauge, hit the turbines, *Fletcher* reared back and took off just like a racehorse leaving the starting gate, immediately pulling out to port to avoid hitting *Monssen*.

S1 Don Dahlke, the 20mm gunner who had shot down a Betty bomber in the late afternoon, was startled to see another destroyer suddenly appear out of the gloom to starboard. Dahlke had no sense of having come up alongside *Monssen;* he and many others thought the other ship was Japanese. Yet more startling was the sudden spray of automatic weapons fire that burst from the after part of the phantom ship directly into the water around her own stern. In fact, the 20mm gunners atop *Monssen's* after deckhouse were trying to hit a passing torpedo. As *Fletcher* passed *Monssen,* her own lookouts saw four torpedoes heading right for the starboard side of the ship. As everyone aboard *Fletcher* who could see sucked in his breath, one torpedo broached and porpoised about 50 yards ahead of *Fletcher,* two disappeared beneath the ship and reemerged to port, and the last passed astern on the surface. At the same time, a number of medium-caliber shells splashed harmlessly into the water on both sides of the American rearguard destroyer.

As *Fletcher* followed through on her leftward swing to avoid *Barton* survivors, her five 5-inch guns were brought to bear on a new target formerly ahead but by now well to starboard. As

Fletcher was about to open fire on the new target, her guns were masked by one of the rear American cruisers, probably *Portland*. This obliged *Fletcher*'s main battery director to lay the destroyer's still-traversing guns upon yet another of the ample targets scattered across the entire area ahead and to starboard. As the quick-firing guns shifted rapidly from one target to the next, and the next, lookouts reported seeing fires break out on several ships nearby, but Commander Cole was unwilling to take credit for any of the hits.

By then, *Fletcher* was surging more or less westward at least at her top-rated speed of 36 knots, and probably several knots faster. All the guns were on full automatic, firing randomly at targets from the starboard beam to the starboard quarter as they appeared on the FD radar scope in the gun director. In this manner, *Fletcher* threaded her way between numerous unidentified warships along the southern and western boundaries of the diffusing central melee. After some minutes of running above her top-rated speed, *Fletcher* passed completely beyond the battle. However, as soon as the ship was in the clear, Commander Cole ordered the rudder put over hard to port. At the same time, while the starboard engine continued at full speed ahead, MM1 Millard Blevins, the port throttleman, shifted the port propeller to full speed astern. This maneuver pivoted the ship sharply to the left and brought her about virtually within her own length. Then she was off again at top speed, this time cutting back through the edge of the diffusing central melee toward the south-southeast. Once again, all her 5-inch guns fired on full automatic at numerous targets as she retraced her earlier route for 6,000 yards.

In the midst of the exciting run, a dead calm Cdr William Cole spoke through the louvered porthole between the bridge and the charthouse to let his exec, LCdr Joe Wylie, know how things were going. "You ought to see this. It looks like the Fourth of July out here." A few moments later, the captain added, "Aren't you glad our wives don't know where we are tonight?"

30

When *San Francisco* emerged from her crippling battle in the central melee several minutes after 0200, her crew was fighting numerous local topside fires and degrees of damage far too complex to fully perceive, much less set aright. Of major importance was the fact that her steering control was in the hands of one machinist's mate manning the sweltering, solitary, blind tertiary steering-control compartment just forward of the rudder and that one of her two engine rooms had been shut down by an oil fire on one of her massive generators. Thus, for all practical purposes, LCdr Bruce McCandless, *San Francisco's* third-senior surviving officer, was conning a weakened cripple through a maze of ships, each one fighting for her life and each one prone to shoot first and ask questions later. Though most of the U.S. flagship's 5-inch, 1.1-inch, and 20mm antiaircraft guns had been destroyed or disabled during her first confrontation with a Japanese battleship, her three triple 8-inch turrets all appeared to be in fighting trim.

Unbeknownst to anyone aboard *San Francisco*, a destroyer looking for a fight was attracted to "two black objects [that] were observed on the port bow at approximately 3,000 yards." The author of that report, destroyer *O'Bannon's* exec, LCdr Donald Mac-

Donald, could see black smoke pouring from one of the "objects."
When the target was pointed out to *O'Bannon*'s skipper, Cdr Edwin
Wilkinson, he ordered Lieutenant Commander MacDonald to conn
the ship toward a confrontation while her two quintuple torpedo
mounts were trained out. Fortunately, lookouts and officers agreed
that the smoking target, which was heading away to the northeast,
looked like a transport departing the area. It was decided to forego
the easy shot at an unworthy target and *O'Bannon* headed south to
scout Cape Esperance for fully loaded transports that might be arriving or at anchor unloading.

卍

As LCdr Bruce McCandless, LCdr Rocky Schonland, and the
other surviving senior officers tried to pull the shattered ship back
together, many junior officers and scores of ratings were fighting
fires and rescuing their injured and burned shipmates.

During one quick peek from the doorway of the well-deck gear
locker in which he and others had sought refuge, S1 Willie Boyce
heard that a fire had erupted in the starboard midships aircraft hangar. Like most members of the aviation division, Boyce had no specific battle station, hence his presence in the gear locker. However,
the burning hangar was a call to action; it definitely was Boyce's
responsibility.

The hangar was a 10-foot-wide, 25-foot-high steel silo topped
with a catapult from which one of the cruiser's three scout planes
could be launched. An exact duplicate was mounted on the port
side of the well deck. The three SOC scout-observation planes
were extremely flammable and had been flown off *San Francisco*
during the day by three of the six pilots assigned to the ship.
Though the flammable aircraft were gone and the hangar doors
were securely dogged, no amount of cleaning and stowing could
completely rid the well-vented hangars and the area around them of
volatile fluids and materials. The fire was a clear danger to the well-
being of the entire ship.

At the time S1 Boyce started toward the hangar fire, BM1
Reinhardt Keppler was wrested from his self-imposed task of rescuing wounded gunners from the wreckage of the shell-ravaged after
1.1-inch antiaircraft mounts. As Keppler was leaving the fantail for

the well deck, he dropped down to ask GM3 George Murphy to join him. Murphy had been knocked senseless when his mount had been hit, but he felt he was fully recovered and so decided to join Keppler. As Murphy rose from the deck for the first time since coming to, he instantly fell flat on his face; his left leg had been shattered, but he hadn't felt a thing. BM1 Keppler left Murphy to others and made a beeline for the burning hangar.

San Francisco's damage-control parties had prepared well. Before the fight had even begun, fire hoses had been played out and fire mains had been turned on. Thus, as S1 Willie Boyce raced across the well deck to the burning hangar, he had to hop and dance across the writhing, pressurized hoses until he reached the nozzle of the one nearest the fire. When Boyce got to the hangar, he found that another sailor had undogged the hatch to reveal a blazing inferno within. As bad as the flames was the amount of light the fire projected through the open hatchway and around the edges of a large roll-up door. Boyce reached down for the nozzle at his feet and turned it on as he lifted it to hip level. An intense spray of seawater engulfed the cavernous silo. BM1 Reinhardt Keppler joined the small group of volunteer fire fighters that was forming around the intensely burning hangar and immediately took charge.

Later, searchers probing the fire-blackened interior deduced that one of *Hiei*'s 6-inch rounds had detonated inside the hangar and started a smoldering fire in a pile of kapok life jackets that took many minutes to get out of control. Beneath the burned jackets the searchers found the charred remains of a junior pilot who had sought refuge in the hangar.

៵

Several minutes into the lull following *San Francisco*'s direct encounter with *Hiei*, her gunnery officer, LCdr Willie Wilbourne, and many others spotted searchlights and muzzle flashes well to the north. As a precaution, Wilbourne ordered all the remaining guns that could bear to train out on the bright lights. One of the 5-inch guns, which was operating on local control, fired on its own, and that apparently drew searchlight-directed fire from an unseen ship much closer in.

At about 0210, Cdr Tameichi Hara's *Amatsukaze* was heading northwest into the lull on the far side of the diffused central melee. As his ship sailed on into the void, Commander Hara found it increasingly strange to be in so complete a lull so soon after destroying *Barton* and ruining the cohesion of the American rearguard, and he found it worrisome that he had received no messages from *Hiei* since the battle had begun about twenty minutes earlier. Soon, however, a lookout spotted a large burning ship dead ahead that was immediately identified as *Hiei*. Commander Hara decided to join on the flagship to offer what protection he could.

Hara's watch showed 0213 when he spotted a huge red flash to the west. Certainly another ship had met her fate, though Hara had no idea whose it might be. Before he could give the matter more of his time, a dark shape loomed out of the blackness right in front of *Amatsukaze*. Instantly, *Amatsukaze*'s officer-steersman swung the helm hard to the right while everyone else watched in helpless terror as the dark thing approached and slowly swung away to starboard. A collision with *San Francisco*—which no one aboard *San Francisco* seems to have noticed—was averted by the narrowest of margins.

Like *O'Bannon*'s Lieutenant Commander MacDonald, Commander Hara was certain that the smoke-shrouded American flagship was an unarmed noncombatant. Unlike MacDonald, who thought he saw a transport, Hara thought he saw an unarmed Japanese submarine tender, and he paused for some moments to try to figure out what she was doing there without his having been briefed. Then Hara realized that it was probably an American ship of some sort, so he ordered his gunners and torpedomen to stand by for action to port.

Within seconds, the torpedo and gunnery officers bellowed the news that they were ready to commence firing. Hara was on the verge of letting them do so, but he wavered; he was still not convinced the target was American. Finally, *Amatsukaze*'s captain ordered the searchlight trained out and flicked on. Certain he saw an American cruiser squirming in the blinding light, Hara finally ordered, "Commence firing!" All three of *Amatsukaze*'s dual 5-inch mounts lashed out in unison. Commander Hara and his gunnery officer both exclaimed at the immediacy of the numerous hits they observed.

※

After fighting the stubborn aircraft-hangar fire until he could no longer bear the intense smoke, S1 Willie Boyce turned his hose over to another volunteer and returned to the well-deck gear locker to watch the ongoing action. However, he had remained there for only a minute before being forced by a strong compulsion to head aft. Boyce was just coming abreast the port hangar when *Amatsukaze* opened fire. The very first of the 5-inch rounds to strike *San Francisco* from starboard caromed off the teak deck no more than 2 feet in front of Boyce's shoes and skittered over the port gunwale. (A thoroughly disbelieving Boyce found a charred groove in the deck at just the right spot when he returned in the morning to check his own credibility.)

Though S1 Boyce and others were eventually overcome by the smoke billowing from the aircraft hangar, BM1 Reinhardt Keppler refused relief. Even when many others ducked to evade *Amatsukaze*'s 5-inch rounds, which fell all around the lighted area, Keppler barely flinched. He never gave in, even when he was struck and seriously wounded by shell fragments. Rather, he directed the fire fighters even as he single-handedly dragged wounded shipmates to protected spots outside the limelight.

※

No more than thirty seconds after *Amatsukaze* fired her last four torpedoes, Commander Hara was certain that he heard all of the fish strike home against *San Francisco*'s hull. Perhaps, but even Hara realized that the fish had not detonated because he—Japan's leading torpedo tactician—had impetuously ordered them fired while his ship was still within the 500-yard arming range of the warhead safety devices.

As Hara stood clutching the bridge railing in total frustration with himself—as *San Francisco*'s second ragged salvo passed right over his ship without scoring any hits—*Amatsukaze* was suddenly buffeted by numerous near misses falling all around her. Commander Hara at first thought that *San Francisco*'s pathetic return fire—just two ragged 8-inch salvos thus far—had somehow been revitalized, but the warrant officer manning the rangefinder, also on the bridge, called out that a large ship was approaching from about 70 degrees to port. Hara turned his head and immediately saw distant muzzle flashes. "Douse the searchlight," he screamed, "Stop shelling! Spread the smoke screen!" But all the precautions were late.

The encounter between *Amatsukaze* and the barely perceived intruder to port had begun long minutes earlier, when *Helena* had passed circling *Portland* and joined up far behind *San Francisco* just as the flagship was running out of the far side of the central melee. No one aboard *San Francisco* had any idea that *Helena* was there.

As *Helena* raced to catch up with the burning and fleeing flagship, her forward main-battery directors located a receding target 8,800 yards to starboard. Less than a half minute later, the as yet unidentified target opened fire on *San Francisco*. Instantly, *Helena* turned slightly to bring all five of her triple 6-inch turrets to bear on *San Francisco*'s assailant. When all the guns were locked on, the light cruiser's main-battery assistant, Lt Warren Boles, ordered them to commence firing on continuous automatic.

Two near misses, one right behind the other, nearly threw Commander Hara from his feet; only his tight grip upon the bridge railing saved him from a painful spill upon the steel deck. Nevertheless, the shock wave was so strong that Hara was briefly stunned out of his mind. When he came to several seconds later, he reflexively felt all over his aching body in search of wounds or broken bones. Satisfied that he was intact, Hara glanced around the bridge to see about the others. The officer-steersman was on his feet, hard at work bringing the ship to a new heading, but the warrant officer manning the rangefinder was sprawled in a bloody heap across the rangefinder. Shocked, Hara ran over to shake him, but he soon saw that a large steel sliver had pierced the man's skull. With that, Hara realized that a round must have penetrated the bridge by way of the gun director, directly overhead. Hara leaned over the voice tube that normally connected him with his gunnery officer, but his frantic calls for attention went unanswered. As Hara reeled from this blow, he learned that another 6-inch round had penetrated the radio room, immediately beneath the bridge, and had killed everyone there.

At that point, *Amatsukaze*'s shocked captain realized that the ship had not yet recovered from its sharp turn to starboard. He shouted an order at the officer-steersman, telling him to recover and come left. The young officer said that he was already trying to but that the rudder was not responding.

Commander Hara was determined to go down fighting; if he could not run from *Helena*'s unremitting bombardment, he could certainly return her fire. This he ordered, but nothing happened. "Damn it," he bellowed, "let's return fire!" Instantly, a gunner with a wounded and bleeding shoulder appeared and told Hara that the gun mounts were frozen in place by a total hydraulic-system failure. An engine-room orderly arrived as this news was sinking in; he told Hara that the rudder was also jammed because the hydraulic system had been destroyed.

Hara asked the gunner what had happened to the gunnery officer, who had not answered his call over the voice tube. The sailor replied that his officer had been blown over the side by a direct hit on the gun director, the same hit that had killed the warrant range-finder operator. The engine-room orderly was asked if the engine was still intact and if there were any fuel fires. For the first time in many minutes, the news was promising; at the time the orderly had left the engine room for the bridge, the engine was unscathed and no fuel tanks had been breached.

By then, *Amatsukaze* had sailed in a complete circle. As *Helena*'s deadly shells continued to rain out of the night sky, Hara sent the wounded gunner to the medical station and ordered the officer-steersman to go to the engine room to check on the orderly's report. By then, damage parties had broken out fire hoses and were hard at work quelling the most serious blazes. But *Amatsukaze* was helpless; all her torpedoes had been fired and none of her guns could be trained on *Helena*. The end seemed near.

❧

Helena held *Amatsukaze* under her fifteen main-battery guns for about ninety seconds. As *Helena* diverged from *Amatsukaze*'s course and the range opened to 9,400 yards, *San Francisco* suddenly crossed into *Helena*'s line of fire from starboard, obliging Capt Gib Hoover to order, "Cease fire!" In all, *Helena* had fired 125 6-inch rounds at *Amatsukaze*, and her lookouts had seen many of them strike home. Indeed, Commander Hara's prized command had clearly been reduced to a floating debris pile.

As *Amatsukaze* completed her second erratic circle, *Helena*'s two starboard dual 5-inch mounts opened fire on an unidentified ship that simultaneously opened fire on *Helena*. The 5-inchers expended a total of forty rounds and apparently drew blood before they, too, were obliged to cease firing when *San Francisco* crossed into their line of fire.

❧

San Francisco was in full retreat. As soon as *Helena* opened fire on *Amatsukaze*, LCdr Bruce McCandless ordered his gunnery officer, LCdr Willie Wilbourne, to cease firing and maintain a wary vigil; all McCandless wanted to do was clear the area with the least amount of new damage. Unfortunately, *San Francisco* was heading in the wrong direction if all McCandless wanted to do was reach safe waters. While recoiling from *Hiei*'s overwhelming main-battery drubbing, the path of least resistance had been to the north and west, between Cape Esperance and Savo. Like *Amatsukaze*, the Japanese ships that were by then retiring were all headed to the north and east, between Savo and Florida. It was thus inevitable that they and *San Francisco* should brush against each other in the dark. As luck would have it, the next Japanese ship to be encountered was *Kirishima*, which had already gotten a few rounds into the punch-drunk American flagship during an earlier exchange.

From a distance of about 2,500 yards—point-blank—the virtually unscathed Japanese behemoth fired a main-battery salvo down *San Francisco*'s starboard side; all of the 14-inch rounds fell close aboard the target, but not one of them struck home. As *San Francisco* returned the fire, one of *Kirishima*'s bombardment rounds struck the cruiser's deck right outside Turret-2. The main force of the fallout was directed outboard, but Turret-2 was laid low by a bizarre series of events beginning when a splash of hot shell fragments obliged the gunnery officer to order the Turret-2 powder magazine flooded.

Just as the powder passers from the flooded powder magazine were settling in with the forward repair party, another 14-inch round penetrated their compartment and bored into Turret-2's armored barbette, just outside the gun chamber. BM2 Vance Carter, the Turret-2 trainer, was sitting inside the turret exactly opposite the point of impact. Though Carter was lifted right out of his seat, neither he nor anyone in the gun chamber was injured. However, fallout from the soft-skinned antipersonnel round sprayed back from the impenetrable barbette and cut through the thirty-five repairmen and ammunition handlers like a blast from a shotgun—which is about what it had become. Nearly all were killed or crippled by grievous wounds, and *San Francisco*'s ability to fight fires forward was severely diminished by the loss of so many trained and knowledgeable specialists.

A single sliver of shrapnel from the 14-inch hit on Turret-2's barbette lodged in the electrical panel that controlled the flooding of Turret-2's lower handling room and both magazines. Thus, though one powder magazine was being flooded voluntarily, suddenly all of the ammunition and powder meant for Turret-2 was placed beyond reach. The turret's three 8-inch guns and entire crew had not been affected by the two direct hits, but the turret was nevertheless out of action.

From his position in the armored conning tower, LCdr Bruce McCandless immediately perceived the loss of Turret-2, though he had no idea why its guns stopped firing nor the extent of human losses. At precisely the moment the forward repair party was gutted, McCandless had to decide how best to avoid a collision with *Kirishima*, so he swung wide to the left, as much to avoid the battleship as to help Turret-3 bear more easily on the huge target.

The exchange was as if between two staggering, punch-drunk fighters: Though the two warships continued to scrap, neither could lay an effective salvo upon the other, even at such close range. After the two successful early hits forward, *Kirishima*'s rounds continued to fall short, though shrapnel from additional near misses caused some damage. And the best *San Francisco*'s guns could score was one grazing 8-inch hit on *Kirishima*'s upper works. Though LCdr Bruce McCandless was certain that the battleship would soon get her main guns on target, the Japanese captain astonished him by turning away at high speed.

As the duel with *Kirishima* had intensified, Lt(jg) Jack Bennett had clung to the exposed fantail and continued to administer first aid to wounded antiaircraft gunners beside the twisted wreckage of the two after 1.1-inch mounts. As *Kirishima* departed, Turret-3, which had lost its director in the afternoon air attack and had thus been firing on local control, swung directly aft, right over Bennett's head just as the officer bent over a screaming gunner. Before Bennett realized what the main guns were doing, all three of them were depressed as far as they would go before firing *San Francisco*'s last salvo of the battle. The round from the center gun scorched a trail only a foot above Jack Bennett's back; had he not bent over, he would have been decapitated by the round.

The last Japanese rounds fired at *San Francisco* were a pair of 14-inchers hurled straight back over *Kirishima*'s fantail by her after turret. Both missed.

卍

Even as *Helena*'s main and secondary batteries were firing at *Amatsukaze* and the unidentified target to starboard, the aggressively managed light cruiser's automatic-weapons control officer observed, in the dim light of passing tracer, a large ship with four stacks sailing by about 3,000 yards to starboard and on a diverging course. There being no other way to interdict the target—*Kirishima*—the starboard 40mm guns were trained out and fired. From his place in the masthead antiaircraft director, the control officer clearly saw at least two-thirds of the 40mm tracer striking in and around the battleship's bridge area. *Kirishima* answered the 40mm fire with one two-gun 14-inch salvo. One of the thin-skinned bombardment rounds struck *Helena*'s Turret-4 directly on the face plate. Though the hit only jarred the gunners in the turret, shrapnel struck numerous fittings all around the turret, including a 20mm gun shield. Miraculously, no one was as much as scratched by the fallout from the huge antipersonnel round. Immediately, the 40mm guns were ordered to cease firing; no matter how many hits they scored, the damage could not be worth raising the battleship's full ire.

As the 40mm guns were being taken in hand, *San Francisco* cleared out from in front of *Helena's* 5-inch and 6-inch guns, so the light cruiser's main battery retrained on yet another unidentified target, this one 16,400 yards out and receding. Rapid continuous fire was maintained for about one minute, until another unidentified ship passed into the line of fire and obliged the 6-inchers to shut down. Withal, a number of the sixty 6-inch rounds that were fired appeared to have struck the target, which seemed to be engulfed in flames. At the same time the 6-inch guns were firing, the starboard 5-inch mounts were trained on a destroyer-size target about 5,000 yards forward of *Helena's* starboard beam. Once again, hits and fires were observed, but only about forty rounds were fired before turning *San Francisco* once again shifted into the line of fire. With that, *Helena* secured her guns and turned to follow *San Francisco* away from the fight.

⇌

LCdr Bruce McCandless's wide left turn to avoid a collision with *Kirishima* found *San Francisco* finally headed in the "right" direction, back toward Guadalcanal on a southerly course.

At about the time *San Francisco* turned south and east, *Fletcher* reached the end of her breathtaking passage across the edge of the central battle arena. As she came into the clear again, Cdr William Cole ordered his torpedomen to prepare to fire all ten of their fish at a large target that lookouts had seen emerging from the mass of ships a short distant to the north. The target, which was northeast of *Fletcher*, was moving at an estimated 20 knots on a southeasterly course—away from the fight, which appeared to be drifting away to the northwest.

As the destroyer's two quintuple torpedo mounts were being trained out, *Fletcher's* gunnery radar was rematched with the SG-radar fix and all guns were thus brought to bear on the large new target. At that moment, the firing around the moving central melee suddenly slackened and became sporadic. *Fletcher* raced ahead at 35 knots in the hope of turning ahead of the target's bows. After a five-minute chase, *Fletcher* came up on her firing position. The quarry had slowed to about 17 knots but had not appreciably altered course. At that time, she was firing what appeared to be white large-caliber tracer rounds at an unseen target of her own far to the north. This fire was being returned, albeit in the form of what appeared to be large- or medium-caliber shells, apparently from as many as two or three sources.

When the target was 7,300 yards to starboard, almost due east of *Fletcher*, Commander Cole ordered his ship to slow to 15 knots. As *Fletcher* settled down to her new speed, the captain ordered his torpedo officer to fire all five fish in the forward torpedo mount.

⌖

Seconds after the fish were away, TM3 Ev Hurley, the mount trainer, looked down at his assistant, whose head was bowed in fervent prayer.

"It's a good thing you're doing that," Hurley tartly observed, "I didn't have the time."

"Don't worry," the unabashed assistant shot back, "I did enough for both of us."

⌖

About thirty seconds later, at Commander Cole's order, all five torpedoes in *Fletcher*'s after mount were expended. For the next six minutes, *Fletcher* hovered in the area while Cole and his torpedo officer counted off the minutes and seconds until the fish were due to strike the target. At about the right moment, a series of increasingly large explosions appeared to rock the distant warship. *Fletcher*'s exec, LCdr Joe Wylie, had left the SG radar to watch from the bridge; he saw two dull flashes and, several seconds later, heard the thump of at least two large detonations. These were followed by a continuous blaze along the top of the apparently stricken warship. Since the action had all but ended, *Fletcher* remained on the scene, observing the burning ship as it limped off to the southeast. After about twenty minutes, a huge explosion appeared to engulf the target. Many of *Fletcher*'s topside officers and crewmen swore the burning ship blew up and completely disintegrated.

If *Fletcher*'s initial visual fix was correct, the target could not have been *Hiei*, as was thought at the time; the Japanese flagship was by then limping away more or less toward the north. *Kirishima* did loop back within the moving central melee after her initial run away from the battle, but the second Japanese battleship did not completely traverse the battle arena so could not have emerged from it through any southern quadrant. Moreover, *Kirishima* was not struck by any torpedoes that night and, indeed, suffered no damage of remotely the magnitude observed by *Fletcher*'s topside crew. That leaves just one possibility: *San Francisco*. She traversed these waters on a southerly and southeasterly heading, she was the victim of numerous visible topside fires throughout her retirement, and she did exchange gunfire with distant warships. If the target was indeed *San Francisco*, then *Fletcher*'s ten torpedoes certainly missed altogether, for the flagship was not struck even by dud torpedoes. Indeed, no one aboard *San Francisco* was aware that any torpedoes had passed her.

Immediately after *Fletcher*'s topside crew saw whatever it saw, Commander Cole ordered his ship to retire east through Sealark Channel. Alone among the thirteen American warships under Dan Callaghan, aggressively handled *Fletcher* was unscathed; she had sustained no casualties and had not suffered as much as a scratch in her paintwork.

卐

As soon as *San Francisco* was in the clear—relatively safe from Japanese *and* American ships—LCdr Bruce McCandless cut her speed to 10 knots to reduce flooding through numerous holes at the water line and to allow repair parties to plug the more accessible holes with mattresses and other such materials. Though fires were neither as numerous nor as intense as they had been, they still posed a serious threat—as much from the beacons they provided as from the damage they caused.

S1 Willie Boyce joined up with an aviation ordnanceman, a character who sported a magnificent Van Dyke beard and incessantly sang "The Wabash Cannonball." However, before the two could do more than nod a mutual greeting, they witnessed a bright flash atop the ruined after control tower; apparently a smoldering fire had fully erupted in the flag bag in the signal station atop Battle-2. The two climbed the ladder at the edge of the port hangar to the boat deck and then shinnied up a pair of broken ladders to the signal platform. By the time they reached the flag bag—a light metal bin filled with flags and pennants made of light cotton bunting—a large and widely visible fire was raging. As they approached the fire, both men realized that they had no means for fighting it. Without a word, however, they both vaulted right into the metal container and proceeded to stomp the flames. Willie Boyce's only thought was that the fire—and the embers he and the other sailor were kicking into the night sky—would pinpoint the ship for enemy gunners. It never occurred to Boyce that that was the least of *San Francisco's* problems; other, larger fires were out of control all along her main deck. After several smoky minutes, Boyce and the other man overcame the flag-bag fire and climbed back to the main deck.

As hundreds of designated or volunteer fire fighters and repairmen fought the ongoing blazes and tried to restore vital services, BM1 Reinhardt Keppler succored the wounded. Though severely injured himself by *Amatsukaze* while directing the fight against the aircraft-hangar fire, Keppler hid his bleeding wounds and intense pain from the corpsmen he was assisting. Finally, however, as *San Francisco* neared safe waters, Keppler collapsed from shock and the loss of massive amounts of blood. Though heroic efforts were expended in trying to control the shock, he died without regaining consciousness.

Simply sailing *San Francisco* was a chore. At least 500 tons of water was sloshing freely through the forward magazines and numerous other below-decks spaces, thereby reducing stability and making her sluggish at the helm. More to the point, the rapid approach of Guadalcanal's darkened shoreline was a daunting challenge for a communicator who considered his navigational expertise to be wanting—particularly since he had no charts, compass, radar, or fathometer. Fearful of running aground—or being obliged to run aground—on a Japanese-held beach near Cape Esperance, Mc-

Candless opted to follow the dimly perceived shoreline toward the Marine-held Lunga Perimeter, about 40 miles to the east.

Helena was about 800 yards behind *San Francisco*. Her skipper, Capt Gib Hoover, was content to follow the flagship at a leisurely pace while maintaining a vigilant watch to ward off any last-ditch attacks upon the cripple. The vigilance paid off, for a large dark form suddenly loomed up from *Helena's* inshore side, from off her starboard bow. The intruder appeared to be cockeyed; her keel seemed to be broken and her forward and after halves seemed to be slightly askew. Before the light cruiser's deadly guns could be brought to bear, however, the intruder was identified as an *Atlanta*-class antiaircraft cruiser—*Juneau*. Still, the danger of collision was imminent, so Captain Hoover ordered "Right full rudder," and *Helena* turned into the encroaching ship.

From his place beside the captain, Ens Bin Cochran tensed for the collision, certain that the friendly ship was about to crunch into *Helena's* starboard quarter. But the other ship turned away at the last possible interval and the two light cruisers passed from danger. Unbelievably, *Juneau's* topside watch never saw *Helena;* the last-instant turn had been coincidental.

As *Juneau* blindly struggled back into the blackness, Capt Gib Hoover turned the conn over to his senior officer of the deck and went straight back to his cabin for a nap. So far as Hoover was concerned, the battle was over.

31

Destroyer *Sterett* had started out as the third ship in the American column. She had first opened fire to starboard, at *Nagara*, and had clearly hit the Japanese light cruiser with a full salvo of starshells followed by fresh salvos of 5-inch armor-piercing rounds. In return, *Sterett* had suffered several minor hits which, among other things, had parted one of her steering cables and sent her briefly out of control. The brief struggle to regain her position in the U.S. column had seen *Sterett* overtaken and passed by *O'Bannon*, following which she had been hit and near-missed by 14-inch and 6-inch rounds put out by *Hiei*. In return, *Sterett* had fired her four port torpedoes at *Hiei*—she claimed two positive hits—following which she had hit the Japanese battleship with eight full four-gun main-battery salvos, had barely avoided being struck by *Hiei*'s towering bows, and had inadvertently run into a lull astern of the Japanese flagship.

After crisscrossing the void on the side of the then-spreading central melee for as long as fifteen minutes, *Sterett*'s fully alert topside lookouts located a choice target, a large, well-silhouetted destroyer about 1,000 yards off the starboard bow. *Sterett* was off the other ship's starboard quarter.

As he stared at the other ship from his open hatchway in the shell-damaged main-battery director, Lt Cal Calhoun, *Sterett*'s gunnery officer, counted three gun mounts, one forward and two aft, a typical Japanese layout. All the Japanese guns were at rest and centered, and the ship was darkened. She showed no recognition lights, indicating that *Sterett*'s approach had not yet been detected. The American director trainer, who had been wounded in the neck during the earlier exchange with *Hiei*, coolly locked his sights onto the target, thus bringing all of *Sterett*'s guns to bear. At the same time, the rangefinder operator, who was still bleeding from a severe wound in the back, confirmed Lieutenant Calhoun's range estimate and noted that the target was indeed Japanese.

As soon as the range and firing angle—and identity—had been confirmed, *Sterett*'s skipper, Cdr Jesse Coward, ordered the starboard torpedo mount to fire two of its four fish while all four 5-inch mounts opened fire with armor-piercing ammunition. The setup was perfect.

The guns opened fire as ordered, two full-battery salvos five seconds apart. All four rounds from the first salvo were observed as they detonated in the Japanese destroyer's superstructure, and all four rounds from the second salvo were observed striking in and around the two after gun mounts. Immediately, one and possibly two large explosions rocked the target. Lt Cal Calhoun watched in awe as a huge billow of orange flame rose hundreds of feet into the night sky, carrying a great volume of debris with it. The spectacle was so awesome that Calhoun called down to his handling rooms and magazines to invite the ammunition handlers to stick their heads into the night air to observe the fruits of their labors. All the guns instantly ceased firing as the gunnery officer's once-in-a-lifetime offer was accepted with stunning alacrity.

As Lieutenant Calhoun lifted his eyes to follow the towering flames, other observers aboard *Sterett* distinctly saw the Japanese warship briefly rise out of the water with numerous fires raging forward as well as aft. Then Lieutenant Calhoun and other observers, including Commander Coward, saw the target sink as soon as it settled back into the water.

Though Lieutenant Calhoun and other observers identified the target as a *Fubuki*-class destroyer, no ships of that class were anywhere near Guadalcanal this night. However, if the next-to-aftmost mount was in fact a single mount, the ship was one of four *Shiratsuyu*-class destroyers. If so, she was certainly *Yudachi*, which was indeed assaulted by an unseen American ship at about that time. Moreover, *Yudachi* had no targets in sight when she was struck from out of the night; all her guns were at rest and centered. Though *Yudachi* did not immediately sink, she was so badly damaged and her demise seemed so imminent that Cdr Kiyoshi Kiikawa and all his surviving officers and crewmen immediately took to the water.

࿗

Whatever really occurred on *Sterett's* starboard side, the American destroyer was herself amply silhouetted for at least one Japanese warship to port. Approximately seven minutes after *Sterett* first located the target to starboard, she was herself struck by a hail of rounds from off her own port beam. Separate hits were simultaneously scored in the port side of the Mount-3 handling room, the Mount-3 shelter, and the Mount-4 handling room. Several ready-service powder tanks were ignited in each of the stricken handling rooms, where flash fires caused numerous casualties, including six deaths in the Mount-4 handling room and two deaths in the Mount-3 handling room. The powder fires and at least one shrapnel-induced electrical fire put both of *Sterett's* after mounts out of action. At least one additional hit in the vicinity of the Mount-3 handling room caused additional extensive damage and at least five additional deaths, and two more hits in or near the Mount-4 handling room did about the same. In addition to the numerous deaths, these hits left numerous wounded sailors in their wakes. At least four crewmen jumped overboard to extinguish their flaming clothing.

No sooner had the after mounts gone down than a second salvo struck the ship in the quarterdeck area. One round pierced the inboard corner of the starboard torpedo mount, killing two men, seriously injuring two men, and putting the mount out of action. At least two other rounds detonated in the 20mm clipping room, where six ammunition handlers were wounded and one was killed. One of these rounds also caused as yet unperceived damage to the forward fire room's cooling system.

After the action, an unexploded 3.9-inch round was recovered from one of *Sterett's* flooded handling rooms. This, combined with the awesome rate of fire, the clustered salvos, and the fact that at least three rounds had point-contact—antiaircraft—detonators points to just one possible culprit. The only Japanese ship firing 3.9-inch rounds that night was *Teruzuki*, the Japanese antiaircraft destroyer.

⇄

Damage-control measures were swift and certain. Ens Perry Hall, the assistant damage-control officer, had been overseeing several 20mm guns early in the action, but he happened to be on his way to the after repair station when the ship was engaged by *Teruzuki*. After being thrown to the deck and slightly injured, Hall regained his feet and went directly forward to the wardroom to confer with the first lieutenant, who told Hall to "take charge of the after repair party." Hall rushed back outside to do just that.

By the time Ensign Hall made his way aft, both after magazines had been flooded to prevent the fires in handling rooms from reaching the main ammunition and powder supplies. At the same time, all electrical power to the after mounts was shut off to prevent the possible ignition of volatile debris by errant electrical charges. The deck around the damaged area was slick with congealing blood and strewn with potatoes that had been blown out of the nearby spud locker. The precarious footing was made more precarious as the ship veered through a series of sharp turns to evade yet more hits.

The immediate danger was from ammunition and powder that was bound to begin cooking off in the two fire-ravaged after handling rooms. Quick action was needed, and two of *Sterett's* chiefs showed all others the way. As CTM L. G. Keenum grabbed the nearest fire hose, CGM H. J. Hodge darted into the burning Mount-3 handling room and picked up an armload of hot powder tanks. Then, as Keenum trained the hose right at him, Hodge dashed back out onto the main deck and threw the powder straight over the side. Without pausing, Hodge ran right back into the handling room for another load.

Within seconds, as more fire hoses and carbon-dioxide fire extinguishers were broken out and trained on both burning handling rooms, gunners, surviving ammunition handlers, and damage controlmen followed Chief Hodge's example and passed up hot 5-inch rounds and ready-service powder tanks. As the emerging volatiles were carried straight to the port and starboard rails to be dumped over the side, some men could hear sizzling noises within the hot powder cans. Indeed, two of the powder cans exploded in midair before they hit the water.

All of the dead, wounded, and burned crewmen who could be reached through the intense heat and flames were rapidly carried straight to either of two emergency medical stations, one in the crew's mess hall, aft, and the other in the wardroom, forward. Meantime, the fire in the Mount-3 handling room was quickly brought under control, but the larger conflagration in the Mount-4 handling room persisted.

The fire in the Mount-4 handling room was being fed not only by the volatiles stored there but by bedding and clothing that had been blown into it from an adjacent berthing compartment. It appeared that several unrecoverable bodies were also roasting in the burning compartment; certainly the stench of burning blood and flesh made the fire-fighting job all but unbearable.

As the fire fighters fought the blaze, Ens Perry Hall supervised the temporary repair of several holes in the ship's side. Most of the holes were small, matching the diameter of *Teruzuki*'s 3.9-inch shells, but one was about 15 inches in diameter. All were stuffed with mattresses carried aft from an untouched berthing compartment, and the mattresses were braced by shoring materials stored throughout the ship for just such emergencies.

In the meantime, Cdr Jesse Coward's attention had become firmly focused upon guiding his ship to safety. That was no easy task, for the fires aft clearly illuminated not only the ship herself but her colors as well; any passing ship could easily have seen *Sterett* and identified her as an American ship, a mixed blessing in those roiling waters.

Sterett was not totally defenseless, but only her two forward guns remained in service. Of her eight torpedoes, six had been expended and two remained in the unserviceable shell-damaged starboard mount. Given these factors, ongoing problems with the fires aft, and a jury-rigged steering system, Commander Coward decided that it was high time for *Sterett* to retire from the area. She initially headed northeast toward Tulagi, but she soon angled away to the southeast, toward Guadalcanal. Finally, sometime around 0230, *Sterett* came due east and sailed straight up Lengo Channel at high speed.

Many minutes after leaving the battle area, *Sterett* was beset by a single torpedo that crossed her bows from port to starboard. At that point speed was increased to 23 knots to clear the area once and for all. However, as quickly as Commander Coward wanted to exit the area, he was obliged to slow to as little as 10 knots from time to time to reduce the stiff breeze that was feeding the still-raging fire in the Mount-4 handling room.

Though *Sterett* was in the clear, running close inshore along Guadalcanal's northern coast, old problems persisted and new problems arose. Eventually, the two boilers in the forward fire room had to be shut down because of a series of cooling-system failures caused by shrapnel damage. Sometime after 0300, the jury-rigged steering gear failed and the rudder jammed hard right. Within minutes, Commander Coward had to back both engines at full power to keep *Sterett* from running aground on a Guadalcanal beach. From then on, Commander Coward had to steer by means of every trick in the book—and invent a few besides—to avoid having to stop to fix the damaged steering cables.

In time, all the fires were quelled and all the holes in *Sterett*'s hull were stuffed with lumber-braced mattresses. As the last fire fighter made his report, Ens Perry Hall lifted his head from the smoky innards of the Mount-4 handling room and breathed air so fresh that he nearly passed out. The last of the charred corpses had been removed and pumps were already at work emptying the compartments Hall and his repair parties had expended so much energy to fill. So far as Perry Hall could influence the matter, *Sterett* was out of danger. With that thought, Hall realized that he was also out of danger. Immediately, the stark terror he had been bottling up during the past hour overtook him in the form of a violent retching heave all the way from the pit of his stomach to the blood-stained deck. Weak but relieved, Hall staggered forward to make his report to the captain.

In all, 28 members of *Sterett*'s 250-man crew had been killed, 13 had been seriously wounded, 5 had been lightly wounded, and 4 had jumped overboard to save themselves from burning to death. For the time being, as far as anyone aboard the wounded *Sterett* could determine, they were the only American sailors who had survived the night's terrible ordeal at sea.

32

Aaron Ward emerged from the disaster of *Amatsukaze*'s and *Yudachi*'s attacks upon the American column's rear without damage and in the clear. Thoroughly at a loss about which of the many potential targets all around were in fact hostile ships, Cdr Orville Gregor opted to take the middle course and ordered his ship to come to a due northerly heading, which was the last course ordered by the now-dead task force commander. Speed was reduced to a cautious 18 knots, which was the last speed requirement anyone could recall receiving from Admiral Callaghan.

Within the minute, at about 0203, *Aaron Ward*'s lookouts spotted a large target off her port beam; the other ship was pointed almost due east and heading away from *Aaron Ward*. It is likely that the large target was *Kirishima*. At Commander Gregor's order, the destroyer's quintuple torpedo mount was trained to port and the torpedo officer, Lt(jg) John Drew, aligned the sights of the port director on the target's receding stern. Just as Drew was about to fire, lookouts cautioned that a burning vessel was sailing out of the gloom about 1,500 yards to port and that it would soon be crossing the projected track of *Aaron Ward*'s torpedoes. The interloper was almost immediately identified as *San Francisco*. Since there was no way to fire the fish at *Kirishima* without endangering the burning flagship, Commander Gregor reluctantly spared his large target. Unable to reach a position from which she could retrain her torpedo tubes on the receding battleship, *Aaron Ward* sailed into the void.

Aaron Ward skirted the diffusing central melee for about four minutes, withholding fire because her officers and lookouts were quite unable to separate friend from foe. Suddenly, Lt(jg) John Drew, the torpedo officer, was certain he saw another darkened ship approaching from his ship's blind side. Without consulting the captain—there was no time—Drew bellowed, "Left full rudder. Come left! Come left!" Instantly, the captain's talker repeated Drew's words right in Commander Gregor's ear. The startled skipper looked out to port, saw the approaching ship and yelled, "Left full rudder!" No sooner said than the helmsman spun the steering wheel all the way to the left.

Even as the terror and excitement on the bridge were still building, lookouts identified the intruder as *Sterett*, which never wavered from her course but backed at full throttle to avoid collision. A collision was narrowly avoided; *Sterett* passed *Aaron Ward* close aboard.

Coincidentally, *Aaron Ward* 's turn and recovery brought her within range of *Yudachi*, which was then about 10 degrees off *Aaron Ward* 's starboard bow. Having just recovered from a close encounter with a friendly ship, Commander Gregor was not initially willing to concede that the new target was indeed hostile. Fortunately, *Yudachi* was showing her recognition lights—green over white over red. Commander Gregor called out to CSM Fred Hart and asked, "Is that one of our ships, Hart?"

"No, Captain."

"Are you sure?"

"Yes, Captain, I'm sure."

Gregor looked at the forward mounts, below the bridge, and saw that the gunnery officer, Lt(jg) Bill LeBaron, had already brought them to bear on the Japanese destroyer.

"Open fire!"

Commander Gregor's inadvertent timing was exquisite. Apparently, *Sterett* and *Aaron Ward* opened fire at precisely the same moment, each without observing the other. As *Sterett's* topside crew was watching the huge fireball emerge from *Yudachi* 's after gun mounts, observers aboard *Aaron Ward* saw exactly the same thing. Many members of *Aaron Ward* 's crew even thought they saw *Yudachi* sink, though she did not do so.

⇄

As *Sterett's* crew turned its attention to fighting off *Teruzuki*, on her starboard side, *Aaron Ward* 's crew shifted its attention to a searchlight that suddenly probed the darkness from off her port bow. The two U.S. destroyers thus separated without anyone having realized that they had teamed up to mortally damage *Yudachi*.

For the two minutes after *Yudachi* 's virtual destruction, *Aaron Ward* shifted around to evade the probing searchlight as well as to bring all her guns to bear. The ship with the searchlight, which remained about 3,000 yards out, moved in such a way as to confound Commander Gregor's best efforts to attain an optimal firing position. Moreover, the blinding beam prevented anyone aboard *Aaron Ward* from identifying the other ship. At last, the main-battery director locked all four of *Aaron Ward* 's guns on the searchlight—all that could be seen of the target, which was probably *Kirishima*—and the fire controlman closed the firing key. The first of four salvos was sent out just as the other ship opened fire on *Aaron Ward*.

⇄

PhM1 Frenchy Prevost was manning the after emergency battle-dressing station, on the port side directly beneath Mount-3. As soon as the duel commenced, Prevost heard someone inside the mount scream, "Get those fucking shells up here faster!" Before the corpsman could react with so much as a knowing smile, he heard the sickening crunch of a direct hit on the nearby emergency radio room. In one fluid motion, Doc Prevost slung his first-aid pouch over his shoulder and reached out to open the door into the stricken compartment. As the door opened, the blackout switch instantaneously killed the bright light inside. Prevost shut the door, which turned the light back on, and immediately saw that one radioman was clearly dead and the other, RM1 George Haines, had been ripped open from shoulder to hip.

Doc Prevost, who was already functioning at a super-pitched state, plucked a morphine syrette from a pouch on his belt and plunged the needle into the wounded man's buttocks. Then he withdrew gauze pads from his first-aid pouch, fought to control the bleeding, laved the wound with distilled water, sprinkled in a dose of sulfa powder, taped the edge of the torn flesh together, and stitched the gaping wound shut. After applying sterile gauze pads and a roll bandage, Prevost lifted RM1 Haines to his feet and helped him stagger forward along the main deck.

⚛

While Doc Prevost was still working on RM1 Haines in the emergency radio shack, and after *Aaron Ward* had fired only four four-gun salvos, a 6-inch round tore through the fire-control radar dish atop the main-battery director. In the next instant, as the rangefinder operator moved to assume control of the guns by means of his optical rangefinder, a 6-inch round burst on the port side of the director shield. The rangefinder operator was mortally wounded by shrapnel, another director crewman was killed, and the optical sight was shattered. The director was no longer able to automatically direct the guns.

At almost the same instant, a 14-inch bombardment round burst in a stateroom directly above the ship's galley, seriously wounding CCstd Ivory Benegar. OC1 Marion Green instantly dropped to Benegar's side and said, "Come on, Chief, let's get out of here." Then Green lifted Benegar to his back and started for the hatchway. The two had no sooner risen when yet another 14-inch bombardment shell detonated right in the galley. Chief Benegar was killed by shrapnel and OC1 Green sustained seventy-two separate wounds.

⚛

It took several moments for *Aaron Ward*'s gunners to realize that the director was down and to assume local control. Since the ship was moving, the guns were temporarily pulled from their target and had to be realigned. The exchange continued for several minutes under the loose verbal control of the gunnery officer, Lt(jg) Bill LeBaron, until yet another searchlight probed *Aaron Ward* from about 3,000 yards off her starboard quarter. As Mount-1 and Mount-3 maintained a steady fire at *Kirishima*, LeBaron verbally coached Mount-2 and Mount-4 onto the new target, a destroyer. It took some steadying up, but the two mount trainers soon had a lock on the new target and hits and small fires were immediately observed.

Any hopes Commander Gregor had of firing *Aaron Ward* 's five torpedoes were dashed when an incoming round struck the weather deck above the engine room and torpedo workshop. Among many other forms of damage, fallout from the detonation severed the fire-control cables to the torpedo mount, dented all the tubes, and punctured two of them.

Yet another round scored a direct hit on *Aaron Ward* 's quadruple 1.1-inch antiaircraft mount, located on the after deckhouse just forward of Mount-3. In addition to wrecking the breeches of all four guns, the shrapnel killed or wounded everyone in the mount and ignited several local fires.

֎

Moments after PhM1 Frenchy Prevost left RM1 George Haines stretched out on a bunk in an officer's stateroom, he heard there were many more wounded men aft. As Prevost was passing through the wardroom, where the ship's senior medico, a chief corpsman, was working, someone in the crowd cautioned, "You better stay under cover, Doc. You'll never get anywhere with all that firing going on." As Prevost made his way to the hatchway, pointedly ignoring the advice, someone else called, "Good luck, Doc."

After leaving the relative safety of the wardroom, Doc Prevost made his way straight to the stricken antiaircraft mount. He was halfway up the deckhouse ladder when yet another round detonated nearby. Then someone yelled, "They're all dead up there, Doc," but Prevost had to see for himself. He arrived outside the open mount in a moment of pitch blackness, so he settled to his knees and began groping forward. He found a leg and jerked, but there was no response. Then he found another leg; no response there, either. When he jerked an arm, it came away in his hand. Grimly determined to complete the gruesome task, Prevost jerked yet another leg. In the light of a fresh starshell, Doc Prevost saw a stirring and heard a welcome voice: "Doc? It's me, Griffin." A quick inspection of SM2 Melvin Griffin's mangled leg convinced Doc Prevost that saving the limb was hopeless; all he could hope to do was save the young signalman from bleeding to death. Without hesitating, Doc Prevost administered a large dose of morphine and rigged a tourniquet. Then, in the continuous light of Japanese starshells, he amputated Griffin's leg, right on the bloody steel deck beside the shattered 1.1-inch mount.

꘎

Five minutes after the first target was spotted, both Japanese searchlights went out—or were shot out—and all three combatants immediately ceased firing, each one recoiling to lick her wounds. However, after less than a minute's respite, *Aaron Ward* was brilliantly illuminated by several starshells and a searchlight aimed from off her port quarter. Immediately, numerous 14-inch and 6-inch rounds fired from port began falling into the water all around her. One of the 6-inch rounds ripped through the canvas windscreen at the after end of the bridge, apparently passed between the legs of Lt(jg) John Drew, the torpedo officer, and severed one of the legs supporting the gun director.

Cdr Orville Gregor was certain that *Aaron Ward* had reached the limit of her relative good fortune, that the Japanese ships would soon have a firm lock on his ship. He ordered the engine room to come to flank speed as he pointed his outclassed destroyer dead ahead. With that, Gregor turned to Capt Robert Tobin, the Destroyer Division 12 commander, and said, "Commodore, I'm going to head north for the present." Tobin, who had not interfered with any of Gregor's decisions thus far, nodded his head and answered, "I agree." Though the Japanese ships continued to hurl rounds after *Aaron Ward* for some minutes, they apparently did not follow.

At about 0220, *Aaron Ward*'s lookouts observed one torpedo crossing about 50 feet ahead of the ship's bows, from port to starboard. Five minutes later, as *Aaron Ward* plunged ahead into the clear, the helmsman suddenly told the captain that he had lost steering control. After exhausting all the backup systems, which did not work, Commander Gregor tried steering the ship on her engines. Minutes later, as the stricken vessel proceeded gingerly on an eastward heading toward Lengo Channel, all hands topside realized that the pyrotechnics display near Savo had abated. Burning vessels could be seen right across the after quadrants, but no gunfire was apparent.

Despite the nagging problem with her steering, *Aaron Ward* appeared to be about to reach certain safety when, at about 0240, she lost all power and went dead in the water. The baffling condition was only partially illuminated for the captain and bridge watch when, moments later, the engineer officer called up by means of the voice tube, "Captain, we have trouble in the fire rooms."

LCdr Julian Becton, who had recently been fleeted up from engineer officer to exec, immediately volunteered to go learn what that cryptic and self-evident message might mean. The captain agreed with a nod and Becton went straight below. When he reached the main deck, the exec was told that the distilled feed water used to make steam and run the turbines had somehow escaped—or, as the engineering officer said, "We're out of feed water." Since the chief engineer appeared reticent about explaining how this unlikely event had occurred, Becton ordered the watertenders and firemen to remove the cover of a water tank, which was located in the forward fire room. Without further ado, Becton issued a series of orders that launched an instant effort to form a bucket brigade from the after main deck to the fire room. As most of the black gang and members of the after repair party who could be spared rounded up all the available buckets and formed themselves into a line, the remaining firemen and watertenders frantically worked to loosen all the nuts holding down the cover of the 2,000-gallon water tank.

It would be hours, at least, before *Aaron Ward* would be able to take herself from these quiescent but thoroughly dangerous straits.

PART V

Salvation and Sinkings

33

tlanta was burning and adrift. Following her violent encounters during the first minutes of the melee, she was mercifully bypassed by many ships, both Japanese and American. Slowly, her shocked and badly hurt crew recovered to fight the fires, succor the wounded, and try to restore power to her battered engineering plant.

When the firing finally stopped, BM1 Leighton Spadone, who was crouched behind the splinter shield of the starboard midships 1.1-inch mount, asked his crew if anyone was hurt. A voice from the darkness said, "I'm hit in the neck," and another said, "I'm hit in the leg." By the time all hands had reported, Spadone realized that half had been injured by shrapnel and flying debris. He stood up to retrieve the mount's first-aid bag, but his right leg did not do exactly what he wanted it to do. A quick self-examination revealed that Spadone had acquired but had not felt a through-and-through shrapnel wound above the right knee, another wound in the crotch, and a third in the right ankle.

By the time everyone's wounds had been bound, Spadone had

determined that he was the senior petty officer in the area and that there were no officers present. Despite the darkness that shrouded Spadone's immediate surroundings, he could see that the ship's foremast was down and that there was massive damage all around the superstructure. No one seemed to be out and about, and he located other men only after he had climbed down to the main deck to learn what was going on.

A check of the ship's boats revealed that only one, the starboard lifeboat, was still seaworthy. During the search, Spadone located one officer, but the man was in a state of utter despondency and refused to come away from the bulkhead against which he was leaning.

Out of touch with higher authority and isolated from the main action to port, BM1 Spadone decided that it was up to him to get the ball rolling. His first act was to order the most seriously wounded sailors placed aboard the starboard lifeboat and lowered away from the burning ship. The forward line controlling the descent of the lifeboat briefly got away from the handlers, but the boat was righted before the wounded men were dumped into the water.

As soon as the lifeboat was away, Spadone decided to try to find his younger brother, Phil, a coxswain whose battle station was in the port after 1.1-inch mount. He made his way quickly down the nearly deserted starboard main deck toward the stern and found a member of his division who knew that Phil had been wounded and evacuated to the vicinity of the after gunnery control station. Despite the fact that his injured leg was stiff and that he was bleeding from his wounds, BM1 Spadone climbed up to the after control station to find his brother. There, he was told that Phil had been taken below to the after mess hall, which housed the after emergency medical team.

The after mess hall was a huge compartment, and it was filled with wounded men. A long, hard search was finally rewarded when Leighton Spadone found Phil in the berthing compartment just aft of the mess hall—their own living quarters, in fact. The younger Spadone was in much worse shape than his older brother. Phil was on his back and looked quite relaxed, but that was merely the effect of a large dose of morphine. His speech was slurred, but

Above
Heavy cruiser *Portland* in June 1942. *(Official U.S.N. Photo)*

Below
Portland's torpedo-damaged fantail area. *(Compliments of K. West)*

Lt(jg) George Hamm, destroyer *Monssen*'s first lieutenant. *(Compliments of G. S. Hamm)*

U.S. Navy torpedo is expelled from one of *Monssen*'s quintuple torpedo mounts during a daytime exercise in mid-1942. *(Compliments of G. S. Hamm)*

Capt George Dooley, flight commander of VMSB-131 torpedo bombers. *(Compliments of G. E. Dooley)*

Left, above

Light cruiser *Helena* in late 1940. *(Official U.S.N. Photo)*

Left, below

Destroyer *Aaron Ward* in early 1943. *(Official U.S.N. Photo)*

Lt(jg) Bob Gibson, of *Enterprise*'s Bombing-10. *(Compliments of R. D. Gibson)*

Battleship *Washington* in August 1942. *(Official U.S.N. Photo)*

RAdm Willis Lee. *(Released by the U.S. Navy courtesy of the S. E. Morison Collection)*

VAdm Nobutake Kondo. *(Official U.S.N. Photo)*

Battleship *Kirishima* in 1937. *(Released by the U.S. Navy courtesy of K. Hando)*

Survivors. *(Official U.S.N. Photo)*

Bombing-10 SBD Dauntless dive-bomber, with 500-pound bomb aboard, prepares to attack the burning Japanese transports beached at Doma Cove and Tassafaronga on November 15, 1942. *(Official U.S.N. Photo by Lt(jg) R. D. Gibson)*

Kinugawa Maru, one of the four Japanese transports and cargomen deliberately run aground at Doma Cove and Tassafaronga. *(Official U.S.N. Photo by VAdm J. T. Hayward)*

he did greet his older brother, attempt a smile, and tightly clasp Leighton's hand. Phil was extremely pallid and obviously quite weak. Leighton decided to stay with him.

Later, Leighton learned that Phil had been hit in the lower left leg, lower back, and throughout the pelvic region. Most of Phil's outer left leg adjacent to the calf had been ripped away.

Lt Stew Moredock was the only member of RAdm Norman Scott's staff to escape the direct hits on *Atlanta*'s bridge with his life. When the shooting finally stopped and *Atlanta* was bypassed, Moredock saw that the ship was dead in the water and on fire. The only other person Moredock encountered who was capable of moving through the wreckage of the bridge was Capt Samuel Jenkins, the light cruiser's skipper. When the two met, Jenkins, who had shrapnel in one foot, told Moredock, whose right hand was shattered and who was wounded in the arm and side, "Let's get below. There's nothing we can do up here."

The two split up and went their separate ways to try to find an intact ladder to the main deck. Failing to do so, Lieutenant Moredock decided to climb over the bridge railing and lower himself to the main deck. This, despite his broken and useless right hand. However, when Moredock crawled over the barrier, he held on too long and the weight of his twisting, falling body snapped his left wrist. With that, Moredock plummeted right down on top of a pile of gunners who had apparently been killed as they fled out the back of Mount-3. In the early stages of shock from his injuries and extremely upset by what it had taken to cushion his fall, Moredock was unable to lift himself to his feet or even crawl away, so he leaned back among the dead gunners to recompose himself.

The entire ship was eerily still for several minutes, then some survivors slowly began to arrive on the main deck to assess the damage and locate living shipmates in darkened corners and along the darkened passageways. One such group finally found the pile of dead gunners behind Mount-3. When Stew Moredock heard the rescuers talking among themselves, he snapped out of his lethargy and yelled to attract their attention.

Before Lieutenant Moredock would submit to receiving any

aid, he insisted that his rescuers check through the bodies on which he lay to see if anyone else was alive. The sailors complied, but they found that everyone else was dead. After one of the sailors administered a syrette of morphine, all hands picked Moredock up and carried him to a collecting point in a forward berthing compartment. The lieutenant's wounds were swathed in bandages and he was set aside with the other noncritical cases.

卐

MM1 Ross Hilton, the machine-shop supervisor, joined a makeshift damage-control party on its way forward to Central Station, the nexus of the ship's damage-control system. No one had been able to reach Central Station, which was forward of the forward engine room, by any means, including battle phones or the intercom, since the torpedo hit. By chance, Hilton was the first to reach the watertight door of the crew's midships mess hall, so he was ordered by the senior officer present to open it and see what was on the other side. As Hilton opened the door, he was nearly overcome by a ferocious shot of heat and a cloud of acrid smoke, so he slammed it shut right away. When someone suggested that Hilton acquire a rescue breather a senior petty officer way back in the line said he already had an RBA on and that he would be happy to make his way through the mess hall. The officer, who had earlier been on the verge of panic, opened the hatch and literally threw the petty officer into the flames before the petty officer even had an opportunity to pull the RBA mask up over his nose and mouth or before he could borrow a flashlight.

The mess hall was burning because the torpedo had detonated right beneath it and had blown a hole in the deck between it and the forward engine room. All hands manning a damage-control station in the mess hall had been killed outright by the blast or from burns or smoke inhalation. Despite the heat and smoke and water, which was two or three feet deep on the deck, the petty officer with the RBA stayed long enough to ascertain that everyone within reach was dead and that the makeshift damage party would not be able to get through that way.

With that, the officer ordered MM1 Ross Hilton to climb to the main deck and make his way forward and then back down to

Central Station. Once Hilton found out what was wrong, he was to retrace his steps and report his findings to the officer. With that, Hilton turned aft, passed the machine shop, traversed the after mess hall, climbed to the level of the main deck, and stepped out on the starboard side. The hatch Hilton used was right beside Mount-5, which earlier had been squeezed open by the internal detonation of a Japanese shell. As Hilton stepped onto the main deck through smoke billowing out of the shattered mount, he felt his foot come down on something soft. He looked down and found that he was standing on the unfurled intestines of a seaman he knew; in fact, Hilton had given the kid hell that very afternoon for crowding in front of him as he waited in line at the soda fountain. With that, Hilton pulled his foot back inside, closed the hatch, and went out to the port main deck, beside Mount-4. There, to his amazement, he found that the ship was listing badly and that there was only about 3 feet of freeboard to port. It was too dark to see, so Hilton had to feel his way forward by carefully sliding one foot in front of the other. At the least, there was no way he was going to step on a mangled corpse again.

As Hilton slid-walked forward, one of several sailors running past him in the opposite direction yelled, "Let's get off this damn thing. It's sinking!"

"No," Hilton said in a voice he hoped would not belie his own fear, "we better all wait until we get an order to leave."

"To hell with you, Jack," the sailor answered, "We're leaving." And with that, the entire group ran right over the side into the water.

Twenty feet farther on, someone lying on the deck grabbed Hilton by the ankles and mewled a weak little "Help." Hilton bent over to see who it was or what was wrong, but could not see a thing. "Who are you," Hilton asked, "and what's wrong with you?"

The sailor identified himself and added, "My throat's cut and I'm bleeding to death."

Hilton sat the sailor up and dimly perceived a broad gash along the man's right jawline, where a sliver of shrapnel had cut him. The wound was big and ugly, but the sailor was not bleeding at all. The white-hot shrapnel had cauterized the wound while it was cutting. No sooner did Hilton give out the good news than a chief pharmacist's mate came by. Hilton asked the senior corpsman to help him carry the sailor back to the emergency medical station in the after mess hall, but the doc was in a state of shock and only stared vacantly at the source of the request. Before Hilton could think about what to do next, two sailors who seemed in control of their faculties came by and offered to help. However, when Hilton suggested that they carry the wounded man below to the mess hall, the wounded youngster came unglued and yelled, "Don't put me down there! We'll sink! I'll drown down there!" Hilton, who was dead calm, spoke soothingly to the young man and got him calmed down enough to agree to be treated below. With that, Hilton left the wounded man to the two volunteers and continued forward.

After climbing over the wreckage of the severed foremast, Hilton was accosted by a friend who told him that everyone in Central Station, including refugees from the forward fire room, had been wiped out by a direct hit. With that, Hilton returned to the makeshift damage party he had left earlier and reported his findings. The officer in charge, who had not moved or done anything in many minutes, came to life and ordered everyone topside to help fight fires.

卍

After redogging hatches over the flooded engineering spaces, S2 Don McKay and several companions stood around for several minutes, awaiting orders. During the wait, they felt the impact of numerous hits, but they were not molested by the fallout. Finally, certain he had been forgotten, one of the sailors decided to open an escape hatch overhead and climb up to see what was going on topside. He immediately yelled back, "The whole ship is on fire!" The others scrambled up the ladder and most of them ran to the nearest water main to help bring the flames under control. By then, though there was no water pressure in the mains, fighting fires by one means or another was becoming the job of choice for most of the able-bodied seamen aboard *Atlanta*.

S2 Don McKay and another sailor bypassed the fire main and made their way up toward the bridge. On the way, they saw wounded and burned officers and sailors moaning and crying over their untreated wounds. Dead men lay everywhere. When the two reached the bridge, McKay found a living man whose four limbs had been torn from his body. As soon as McKay knelt to offer aid, however, his companion pulled him away and whispered, "He's beyond help." The two climbed back down to the main deck to join the bucket brigade that was fighting a fire in the Mount-3 handling room. As the fire fighters stepped nimbly to evade rounds that were cooking off like firecrackers, they had to step back and forth across the shattered bodies of officers and sailors who had apparently been blown out of battle stations higher up.

࿕

EM3 Bill McKinney and S2 Dan Curtin remained at their post in the darkened, isolated berthing compartment below Mount-3. McKinney had no idea what was expected of him, so at one point he banged on the watertight hatch forward just to make contact with other human beings. The bang was answered, so McKinney yelled to ask what was going on. The larger repair party in the next compartment forward was also in the dark and out of touch; no one there knew what to do either.

Next, McKinney heard someone in the compartment directly overhead throw a violent coughing fit. Then he heard nothing for many minutes. He knew that *Atlanta* was dead in the water and he measured her increasing list by hanging a strap from the overhead and watching it ease farther and farther away from "straight down."

Finally, someone in the compartment forward banged on the watertight door and yelled that fire had eaten through the upper forward corner of his compartment and that he and his companions could see blood running down through the opening. When the voice told McKinney that he and his companions were leaving, McKinney thought of bolting too, but he had orders to maintain the watertight integrity of the large berthing compartment, which was one of the main factors in keeping the ship buoyant.

By then, the desperate coughing from the compartment overhead had stopped. McKinney climbed up into the escape scuttle in the overhead and peered through. The space was filled with thick, yellow, acrid smoke.

After fumbling around for some precious minutes trying to

figure out how to use their RBA packs, McKinney and Curtin squeezed through the escape scuttle in the overhead and entered the compartment above, on their way topside. The beam of McKinney's flashlight, which barely penetrated 2 feet through the thick yellow smoke, revealed the body of a sailor who had apparently been asphyxiated following his desperate coughing fit.

From there, McKinney and Curtin entered the wardroom and breasted several smoky fires in there. As his attention wandered to a string of fireflylike lights winking on and off against the wardroom bulkheads—1.1-inch ammunition cooking off in an adjacent clipping room—McKinney tripped over a chair he could not see in the murky gloom and nearly collapsed the rubber rebreathing chamber of his RBA. However, he recovered his balance and led Curtin through the starboard watertight door and out onto the main deck. By then, the two had breathed the last of the air in their RBA air cartridges, and both were actually choking when they emerged. McKinney pulled off his RBA mask as soon as he stepped out on deck and was belted in the face by what seemed to him like frigid fresh air.

As McKinney recovered and looked around, he thought that the ship had been abandoned. He could not see or hear a soul. Suddenly, someone ran by shouting, "Get off! She's going to blow!" McKinney and Curtin debated the matter for some seconds, and one of them mentioned the possibility of encountering sharks if they went into the water. Put that way, McKinney decided that blowing up was better than being eaten up, and Curtin agreed. With that, the two decided to help fight fires as a means of rendering moot their Hobson's choice.

After finding new air canisters for their RBAs, the two returned to their battle station below to collect carbon-dioxide fire extinguishers and see to the condition of a 2½-inch hose stored there. Then they returned to the main deck. Immediately, they encountered two sailors who were just standing around watching the fires spread. McKinney urged the two to take several fire extinguishers and try to stop the spread of the flames, but the two just looked at McKinney and Curtin without saying a word. Finally, McKinney and Curtin shoved the two zombies toward the fire, and

that snapped them out of their lethargy. The two grabbed the prof-
fered fire extinguishers and went to work.

McKinney and Curtin next grabbed several fresh air canisters
from a stack they found beside the wardroom and returned below
again to begin manhandling the heavy 2½-inch hose up two decks
to the main deck. Earlier, McKinney had found a water main that
seemed to be functioning, so the effort and danger made sense.
When the two finally wrestled the hose to the main deck, they saw
MM1 Ross Hilton setting up a handy-billy gasoline pump to fight
the persistent fire in Mount-5.

To McKinney's amazement, Hilton was being hampered by
several spectators, none of whom stooped to help Hilton. In fact,
the spectators were so close that when Hilton yanked the cord to
start the pump, he inadvertently slugged one of the rubberneckers
right on the point of his chin. As McKinney and Curtin waded in
and dispersed the crowd, Hilton got the pump running and beat
down the fire in Mount-5 with water from a 1½-inch hose.

McKinney offered Hilton the 2½-inch hose he had just wrestled up from below, and he told Hilton that he had tested the nearest fire main. However, Hilton pointed out that all the ship's fire
mains were inoperative because there was no steam to power the
water system; if McKinney had drawn water from one, it was because the system was open to the sea somewhere well below sea
level.

🌀

Shortly after EM3 Bill McKinney met up with MM1 Ross
Hilton, several senior officers began making great strides toward
exerting complete control over the hitherto fragmented rescue and
damage-control efforts. While many panicked officers and sailors
continued to leave the ship, the senior officers organized work parties to try, among other things, to lighten the port side of the ship to
correct the worrisome and extremely dangerous list. A large work
party tried to jettison the heavy port quadruple torpedo mount,
complete with its four torpedoes. However, there was no chain
aboard the ship strong enough to take the weight of the loaded
mount, so the effort was wasted. On the other hand, the port an-

chor and its entire chain were easily dropped over the side, and volunteers dumped a vast number of 5-inch shells and powder cans into the water from portside locations—as much to deprive some fires of volatile fuel as to level the ship. Portable pumps employed in the firefighting effort often drew their water from flooded compartments.

Unauthorized departures had been set in motion just after the battle passed *Atlanta* by orders issued by a panicked lieutenant commander. It did not abate until Capt Samuel Jenkins dragged himself all the way around the main deck on his wounded foot and personally ordered all hands to remain aboard the ship. However, Jenkins did not leave it at that; he tracked down the officer who had given the order and opened an acid exchange that instantly broadcast his feelings about perceived cowardice to the entire crew. Only after he had reasserted his unquestioned authority and stopped the flow of men into the water did Captain Jenkins take a few minutes to have his wounds cleaned and bandaged.

🜨

As the first gray streaks of the new dawn broke through the fire-tinged darkness on the eastern horizon, all hands still aboard *Atlanta* pretty much acknowledged that they stood a good chance of saving their ship. The fires were under control and the list was at least stable—barring a buildup in the calm sea, which would have capsized the vessel in a matter of minutes. There was no time for breathers, but sighs of relief were heaved by many of *Atlanta*'s exhausted officers and crewmen.

Other wounded and crippled ships were more and less fortunate.

34

Akatsuki was sunk with all hands. *Yudachi* was so badly crippled by *Sterett* and *Aaron Ward* that she was abandoned and cast adrift. *Hiei*, reeling under the impact of dozens of hits topside and at least two torpedo detonations that destroyed her rudder and steering control, limped away from the melee under her own power and was briefly towed by *Kirishima* to the northern side of Savo. There she was cast off by her slightly damaged sister battleship and left to her fate in the care of *Yukikaze* and a unit of three unengaged destroyers that arrived on the scene late. *Nagara* and nearly all the surviving destroyers, most of which had suffered some damage, beat a hasty retreat to the north, back through the Slot, toward the Shortlands anchorages. Following her brutal pummeling at *Helena*'s hands, *Amatsukaze* barely regained steering control by manual means and limped north under her own power well behind the retiring main body. Though grievously damaged and in need of massive and lengthy repairs, she would survive to fight another day.

On the American side, *Laffey* and *Barton* were sunk in the night and *Cushing* and *Monssen* were set afire and abandoned by their crews, all with great loss of life. *Portland* was steaming in slow circles in the channel, *Atlanta* was afire and dead in the water, and *Aaron Ward* was damaged and dead in the water, the victim of a freakish loss of the feed water she needed to run her engines. *San Francisco*, which was retiring, was severely damaged by dozens of Japanese shells, and *Juneau* was steaming away more or less in her company with a broken keel and with her power supply severely diminished. *Sterett* was also retiring with severe damage. *Helena*, which was accompanying *San Francisco* and *Juneau*, was only superficially damaged, as was *O'Bannon*, which was going it alone. Of all the American warships engaged that night, only *Fletcher*, which was retiring alone, was totally unscathed; not one of her crew was hurt.

Though the battle was over and the survivors of both forces were separating, there were still places where action might flare. Several of the wounded or crippled combatants that had been left in or near the contested waters remained within gunnery range of other combatants, and it would only take a little sunlight to make their crews realize this.

卍

Though salt water was about the last substance recommended for use as feed water, LCdr Julian Becton, *Aaron Ward* 's exec and former chief engineer, learned that there was no means for distilling fresh feed water. Earlier, the destroyer's electrician's mates had had to redistribute the ship's electrical power to bypass an electrical distribution board that had been smashed by a Japanese shell. When the entire load was passed through the after generator, the ship's entire electrical system had shut down; the single generator could not handle the load. Though this was by no means the reason *Aaron Ward* had lost her feed water to begin with, the electricians had to close down the electrically powered evaporators to conserve power. Until the steam-powered electrical system could be restarted, there was no way to distill fresh water. Thus, Lieutenant Commander Becton had no choice except to "jump start" the entire process with salt water. The process of filling the 2,000-gallon feed-water tank in the forward engine room began with the formation of a bucket brigade, but a gasoline-powered handy-billy pump was soon rigged.

Adding appreciably to the problem of restarting the engines was the fact that there was no power to operate the ventilators. As *Aaron Ward*'s watertenders and firemen pumped the salt water into the boilers, temperatures rose significantly throughout the enclosed, unventilated engineering spaces. Soon, firemen and watertenders on their way topside for cooling breathers had to wear thick gloves to climb the steel ladders, which were too hot to touch with bare hands. As if these problems were not sufficient, the forward engine room was slowly flooded by a breach in the hull, a leaky pipe, or "something" that defied discovery.

Aaron Ward had also suffered a steering breakdown and the job of working through the problem was handed to Lt Bob Weatherup, the Destroyer Division 12 staff communicator. Weatherup had served aboard a similar *Benson*-class destroyer whose crew had been drilled to overcome such a breakdown, and only he seemed to know the secret solution. Since many of the control and power cables had been severed and could not be readily repaired, Weatherup had the rudder unlocked from the power drive and switched to its emergency-manpower mode—that is, muscle power was used to replace steam and electrical power. (Coincidentally, this rarely used technique was being employed aboard fleeing *Amatsukaze*, whose rudder-control cables had also been severed in the night action.)

The feed-water tank was finally filled at 0500, by which time the watertenders had enough steam pressure up to get the turbines going. Everyone knew that it would just be a matter of time before the minerals distilled out of the salt water clogged the boiler tubes, but it was hoped that *Aaron Ward* would be safely at anchor in Tulagi Harbor before that happened.

At 0510, after *Aaron Ward* had been underway for ten minutes, several Tulagi-based PT boats overtook her on their way up the channel from the direction of Savo. The destroyer's chief signalman contacted the speedy plywood boats by blinker tube and asked that they request the Tulagi base to dispatch a tug. Twenty minutes later, at 0530, *Aaron Ward* was again dead in the water.

At 0600, lookouts spotted what appeared to be a Japanese battleship—*Hiei*—steaming in slow circles about 26,000 yards away, between Savo and Florida. At about the same time, lookouts spotted *Monssen*, *Portland*, *Cushing*, and *Atlanta*. *Monssen* and *Cushing* were both burning. Finally, a Japanese destroyer—*Yudachi*—was spotted drifting well to the left of the battleship, near Cape Esperance. She was also burning.

The engineering department's frantic efforts continued to raise enough steam to allow *Aaron Ward* to get slowly underway again at 0618. At 0620, *Bobolink*, an ocean-going fleet tug, was spotted on the way out from Tulagi. *Aaron Ward*'s chief signalman flashed a blinker message asking that the tug stand by to take the destroyer in tow.

Hiei awoke from her introspective somnolence at about 0630 and fired a two-gun 14-inch salvo at *Aaron Ward*. From his place on the destroyer's bridge, LCdr Julian Becton distinctly saw the ominous flash of the battleship's guns.

When the two 1-ton shells plunged into the calm water 1,000 yards west of *Aaron Ward*, Capt Robert Tobin, the destroyer-division commander, leaned over and said in a low voice, "Julie, I think she's firing at us."

"I agree, Commodore, but our gunnery officer reports that she's thirteen miles away; we can't reach her with our guns or torpedoes."

With that, two more rounds splashed into the water, nearer to *Aaron Ward* than the first two. And then two more 14-inch shells arrived; one fell a little short of the ship, and the other fell a little beyond the ship. This was a straddle, a gunner's dream. All the Japanese had to do was "rock the ladder"—bring the range down about 50 yards. Everyone aboard *Aaron Ward* who knew what was about to happen reflexively ducked his head into his shoulders.

And then the cavalry arrived. A bomber strike launched minutes earlier from Henderson Field swooped out of the sky and went right for *Hiei*, whose gunners lost interest in *Aaron Ward*.

As soon as the shooting stopped at 0635, *Aaron Ward* went dead in the water again. *Bobolink* approached and passed across a towline. At 0650, *YC 236*, a commandeered California tuna boat grandiosely designated a "yacht-patrol" vessel, arrived and assumed the tow from *Bobolink*, which had been dispatched to assist *Atlanta*. *Aaron Ward* finally arrived in Tulagi Harbor at 0830 and was moored to coconut trees growing on tiny Makambo Island.

꘏

Circling *Portland* launched one of her small boats at about 0430, when the topside crew heard cries for help in the darkness. When it became light at about 0530, more boats were launched and the haul increased. Also at about 0530, *Portland* 's lookouts spotted and reported all the other ships that appeared to be adrift in the area. *Hiei* was easily identified, as were *Aaron Ward, Atlanta, Monssen,* and *Cushing.* However, *Portland* 's lookouts were unable to determine the identity of a destroyer-size warship drifting and burning south of Savo. *Portland* 's signalmen requested help from *Atlanta,* but the light cruiser did not respond until one of her signalmen asked *Portland* to confirm her own identity. (Until the word arrived, *Atlanta*'s torpedomen were actually drawing a bead on the circling heavy cruiser.) As soon as that formality was out of the way, the *Atlanta* signalman told *Portland* that the burning destroyer was Japanese—*Yudachi.*

Of the two Japanese cripples, only *Yudachi*—and two small boats that were standing beside her—appeared to be in range of *Portland* 's 8-inch guns. Though the Japanese cripple was adrift and burning—and abandoned, a factor that could not be discerned from *Portland*—Capt Laurence DuBose was too angry with the lot the Fates had cast him and too aggressive in any case to withhold fire. So, as *Portland* steamed in slow circles to the right, her main battery director locked onto the stationary target at a range of 12,500 yards and fired one six-gun salvo to test the waters. The fall of the shells was close enough to *Yudachi* to provide encouragement, so another salvo was fired. This was a little off because of the need to traverse the two forward turrets through the heavy cruiser's involuntary and uncontrollable turn away from the target.

During her next turn, *Portland* fired two more six-gun salvos at *Yudachi,* but only several shells hit home and only minor damage was observed. The fifth salvo, fired during the next turn, missed, but *Portland* 's sixth salvo was dead on. Several rounds apparently detonated in the destroyer's after magazine. As cheering gunners left their turrets to watch, *Yudachi* blazed anew and, within five minutes, rolled over and sank from sight.

At 0658, the Guadalcanal radio station reported Japanese aircraft at a range of 42 miles and closing. *Portland* went to full battle alert; all the antiaircraft guns that had not been damaged in the night action were manned by their crews or uninjured volunteers. *Portland* was the next best thing to a sitting duck, but there was no doubt among her officers and crew that she was still very much a fighting ship. (She was not molested by these incoming Japanese bombers, nor threatened by any that followed during the course of the day.)

As *Portland*'s small boats continued to bring in waterlogged American survivors, Captain DuBose requested the aid of a tug. *Bobolink* was spotted on the horizon at 0805, but she did not close on *Portland* until 0953. However, as the tug completed her approach, Captain DuBose ordered her to proceed to *Atlanta* and tow her instead. Several large tank lighters sent out by the Lunga Boat Pool to rescue survivors were commandeered to help pull *Portland* while the cruiser maneuvered on her engines. At length, one of the tank lighters eased up to *Portland*'s starboard bow and pushed with all its might. The maneuver aimed the cruiser toward Kukum, just west of friendly Lunga Point. Later, *Bobolink* and *YC 236* shoved *Portland*'s bows around so that the cruiser was aimed toward Tulagi.

Efforts to tow and push *Portland* to Tulagi were undertaken through the entire day by the tank lighters, *YC 236*, and *Bobolink*. *Portland* finally dropped her anchor in Tulagi Harbor at 0118, more than twenty-three hours after she had been torpedoed.

꙰

It looked for many hours as if *Atlanta* might be saved. As wounded and injured crewmen were plucked from the fantail by a stream of landing boats out of Kukum—and as her many dead crewmen were expediently buried over the side—efforts to fight the light cruiser's many topside and internal fires to a standstill were successful, and there was even some hope that her disabled engineering plant might be partially resuscitated.

Bobolink, which had been sent by *Portland*'s Capt Laurence DuBose, arrived at about 1030 to tow *Atlanta* to relatively safe waters off Kukum, where at least she would be close to friendly territory. However, *Bobolink* needed to confirm her identity before she was allowed to approach, for she did not look like any U.S. Navy ship anyone aboard *Atlanta* had ever seen. Usually tied up close in to Tulagi, the tug had had to adopt a unique camouflage paint job: dark green overlaid with black streaks. As *Bobolink* came close aboard *Atlanta*, the light cruiser's topside crew saw that the strange black streaks spelled out the names of *Bobolink*'s women.

The towing effort got off to a slow start because the cruiser's crew had to manhandle 90 fathoms of anchor chain back aboard the ship. The starboard anchor had had to be dropped during the night to prevent *Atlanta* from drifting up onto a Japanese-occupied beach. The anchor and chain could not be jettisoned because the port anchor and chain had been let go to help correct *Atlanta*'s port list; the remaining anchor would certainly be needed to hold the ship off Kukum when she finally arrived. The grueling, backbreaking task took time and diverted previous manpower from critical work elsewhere, but there was nothing else to be done.

At 1115, Capt Samuel Jenkins informed *Portland*'s Capt Laurence DuBose, the senior naval officer present in the area, that flooding was beyond the light cruiser's pumping capacity and that *Atlanta* had entered a downhill slide in her fight for life. However, Jenkins was not ready to concede defeat and proved it by outlining a plan to jettison heavy equipment to counteract the flooding.

Before anchoring off Kukum at about 1400, *Atlanta* was checked over by a low-flying Betty, which was fired on by Mount-8, the cruiser's only 5-inch mount with power. No hits were scored, but the Betty ran.

Atlanta's crew worked without respite as the day wore on, but the cripple's fate was sealed by reports from the north indicating that a powerful Japanese surface battle force was approaching and might arrive after nightfall. With that Captain Jenkins grew fearful that *Atlanta* might actually be captured and towed away by the Japanese. Thus, early in the afternoon, Jenkins radioed *Portland*'s Captain DuBose to ask if he might take off the rest of his crew and scuttle the remains. DuBose told Jenkins to do what he had to do.

Every landing boat that could be spared was sent to *Atlanta* in the early evening, and 470 uninjured crewmen were quickly taken off. The final evacuation went so smoothly that service records and pay accounts were also saved, and many sailors brought away whatever personal possessions or ship's stores they could carry, though doing so was emphatically unauthorized. As the last crewmen were leaving the ship, *Bobolink* returned and signaled that she was prepared to tow *Atlanta* out to deeper water.

S2 Dave Driscoll was just lowering himself into a landing boat when a first-class boatswain's mate ordered him to return to the main deck to help with the scuttling. When Driscoll had climbed back aboard the ship, he found that only Captain Jenkins, the first-class boatswain's mate, three other sailors, and several officers were still aboard. The five sailors and officers stationed themselves along the main deck and in the after steering-control room so that Captain Jenkins could help *Bobolink* by steering his own ship to her final resting place. When the captain was finally pleased with the location, a bucket filled with explosives was lowered into the after steering-control room and a pair of wires that was unreeled from the bucket to the forecastle was rigged to a detonation plunger.

The captain was not quite ready to destroy his ship. While he ruminated, the five sailors were given an opportunity to go to their lockers and remove prized valuables. S2 Dave Driscoll took the opportunity to exchange his oil-soaked work clothes for a clean set and retrieve a photo album and a meager collection of other belongings. In minutes, *Atlanta*'s last crew was mustered on the starboard side of the forecastle and ordered to climb into a waiting landing boat by rank, senior men last. Thus, S2 Driscoll went over the side first. At last, at 1830, as Captain Jenkins left the ship, he pushed the plunger wired to the bucketful of explosives in the after steering-control room. All hands heard a muffled explosion, but S2 Driscoll felt nothing.

Captain Jenkins ordered the crew of the landing boat to circle around and around the ship so that he could watch her final plunge. However, though the demolition charge had certainly opened her bottom to the sea, *Atlanta* took a very long time to die. Finally, at 2015, the namesake of her new class of light antiaircraft cruisers sank off Kukum, approximately 3 miles west of Lunga Point. S2 Dave Driscoll, who was still aboard the landing boat, missed the event; continuously awake for the twenty-four worst hours of his life, he simply nodded off before the final act.

Of 675 officers and sailors embarked in *Atlanta*, 14 of 45 officers had been killed and 7 had been wounded, and 158 enlisted men had been killed and 76 wounded. That is a total of 255 casualties, more than one in three.

35

Cdr Butch Parker wanted to be the last man to leave *Cushing*—so much so that he wound up staying aboard for more than an hour after all the wounded and living sailors anyone knew about swam away or had been cast off in life rafts. When Parker thought everyone who was getting off was gone, he set off alone to carry out a final inspection of the ship.

Cushing was no longer under fire, but there were fires and danger aplenty to be had. A particularly large inferno was raging in the open Mount-2 crew shelter and a smaller fire was visible around the Mount-1 shelter. In the flickering flames of those and other fires, Parker clearly saw smoke pouring through hatches leading to the crews' quarters, but he could see no flames from below.

As Parker made his way aft, EM1 Ernest Johnson returned alone in a life raft and joined Parker for the captain's final tour of the ship. When the two located a pair of injured sailors, they carried them to the side of the ship and lowered them into the raft. Then, because Parker still was not satisfied that *Cushing* was a total loss, he ordered EM1 Johnson to paddle the injured men to safety. Johnson refused to leave his captain alone, so the raft was cast off and the two wounded sailors feebly paddled themselves out of immediate danger.

As Parker and Johnson continued to survey the ship, the fire in Mount-2 spread to a cache of ready ammunition and a tremendous new conflagration burst out. The two next strode briskly to the fantail to be certain that all the depth charges had been set on safe.

By the time they had checked the depth charges, it was after 0300. Lieutenant Commander Parker had thought of no viable solutions for saving the ship, and it was time to leave. The fires were raging out of control. He and Johnson each tied a pair of powder tanks together and threw them over the side. Then they jumped into the water, put one powder tank under each arm and kicked away from *Cushing*.

As the two got farther from the ship, Parker looked back and saw that *Cushing*'s two forward gun mounts were engulfed totally in towering flames and that an unbroken chain of smaller fires ran back to nearly amidships. Suddenly, there was a huge explosion from beneath the forecastle that hurled debris several hundred feet in the air. Throughout the ship, 5-inch and 20mm rounds continually cooked off and burning oil from breached fuel tanks was rapidly spreading to engulf the entire ship, and this apparently ignited fires below decks aft.

With that, Butch Parker finally gave up any notion he still had about saving *Cushing*—the third destroyer he had commanded in a night action against the Japanese, and the first he had lost.

꘡

After an hour in the water, LCdr Butch Parker and EM1 Ernest Johnson, the last men off *Cushing*, located one of their ship's life rafts, which was filled with injured men and surrounded by many men hanging on to lines secured to it. Later, another raft with Cdr Murray Stokes, the Destroyer Division 10 commander, drifted by and the two rafts were tied together. Until well after sunrise, all of *Cushing*'s living paddled or kicked away from the burning ship, which everyone expected to blow up at any moment.

꘡

WT1 Dennis Behl could not see where he was going, but every time he thought he saw a shadow that might be land, he swam as hard as he could in the opposite direction. Behl had been told that most of Guadalcanal was in Japanese hands, and he frankly preferred drowning to capture. When it became light enough for Behl to be able to see *Portland* circling in the distance, he shaped a course straight for her. However, long before Behl reached the cruiser, one of the first landing craft sent out by the Kukum-based Lunga Boat Pool arrived. There were several awkward moments in which the boat crewmen tried to identify oil-covered swimmers and the swimmers tried to ascertain the nationality of the boat crewmen. When enough had been said to satisfy all parties, Behl and other swimmers nearby allowed themselves to be rescued. When the Higgins boat was full, it returned to Kukum to drop off the survivors and then ventured out again.

卐

Y2 Tom Foreman, *Cushing*'s doctor, and two wounded sailors all found themselves on a tiny upside-down balsa raft floating inshore toward a light. Their feelings were exactly contrary to WT1 Dennis Behl's; they wanted to get ashore. Though Y2 Foreman had been badly wounded in one leg, he was in better shape than the other two sailors. He retrieved two paddles from beneath the water and helped the doctor, who was also wounded, to paddle the raft toward the light. When the sun came up, Foreman saw several other rafts far ahead of his and a large ship in the distance behind him. At first, Foreman thought the ship was Japanese, but he soon realized that it was *Portland*. There were several scary minutes when *Portland* opened fire at a target Foreman could not see; he thought a Japanese battle force was steaming into the area. Foreman remained wary even after seeing a column of smoke from what must have been *Portland*'s target, but at least no Japanese ships sailed into view.

Fortunately for Foreman and the *Cushing* sailors in the other rafts, they were held offshore by the tide. Eventually, all the rafts were scooped up by a ramped landing craft—literally scooped up; the ramp was dropped and the rafts rode in on the bow wave, then the ramp was raised, and the troop compartment was pumped out. When the landing boat was full, it turned for Kukum.

༝

Upside-down life rafts were the bane—and the death—of many survivors. The raft on which GM2 Jim Tooker joined a score of other *Cushing* survivors was upside down. Cox John Bilyeau, who had so masterfully aimed Mount-3 during the latter part of the battle with *Nagara*, again rose to the occasion by diving under fuel-filled water to retrieve the first-aid kit, boxes of food and tins of water. The morphine in the aid kit was a godsend for a seaman whose lower right arm had been blown away, and for a second-class machinist's mate who had suffered a blindingly painful compound fracture of his thigh.

There being no splints aboard to immobilize the machinist's mate's thigh, GM2 Tooker slipped into the water and became a human traction machine; despite several painful wounds in one leg and the ache of a piece of shrapnel that had struck him in the back and lodged in his chest, Tooker immobilized the machinist's mate's broken femur against the edge of the raft until the raft was located by a landing boat out of Kukum.

༝

When S2 Felton Maillot, of *Cushing*, came to his senses, he was in the water, afloat in his life jacket. Maillot's last memory was of being overwhelmed by a large explosion as he was setting fuses for starshell rounds going into *Cushing*'s forward 5-inch gun. As Maillot's senses returned, he saw that *Cushing* was drifting along beside him. The ship appeared to be burning down her entire length. He had no idea how long he had been in the water, but he did learn that there was no one else within shouting distance.

When Maillot realized that about half his kapok life jacket had been burned or blown away, he slipped his shoes off and began treading water despite a right knee made stiff by several shrapnel wounds. He could see a dark silhouette to one side, which he took to be Guadalcanal. There being no other options, he turned toward the island and pulled himself along in a series of strength-conserving strokes. After a time, he bumped into a large shoring timber.

He pulled himself out of the water and rested his tall body length-wise along the wood, then paddled it toward the island.

When the sun rose, Maillot saw a life raft brimming full of sailors. To reach them, he had to paddle his length of lumber through a pool of fuel oil, but he counted the effort as worthwhile. It turned out that the raft was manned by sailors who had abandoned *Atlanta* during the night. They were just about to head back to their ship, which was still afloat nearby, and they offered Maillot a ride. He released the lumber that had carried him for hours and trailed along grasping a line hanging over the raft's side. A quarter hour later, he climbed aboard *Atlanta* and allowed himself to be eased down to a spot on her fantail among scores of recumbent men.

⮔

The spark plug behind the orderly collection of most of the *Laffey* survivors turned out to be Lt Eugene Barham, the chief engineer. After the ship went down, Barham was extremely surprised to see that the swimming party he led, which had been a highly compact unit moments earlier, had spread out over a wide area. As Barham was pondering this strange turn of events, he heard the sound of a small engine, so he reached into his pocket for a small flashlight, which he flicked on and off in the direction of the sound. Soon, one of *Laffey*'s two whaleboats emerged from the gloom. When Barham heaved himself into the boat, he found it occupied by only three men. One, the chief quartermaster, was unhurt but virtually comatose. The next, a gunner's mate, had had his arm nearly severed. And the third, a fireman, was unscathed. A quick check of the boat revealed that it was slightly damaged but completely serviceable.

After checking the boat and its three occupants, Lieutenant Barham slipped back into the water to fully engage the rudder, then heaved himself back into the boat and assumed duties as its coxswain. His immediate task was to gather up all the loose swimmers he could find. However, as he proceeded, he quickly came upon several more or less filled life rafts, which he ordered secured to the whaleboat for towing.

One of the first rafts Barham found contained the prostrate

form of Lt(jg) Tom Evins, who had been severely wounded by debris from the final explosion that sank *Laffey*. When Evins begged to be taken aboard the more stable whaleboat, Barham made his single exception to a strict code of impartiality he had imposed. Once Evins was in a secure spot, someone aboard the whaleboat dosed him with one of the few morphine syrettes that had been carried away from the ship, and that induced merciful slumber.

By daylight, Lieutenant Barham had located and reeled in all but two of *Laffey*'s life rafts, and the destroyer's second whaleboat. The second whaleboat's stern area had been splintered and its motor had been damaged, but it was otherwise seaworthy. Though Lieutenant Barham found *Laffey*'s executive officer, the lieutenant commander refused to assume command of the expedition and, indeed, offered no constructive advice.

There was much pain and suffering among the wounded and injured survivors. And there were deaths. S1 Ward Casey, *Laffey*'s only living medico, took charge of a young seaman who had a gaping shrapnel hole in his throat. All Casey could do for the man was give him a shot of morphine, the only drug he had carried into the water. The seaman eventually died as he lay with his head in Casey's lap. Casey later learned that one of the two sailors he had placed aboard a life raft just before the ship blew up had also died in the night. And so did TM1 Frederick Sanderson, who had been mortally wounded when the ship blew up moments after he had helped free a trapped and injured gunner from the wreckage of Mount-4.

Shortly after daybreak, the *Laffey* procession came upon a burning destroyer lying very low on the water. Soon, Lieutenant Barham recognized the ship as *Cushing*, which was in much the same condition as when LCdr Butch Parker had left her after 0300. Sensing a unique opportunity, Barham headed right for her, came alongside, and jumped out of the whaleboat to her main deck. A quick check of the ship bolstered Barham's suspicion that he could get her underway, but he was arrested in his thinking by demands from his own shipmates that he reboard the whaleboat and resume the journey toward Guadalcanal. Reluctantly, Barham acceded; most of the men in the whaleboats and life rafts were wounded— some were dying—and it was best to get on with the rescue.

Shortly after leaving *Cushing*, the *Laffey* survivors heard someone hail them. Lieutenant Barham stopped the whaleboat to listen, and soon a solitary sailor swam up, grasped the gunwale, and hoisted himself aboard. When Barham asked what ship he was from the sailor said he had been aboard *San Francisco*, but he would not speak further and went right to sleep. About fifteen minutes later, when Lieutenant Barham went forward to check on the sailor, he found the man had died. A quick check of the sailor's body revealed no sign of wounds.

After more long hours underway beneath the hot sun, the *Laffey* procession was approached by a Higgins boat from the Lunga Boat Pool. The landing craft made a wide circle around the string of whaleboats and rafts and someone called out to ask the castaways to identify themselves. The request seemed strange at first, but most of the survivors were coated with thick black fuel oil and might just as easily have been Japanese. As soon as the landing-craft crew was satisfied it was dealing with friendlies, it brought the Higgins boat alongside the whaleboats. The wounded were offloaded first, then the able-bodied followed. Many of the survivors were amazed that all of them together did not quite fill the smallish Higgins boat.

⌘

Despite Lieutenant Barham's best efforts to gather in all the *Laffey* survivors, two life rafts and several swimmers were missed in the search in the dark. S1 John Jenkins heard the whaleboat's motor in the distance, but he could not determine from which direction the noise was coming. He joined up with several other castaways and watched the battle as it ebbed and flared in the near distance. With the aid of air they trapped now and again in their shirts, Jenkins and his fellow castaways floated on their backs until, at dawn, they spotted a life raft about a half mile away. They swam to the raft, which was filled with wounded, and hung on for dear life. Soon, Jenkins and another sailor started singing a song to raise morale, and many of the others, who had been sullen to that point, joined in. When the first song was finished, someone started singing another song, and so on.

When the dozen *Laffey* survivors aboard the overlooked life raft saw *Portland*'s rounds strike *Yudachi*, they stopped their rollicking songfest to cheer themselves hoarse. Then they began singing hymns and spirituals. But salvation was still hours in coming. The raft was finally spotted by the pilot of a Marine dive-bomber out of Henderson Field. Word was quickly passed to the Lunga Boat Pool and a landing boat was diverted to the correct spot.

⇄

Most of the forty or so *Barton* survivors managed to stay together in the wake of the nightmare loss of their ship. Several died from the effects of the depth charges that went off beneath them, and several others died from massive injuries sustained while being dragged through *O'Bannon*'s propellers when that destroyer overran them.

M1 Wayne Clark managed to find a balsa life raft and pulled himself aboard. Two of the sailors already on the raft had had their guts tied in knots by the depth charges. Those two, and others in the water, spent the night trying to vomit or pass gas trapped by the new kinks in their intestines, but to no avail. (It was common for the survivors of such awesome underwater compression to succumb.)

Another large group of *Barton* survivors spent the night in the water, kept afloat by their kapok life jackets. One member of the group, S2 Harold Bone, had been severely wounded in the leg by *O'Bannon*'s propellers, and he moaned and groaned for hours. Eventually, another member of the group became so irate over Bone's incessant complaining that he loudly demanded that Bone shut up. Bone never made another sound that night. When a large ammunition case floated by, six of the swimmers grabbed that number of handles around its side and, even though only an inch of the sealed metal canister showed above the water, the six were able to stay afloat without difficulty.

Like many other swimmers throughout the area, RM2 Jack Slack inadvertently swallowed seawater mixed with fuel oil. Slack spent the rest of the night and morning hours retching and vomiting on an empty stomach.

Many of the *Barton* survivors were picked up by whaleboats launched by circling *Portland*. As soon as M1 Wayne Clark boarded the heavy cruiser by way of a cargo net rigged over her side, *Portland* crewmen helped him strip off his oil-soaked clothing, which he threw over the side. He was given a pair of dungarees, a T-shirt, and a pair of tennis shoes from a pile of clothing donated by the cruiser's crew. As soon as RM2 Jack Slack pulled himself to *Portland* 's deck, he wandered off to find an isolated spot and immediately fell asleep. When Slack awoke the *next* morning, he was in a bunk in one of the crew's berthing compartments.

╬

Lt(jg) George Hamm, the last able-bodied member of *Monssen's* crew to leave the ship, joined up with a seaman and both tried to swim away from the burning ship on Hamm's watertight powder can. They made some progress for an hour, until the wind and tide changed. Then they were slowly driven back toward *Monssen*, which Hamm was sure would blow up any minute. As Hamm and the seaman swam hard to escape—they eventually opened the distance—feelings of gloom Hamm had experienced early in the action were overwhelmed by a sense of well-being and renewal; George Hamm was sure he would survive the ordeal, which indeed he did. The two joined a raft filled with about twenty-five other *Monssen* survivors—two of whom died in the night—and were in voice contact in the dark with others.

Another raft within visual distance of Hamm's had been thrown into the water upside down, so none of the emergency supplies or paddles could be reached. It probably made no difference in the end, but lack of medical supplies prevented anyone from treating the two crewmen with the worst injuries. One was a fireman whose feet had nearly been severed. He went into a coma early in the ordeal and no one knew or cared to find out if he was dead. Though another man, who was clinging to the side of the raft, did not look especially ill, he suddenly stiffened and sank from sight before anyone nearby could reach out to help.

At sunrise, several medium-size sharks arrived to scavenge the remains of especially crumbly biscuits the crew of one raft was eating for breakfast. After devouring all the biscuit crumbs in the water, the sharks took an interest in the men themselves. Many of the men clinging to the raft kicked the water and raised a fuss, and that sent the sharks away. However, Lt(jg) George Hamm, whose earlier sense of well-being was put on hold, tried to shinny into the fully loaded life raft. All he could get in was his head and chest. Telling himself the two "monsters" were probably not man-eaters, Hamm gritted his teeth and maintained his balance until someone told him the intruders were gone.

Monssen's acting skipper, LCdr Charlie McCombs, spent the dark hours alone, clinging to a portion of a shattered balsa life raft. After sunrise, he located several survivors who had fashioned a makeshift raft out of cushions from the ship's gig and some powder cans. All hands but one, who was on top of the flimsy raft, were in good shape, though tired and full of salt water and fuel oil. The small group spent the early morning hours kicking feebly toward what they hoped would be an American-held portion of Guadalcanal, and they were all picked up by a landing boat at about 0930.

A floatplane found the main body of *Monssen* survivors in two separated rafts late in the morning, and two landing craft finally arrived a little after noon. One of the Higgins boats began pulling in sailors from one group while the boat closest to Lt(jg) George Hamm's raft stopped short to allow one of the crewmen to fire his pistol at several sharks. Hamm asked the boat crew to at least fish him out of the water before riling the sharks. This was done and a Navy doctor aboard Hamm's boat went right to work treating the wounded—a job he did without letup during the entire two-hour trip to Kukum. The sailor whose feet had nearly been severed was pronounced dead on the beach.

When LCdr Charlie McCombs mustered all the known *Monssen* survivors on the beach later that morning, about 100 of 226 reported themselves present or gave details about wounded shipmates being treated at the nearby field hospital. Seven men were known to have died in the water. Over the next few days, several more *Monssen* survivors drifted in, but the losses nevertheless remained above 50 percent. Of 18 officers aboard *Monssen* at the start of the action, 8 left the ship and 1 died in the attempt.

卐

As the lights slowly went on in his head, S1 Bert Doughty, of *Monssen*, looked into the eyes of another sailor. The other man was speaking, but Doughty could not hear the words. After a moment or two, the darkness once again enfolded him.

Doughty had received severe head wounds, which also knocked him unconscious, as he was launching a life raft from *Monssen*'s fantail in the closing moments of the action. Somehow, he had been left aboard the ship when most of the survivors evacuated the fantail.

The man who had briefly appeared before S1 Doughty was BM2 Clyde Storey, one of the last men off the ship during the night. Storey had spent the remaining dark hours clinging to an empty powder can along with GM2 Leo Spurgeon and F1 Joe Hughes. By sunrise, the three had smoked up the last of the cigarettes Spurgeon had thoughtfully thrown into the waterproof powder can. About then, a pair of torpedo boats from the Tulagi PT-boat base passed close by on their way to look over Japanese cripples. The three sailors in the water yelled themselves hoarse trying to attract the powerful boats, but to no avail.

As soon as the PT boats passed, three huge sharks appeared on the scene and slowly circled the three swimmers three times. The sharks left, but the first words out of everyone's mouth amounted to a unanimous vote to swim back to the burning, drifting ship; each preferred blowing up to being eaten up, a decision many survivors of the action had been making all night. The three immediately swam back to *Monssen*, which was only a quarter mile away.

The first survivor the three found aboard the burning ship was an uninjured mess attendant who was standing tall on the forecastle, screaming and begging for help. He was coaxed to the fantail and calmed down. Then they found S1 Bert Doughty, who came to for a moment and then lapsed back into unconsciousness. As Spurgeon, Storey, and Hughes scouted through the ship, they located six injured sailors in addition to Doughty and the uninjured mess attendant.

Several small floatplanes were buzzing about over the battle area, so F1 Joe Hughes went below and pulled a white mattress cover from an officer's bunk. He waved the cover and soon attracted a SOC observation plane, one of three that had flown off *San Francisco* to Tulagi the previous afternoon. The SOC landed in the water beside *Monssen*. The aircrewman opened his canopy and listened intently as Hughes told him there were wounded aboard the ship and that he needed a boat sent out immediately. The air-crewman waved to signal his comprehension, and the SOC took off and flew toward Guadalcanal.

While awaiting a boat of some sort, one of the three rescuers reminded the others that *Monssen*'s crew had not drawn pay for months, and conjectured that all the payroll money—they figured it was $500,000 in small bills—was locked away in the ship's safe. There was a little joking about salvage rights before the idle talk became serious. F1 Hughes thought of getting an axe he knew was stored in one of the gun mounts, but neither he nor Storey and Spurgeon wanted to leave the open deck when the ship might sink at any moment.

At last, well after noon, a small landing boat appeared off *Monssen*'s beam. Hughes, Storey, and Spurgeon waved their arms and yelled to attract attention, but the coxswain did his best to ignore them. Finally, the coxswain admitted that he was afraid the destroyer would roll over on his landing craft if he came too close. There was ample cause for concern. *Monssen* was burning and listing far to port. If the landing craft came alongside, it would have to do so to port because the starboard side was too high out of the water. If the ship capsized with the landing craft alongside, the landing craft would probably be captured by some topside equipment. The men aboard *Monssen* sympathized with the coxswain's feelings, but they had strong views of their own. BM2 Storey yanked out the .45-caliber pistol he had salvaged from the body of a dead officer and calmly aimed it at the coxswain. "You son-of-a-bitch," he yelled. "You get that goddamned boat over here right now or I'll kill you." The boat immediately closed on the destroyer. The men aboard *Monssen*, eleven in all, were quickly helped aboard the landing boat, which pulled away with alacrity and headed for Kukum. About thirty minutes later, *Monssen* blew up and sank.

S1 Bert Doughty did not fully regain his senses for several days after he had been evacuated by air to a hospital on Efate.

The vast influx of injured and sick survivors—over 1,000 from *Laffey*, *Cushing*, *Barton*, *Monssen*, and *Atlanta*—totally overwhelmed medical facilities ashore that had trouble coping with injuries and illnesses incurred by the island's aviation and ground-based garrisons. There was no shortage of compassion; hundreds of grimy, underweight Marines volunteered to help care for the survivors of the night battle and thousands of garments were donated by men who barely had shirts on their own backs. But the hospital wards were over-filled before noon and aid stations dedicated to serving infantry battalions and air squadrons were pressed into service. Every transport plane in the South Pacific Area was sent to Henderson Field to start a days-long, around-the-clock evacuation of the most seriously wounded. Army and Navy hospitals and hospital ships and even some French and British civilian facilities as far away as Fiji were caring for patients by late the next afternoon. Inevitably, dozens and perhaps scores of sailors died of their wounds before the doctors could get to them or before they could be gotten to the doctors.

The medical rescue effort was unprecedented in the annals of the military medical services, but it was largely undertaken in an impoverished active war zone where shortages of all types, including medical supply shortages, were the norm. For all that, hundreds of lives that were in extreme jeopardy were saved, often as a result of heroic efforts by shipmates, the boat crews, and the doctors, corpsmen, medics, and nurses from a score of Army and Navy medical units.

For most of the uninjured or ambulatory survivors, the greatest effort went into scrubbing themselves free of thick coatings of fuel oil. There was virtually no sure cure for the clinging gunk, and all the cures, viable or not, caused pain. But it was no laughing matter. Y2 Tom Foreman, of *Cushing*, watched a close friend who had inhaled some fuel oil suffocate in slow agony despite the best efforts of a medical team that was really in over its head. (Foreman himself nearly died from a reaction to the antitetanus shot he was given). S1 Hugh O'Fallon, also of *Cushing*, spent days hunched over in a jungle outhouse, purging oil from his system; the only nourishment worth taking during that time was fruit juice. Hundreds of survivors suffered similar fates, and some died from the rigors, mostly because of dehydration. Many sailors who swallowed fuel oil swear that their bodies smelled of it for many years after, or that it seriously impaired their lives and well-being.

It is estimated that between 700 and 900 American officers and sailors and Marines met their deaths during or as a direct result of the surface action off Savo on November 13, 1942. Over 600 other men who survived the carnage were fated to die as the surviving American warships retired toward Espiritu Santo.

36

San Francisco was nearly done in by *Helena* as the three underway American cruisers fled the battle along Guadalcanal's
northern shore in an unorganized strung-out gaggle. At one
point, *San Francisco*'s radar image merged with that of the land mass
to port. When the wounded flagship reappeared it was by no means
a matter of consensus on *Helena*'s bridge that she was a friendly
vessel. Indeed, *Helena*'s bridge watch had never really been sure
who their ship was following, for the light cruiser's lookouts had
reported *San Francisco*'s demise early in the action. A rather tart
blinker-light challenge was issued, but *San Francisco* was unable
to answer in the required form because no one alive on her bridge
had been privy to or could recall the night's official countersign.
Quickly, a signalman was outfitted with a powerful flashlight and
sent aft to the well deck to repeat, over and over, *San Francisco*'s bow
number: "CA 38 . . . CA 38 . . . CA 38." At length, *Helena* acknowledged and her skipper, Capt Gib Hoover requested instructions from RAdm Dan Callaghan. Hoover was immediately
informed that Callaghan was dead and that *San Francisco*'s acting
captain was a lieutenant commander. Only then did Hoover as-

sume command, a ritual that included replacing *San Francisco* at the head of the loose column of cruisers with *Helena*.

Lt(jg) Jack Bennett joined LCdr Bruce McCandless in *San Francisco's* armored conning tower sometime around 0300 and thereafter shared responsibility for guiding the grievously wounded heavy cruiser along Guadalcanal's northern shore and on to safety. Among the ship's countless unperceived malfunctions was a 15-degree mismatch between the compass in the conning tower and the one in the after emergency steering-control room. Somehow, Lieutenant Commander McCandless avoided tight situations arising from the mismatch, but after he left to have his wounds treated, Lieutenant (jg) Bennett inadvertently steered the ship toward the dark silhouette of Malaita when *Helena's* silhouette merged with the shoreline. Bennett, who was certain he was paralleling the beach, would have run the ship aground had not a sharper-eyed officer called down from Sky Control to apprise Bennett of the imminent danger. This incident was about par for the course, though augmented repair parties working under the skilled and calm leadership of LCdr Rocky Schonland were making enormous strides in correcting the most serious defects. As soon as the compass mismatch was discerned, it was corrected.

Slowly, all the survivors—*Helena, San Francisco, Juneau, Sterett, O'Bannon,* and *Fletcher*—found one another in the dark and in the hour after sunrise. *Juneau,* whose keel had been severed and whose two halves were slightly twisted in opposite directions, set the pace of the retirement; no ship could lay on more speed than her captain felt it was safe for her to steam.

By dawn, *San Francisco's* medical department was ready to concede that it could not effectively handle the flood of wounded officers and sailors, many of whom only turned themselves in for treatment after the danger had passed. Among those who slipped away were the heavy cruiser's new skipper, Capt Cassin Young, and her exec, Cdr Mark Crouter, who had apparently been killed as he lay in his bunk sleeping off some of the effects of extensive burns sustained by the Betty bomber's flaming crash into Battle-2 the afternoon of November 12. News of the urgent need for medical assistance caused Capt Gib Hoover to stop the procession dead in the water and send *Helena*'s junior doctor and several corpsmen to help *San Francisco*'s doctors and corpsmen. *Juneau* was ordered to do the same, and she complied at the same time. The brief pause at about 0800 caused no end of consternation and apoplexy among the skittish, overtired survivors of the night action, but it was a humanitarian gesture all hands aboard all the ships would have expected to be made in their behalf.

卍

Late in the morning, as the force of survivors steamed along San Cristobal's southeast coast, the damage-control parties in charge of bracing *Juneau*'s fractured keel urged their skipper, Capt Lyman Swenson, to ask the other ships for welding tools and the specialists to run them. The blinkered message brought forth numerous volunteers, so Capt Gib Hoover slowed the force to allow the transfers to proceed. At 1035, as the volunteers bound for *Juneau* were assembling their equipment, many lookouts spotted an unidentified airplane dodging through some clouds to starboard. There had been rumors that the Japanese had set up a patrol-plane base near San Cristobal, so Captain Hoover routinely ordered the ships to switch from a wide antisubmarine formation to a close-in antiaircraft formation.

The unidentified multi-engine airplane played cat-and-mouse with the ships until it was positively identified as a friendly Army Air Forces B-17, no doubt on patrol out of Espiritu Santo. At 1058, Captain Hoover ordered all ships to resume the antisubmarine formation while a *Helena* signalman tried to exchange identities with the bomber by means of a blinker tube.

Before the antisubmarine deployment could be reinstituted, and as the formation slowed so several ships could get boats away to *Juneau*, *I-26*, one of the numerous picket submarines the Japanese had deployed along all the routes leading to Guadalcanal, fired as many as six torpedoes from very close range at the virtual wall of gray-hulled American ships in her sights. Moments after that, at precisely 1100, *San Francisco*'s and *Helena*'s lookouts saw torpedo wakes heading for each of their ships from port. Though an instant alert was broadcast, there was no time for any ship to react. Two torpedoes missed *San Francisco*'s bow by a hair and at least one other passed right astern of *Helena*. About 1,000 yards beyond *San Francisco's* starboard beam and about 800 yards beyond *Helena*, one of the fish that had passed ahead of *San Francisco* passed right ahead of *Juneau*. Then the second torpedo that missed *San Francisco* struck *Juneau* on her port side, nearly amidships.

Juneau simply vaporized; it happened that quickly. Apparently, one torpedo entered one of her numerous magazines—the *Atlanta*-class light antiaircraft cruisers were essentially high-speed ammunition dumps—through the thin skin beneath her narrow armor belt. There is no other explanation for the violence and magnitude of the explosion that instantaneously engulfed the broken-backed ship.

A signalman aboard *Helena* who was taking down a message from *Juneau* had his glass trained on the *Juneau* signalman and saw him thrown at least 30 feet in the air by the initial force of the torpedo detonation. An instant later, as scores of inadvertent onlookers gaped and gasped in awe, a vast, violent secondary detonation spread a huge ball of dirty brown and yellow-gray smoke hundreds of feet across the surface. A vast column of white water, more brown and yellow-gray smoke, and gray-painted debris climbed hundreds of feet in the air. One of *Juneau's* dual 5-inch mounts tumbled slowly upward at the crown of the rising column and then plunged into the water hundreds of yards from the center of the blast—right into *Fletcher's* wake, only about 100 feet astern of the destroyer.

No one who saw the display was anything less than speechless, and several onlookers went into shock. Pieces of the demolished ship, a black shower of fuel oil, and parts of people cascaded into the water and as far away as *San Francisco's* main deck for many minutes. A piece of steel plating the size of a door smashed into *San Francisco* only a few feet from where LCdr Rocky Schonland was conferring with LCdr Bruce McCandless and the ship's gunnery officer, by then her third exec in twenty-four hours. The shock of the blast was so great that *San Francisco's* Lt Howard Westin, who was recuperating from his wounds in a bunk below decks, was sure that his ship had been torpedoed.

When the bottom of the smoke cloud lifted from the surface moments after the blast, there was nothing to be seen of *Juneau*. She and all her crew seemed to have vanished. It was as if she had never existed.

Capt Gib Hoover had a split second in which to decide what to do. A brilliant officer—he was under consideration for advancement to flag rank—and an avid student of naval history and tactics, Hoover knew that stopping or even slowing to help would place the entire force in jeopardy. *Juneau's* instantaneous catastrophic demise was more than enough to overcome Hoover's initial compassionate urge to stop. Moreover, the force had little in the way of effective antisubmarine equipment or weapons. *O'Bannon* had been sent to a distant location so the force could not be pinpointed by Japanese radio-direction-finding equipment while she transmitted news of the night battle to higher headquarters. Of the two destroyers present, only *Fletcher* had depth charges aboard; *Sterett* had had to jettison hers when they were threatened by fire from hits she had sustained around her fantail. *San Francisco* was a virtual cripple, *Sterett* could only steer on her engines, and *Helena* didn't have the means to duel with a submarine, even assuming the submarine could be located. With Captain Hoover's initially tacit approval, three of the four survivors laid on their best speeds to clear the area and maneuvered radically to throw off the aim of any follow-up torpedo spreads.

Fletcher's topside crew had not seen the torpedoes nor been warned that there was a submarine on the loose. Cdr William Cole, who assumed the blast had been touched off by a spark from a welder's torch, instinctively turned *Fletcher* toward the center of the blast in the hope of rendering aid. *Fletcher* had only just begun to turn when she was arrested by a message from *Helena* that ordered her to resume her station in the screen. Commander Cole was disconcerted by the order, but *Helena* followed up with a blinker-tube message explaining that torpedo wakes had been sighted and that *Helena* had information that several Japanese submarines were thought to be on station in the vicinity.

The Army Air Forces B-17, which closed on the fleeing warships again at about 1125, provided Captain Hoover with a reasonable alternative to returning to *Juneau's* grave and risking the loss of more precious warships. A *Helena* signalman blinkered an urgent request that the B-17 fly away from the friendly surface force—to throw off Japanese radio-direction-finding efforts—and radio news of the tragedy and a request for assistance to its base at Espiritu Santo. No one who witnessed the demolition of *Juneau* really believed that there was even one survivor, but the effort had to be made. When the *Helena* signalman reported that he had received an acknowledgment from the bomber, Captain Hoover ordered all the survivors to maintain the antisubmarine formation and continue sailing away from *Juneau's* grave at the best speed of the slowest ship, still well over 20 knots.

The B-17 dropped its crew's life rafts to swimmers the aircrew spotted in the water—but it did not send the message *Helena's* signalman had asked it to send. It maintained strict radio silence as it continued to patrol its assigned sector for many hours. When the B-17 finally did return to its base, the pilot's rather laconic report was never transmitted to any headquarters that might have set a rescue effort in motion.

৵

Unbelievably, about 100 members of *Juneau's* crew survived the detonation and instantaneous loss of their ship. S1 Wy Butterfield, a 5-inch mount trainer, was catapulted out of his mount when its roof was blown off, but he persisted in trying to make his way to the mount's hatchway until he realized that he was underwater and in the clear. He involuntarily gasped in huge amounts of salt water and fuel oil until he surfaced right next to a doughnut-shaped balsa life raft. Butterfield crawled into the net-bottomed raft and threw up salt water and oil as heads popped out of the water all around him. When Butterfield recovered somewhat from the retching fit, he paddled as well as he could with his hands. Everyone he found was wounded. In very little time, Butterfield helped load three balsa rafts and a large net that was buoyed up with flotation tanks.

SM2 Joseph Hartney heard a Condition-I signal sound and was just stepping from the after gun-director trunk to the main deck when he was engulfed in a tremendous explosion. His eyes were immediately dosed with fuel oil and he was catapulted high into the air, unable to see where he was or what was going on. Hartney fell to the deck and, as his senses cleared, he heard the cries of men he could not see. He tried to stand, but one of his dungaree cuffs caught on a piece of metal, and that held him down. When Hartney blindly groped at the cuff of his dungarees, he felt water around his feet and thus learned that the ship was sinking. Before he could act, he was pulled beneath the waves as the ship took her astoundingly rapid plunge. Pain from water pressure was building up around Hartney's head and he had about reached the limit of his endurance when he suddenly began floating upward. He surfaced next to a large piece of shoring timber and latched on for dear life. He was just in time, for the suction created by the descending cruiser all but pulled him down again; it took with it a shipmate whom he had briefly seen struggling in the water only a few feet away. Hartney kicked through a thick film of fuel oil cluttered with broken debris and bodies until he came upon a balsa raft completely filled with sailors. He let his timber go and clung to a rope attached to the raft, shouldering in among other uninjured survivors.

GM2 Allen Heyn was relieving another member of his crew for the after 1.1-inch mount when the other man stopped talking and stared at something behind Heyn's back. Before Heyn could turn, the torpedo struck the ship and Heyn was thrown headfirst against the mount. When Heyn came to a moment later, everything he could see was broken or breaking and fuel oil was falling on him in a heavy downpour. Through the murk of smoke and the fuel oil, Heyn saw that the fantail was sticking straight up in the air, and that men were trying to pull themselves up the oil-slick deck toward the railing by means of a life line. There seemed to be dead and dying men everywhere. When Heyn finally moved to save himself, he found that one of his feet was caught in the twisted gun shield. By then, the water was up around his chest. He instinctively grabbed one of numerous kapok life jackets that were lying loose on the deck and pulled it close to his chest. The water went over Heyn's head and he gave in to the certainty of his death. Suddenly, the gun shield moved and released his broken foot, and the life jacket carried him straight toward the surface. He shot through a film of oil that was at least two inches thick and surfaced amid a collection of blueprints and drawings of ships and roll upon roll of toilet paper. As Heyn tried to clear his head and figure a way out of his predicament, a doughnut life raft popped out of the water right beside him. Heyn grasped the life line around the raft just as he heard the desperate cries of a shipmate, one of the ship's postal clerks. The other man said he could not swim and that one of his legs had been blown off. Heyn helped him into the raft, by which time other shipmates were straggling in from all over the place. By the time the group settled down, the masts of all the other ships had disappeared over the horizon.

卍

All of the surviving warships buried their dead at sea off San Cristobal on the afternoon of November 13, and all arrived safely at Espiritu Santo on the afternoon of November 14. As the survivors sailed into the harbor, thousands of sailors aboard ships of every description came to attention and saluted the battered veterans of the battle of Friday the Thirteenth.

Shortly after Capt Gib Hoover conned *Helena* on to Noumea, the seat of VAdm Bill Halsey's South Pacific command, he was summarily relieved of his command and sent home in disgrace. The immediate cause of the relief and destruction of Hoover's career was his so-called abandonment of the *Juneau* survivors. Admiral Halsey admitted years later that he might have acted hastily in relieving one of the U.S. Navy's most aggressive and most experienced combat commanders. Rumor has it that Halsey was unduly influenced by his chief of staff, a psychotic misanthrope who is said to have harbored a grudge against Hoover from their Annapolis days. Whatever the actual cause, the result devastated the morale of *Helena*'s crew and deprived the U.S. Navy of one of her best potential admirals.

In fact, there was some reason to be emotional. Approximately 100 officers and men made it off *Juneau*, but as many as 90 died from their wounds or as a result of the extreme privations they suffered while adrift in the sun-swept sea. Many survivors went berserk in the intense sunlight or became crazed from the lack of fresh water. The wounded died off early, though the only officer to survive did so despite severe injuries sustained in the blast. A number of the survivors committed suicide, others drank salt water and died, and several died from despondency. Most of the dead certainly succumbed to extreme dehydration, and many drowned because they were too weak to hold on to flotation devices or, in some cases, because they fell asleep with their heads in the water. Every death was the culmination of intense agony and the most brutal mental and physical suffering imaginable.

The large group that initially included GM2 Allen Heyn and SM2 Joseph Hartney dwindled rapidly during the first few days. The rafts were overflown several times by B-17s, transport planes, and PBYs, and sometimes pilots and aircrewmen even waved to the shipwrecked sailors. But no help arrived.

After several days with the large group, GM2 Heyn drifted off with two other sailors, both of whom went mad and died the next day. The day after that, a PBY circled over him. He waved with what felt like the last of his energy, but the airplane left. Heyn was about to give up, but the PBY returned hours later and dropped smoke pots near his raft. Several minutes later, *Ballard*, a PBY tender out of Tulagi, steamed up over the horizon and made a beeline for GM2 Heyn's raft. He was between clean sheets within the half hour.

After several days afloat, the seven survivors of a much larger number that had started out with S1 Wy Butterfield spotted a PBY high overhead. When the patrol bomber began circling the raft, SM1 Lester Zook, the only signalman in the group, passed semaphore signals to identify the group and ask for help. A blinker signal from the PBY explained that the airplane was not allowed to land but that a life jacket and some food and water would be dropped. The airplane circled once more, then came in low and slow. The parcel landed about 40 feet from the raft, and Wy Butterfield swam out to retrieve it. He had to fight for the manna with three sharks. Flailing for all he was worth, Butterfield landed a few good punches with his belt knife and ran the sharks off. He was certain he had been chewed up, but he found only a small cut on his foot. By the time Butterfield returned to the raft, the PBY pilot, who had witnessed the desperate shark fight, had decided to ignore his orders. The PBY landed and taxied up to the raft. One of the aircrewmen climbed out onto the starboard wing and dropped a life ring, which one of the shipwrecked sailors eagerly grabbed. The raft was then hauled to the PBY's opened waist gun blister, and all seven *Juneau* sailors were taken aboard the amphibious bomber.

This was by far the largest single group of rescued survivors, over half the total. The PBY flew them back to Tulagi for treatment and eventual evacuation.

Three men from the large group that had included GM2 Allen Heyn set out alone in one of the rubber rafts the B-17 had dropped right after *Juneau* went down. The three—SM2 Joseph Hartney, S1 Jimmy Fitzgerald, and Lt(jg) Charles Wang—told the others that they were going to paddle to the nearest island and await rescue or sit out the war. Everyone else thought the three were crazy and elected to stay in the large group. By November 20, Lieutenant (jg) Wang, who had been severely wounded, was nearly out of his head, and Hartney and Fitzgerald were not far behind. The three survived on rain water captured in a small rubber bag meant for bailing and on a pouch of rations they found attached to the raft. Hartney did most of the navigating from memory, and he and Fitzgerald did all the paddling since Wang was too badly hurt to help. The raft was found on November 20 by a PBY, which circled, dropped smoke pots, and looked like it was about to land. However, a heavy squall suddenly came up and sent the bomber scurrying to a safe altitude. The heavy wind drove the raft away and, perhaps, the PBY ran low on fuel. Whatever the reason, the PBY was not there when the squall passed, and it did not return. That night, the raft bumped into a coral reef and was eventually driven to the beach of a tiny island by the morning tide. Hartney and Fitzgerald left Wang on the beach while they explored the island. They found a stream in short order and were found in turn by several islanders. One of the islanders, who spoke broken English, told the three that a European resided on the next island, Santa Ana, and he volunteered to carry word of the shipwrecked sailors to him. Next day, November 22, the half-caste son of a German planter arrived to take Wang, Hartney, and Fitzgerald to his father. From then on, the three were on the road to recovery. The German and his son had nursed the three back to a semblance of good health by the time a PBY arrived two days later. The three were receiving intense medical treatment at Espiritu Santo by the end of the day.

In all, including the doctor and three corpsmen dispatched to *San Francisco* before *Juneau* was sunk, just fifteen of the light anti-aircraft cruiser's 650-plus officers and men survived.

Among those who died while adrift was the oldest of five brothers named Sullivan who were serving aboard *Juneau* when she was torpedoed. The loss of all five Sullivan brothers in one catastrophe became a national sensation, and Captain Hoover's already-severed head was offered up by the Navy. There was thus no way to reinstate *Helena*'s captain even after he had been exonerated by a board of inquiry.

37

Dawn of November 13 found *Hiei* virtually dead in the water behind Savo Island. Her steering control had been destroyed by one of several American torpedo hits during the wild night melee, she had suffered innumerable small- and medium-caliber shell hits throughout her upper works, her captain was dead, her sister battleship and all her smaller consorts but one—destroyer *Yukikaze*—had fled. Given the right circumstances, *Hiei* was salvageable, but the rising sun exposed her to a danger every bit as fearsome as any she or any of her kind had ever faced: Only 50 miles away, a thoroughly aroused Cactus Air Force was awakening to the new day and new possibilities, and fleet carrier *Enterprise* was nearly close enough to begin launching elements of her air group in the direction of Guadalcanal.

The two-man crew of a Marine SBD Dauntless dive-bomber found the crippled behemoth just after sunrise. The Dauntless was on its way through low clouds and intermittent squalls to nearby Santa Ysabel to look for oncoming Japanese ships, but the pilot could not resist attacking what surely seemed to be the target of a lifetime. As the SBD's radioman-gunner keyed a sighting report to the Cactus Air Operations center—Cactus Air Ops—at Henderson Field, the pilot maneuvered through streams of rising 25 mm tracer to drop his 500-pound general purpose bomb. Thick, dark smoke was billowing from both of *Hiei*'s forward main turrets, and the guns in several of her after 6-inch mounts appeared to be dangling precariously over the water. The pilot estimated that his target was making all of about 5 knots.

The attack on what appeared to be all but a huge sitting duck came to nothing; the bomb exploded in the water, causing no apparent damage. As the Dauntless's radioman-gunner repeated the sighting report, the pilot resumed his course toward Santa Ysabel.

Cactus Air Ops went all aflutter at the news of a crippled battleship off Savo. Immediately, the first three SBDs that could be readied were launched to search for more cripples, and Capt Joe Foss, of VMF-121, was dispatched aboard an F4F Wildcat fighter to make a close inspection of the battleship.

The Dauntlesses, which were led by Maj Joe Sailer, the skipper of Marine Scout-Bomber Squadron 132 (VMSB-132), made low passes over all the cripples they could find beneath the low clouds. No shots were exchanged, though there were some mighty untrusting sailors aboard the American cripples and the airmen were not always sure whose side any given ship might represent. The three brought back an accurate enough report on the friendly cripples—*Aaron Ward, Atlanta,* and *Portland*—for the fledgling naval-base command at Tulagi to act upon.

By the time Captain Foss arrived over *Hiei* in his F4F, the battleship was flanked by three destroyers. Apparently, *Yukikaze*, which was over-filled with wounded and nonessential battleship crewmen and RAdm Hiroaki Abe, had been relieved by destroyers *Shigure, Shiratsuyu,* and *Yugure*, comprising Capt Yasuhide Setoyama's Destroyer Division 27. Foss looked the cripple over from a safe distance outside the ample antiaircraft umbrella, noted a great deal of damage, and hightailed it straight back to Henderson Field to report to Air Ops.

Marine BGen Lou Woods, the Cactus Air Force commander, ordered an instant strike against *Hiei* by six SBDs that happened to be ready to go. At the same time, all the other available Dauntlesses and a newly arrived six-plane division of Marine TBF Avenger torpedo bombers were to be readied to undertake follow-on strikes.

The day's agenda was clearly set: Without news from searchers that a fresh Japanese surface force was on the way toward Guadalcanal, all available assets would be directed against *Hiei* until she was laid to rest.

The six SBDs, which launched at about 0600, were all from VMSB-142, a squadron that had arrived at Henderson Field only the day before, in the midst of the Betty torpedo attack on the shipping in the channel. By 0615, the six novices, including Maj Bob Richard, the squadron commander, were set to commence their premier combat dives against the many-horned cripple. The SBDs were brand-new and each was equipped with an electric bomb release, an innovation that was just finding its way into Marine squadrons after several months of use in Navy Dauntless squadrons. During the final approach, Major Richard, an old hand who should have known better, checked the new bomb release one last time and inadvertently dumped his 1,000-pound bomb into the water.

During the final approach, MTSgt Don Thornbury, another old hand, saw a single-engine airplane far below his SBD and paused to wonder what an old Navy trainer was doing out over Savo; then he realized he was looking down at a Zero fighter. When Thornbury looked again, the Zero was gone. By then, the main concern was from a rather unhealthy dose of 25mm and 13mm gunfire that was being put up by the battleship and her three destroyer consorts. Thornbury put aside all thoughts of mortality and tipped over into the first live combat dive of his seven-year career.

Riding in Thornbury's rear seat was another breed of Marine, Pvt John Audas, the youngest and most junior man in the entire squadron. Unlike Thornbury, Audas had nothing to do except look back over the sights of his twin .30-caliber in the unlikely event a Zero followed the Dauntless into the dive. As usual, young John Audas floated somewhere between the back of his seat and his shoulder harness. What was unusual was the array of black antiaircraft bursts blossoming close behind his Dauntless's tail. Audas did not even know that he was plummeting down upon a Japanese battleship until he was pushed hard against his shoulder straps by the terrific gravitational forces generated by Don Thornbury's perfect recovery from the dive. Only then did Private Audas see *Hiei*.

Seconds later he also saw the 1,000-pound bomb from his own dive-bomber strike the Japanese cripple squarely amidships.

Of the five VMSB-142 pilots who released their bombs over *Hiei*, only MTSgt Don Thornbury got a direct hit, and another was credited with a near miss. Though Thornbury's direct hit was far from debilitating—much less mortal—this strike set *Hiei*'s life clock ticking toward zero.

卐

It took another hour for Cactus to get another strike away. Part of the problem was the ongoing heavy demand for searchers to cover all the possible approach sectors leading to the American-held portion of Guadalcanal. For example, MTSgt Don Thornbury, a proven hitter, was pulled from the ranks of pilots set to go after *Hiei*, and sent on a fruitless search over a neighboring island. Another problem was the massive infusion of fresh squadrons that had bolstered the Cactus Air Force in only two days' time; many of the new airplanes and their crews were operating below peak performance for combat, maintenance crews and spare parts were in excessively high demand, and Henderson Field's rather crude facilities were generally overtaxed.

The second formal strike of the day against *Hiei* involved another combat debut. In this case, newly arrived VMSB-131, the Marine Corps's first and only torpedo-bomber unit, got four TBF Avengers aloft at about 0700. The four were led by Capt George Dooley, who had assumed command of the Marine torpedo contingent literally upon arrival at Guadalcanal on November 12 because the VMSB-131 skipper, LtCol Pat Moret, had been dragged kicking and screaming to replace the Marine Air Group 14 (MAG-14) operations officer.

George Dooley was already a legend. He had entered flight school right out of college in 1940, but before earning his wings he had been grievously burned in a midair collision. Dooley should have been surveyed out of the Marine Corps after undergoing numerous skin grafts over most of his body, but he rehabilitated himself through force of will. Though badly scarred and a full year behind his classmates, Dooley went on to earn his wings and the

334

gold bars of a second lieutenant. Eventually, he helped form VMSB-131 and was officially its flight (operations) officer when it deployed to Guadalcanal on November 12.

Captain Dooley's flight of four TBFs experienced some difficulty in finding *Hiei* because the sea around Savo was both obscured by low clouds and covered with burning, smoking ships. More to the point, the newly arrived Marine torpedo pilots were not particularly familiar with major landmarks such as Savo and nearby Cape Esperance. However, at about 0715, Dooley was reasonably certain he knew which burning ship was the correct target.

Also aloft at that moment were seven Marine SBD dive-bombers under the VMSB-132 commander, Maj Joe Sailer. Prior to takeoff, Sailer, a veteran of nearly two hectic weeks on Guadalcanal, had arranged to launch his attack at the same time Dooley's TBFs were releasing their fish. Thus, as Dooley led his flight toward *Hiei*, Sailer's voice came up on the tactical network: "Mark five, Dool. Mark five," by which he meant that the dive-bombers would be in position to release their bombs in five minutes.

Everything seemed to be going great, but Dooley suddenly realized that there was some sort of action erupting dead ahead. In fact, eight Marine Wildcats returning from an abortive strike against a nonexistent Japanese carrier were tangling with a newly arrived squadron of Zero fighters that had been set out to guard the cripple. In a whirling, swirling melee right over *Hiei*, the American veterans—a mixed bag from three squadrons—claimed seven confirmed kills and two probables.

Just as the four Marine TBFs were about to begin their final run on the battleship—their first combat strike ever—1stLt Doug Bangert brushed against the edge of the moving fighter scrap. Suddenly, Bangert's turret gunner, TSgt John Dewey, sang out, "Bandit at twelve o'clock," as he opened fire with his single power-operated .50-caliber machine gun.

Dewey was overexcited. The Zero was dead on Bangert's tail, which was straight "ahead" for the man in the rear-facing turret. The erroneous call arrested the attention of all four Avenger pilots at a critical moment, and that nearly aborted the approach. The Zero bored in from directly behind Bangert's TBF and opened fire. The Marine manning the TBF's .30-caliber ventral stinger was superficially wounded, but Technical Sergeant Dewey cleared his slate by shooting the Japanese fighter out of the sky.

By then, *Hiei* was looming in the pilots' sights, and the thick cones of tracer rising from the three destroyers forced Dooley and the other plots to undertake no end of twisting and jinking. As if this was not enough, all four of *Hiei* 's main turrets swung outboard to bear on the four Avengers, and all eight guns fired at once. All of the 14-inch rounds appeared to land short, thus raising a curtain of water that left behind a persistent rainbow-hued film of spume perhaps wittingly designed to throw off the aim of the torpedo pilots. Nevertheless, Captain Dooley released his fish, and the others followed suit. Or tried to. In the end, Lieutenant Bangert could not get his bomb bay to open because his hydraulics had been damaged moments before by the attacking Zero. Another torpedo porpoised when it hit the water and then circled harmlessly well short of the target. Of the two fish that ran true, only one detonated. On the basis of a confirmation rendered by Lieutenant Bangert, credit for the hit was given to Captain Dooley.

Maj Joe Sailer's seven-plane SBD strike went off more or less in conjunction with Captain Dooley's torpedo attack, but the Dauntlesses went scoreless.

卍

At 1010, Capt George Dooley returned with three other Marine TBFs and six F4Fs led by Capt Joe Foss. As the Avengers dropped down to line up on the smoking cripple, Foss's fighters streaked in to engage one of the destroyers before passing low over *Hiei* to deliver an attention-arresting strafing attack that sent many of the battleship's antiaircraft gunners scurrying or ducking for cover. The diversion gave Dooley's torpedo bombers an ample edge, and though under continuous heavy fire from the destroyers, they launched clean and followed through right over their target. Dooley's second torpedo of the day detonated against the cripple's flank and sent a devastating shock wave through her abused frame. As Dooley's flight receded, Joe Foss returned to execute a breathtaking pylon turn right in front of the battleship's shattered pagoda bridge. During the turn, Foss executed an emphatic one-finger salute for the benefit of any Japanese who might have been watching.

336

꙰

Earlier, at 0722, and nearly two hours after launching numerous searchers to look for Japanese warships, fleet carrier *Enterprise* had turned into the wind 280 miles south of Guadalcanal and launched ten Fighting Squadron 10 (Fighting-10) Wildcats and nine Torpedo Squadron 10 (Torpedo-10) Avengers. After orbiting once, the two groups turned toward Henderson Field.

Enterprise's presence in these hostile waters was both a compromise and an indication of how seriously the U.S. South Pacific command viewed the renewed Japanese push to interdict Henderson Field and reinforce their ground forces ashore on Guadalcanal. On October 26, off the Santa Cruz Islands, *Enterprise* had emerged from a direct confrontation with four Japanese carriers as America's only *marginally* operational fleet carrier. Among many other ailments caused by Japanese bombs on October 26 was a severely damaged forward elevator. Though fortunately the elevator had been jammed in the up position, thus allowing *Enterprise* to launch and recover aircraft, the carrier's capacity for lowering and raising warplanes between her flight deck and hangar deck was severely impaired. Under certain conditions, she had to stop launch and recovery operations altogether so that her midships and after elevators could do the job.

The mid-November alarm had caught *Enterprise* undergoing temporary repairs in Noumea, and she had been reluctantly released to join the fight. Her remaining damage was so severe that most of a battalion of Seabees that had been hurrying to complete the repairs had remained aboard the carrier as she raced toward Guadalcanal. Withal, though her Air Group 10 and her mobility might become critical factors in the expanding conflict, *Enterprise* would, under all conditions but the most dire emergency, be held at a safe distance from Guadalcanal. Eventually, if the rumored Japanese carriers were not found and attacked, most of Air Group 10 would shuttle to Henderson Field to bolster the Cactus Air Force. However, if the Japanese carriers were found or launched an attack against Allied shipping, even priceless *Enterprise* would be hurled into the breech.

Just after noon, a four-plane Wildcat division from Fighting-10 was vectored out on a radar heading and found a Japanese four-engine patrol bomber edging toward their ship. The flying boat was instantly shot down. There was a brief discussion on the precious carrier's bridge about whether it was best to turn away from Guadalcanal or brazen it out. When RAdm Thomas Kinkaid thought about what his boss, VAdm Bill Halsey, might have to add to the discussion, brazening it out became the order of the day. It was a good choice; apparently, the flying boat did not transmit a sighting report before it was destroyed.

卍

The first Air Group 10 strike aircraft to be committed to Cactus were the nine Torpedo-10 TBFs. These were led by Lt Scoofer Coffin, the Torpedo-10 skipper. The ten Fighting-10 Wildcats were led by Lt John Sutherland, the senior of several *Hornet* fighter pilots temporarily transferred to Fighting-10 following the sinking of their ship on October 26. Rather than waste fuel on a long climb and because the cloud base was quite low, Lieutenant Coffin's Avengers held at 500 feet. Sutherland's much faster fighters, which were grouped in two four-plane divisions and one two-plane section, were obliged to weave overhead and below to match speed with the slower torpedo bombers.

At about 1020, as the boringly routine journey was nearing its conclusion, the mixed flight rounded Cape Esperance to begin its final approach on Henderson Field. Though Scoofer Coffin had no inkling that *Hiei* was virtually adrift behind Savo, he improvised an attack the moment he sized up the situation as it appeared before his eyes.

As Lieutenant Sutherland's Wildcats deployed to screen the Avengers from orbiting Zeros—there were none present at that time—Lieutenant Coffin led seven other bombers—the last was equipped with four 500-pound bombs—up to 5,000 feet. The extra time was well spent, for a nose-down approach from relatively high altitude would pay for itself in the extra speed the TBFs would accumulate on the way to launch altitude, only 150 feet above the waves. When the Avengers reached altitude, they split off into two groups of four planes each to deliver a textbook hammer-and-anvil attack against the battleship's port and starboard bows.

The torpedo bombers flew through the bottom of the thick clouds as they passed beneath 1,000 feet, and *Hiei* loomed dead ahead. At about the same moment, the battleship's stunned, beleaguered gunners traversed both forward 14-inch turrets to bear on Coffin's element, which was approaching from port. All four guns spat smoke and flames, and pilots and aircrewmen watched in breathless, silent awe as the huge shells passed them by to raise huge harmless geysers miles away. As the two line-abreast Avenger formations came within 1,000 yards of the helpless target, each pilot toggled his torpedo by means of the electric release, and then each activated his emergency manual release for good measure.

All eight fish slid into the water as all eight Avengers pulled up and away to evade the rising tracer put up by *Hiei* and her three consorts. Within the minute, three of the eight torpedoes detonated against *Hiei* 's hull. One each tore gaping holes in the port and starboard bows, and the third, from the port group, wreaked further havoc astern, abreast the already damaged rudder. Perhaps other torpedoes struck *Hiei*, but the same problems that plagued ship-launched torpedoes dogged the determined, brave torpedo-bomber crews. Three detonations for eight launches was about as good as it got. The ninth TBF, with four bombs aboard, delivered a glide-bombing attack against the battleship, but none of the bombs struck home.

As the Torpedo-10 contingent smartly reformed beyond the Japanese antiaircraft umbrella, Lieutenant Coffin flew back over *Hiei* to take pictures. Then the TBFs entered the traffic circle over Henderson Field and landed. As soon as Coffin's contingent had landed, BGen Lou Woods arrived to see who they were; the Cactus Air commander had no idea who had sent the Avengers, so secret had been *Enterprise*'s approach.

⌗

At 1110, *Hiei* was visited by fourteen Army Air Forces B-17 heavy bombers of the 11th Heavy Bombardment Group's 72nd Bomb Squadron. Following long search flights out of Espiritu Santo, the B-17s had assembled over San Cristobal and then had proceeded to Savo to jettison the four 500-pound bombs each normally carried on search hops. Thus the majestically wheeling B-17 formation—the largest to appear thus far over Guadalcanal—found *Hiei* at 1110. At the right moment, Maj Donald Ridings, the 72nd Bomb Squadron's skipper, turned the entire flight over to his bombardier, who acquired the huge target through his Norden bomb sight and followed through to release his bomber's payload. Each of the trailing Flying Fortresses followed suit, and a total of fifty-six 500-pound bombs cascaded toward the helpless target from 14,000 feet.

B-17s had been undertaking antishipping missions since the first day of the war. The results had been mixed. Only a few weeks earlier, an 11th Bombardment Group B-17 had been instrumental in sinking a Japanese cruiser. However, of the fifty-six 500-pound bombs the B-17s dropped against *Hiei*, only one was scored a direct hit and only one other was rated a near miss.

卍

At 1120, as the B-17s receded from view, Maj Joe Sailer, the VMSB-132 skipper, returned with six of his Dauntlesses to try to break the pattern of the squadron's scoreless first strike. Sailer and two of his pilots planted their 1,000-pound bombs on the battered target; the other three missed altogether.

No sooner had Joe Sailer's Dauntlesses dropped and scored than Lt Swede Larsen arrived with three other Navy Avengers from his Torpedo-8 and two Marine Avengers from VMSB-131.

This was to be Torpedo-8's last strike of the campaign. The squadron's first strike over Guadalcanal had been launched from *Saratoga's* flight deck on August 7—D-Day—and Torpedo-8 Avengers had flown against the Japanese on August 24, during the Eastern Solomons carrier battle. In mid-September, several weeks after *Saratoga* had been damaged by a Japanese submarine torpedo, Larsen had led his bolstered squadron to Henderson Field. Until the arrival of the Marine Avengers on November 12, Torpedo-8 had been the Cactus Air Force's first and only torpedo unit. The remnant of the squadron—four crews and four airplanes—was to have stood down that morning, but Larsen—who had rebuilt Torpedo-8 after its nearly total annihilation at Midway—had begged for one last mission.

Swede Larsen's last attack out of Cactus started at about 8,000 feet, from which the four Navy and two Marine TBFs descended to about 200 feet before leveling off at a speed of 180 to 200 knots. Major Sailer's six dive-bombers were just pulling out of their dives as the three pairs of Avengers began their final approaches from three different angles.

The antiaircraft fire, which had been following the Dauntlesses, suddenly switched to the Avengers. Sgt Dominick Pace, the .50-caliber turret gunner aboard 1stLt Martin Roush's VMSB-131 TBF had swung his turret as far around to the left as he could in the hope of being able to get rounds into the battleship. Pace could not quite get the gun to bear, but he could see "red golf balls" streaking past him. Despite the intense antiaircraft barrage, all the TBFs held to their courses and dropped their fish inside of 1,000 yards from the target. Momentum carried several of the Avengers right over the huge ship's main deck, while others, like Lieutenant Roush's, swung out and passed right up *Hiei*'s side. At that point, Sergeant Pace was able to get his machine gun to bear. As Pace watched Japanese gunners firing right at him, he simply triggered rapid short bursts at the huge gray vessel.

Two hits were credited, one to Lt Swede Larsen, whose fish bored right into *Hiei*'s side amidships, and the other to 1stLt Martin Roush, who put his torpedo into the battleship's port bow. Two of the remaining four fish missed the target, and two hung up in their bomb bays and had to be hauled back to the field.

卍

For the next three hours, *Hiei* was spared further bombing because the bomber crews needed to bolster search elements and rest. However, the respite was broken when Lt Scoofer Coffin led five other Torpedo-10 Avengers back to Savo at 1435. Of the six torpedoes launched, three hit and three missed.

The last strike against *Hiei* was launched just before sunset by a mixed bag of four VMSB-132 and VMSB-141 SBDs under Maj Joe Sailer, back for his fourth mission and third strike of the day. By then, the day's marginal flying weather had all but shut *Hiei* in. Indeed, the weather was so bad that the tiny dive-bomber formation came unglued and only Sailer found the primary target. However, Sailer could not get lined up on *Hiei;* his best shot was a near miss beside one of the battleship's screening destroyers. After the drop, Sailer nearly became lost in the bad weather; he was lucky to get home to Henderson Field alive.

MTSgt Ed Waloff ran straight into a cloud that obscured all the targets, but he recovered in time to redirect his dive at one of the destroyers. Waloff became somewhat disoriented in the rapidly worsening murk and released his 500-pound bomb while his airplane was partially on its back. The bomb did not release and the weather was so bad that Waloff dared not risk a climb back to diving altitude, so he carried the bomb home.

The two VMSB-141 pilots, whose battered squadron had been officially relieved by Maj Bob Richard's VMSB-142, were scheduled to fly to the rear the next morning and were not supposed to have flown at all on November 13. However, the continuous action against *Hiei*, the ongoing searches, and two full-scale air strikes against nonexistent Japanese carriers had created a severe shortage of pilots who were not too tired to fly safely, so the two pilots and their radioman-gunners had agreed to make the one last hop. The two Dauntlesses never completed their dives on *Hiei*, and both pilots and both gunners disappeared without a word or a trace. They were the only Cactus aircrew losses of the day.

彑

In the end, it was the Japanese who delivered the final blow. Unable to sail away under her own waning power and beyond the reach of any ship powerful enough to rig a viable tow, *Hiei* had to be written off along with the 450 officers and sailors who had died aboard her in the face of gunfire and torpedoes from American surface warships and the bombs and torpedoes of American bombers. Late in the night of Friday, November 13, 1942, minutes after the last of her crew was taken off by the last of the three shielding destroyers, scuttling charges laid deep in *Hiei* 's bowels opened gaping holes that ended a life begun on November 21, 1912. *Hiei* was the first Japanese battleship ever to face American surface forces, she was the first battleship the Japanese ever lost in war, and she was the first battleship sunk by the U.S. Navy since 1898.

PART VI

The Slot

38

The Japanese had won a stunning tactical victory over the American surface force they had engaged off Savo—they claimed a far larger victory—but their carefully laid plan of action lay in ruins by the forenoon of November 13.

The Japanese were meticulous planners, but the realities of war against an often desperate adversary had not yet taught them that flexibility was the key to seeing their plans to successful fruition. Time and again at Guadalcanal, on land and at sea, operational difficulties and unforeseen countermoves by American land and naval forces had ruined the outcomes of Japan's best-planned operations. Often as not, the resolve of the Japanese went the way of their rigid plans.

The moment that RAdm Raizo Tanaka heard of the failure of RAdm Hiroaki Abe's bombardment force to bombard Henderson Field to oblivion, he turned his large convoy of transports and destroyers back to the nearest safe haven, Faisi, in the Shortlands, to await a more favorable outcome. Tanaka was among Japan's boldest and most imaginative naval commanders. His reticence about going on is emblematic of the pyrrhic qualities of the outcome of Abe's unexpected engagement with RAdm Dan Callaghan's makeshift surface force: Abe's ships had destroyed more American ships than Abe had lost, but he had been kept from his mission; so long as Henderson Field remained operational, Tanaka's slow transports and the thousands of soldiers they carried would be at risk as soon as they came within range of the Cactus Air Force.

So, the Japanese plan lay in ruins. The only way to retrieve strategic victory from Abe's stunning beside-the-point tactical victory was to send in more powerful surface forces to destroy the Cactus Air Force. This the Japanese did, with alacrity.

VAdm Gunichi Mikawa, the Japanese 8th Fleet commander, was already on the way. His assigned mission had always been to bombard Henderson Field on the night of November 13–14, although the original plan had the bombardment going off in direct support of a contemporaneous unloading operation around Cape Esperance by Tanaka's transports.

Mikawa had never suffered a defeat at the hands of American surface forces. Indeed, his stunning victory off Savo on the night of August 8 had done more to mold the course of the Guadalcanal Campaign than any other single event since. The Savo battle of August 8 had literally tainted the outlooks of all the American admirals charged with keeping the supply lines to Guadalcanal open. Indeed, the nervous tactics employed by Dan Callaghan in the wee hours of Friday the Thirteenth had been shaped by Gunichi Mikawa's brilliant handling of the Savo debacle.

Since August 8, however, Mikawa's powerful 8th Fleet had been steadily whittled down. Only three of the original eight cruisers that had accompanied Mikawa to Savo on August 8 were still with him. Now dubbed the Outer Seas Force, the main body of Mikawa's 8th Fleet—the Support Group—was composed of four heavy cruisers, two light cruisers, and six destroyers. Its mission on November 13 was to slip through the American search umbrella and bombard Henderson Field so heavily that follow-on surface and transport units would be able to advance on Guadalcanal with impunity.

The identical mission, undertaken by Mikawa and others, had been attempted time and again since mid-August with mixed results. Often as not, the approach had been discovered and interdicted by Cactus-based bombers, and no single bombardment had ever quite laid the Cactus Air Force to rest. In light of the mixed results of recent history, the Japanese extemporized a solution that turned Mikawa's effort into the first of a series of two bombardments: one by Mikawa's Outer Seas Force Support Group, and the other by a makeshift force that was forming around the so-called Main Body of two heavy cruisers, one light cruiser, and three destroyers under the direct command of VAdm Nobutake Kondo. It was hoped that Tanaka's troop-laden transports could sail safely between the effects of the two bombardments the Japanese planned on the run—between Mikawa's bombardment on the night of November 13–14 and Kondo's bombardment on the night of November 14–15. If all went well—if the Cactus Air Force could be defanged—Mikawa's bombardment would ensure the success of Tanaka's approach through the Slot, and Kondo's would ensure the safety of the unloading operation near Cape Esperance.

The first requirement was that Mikawa's force arrive safely off Lunga Point. To do so, Mikawa had to evade the thoroughly aroused and massively bolstered Cactus scout-bomber squadrons charged with searching Guadalcanal's adjacent islands and far up the Slot. To accomplish this crucial part of his mission, old hand Mikawa simply sailed where Cactus searchers did not fly—far north of Choiseul and Santa Ysabel.

While Mikawa was making his end-around run, the core of Admiral Kondo's still-forming battle force was located by one of the many 11th Heavy Bombardment Group B-17s dispatched throughout the day from Espiritu Santo. The discovery was made north of Ontong Java Atoll, on the way from Truk, and it led American senior planners to conclude that there would be at least one peaceful night around Henderson Field before the Japanese returned in force. This surmise exactly fit objective reality: Other than the Cactus Air Force, the South Pacific command had nothing with which to defend Henderson Field; no surface force of any size was within reach of the place, and none would be for at least twenty-four hours.

Mikawa's timing was exquisite. He arrived within range of Cactus searchers and strikers only after it was too dark for him to be seen had any of either been aloft. As a result, his formidable surface force slipped in unannounced.

卍

While Mikawa's Main Unit of two heavy cruisers, one light cruiser, and two destroyers searched in vain west of Savo for American surface units that might challenge them, RAdm Shoji Nishimura's Bombardment Unit of two heavy cruisers, one light cruiser, and four destroyers deployed to deliver the blow.

Scout planes off heavy cruisers *Suzuya* and *Maya* were launched well ahead of the start of the bombardment to light the target with magnesium parachute flares. At about 0130, November 14, as the scouts flew over the beach to fix the exact location of Henderson Field, one of them woke 2ndLt Emil Novak, of the Army Air Forces' 67th Pursuit Squadron, a P-39 fighter unit that had been permanently deployed at Cactus since August. Novak, who had arrived for his tour with the 67th only days earlier and who had thus never been shelled, was slow to react to the providential warning because he thought he was hearing one of two amphibious scouts attached to the Cactus Air Force to pick up downed pilots. Moments later, as the first flares brightened the night sky, Novak was thoroughly disabused of his incorrect surmise. He pulled back the mosquito netting over his cot, grabbed his shoes and flight coveralls, and dashed from the tent. Novak was about halfway to the nearest shelter when a tremendous explosion from seaward marked the firing of the first cruiser salvo. He yelled back over his shoulder to alert his three tentmates and dived headfirst into the hole. He was still airborne when the first shells detonated nearby, and he saw the force of the blast hurl the wing of a downed Betty used as a table end-over-end through the air.

One of Lieutenant Novak's three tentmates immediately joined him in the shelter, but another, 2ndLt Bob Tullis, missed the shelter completely as he traversed the camp on his hands and knees. Tullis wound up in a tiny foxhole in which he had to lie prone to avoid the spray of shrapnel that accompanied each of numerous near misses. When one especially close near miss piled dirt and debris atop Tullis's recumbent form, the pilot became overwhelmingly lonely and bawled out in a quavering voice to Lieutenant Novak and his other tentmate, "Hey, fellas, why don't you join me.

There's *plenty* of room over here!" Of course, they were as reticent to move as Tullis was.

As Lieutenant Tullis calmed down a bit, Novak realized that the last of his tentmates, 1stLt Danny Miller, had not yet emerged from the tent. Sick with worry, Novak stood up in his shelter and called Miller's name between deafening detonations. Meanwhile an overly fastidious and weirdly unconcerned Miller was busily rooting through his flight bag in search of a pair of clean socks, without which he did not feel a trip to the shelter would be seemly. For good measure Miller slipped on a clean set of flight overalls, sat down to tie his shoes, and placed his helmet on his head. Only then did he deem himself ready to step out. He finally sauntered out to the shelter as unconcernedly as he might have been had he been taking in the sights on his own street back home.

卐

For all the times Henderson Field and environs had been bombarded over the course of three months, no one who lived there was every fully prepared for the onset of a new bombardment, least of all the new arrivals. Capt George Dooley, the commander of the Marine torpedo-bomber contingent had never been bombarded, but as soon as the first rounds struck, Dooley was on his way to the nearest shelter, an appurtenance whose exact location he had taken the time to fix firmly in his mind before turning in. For all the usual reasons left to the still-civilized new guy, Dooley had the presence of mind as he streaked out of his tent to grab his trousers. Unfortunately, the day's heavy rain had left about eight inches of water in the hole, and Dooley had no way to get his trousers on without immersing them. He tried to solve the problem by climbing back up to dry land, but a fresh salvo struck nearby as he did, and he willingly slipped back into the hole. Dooley tried this approach once more, but the Japanese, who seemed prescient, dropped in another salvo as he did. With that, the torpedo leader decided to spend the balance of the bombardment crouched beneath the shoulder-high parapet of the log-covered hole, his teeth chattering from the cold water lapping around his bare calves. He remained alone until four enlisted Marines who had opted to sleep through the ordeal bolted from their tent after a near miss burst a lister bag that showered them with drinking water. All four hit the entrance to Dooley's shelter at roughly the same instant following a panicked search for the entrance.

Not all of the old hands were as lithe as they once might have been. In a tent on the northern slope of Bloody Ridge, a much fought-over rise just south of Henderson Field, Maj Ben Robertshaw, the VMSB-132 exec, tried to rouse his thoroughly done-in tentmates as the first salvo detonated. Robertshaw and two others left the tent for their shelter, but 2ndLt Hap Simpson was just too bone tired from several long search missions to respond. Simpson was still writhing in indecision upon his cot when an especially loud *bang* engulfed him, and he was thrown to the ground. Simpson was so thoroughly aroused that he would have won the Olympic foxhole crawl hands down. When Simpson arrived, Major Robertshaw was holding forth in a calm voice about the differences between the sound of approaching land-based artillery and naval bombardment shells, and how to tell whether a particular shell would be short, over, or on target. The somewhat pedantic cadences of the exec's discourse did nothing to allay Lieutenant Simpson's rising terror. Fortunately, Robertshaw never had to call a round he thought might be dead on target.

卍

The airfield complex's two fighter strips—Fighter-1, a heavily used, often quagmired dirt strip, and Fighter-2, a brand-new, as yet unused coral-topped all-weather runway—were almost never seriously molested. Indeed, the rounds that usually struck on or near them were probably just fallout from the main effort against the main runway and bomber revetments and workshops around Henderson Field. This night, however, Fighter-1 was definitely an intentional target.

Typically, the new guys had the most profound reactions. Maj Paul Fontana, the VMF-112 skipper, evacuated his tent with alacrity, along with the other three members of his Wildcat division, and they all took shelter in the ubiquitous adjacent covered shelter. Moments after the first rounds struck, 2ndLt Jim Johnson, the major's wingman, started shaking uncontrollably. Fontana, who was battling mosquitoes that seemed the size of bats, peremptorily ordered the lieutenant to "quit shaking," but Johnson averred that the reaction was beyond his control. Before Fontana had an opportunity to make any mock-disparaging comments, Johnson was perversely gratified to feel his normally self-possessed superior begin to shake as well.

Though the fighter pilots, who were chastened, escaped unscathed, two of their Wildcat fighters were destroyed and fifteen others were damaged. In addition, the Fighter-1 runway was amply cratered. Withal, only one ground crewman at Fighter-1 was injured. The main effort against Henderson Field itself netted greater results: In addition to seriously cratering the steel-matted runway, the Japanese 8-inch high-capacity bombardment shells destroyed one Dauntless dive-bomber and fifteen Wildcats and damaged seventeen Wildcats.

Only two classes of Lunga Perimeter citizens bore the brunt of Admiral Nishimura's thirty-seven minute bombardment: weary pilots, aircrew, and ground crewmen, and the several hundred shocked survivors of the night naval melee they were hosting. Many of the airmen were used to such doings and bore the ordeal with relative good humor. The dazed survivors were neither used to being shelled while on land, nor did any of them retain the reservoir of sangfroid required to bear up to such doings with equanimity. However, except for the one ground crewman injured at Fighter-1, and despite many narrow escapes, casualties were nil.

In the midst of the bombardment, two plywood-hulled PT boats from Tulagi launched an exceptionally brave attack upon the Admiral Nishimura's Bombardment Unit, but none of the six torpedoes they launched in three separate runs found a target or detonated, whichever. In the event, the Japanese cruisers and destroyers escaped unscathed, departing at about 0205. Nishimura's Bombardment Unit joined Mikawa's Main Unit west of Savo and both proceeded directly up the Slot.

Most of the exhausted pilots and aircrewmen remained in their shelters for some hours, missing much-needed sleep. In that regard, in addition to gutting the fighter contingent, the bombardment had been a thoroughgoing success. But that was not nearly the degree of success Admiral Tanaka was hoping for.

39

One of the morning searchers out of Henderson Field found VAdm Gunichi Mikawa's retiring Support Group at 0630. The Japanese bombardment force was in the Slot 140 miles northwest of Cape Esperance. The discovery marked the beginning of a brutal process of payback as the Japanese cruisers and destroyers made full speed toward the Shortlands.

The first strike that could be mounted by Cactus Air was a mixed bag of five Marine SBDs led by Maj Joe Sailer plus three VMSB-131 TBFs, three Torpedo-10 TBFs, and two Marine fighters launched at 0715. At 0800, following a full-speed run northwestward from the position at which Mikawa's force had been sighted earlier, Sailer's dive-bombers dived on *Maya*, one of the two heavy cruisers under RAdm Shoji Nishimura that had interrupted the sleep of the Cactus-based pilots and radioman-gunners. No direct hits were observed, but fires were apparently started by the effects of several near misses.

All of the torpedo bombers converged on *Kinugasa*, a heavy cruiser that had participated in the Savo battle on August 9. Capt George Dooley, the Marine torpedo-bomber flight leader, delayed his attack on the cruiser's port side for several minutes to allow the three Navy torpedo bombers, which were led by Lt Jim McConnaughhay, to approach the heavy cruiser from her starboard side.

Captain Dooley's delaying tactics allowed the Japanese to locate his flight, so all their attention was directed at the three Marine TBFs. However, the Japanese reacted somewhat strangely to the approach of the three Marine Avengers. While every gun that could bear opened fire to port, *Kinugasa* did not deviate from her path. That left her starboard flank vulnerable and unprotected.

Dooley played it by the book, a good tactic that had brought him credit for two hits for two tries against *Hiei* the day before. The object of a torpedo attack was to descend at the TBF's top speed of 315 knots and then slow to 200 knots at about 200 feet. The nose and wings of the airplane had to be dead level. At the correct speed, altitude, and attitude, the released torpedo traveled 400 yards through the air. Since the arming mechanism required a hot run of at least 400 yards, the fish could not be dropped within 800 yards if it was to detonate. Captain Dooley had all this on his mind as he was leveling off after his swift descent to build up to maximum speed. Just as Dooley was leveling off, a gunner manning a 13mm machine gun located near the heavy cruiser's bow immediately got his airplane boresighted and cut loose. As streams of the machine gun's red tracer began curling around the lead TBF's left wing, the pilot instinctively pulled up and away. Once clear of the tracer, Dooley tried to level off again, but the machine gun resumed firing, and, once again, Dooley thought about flinching. However, he was nearly within minimum release range, so he decided to let the gunner have his way while he, Dooley, had his. As that decision was being made, the red 13mm tracer rounds—and the many more nontracer rounds—began tearing into the lead Avenger's left wing. Seconds later, Dooley released his fish and pulled away from the pesky machine gun's traverse. One of Dooley's wingmen, 2ndLt Erwin Hatfield, released his fish right behind Dooley, but the third Marine TBF's release shackle malfunctioned and the torpedo remained in the bomb bay.

By the time *Kinugasa*'s captain realized that his ship was the victim of a hammer-and-anvil attack, it was too late for him to turn into or away from either spread of incoming torpedoes. There is some controversy as to whose fish detonated. A departing Marine dive-bomber pilot saw two detonations on either side of the ship, indicating that Dooley and Hatfield and two of the three Navy pilots got hits, but the Navy pilots claimed that they went three hits for three tries, which is also possible. Whether the score was four for five or five for five is immaterial, for *Kinugasa* was beaten to a standstill.

At the last moment, rather belatedly, the bulk of the cruiser's defensive fires had been switched over to the three Navy TBFs. Thus, Lieutenant McConnaughhay and his two wingmen had to fly at full speed and right above the waves between rows of Japanese warships in order to make good their escape. Captain Dooley was certain that his Avenger's wounded left wing might give way at any moment, so he nursed the airplane home with special care.

The departing Cactus pilots and aircrew noted that *Kinugasa* was dead in the water with many fires burning and that *Maya* was also afire and limping along. Soon after the Americans left, however, *Maya*'s crew got all the fires under control and she rejoined Mikawa's receding main body at 30 knots of speed. Miraculously, *Kinugasa* also overcame her far more severe damage and also raced to catch up to the main body.

卍

The next strike against Mikawa's force came from an unexpected source. After launching parts of Torpedo-10 and Fighting-10 toward Henderson Field the previous morning, November 13, *Enterprise* had warily continued toward Guadalcanal from the south and had launched numerous search missions to try to find the Japanese carrier or carriers rumored to be in open waters west of the Solomons. After dark, America's last operational fleet carrier went to 25 knots and made for a point only 200 miles south-southwest of Guadalcanal. From there, at about 0530, *Enterprise* began launching search teams through intermittent rain storms in order to cover a narrow spread of search sectors in the most likely direction, toward the Slot.

Because radio exchanges with Guadalcanal—or any friendly base—had been strictly forbidden as a means of hiding *Enterprise* from Japan's relentless radio-direction-finding efforts, the naval commander, RAdm Thomas Kinkaid, had no information regarding the land-based effort that was then forming against Mikawa's departing surface battle force. Kinkaid was naturally more concerned with the Japanese phantom carriers, and most of his early effort was directed toward finding them, but several search sectors to be covered by *Enterprise* dive-bombers overlapped the land-based effort along the Slot.

It was Kinkaid's decision to launch an immediate strike against any major target the searchers located, so the pilots and aircrews were cautioned to be especially careful in determining the exact location of any targets they found. If they were wrong, the day's effort might be totally wasted.

One side effect of the decision to mount an immediate strike against a major target was the requirement that *Enterprise* expend as few airplanes as possible on the search mission. Thus, only ten of the carrier's thirty-plus Dauntlesses and none of her eight or nine remaining Avengers could be spared to conduct what amounted to a minimum five-sector search. Even so, the tangible results came early, at 0708, when the team of Lt Bill Martin, the Scouting-10 exec, and Ens Chuck Irvine spotted a group of ten warplanes at 2,500 feet, 140 miles out, and bound directly for Task Force 16, the *Enterprise* battle force.

The sighting of the inbound airplanes sent Task Force 16 into a frenzy of defensive and offensive activity. As the irreplaceable carrier steamed directly into the wind to launch all her remaining Wildcat fighters and bomb-equipped Dauntlesses, the cruisers and destroyers charged with providing antiaircraft protection moved in to seal off all possible avenues of approach by the oncoming attackers. As a dozen fully fueled Wildcats joined the eight already aloft, the Dauntlesses and ten more Wildcats formed up and climbed as they shaped a course directly up the heading from which the attackers were coming. This was a tried and true method for finding hitherto unlocated enemy carriers, for carrier strikes rarely deviated from a straight-in course. It had been tried with some success on October 26, during the Santa Cruz carrier battle. If other search teams achieved better, harder sightings elsewhere, Admiral Kinkaid stood ready to divert the strike by means of a radio message.

After the bulk of the air group was launched, Task Force 16

settled down to await the arrival of the inbound strike discovered by Lieutenant Martin and Ensign Irvine. But the strike never materialized and was never even picked up on *Enterprise*'s air-search radar. However, at 0820, the radar did pick up a single bogey, and Lt Macgregor Kilpatrick's four-plane division of Fighting-10 Wildcats was vectored out to make the intercept.

The target, a lumbering four-engine amphibious patrol bomber possibly from as far away as Rabaul, was low on the water and heading in an easterly direction. Lieutenant Kilpatrick, a blooded Santa Cruz veteran, led his division around to deliver a high-side attack from starboard, and the two lead Wildcats came on, each with its six .50-caliber wing guns blazing. The exceptionally flammable bomber caught fire as Kilpatrick's wingman was passing it, so Kilpatrick and the wingman shared credit for the kill. The demise of the Japanese airplane was spectacular. Aviation gasoline in vulnerable tanks within the huge parasol wings and crammed into passageways within the fuselage erupted with frightening swiftness. As Lieutenant Kilpatrick looked on, long tongues of flame shot out of several gun blisters, and the huge bird plummeted straight into the water. Kilpatrick's voice-radio report and a rising pillar of smoke visible from the task force raised a great cheer aboard *Enterprise*, whose crew had borne the brunt of two punishing air strikes since late August.

☸

The next contact report from the searchers arrived at 0821 from a Bombing-10 team, Lt(jg) Bob Gibson and Ens Richard Buchanan. Gibson was one of a handful of *Enterprise* pilots who had been flying in the Solomons since D-Day at Guadalcanal. The two had actually made their first sighting at long distance at about 0800, but Gibson, the veteran of numerous such search missions, had decided to wait about twenty minutes before transmitting his report. What the Bombing-10 searchers had in sight from 0800 on were nine indistinct ships sailing several miles south of New Georgia and about 270 miles northwest of *Enterprise*. It seemed doubtful to Gibson that a carrier would be so close to an island, so he led Buchanan closer to see exactly what they had found. The 0821 report, which was made before the two had quite identified the ships by type, reflects Gibson's sanguinary nature; after giving his position, Gibson had his radioman key the observation that "weather conditions [are] favorable for dive-bombing." By 0835, Gibson was at last ready to commit himself as to the types of ships he had located: "Two battleships, two cruisers, one possible converted carrier, four destroyers." By then, the two SBDs were the targets of heavy shipborne antiaircraft gunnery, no doubt a factor that combined with heavy clouds to cause them to misjudge the size of the ships they were observing. Nevertheless, Gibson and Buchanan had pinpointed the main body of Admiral Mikawa's retiring bombardment force.

There was one problem with Gibson's report. It was standard operating procedure for the carrier searchers to issue their contact reports by Morse signal rather than voice radio because the Morse radios carried to ranges of 300 miles or more, half again as far as the voice radios. By coincidence, the search team in the adjacent sector north-northwest of Gibson's and Buchanan's was transmitting a contact report at the same moment as Gibson's radioman-gunner, ARM2 Cliff Schindele. The exact source of the confusion is not known, but the result was the transposition of a "dit" for a "dah" that rendered Gibson's interpreted sighting report 30 miles off the mark.

As the position report was being keyed by ARM2 Schindele, Lieutenant (jg) Gibson was leading Ensign Buchanan higher and to the optimum position for attacking one of the heavy ships with their 500-pound bombs. The launching of an attack by *Enterprise* searchers who had already reported was traditional. Indeed, Gibson was the veteran of a nearly identical sighting and attack on August 24, during the Eastern Solomons carrier battle.

On the way to higher altitude, Bob Gibson decided to go after one of the largest ships present, a ship that eventually resolved itself into a heavy cruiser with a raked stack—*Kinugasa*. Though certainly game to complete the attack, Gibson experienced some doubts along the way, chiefly the possibility that he might be about to attack a friendly warship that no one had bothered to tell him about. Such attacks had occurred in the past because the Navy rarely told junior officers what was going on around them. The fact that the ships opened fire during Gibson's attempt to fly closer to verify the target's nationality had no bearing on the matter; U.S. ships often shot at friendly aircraft.

The long climb through and around towering clouds to 17,500 feet finally brought Gibson and Buchanan to a good downwind attack position at 0915. There was nothing else left to do. Gibson pointed his Dauntless's nose down at *Kinugasa*, flipped open his diving brakes, and tried to align his bomb sight, a little 1-power telescope, on a vulnerable portion of the twisting target's main deck. Seconds later, Ensign Buchanan did the same. Maneuvering within the little space he had during the steep dive, Gibson both evaded extremely heavy antiaircraft fire and managed to keep the crosshairs in his sight on the target. He released his 500-pound bomb somewhere under 2,000 feet. Buchanan followed suit, and both Dauntlesses recovered from their dives somewhere under 1,000 feet. The two radioman-gunners reported solid hits by both bombs: Gibson's struck *Kinugasa* on the starboard side, forward of the superstructure, and Buchanan's detonated portside amidships. Unbeknownst to Buchanan, his Dauntless had taken a direct hit from an 8-inch shell, which did not detonate. At 0944, ARM2 Cliff Schindele transmitted the first of three similar action reports: "Dive on [heavy] cruiser. Left ship burning. Continuing to Cactus."

꩜

At 0923, minutes after Lieutenant (jg) Gibson and Ensign Buchanan attacked *Kinugasa* and flew from sight, another team of *Enterprise* searchers—Ens Red Hoogerwerf and Ens Paul Halloran, both members of Bombing-10—found the Mikawa force. Strictly obeying their directives, the two circled the targets at medium distance in order to see what they had and where it was so they could transmit an accurate position report.

As the main body of Japanese warships stood off to the northwest at 25 knots, the two Navy pilots saw that *Kinugasa* lay dead in the water, streaming columns of thick black smoke into the sky. Two destroyers appeared to be alongside, fighting fires or taking off survivors. What appeared to be a light cruiser accompanied by one destroyer was about ten miles south of the main body and on a parallel course, and what appeared to be a heavy cruiser accompanied by one destroyer was sailing due west about 12 miles southwest of *Kinugasa*. All this was duly reported by Morse radio while Hoogerwerf led Halloran up to 17,500 feet and into position to deliver their attack on the main body.

The two dives were delivered from east to west against zero opposition; the Japanese gunners did not spot the two Dauntlesses because the sun was behind the attackers all the way. Hoogerwerf's bomb, which was dropped from dead astern a heavy cruiser, detonated in the ship's wake only 15 feet astern; it undoubtedly caused some damage. As Hoogerwerf completed his recovery, he called for Halloran to join up, but there was no response. Seconds later, Hoogerwerf thought he saw a massive explosion rock the light cruiser south of the main body and he let out an exultant whoop of congratulations for his wingman. However, Halloran neither responded nor joined up. Hoogerwerf flew back to *Enterprise* alone and reported all he had seen and done. Neither Ens Paul Halloran nor his radioman-gunner was ever heard from again. It is possible that the explosion witnessed by Ensign Hoogerwerf was the demise of Halloran's Dauntless, for apparently neither of the Japanese light cruisers was struck at this time.

LCdr Bucky Lee, the Scouting-10 commander and leader of the sixteen plane *Enterprise* strike group, overheard Lt(jg) Bob Gibson's initial sighting report at 0821 but failed to understand the coordinates Gibson transmitted. Unable to act, Lee and his fellow pilots had spent a frustrating twenty minutes going nowhere until *Enterprise* herself went on the air for the first time that day to transmit her interpretation of Gibson's garbled report. Thus, at 0844, Lieutenant Commander Lee turned onto a somewhat erroneous heading and began climbing to attack altitude. In addition to receiving an erroneous position report, Lee also made an incorrect surmise. Since no one had advised him to the contrary, he assumed that the Mikawa force was heading *toward* Guadalcanal, and not away.

Soon after turning away from Guadalcanal—which had been in sight when the turn was made—the *Enterprise* strike group passed 15,000 feet over battleships *Washington* and *South Dakota*, which, along with four destroyers, had surged ahead of *Enterprise* the previous afternoon in order to reach Guadalcanal sometime after nightfall on November 14. Later still, Bucky Lee's force arrived at the point over open water at which Lee had surmised he would find the Mikawa force. Of course, nothing was there.

Lieutenant Commander Lee quickly laid out his options and instantly decided that Mikawa was heading away from Guadalcanal after all. He recomputed his navigational requirements and, at 0930, turned to the west to follow the Japanese battle force toward the Shortlands.

Though Lee broadcast a message to all his Dauntlesses, it was not picked up by eight of the ten Fighting-10 Wildcats that had been escorting the dive-bombers all the way from *Enterprise*. The eight fighters, which were behind a bank of clouds when Lee turned, flew on up the original heading on the assumption that Lee might want to strike the Japanese seaplane base at Santa Ysabel's Rekata Bay rather than fly home with his bombs aboard. The fact that the bombers were missing was discovered in short order, but there was nothing for the fighter leader to do except forge ahead and hope he would find them. These fighters eventually returned to *Enterprise*.

At 1005, the first of Lee's sharp-eyed pilots spotted burning *Kinugasa* and two destroyers. However, the strike leader decided to fly on to find the main body. The extra effort was rewarded at 1015 when the additional cruisers and destroyers indeed appeared on the horizon. At this juncture, however, the two remaining Wildcats had to leave the bomber group because their gas tanks were nearly empty. They turned for Guadalcanal and eventually landed safely at Fighter-1 on the last of their fuel.

The strike group finally came up on the Mikawa force—five cruisers and four destroyers—at about 1030. The Japanese force was split into two parallel columns of three ships each surrounded by an outguard of three destroyers, essentially an antiaircraft formation. The targets were all ripe for picking, but Bucky Lee was not quite ready to commit *Enterprise*'s main effort of the day against a surface force when there was still some chance that a Japanese carrier or two might be lurking beneath the clouds in the near distance.

Lee's concern was well founded in recent experiences. During the Santa Cruz battle, the best efforts of the *Enterprise* air group had been frittered away against surface targets that were in effect acting as bait to protect the carriers. Lee himself had been victimized by events on October 26, and his main concern on November 14 was that the best effort be made against the best target.

On the other hand, there was much to be said for taking on this wonderful bird in the hand. Among numerous other concerns was the fact that the Dauntlesses had been aloft for three hours and some would soon be running low on fuel. Moreover, even if there were carriers out there, there was no guarantee that they would be rooted out from beneath the ample cloud cover.

Lee worked a compromise. He ordered LCdr James Thomas, the Bombing-10 skipper, to attack the heavy cruisers with his four other Bombing-10 Dauntlesses. At the same time, Lt Birney Strong would lead five of the eleven Scouting-10 Dauntlesses against the two light cruisers. Finally, Lee would lead the remaining dive-bombers farther on to try to find a carrier or two. If no carriers or other targets were found in time, Lee would turn back and attack Mikawa's main body before flying on to Henderson Field, which was closer than *Enterprise*.

Lieutenant Commander Thomas selected the heavy cruiser leading the right-hand cruiser column. This was *Chokai*, Vice Admiral Mikawa's flagship here and at Savo. Diving through extremely heavy antiaircraft gunfire, all five Bombing-10 pilots misjudged the wind velocity and each scored a near miss that caused some damage but didn't even slow the Japanese flagship.

Lieutenant Strong and his four wingmen went after the lead cruiser in the left-hand column, light cruiser *Isuzu*, which twisted violently to evade the falling bombs. Strong, an iron-willed veteran who had been in the Pacific since the start of the war and who had hit a Japanese carrier on October 26, missed, as did the next two Scouting-10 pilots. But *Isuzu*'s luck ran out beneath the sight of Lt(jg) John Finrow's violently maneuvering SBD; Finrow's 1,000-pound bomb dealt the light cruiser a solid blow. Seconds later, Lt(jg) Howard Burnett, a veteran of both Eastern Solomons and Santa Cruz, caused his bomb to do the same. As Strong's division ran full out to evade the antiaircraft fire, several radioman-gunners reported that the light cruiser rapidly lost way and fell out of the column with thick black smoke billowing up all around her.

As Thomas's and Strong's divisions headed for Henderson Field, LCdr Bucky Lee led his division down to low altitude to peek beneath the clouds ahead of the Japanese cruiser force. There was nothing but bare, empty sea to be seen in all directions, and not much hope of finding anything ahead. Thus, after a relatively short flight, Lee led the other five Dauntlesses back toward Mikawa. Climbing all the way, Lee's division only got to 7,500 feet before the Japanese cruisers and destroyers were reacquired. Fuel was getting low and the pilots were all but burned out, so Lee decided to get on with it rather than spiral all the way up to optimum attack altitude.

The first and best target Lieutenant Commander Lee could acquire was the second light cruiser, *Tenryu*, another Savo veteran. Lee's approach and release were virtually flawless, but the lithe cruiser turned out from under the squadron commander's bomb at the last possible instant, and the bomb detonated inside the turn. Three other 1,000-pound bombs fell in roughly the same spot, and the last two hung up in their slings and had to be carried away toward Henderson Field.

As if Lee's entire day had not been thrilling enough, the Scouting-10 commander's reformed division was passing over crippled *Kinugasa* when the veteran heavy cruiser turned her bottom to the sky and plunged beneath the waves.

All of the *Enterprise* strike bombers reached Henderson Field by 1315 following one of the longest carrier strike missions in history. Once his crews were fed and his Dauntlesses rearmed and refueled, LCdr Bucky Lee willingly allowed his group to be dragooned into the Cactus Air Force to take on the most important target of Henderson Field's busiest day of 1942. For, though the remainder of VAdm Gunichi Mikawa's mauled and battered Support Group had by then escaped beyond range, RAdm Raizo Tanaka's approaching Reinforcement Group of twelve transports and eleven destroyers had been firmly fixed early in the morning by an *Enterprise* search team.

The Cactus Air Force's main battle cry on November 14, 1942, was "Get the transports!"

40

Adm Raizo Tanaka was an authentic war hero, a destroyer enthusiast and leader of enormous stature and skill. Early in the war he had commanded Destroyer Squadron 2 with great distinction in several surface engagements during the East Indies campaign. However, he had also turned in a superb performance as overseer of several complex amphibious troop movements and landings and had thus been saddled with a reputation—earned, to be sure—that took him further and further from destroyer operations. At the outset of the Solomons campaign, Tanaka's veteran Destroyer Squadron 2 had been attached directly to VAdm Gunichi Mikawa's newly formed 8th Fleet, and thus Tanaka had been the right man in the right place when the Imperial Army needed to move troops expeditiously to Guadalcanal. Tanaka's highly innovative solution had been to load infantry units aboard fast destroyers, approach Guadalcanal during the evening, land the troops through the night, shell Henderson Field during the retirement, and sail safely out of range of Cactus bombers before sunrise. This solution had been particularly effective before the Cactus Air Force became a fairly potent weapon, but it still remained the best solution available to the Japanese. Of late, however, Tanaka's so-called Tokyo Express had been sustaining greater losses at the hands of Cactus fighters and bombers, which seemed to be able to undertake night operations with greater skill and in greater numbers.

The tactic that had always failed, the one Tanaka railed against the loudest—for, among his other qualities, Tanaka was as much an iconoclast as any Japanese officer could be—was the movement of troops and materiel aboard slow, fat transports. Tanaka had nearly been killed on the bridge of his flagship by an aerial bomb when the speedy warship was tethered to a slow transport convoy during the Eastern Solomons battle. Indeed, no slow transport convoy had ever gotten to Guadalcanal in good enough shape to have rendered the mission worthwhile.

By mid-November 1942, however, Tanaka's fast destroyer solution was no longer entirely feasible; there had been too many recent unsustainable losses. Nor was it the best solution for the mission at hand; the Imperial Army wanted to move 13,000 soldiers—the bulk of an infantry division—and their heavy equipment and supplies as quickly as possible. Tanaka's fast-destroyer solution was not the best way to move heavy equipment, and it could lift only hundreds of men a night, not the thousands required on short notice.

The entire Japanese mid-November scheme had been planned around the timely arrival of the dozen slow transports with which Tanaka had been saddled. As always, Tanaka had been game to play his part in the plan, and he had left the Shortlands on schedule. In the wee hours of November 13, however, higher headquarters had ordered him to turn back to the Shortlands. The dozen transports and cargomen and Tanaka's now-makeshift Destroyer Squadron 2 arrived in the anchorage at about noon, but they were all on their way again at 1300. By then, any confidence Tanaka had had in the complex plan had dissipated; he knew the outline, if not the details, of the defeat of RAdm Hiroaki Abe's crucial mission off Savo.

In addition to the loss of his initially equivocal confidence in the plan, Tanaka was keenly worried about the relative position of his slow convoy and escorts. The slowest of the transports and cargomen had a top speed of only 11 knots, so the entire convoy was obliged to proceed at 11 knots, though Tanaka well knew that all the ships would thus be exposed to the wrath of Cactus fighters and bombers for nearly all the daylight hours of November 14. Moreover, several light bombing raids over the Shortlands early in the week had convinced Tanaka that the Allies knew of the existence of the transport fleet and that they might very well be shadowing it with submarines or unperceived patrol aircraft. There was no doubt in Tanaka's mind that the path to Guadalcanal lay through a gauntlet of steel.

卍

The Allies did indeed know almost everything there was to know about Tanaka's convoy and its progress to and from the Shortlands, mainly through radio intercepts. Also, however, the crew of an 11th Bombardment Group B-17 out of Espiritu Santo had seen Tanaka slip back toward the Shortlands anchorage on November 13, and the main purpose of Cactus searches up the Slot on the morning of November 14 had been to find the transports. Nevertheless, the honor of pinpointing the oncoming transports fell to a 5th Air Force B-17 out of Port Moresby, New Guinea. At about 0730, the bomber crew transmitted to its distant base a sighting and position report that included news of at least one carrier. Then the heavy bomber attacked with the four 500-pound bombs it had aboard, but it hit nothing.

At 0849, the transports were pinpointed by *Enterprise* searchers, the northernmost of the five teams dispatched from the overburdened carrier before sunrise. Lt(jg) Martin Carmody and Ens William Johnson, who had had no news of the earlier sighting and attack by the B-17s, calmly stood off to ascertain an accurate position fix and to count the numerous ships in the huge formation. The two agreed that there were twelve transports and cargomen, but they overcounted the eleven accompanying warships by one. Typically, they misjudged the size of many of the escorts, reporting six destroyers, three light cruisers, and three heavy cruisers. At the time of the sighting, Admiral Tanaka's transports were between New Georgia and Santa Ysabel, only 120 miles from Guadalcanal. By all estimates, the laden transports and cargomen would be off Cape Esperance by the early evening—unless they were sunk or turned back.

After getting off a detailed message at about 0900, Carmody and Johnson climbed to over 15,000 feet and came up on an attack position over the Japanese convoy. Apparently, a follow-up message transmitted during the long climb interfered with Lt(jg) Bob Gibson's position report on the Mikawa force. At length, for the second time in three weeks—both of them had been separately involved in locating and attacking the Japanese carriers on October 26—the two Scouting-10 pilots tipped the noses of their SBDs down on the quarry.

Carmody nearly missed his transport by only 10 feet, and Johnson also missed, though Carmody was certain he saw his wingman's bomb fall squarely on the fantail of one of the transports. As the two were recovering from their dives, they were jumped by as many as seven Zeros. As Carmody swooped up toward the clouds, his radioman-gunner—ARM2 John Liska, a solid veteran with four Zero kills to his credit—had an opportunity to strafe a destroyer that flashed by out of the corner of his eye. Carmody's Dauntless evaded the Zeros so well that Liska never had a chance to shoot at one. Johnson had no luck at all. He was forced to ditch his bullet-spattered Dauntless. The last Carmody and Liska saw of Johnson's dive-bomber, it was being strafed on the surface by two of the Zeros. Neither Johnson nor his radioman-gunner were ever heard from again.

Carmody and Liska arrived safely aboard *Enterprise* at 1133. They had been airborne for five hours, 21 minutes and had only 5 gallons of fuel aboard when they taxied out of the arresting wires.

After Carmody left the scene, Admiral Tanaka, from the bridge of destroyer *Hayashio*, observed through a break in the intervening clouds the *Enterprise* dive-bombing attack upon the Mikawa force, which was then just over the horizon to the southwest. Though Tanaka's convoy was neither seen nor even closely approached by the American warplanes, the admiral ordered the screening destroyers to make smoke while the four separate three-ship columns of slow, fat transports and cargomen zigzagged along diverging base courses. With that, Tanaka's relative good luck —his convoy had been seen and attacked but had sustained no damage— ran out.

卍

Cactus Air Ops quickly received word of the two sighting reports involving Tanaka, but it took some time for BGen Lou Woods and his strike commander, LtCol Al Cooley, to reconcile the differences and realize that the transports were the day's essential target. At that moment—it was after 1000—Woods and Cooley pulled out all the stops: Cactus Air would devote itself totally to sinking the transports before they could land enough troops and ordnance to endanger the Lunga Perimeter directly.

The second Cactus-launched strike of November 14 was sent off at 1020 under Maj Joe Sailer, who had just returned from his first mission of the day, Guadalcanal's only strike against Mikawa. In addition to several of Sailer's own VMSB-132 Dauntlesses, Maj Bob Richard led off a large group of VMSB-142 Dauntlesses, a total of nineteen dive-bombers in all. Rounding out the strike were eight Navy and Marine TBFs under Torpedo-10's Lt Scoofer Coffin, and ten or twelve Wildcat escorts. At approximately the same time, Espiritu Santo launched a strike of fifteen 11th Bombardment Group B-17s, whose crews thought they were going after the carrier reported by the New Guinea–based B-17. However, the Cactus strike group was hundreds of miles closer to Tanaka, so it would get there hours earlier.

Maj Joe Sailer's strike group, one of the largest ever launched from Henderson Field, found Tanaka's convoy at about 1100 and immediately deployed into three groups—Sailer's VMSB-132 SBDs, Richard's VMSB-142 SBDs, and Coffin's seven TBFs—to attack separate targets among the four columns of transports. The approaching strike aircraft were pointed out to Admiral Tanaka early, and he set all his ships in motion; as the destroyers laid a thick smoke screen, the transport columns turned back to the north along diverging zigzag courses.

All the Dauntlesses fell upon the Japanese from starboard to port to allow the Avengers to make a clear approach from port. Sailer's group of SBDs took on the two lead vessels in the port three-ship transport column, and they scored two 1,000-pound bomb hits on one of them and four 1,000-pound bomb hits on the other. Richard's group got six solid 1,000-pound bomb hits on one transport, but two or three bombs were wasted on a destroyer, which nimbly evaded the attack.

The torpedo bombers drew the bulk of the antiaircraft fire, which was heavy but ineffectual; only two of the lumbering Avengers were lightly hit. For seven torpedoes dropped, Lieutenant Coffin's *Enterprise* Avengers claimed two hits on one transport and one hit on another, both of which had been hit by bombs moments earlier.

During the bombing and torpedo attack, the ample fighter escort tangled with a freshly arrived nine-plane Zero squadron. In a wild, one-sided duel, six of the seven VMF-112 pilots each downed one Zero. The fighter victory was so complete that, as soon as all the Dauntlesses and Avengers were clear, several of the unengaged high-cover Wildcats swooped down to mercilessly strafe the troops crowding the decks of all the transports they could reach.

The two transports bombed by Major Sailer's Dauntlesses and torpedoed by Lieutenant Coffin's Avengers, *Niagara Maru* and *Canberra Maru*, sank before the strike group had flown from sight. After helping to pick up survivors from the two destroyed transports, *Sado Maru*, the transport that had been struck by Major Richard's Dauntlesses, was obliged to drop out of the formation and limp back toward the Shortlands with the convoy's senior Imperial Army commander aboard. Tanaka sent two of his precious destroyers, *Amagiri* and *Mochizuki*, back with *Sado Maru*, both to protect her from carrion-chasing Allied bombers and to rescue survivors if she too was sunk. Thus, the one raid had removed one-fourth of Tanaka's ships and, more important, one-fourth of Tanaka's passengers from the board.

卍

The Cactus flight commanders were really scrambling. In addition to keeping all the search sectors amply covered—everyone was still looking for the phantom carriers—General Woods and Lieutenant Colonel Cooley wanted to press every available operational bomber and fighter into service against the Tanaka convoy. One problem that arose following the departure of Major Sailer's mixed strike was that Lieutenant Coffin's seven TBFs had taken the last of the Cactus Air Force's supply of aerial torpedoes with it. Much to his chagrin, Capt George Dooley had to release three of his six Marine TBFs to fly all the way down to Espiritu Santo to pick up torpedoes they might eventually lug out up the Slot, if Tanaka lasted another full day. At the same time, Cactus Air ordered the VMSB-131 exec—now its skipper—to bring six fresh torpedo-equipped Marine TBFs to more than make good the voluntary loss at Cactus. However, it would be many hours before the replacements and their vitally needed torpedoes would arrive. The supply of 1,000-pound bombs also seemed to be approaching a critical level, but General Woods wisely decided to use them until they were gone rather than switch over to the more plentiful but less effective 500-pound bombs normally carried by searchers to help conserve fuel and stretch operational range.

卐

Lt(jg) Bob Gibson and Ens Richard Buchanan, the *Enterprise* search team that had first found and attacked the Mikawa bombardment force, arrived safely at Henderson Field at 1120, in the midst of a Japanese air raid. After taxiing off the absolutely deserted runway, the two Navy pilots and their aircrewmen were picked up by a jeep and driven to Cactus Air Ops, an underground bunker in which they met General Woods. After Gibson told the Cactus Air commander all he had seen and done, Woods offered to put fresh bombs aboard the two Navy Dauntlesses and send Gibson and Buchanan out with the next large strike he intended to launch against Tanaka. Gibson said, "Fine," and immediately returned to his airplane to find that a Marine ground crew was already hanging on a 1,000-pound bomb and refueling it from 5-gallon gas cans.

The strike to which Gibson and Buchanan were attached was delayed in getting off because of the arrival of a steady stream of other *Enterprise* Dauntlesses; landing aircraft, which might be low on fuel, always had precedence over aircraft waiting to take off. Lt Bill Martin, the Scouting-10 exec, showed up with his wingman shortly after Gibson and Buchanan landed. At about 1130, Ens Len Robinson arrived in a Bombing-10 Dauntless that had had to leave LCdr Bucky Lee's strike group early because of a fuel shortage.

For some reason, Gibson's and Robinson's were the only Navy Dauntlesses that were ready to launch when the next strike left Henderson Field at 1155. The two Navy Dauntlesses were among the last three of seventeen dive-bombers to go, so Gibson took command of a makeshift section composed of himself, Ensign Robinson, and SSgt Albert Beneke, of VMSB-142.

When the large strike group arrived over Tanaka's diminished convoy, the Marine flight leader set up a dive on the lead transport, and all the other Marines followed him down on the one ship. Lt(jg) Bob Gibson shook his head in dismay as his tail-end section arrived over the Japanese ships, and he flew on to deliver his attack, with Ensign Robinson and Staff Sergeant Beneke, against a fat transport in the middle of the formation. Just after Gibson pitched over into a standard 70-degree dive, Robinson was beset by several Zeros and could manage only a much shallower no-flaps 60-degree dive after he evaded them. Beneke followed Robinson's shallow lead in order to avoid getting ahead of the Navy Dauntless. Halfway down, Robinson caught up with Gibson, so he opened his dive flaps and brought his nose down to match Gibson's dive. Beneke loyally followed suit. By then, heavy antiaircraft fire was reaching out toward the unflinching dive-bombers, and a Zero that made a brief pass at Robinson's tail shot away the radio antenna and holed one wing. Gibson's radioman-gunner, ARM2 Cliff Schindele, chased the Zero off with an accurate burst from his twin .30-caliber machine guns.

As Gibson neared the release point, he deliberately opened fire on the transport's crowded main deck with his two cowl-mounted .50-caliber machine guns. When Robinson saw Gibson open fire, he did the same. Beneke withheld his fire, however. Gibson was still firing his guns when he released his bomb beneath 2,000 feet and followed through with his recovery. Robinson followed suit exactly, and Beneke also released under 2,000 feet. As the three Dauntlesses leveled off, all three radioman-gunners cut loose with their pairs of .30-caliber machine guns. As the rearseatmen fired, they saw Gibson's and Robinson's 1,000-pound bombs strike the target, *Brisbane Maru*, dead amidships. Staff Sergeant Beneke's 1,000-pound bomb nearly missed as the large transport simply broke in two and sank with enormous loss of life. It was Gibson's second attack, second direct hit, and second assist in a sinking that day.

Among the fighters escorting this strike was a four-plane division of Army Air Forces P-39 Airacobras from the 67th Pursuit

Squadron, which were on station providing low cover. As 2ndLt Emil Novak was watching Bob Gibson and Len Robinson score their direct hits dead center on *Brisbane Maru*, his element leader, Capt Marty Ryan, reported seeing Zeros just above a low cloud nearby. The first thing Lieutenant Novak knew, smoking shrapnel from a 20mm round that had exploded beneath his fighter's long nose whizzed by both sides of his head. Novak looked around for Captain Ryan, his element leader, and saw him execute a violent evasive turn to the right. Novak followed Ryan through the turn, slid inside Ryan's path, and only then noticed that Ryan was firing head-on at an approaching Zero. Novak got his sights on the Zero, too, and figured he would be able to get as many as five rounds into the Zero's engine from the 20mm cannon protruding from his P-39's propeller spinner. However, as Novak tensed his trigger finger, he saw that Ryan's P-39 was also in his gunsight, though well up around the top right corner. While Novak was trying to decide if he should fire anyway, the Zero roared by within 10 feet of his canopy. When Novak looked around again, he saw that Captain Ryan's P-39 was halfway through an inverted Split-S maneuver and was pulling vapor contrails from halfway up its wings. Novak rejoined on Ryan just as seven Zeros ominously emerged from a nearby cloud, but the two P-39s evaded and headed back toward Guadalcanal with several departing Dauntlesses. On the way, Novak spotted lines of bullet holes running across the wings on either side of his cockpit. Apparently, a Zero he never saw had fired from such close range that its twin streams of 7.7mm bullets had not converged on the cockpit, which had certainly been in the center of the Japanese pilot's gunsight.

Of the fourteen 1,000-pound bombs dropped at the lead transport by the Marine Dauntlesses, several hits were claimed, but Japanese accounts do not support the assertion. As all the American warplanes departed, destroyer *Kawakaze* was detached from the escort unit to rescue what *Brisbane Maru* survivors it could and carry them back to the Shortlands.

༺

After the sinking of *Brisbane Maru*, it is unclear who did what to whom. So many piecemeal attacks were launched by so many groups from so many sources that even the Japanese appear to have lost track of when each attack group arrived and what it hit or missed. By then, certainly, Admiral Tanaka and his subordinates were too busy to keep accurate records of events as they occurred, and so were the overseers of the virtually continuous stream of makeshift strike groups from Cactus.

At 1345, only a half hour after LCdr Bucky Lee led the main body of *Enterprise* dive-bombers into Henderson Field after the big attack on Mikawa's battle force, Lee's and another Scouting-10 Dauntless were getting airborne again with seven VMSB-142 Dauntlesses. Minutes later, another Scouting-10 Dauntless led off three more Marine dive-bombers. Less than an hour after that, the twelve Dauntlesses dived in two groups through moderate antiaircraft fire on various ships around Tanaka's diminished convoy. Bucky Lee claimed a direct hit on a transport, his Navy wingman could not get his bomb to release, the third Navy pilot claimed another direct hit, and many of the Marines thought they scored several hits or near misses. All hands returned safely to Henderson Field around 1530.

Meantime, Lee's exec, Lt Bill Martin, who had led off the main body of Scouting-10 Dauntlesses right behind Lee's 1345 launch, searched for fresh targets—the carriers again—northwest of the Russell Islands. The results were negative, so Martin joined the herd over the beleaguered transports. Once again, several claims of direct hits and near misses were turned in.

Minutes behind Martin's strike, Scouting-10's Ens Chuck Irvine, who had been late getting aloft because of engine trouble, delivered a thrilling solo attack, streaking through a covey of Zero fighters and all the guns in the convoy that could bear to lay his 1,000-pound bomb on one of the wildly shooting transports.

The first squadron of eight B-17s launched from Espiritu Santo at 1018 arrived at about 1500, somewhere in the midst of yet another Cactus-launched dive-bombing attack. Each of the B-17s dropped four 500-pound bombs, but no hits were observed or credited.

A scratch team of five Marine Dauntlesses arrived over the Japanese convoy at about 1515, at the same time Tanaka was being attacked by the second squadron of eight 11th Bombardment

Group B-17s. By then, the heavy bombers were under attack by enough of the Zeros in the area to allow the light bombers to slip in unchallenged. The B-17 gunners claimed several Zeros destroyed or badly damaged. It is unclear if the eight payloads of four 500-pound bombs from the B-17s and the five 1,000-pound bombs from the tiny group of Dauntlesses scored any hits.

卍

As the day wore on and pilots went out on their second and third strikes, the pressure began catching up. Though mainly young, fit men, the pilots had been deprived of their sleep the night before and most spent nearly all their time in the air under the enormous strain of constant concentration. On one early mission that day, the vertical stabilizer of 2ndLt Leon Clark's Wildcat was severed when his wingman lost control of his own Wildcat while adjusting his oxygen mask. Clark immediately aborted and ran for home, but he was barely able to control his fighter by keeping one wing down and both feet firmly on one rudder pedal. Huge thunderheads along the way had to be gingerly circled by the virtually uncontrollable fighter. Once back over the Lunga Perimeter, Lieutenant Clark realized that there was no way he was going to land in one piece, so he decided to bail out over the channel. He flipped the canopy, cut off the fuel and ignition, and fought his way out of the cockpit against a surprising amount of air pressure. By the time Clark disentangled himself from his parachute shroud, a friendly destroyer was already coming alongside; she immediately sent him ashore in her whaleboat. Clark was back in the air as soon as he could rustle up a new fighter. When Maj Paul Fontana, the VMF-112 commander, learned that Clark's wingman had arrived home an hour ahead of Clark in his barely damaged fighter, he all but permanently grounded the wrongdoer, not because he had hit Clark, but because he had not escorted his victim back from enemy territory. Ironically, Clark's first mission after the accident was escorting one of Cactus Air's two Grumman J2F Duck amphibian scout planes to pick up a fellow pilot who had ditched in open water. On the next mission after that, Clark bagged a Zero in a one-on-one duel over the transports. And on yet another mission later in the day, Clark witnessed a head-on collision between another Wildcat and float Zero from which neither pilot emerged.

Adding appreciably to the strain was the tendency of Japanese snipers ensconced just beyond the Marine front lines to fire at both the main runway in general and approaching airplanes in particular. The Marine pilots who lived at Henderson Field and Fighter-1 were used to the danger and made fast straight-in approaches after breaking formation well away from the landing pattern. Incoming *Enterprise* pilots, most of whom had never been to Henderson Field, had a tendency to break formation by means of formal convention. The landing Navy formations looked good, but many shocked carrier-warfare veterans hardly expected to receive single rounds from snipers right over a friendly runway.

In addition, the dirt fighter strip and steel-matted bomber strip were increasingly chewed up by foreign matter hurled in by Japanese 150mm artillery pieces. In one memorable first-time landing, a Navy fighter pilot burst a tire on newly laid shrapnel during his landing and swerved uncontrollably into a debris-strewn grass field another artillery round had just set ablaze. Before the dazed pilot quite knew what was going on, his relatively new Wildcat was already ablaze. After the six fresh Marine TBFs arrived from Espiritu Santo some of the broken-field navigation problems were alleviated by Capt Jens Aggerback, the VMSB-131 exec, who was a qualified carrier-landing signal officer. Speaking a language at least the *Enterprise* pilots could understand, Aggerback broke out his personal set of landing-signal paddles and guided all the returning pilots around potholes and debris that had littered the main runway since they had taken off.

꙲

Enterprise launched every remaining Dauntless she had aboard at 1310—five from Bombing-10 and three from Scouting-10, plus twelve Fighting-10 F4Fs. Then, with only a dozen fighters aboard and aloft to protect her, she withdrew from range in the direction of Noumea. At 1530, the attack group, led by LCdr Jimmy Flatley, the Fighting-10 commander, sighted Tanaka 5 miles north of the Russell Islands. In the half hour it took the *Enterprise* bombers to get into optimum attack position, the previously scattered transports closed ranks behind a tight destroyer screen and all the ships blossomed forth with effective antiaircraft fire. Flatley sent one Dauntless after each of the seven remaining transports and held the last in reserve.

The three Scouting-10 SBDs approached the left column of three transports from astern, but they were jumped by five Zero fighters before they reached their attack positions. The Zeros, which had evaded Lieutenant Commander Flatley's dozen Wildcat escorts, pressed unrelenting attacks, but two were gunned down by ARM2 Wayne Colley and a third was destroyed by ARM2 Ray Reames. The two remaining Japanese fighters withdrew as the three Dauntlesses tipped over into their dives. Each of the Scouting-10 pilots claimed a direct hit on his target.

The right-hand column of four transports was the province of the five Bombing-10 Dauntlesses. The dive-bombers were not threatened by Zeros, but they were obliged to launch difficult crosswind attacks that carried many of their bombs awry. However, two solid bomb hits and three near misses were claimed, and most of the Bombing-10 pilots and radioman-gunners mercilessly strafed the crowded decks of every ship they could reach. The waiting Zeros made the withdrawal by several of the recovering Dauntlesses rather more memorable than the pilots and gunners would have liked.

As soon as the Dauntlesses were clear, Lieutenant Commander Flatley left four of his Wildcats to provide top cover and led the others down to strafe the transports. Flatley's four-plane division, and Lt Dave Pollock's, approached their separate targets from 60-degree dives and poured out hundreds of deadly half-inch bullets between 4,000 and 1,000 feet. Most of the fighter pilots went around again, until they had used up all or nearly all of their ammunition. When Ens Ed Coalson fell behind the rest of Pollock's division, four waiting Zeros pounced—two from below and ahead and two from below and astern. Coalson still had a great deal of speed on from his dive, and he used it to boost his heavy F4F up and over the ahead pair. When Coalson righted his fighter again, he came down dead astern the two Zeros that had been on his tail, and he hammered one of them straight into the water while the other evaded and fled. Meanwhile, the four-plane top-cover division was attacked by a lone Zero that withdrew smoking after only one pass.

All of the *Enterprise* Dauntlesses and Wildcats safely reached Henderson Field beginning at 1615.

卍

Seven Bombing-10 Dauntlesses under LCdr James Thomas, the Bombing-10 skipper, took off from Henderson Field at 1530 and found the remnants of the transport group only 50 miles out. Unfortunately, Thomas was unnaturally sluggish in his leadership role and had led the group to only 9,000 feet by the time the transports were spotted. Compounding matters, Thomas was then slow in arriving at a decision to attack and spiraled the entire group higher at extremely slow speed for about 20 minutes while the numerous Japanese fighters in the vicinity swarmed all over them.

One Zero boldly attacked Thomas's lead section from abeam, and several others streaked by from dead ahead and underneath. Despite heavy damage inflicted upon Thomas's and Lt(jg) Bob Gibson's airplanes, Thomas's radioman-gunner, ACRM G. C. Gardner, put enough rounds into one of the Zeros to send it burning into the sea. Only then did Lieutenant Commander Thomas lead a 70-degree group dive toward the transports.

Thomas got his bomb away without difficulty and pulled out at 800 feet, but Gibson, who was next in line, heard from his radioman-gunner, ARM2 Cliff Schindele, that ten Zeros were coming in against the remaining Dauntlesses from port. Seconds later, two of the Zeros executed swift high-side attacks on Gibson's SBD, which was struck by at least twenty-eight 7.7mm and 20mm rounds. Schindele turned his guns on both of the attackers; one was observed as it fell away into the water, and the other left with smoke trailing from its engine. Meantime, Gibson's plane went into a spin, and it was all the pilot could do to get it under control and headed back toward Henderson Field. The third member of Thomas's lead section claimed a direct hit right on top of Thomas's apparent direct hit, and his rearseatman strafed that and another transport during the recovery.

The second section of four Bombing-10 Dauntlesses under Lt Vivien Welch, the Bombing-10 exec, was attacked by as many as eight Zeros at the same time as Gibson was being attacked by two.

Welch and his wingman, Ens Jeff Carroum, bore on stolidly while their gunners held at bay several Zeros coming up their tails. When one Zero attacked from dead ahead, Welch fired his twin .50-caliber nose guns until it passed by to attack the next pair of Dauntlesses. At the same time, Carroum pulled out of formation to get his nose guns on another Zero that was approaching from the left. By then, Welch and Carroum were directly over the transports, so Welch put his bomber's nose down at the nearest target and dived away. Carroum caught up, popped open his diving flaps, and followed. Welch was so far ahead of Carroum that his bomb detonated on the target before Carroum could get his released. Just before Carroum dropped, he saw scores of Japanese soldiers hurled into the air by the detonation of Welch's bomb, and he even saw the sides of the ship swell outward and give way under the force of the blast. Carroum did not get his bomb away until he was beneath 1,500 feet; it went in only 25 feet from Welch's. Carroum began his recovery beneath 900 feet and pulled right into the converging cones of fire from as many as three Japanese destroyers. The antiaircraft fire, which was way off the mark to begin with, was soon brought directly to bear by gunners who could correct their aim on rounds splashing into the water directly beneath the Dauntless's wings. As Carroum was just getting beyond range, one round struck his engine. Oil and smoke blew back over the windscreen, and Carroum had to ease off the throttle to keep himself airborne. No sooner done than a Zero came in from high and right. Carroum shoved the throttle in his left hand all the way to the fire wall to lay on every ounce of power the faltering Dauntless engine could muster. The Zero opened fire, and Carroum responded with his cowl guns. However, before Carroum could follow through or escape, the Dauntless's abused engine cut out. Carroum, who saw that he was only 100 feet above the water, dropped his tail hook and nosed over to land. The impact carried the pilot into the instrument panel and momentarily knocked him senseless. Water rising above his knees restored him to reasonable awareness, and he yelled back to his gunner, ARM3 Robert Hynson, "Don't inflate the life raft; the Zeros will strafe us." After releasing his heavy pistol belt, which nearly dragged him down, Ensign Carroum, who momentarily blacked out from time to time, began swimming in circles with

ARM3 Hynson. No Zeros came to shoot them and the running air battle passed them by.

Ens Len Robinson, who had been out against the transports once already, was flying wing on Lt(jg) Don Wakeham, behind Welch and Carroum, when they were attacked simultaneously from dead ahead and dead astern by two of the swift Japanese fighters. Robinson opened fire at the ahead Zero with his cowl-mounted .50-caliber machine guns and immediately saw his tracer going in, but he also saw hits from the astern Zero going into Wakeham's SBD. Seconds later, Wakeham's rear guns stopped firing and, at the same moment, a 20mm round in Robinson's engine forced him to belly out of the formation; he had to sideslip violently to put out the fire that instantly erupted ahead of his cockpit. A second fire that had taken hold in the rear cockpit was also quelled. Next, Robinson's engine died, and he had to restart it in a steep involuntary dive. All the while, the Zero remained fastened to his tail, slinging lead at the hapless Dauntless at every opportunity. Ensign Robinson tried rolling away to the right, but his recovery to the left brought a fresh fusillade of hits, as did another feint to the right. Finally, Robinson did what he knew best; he pointed the Dauntless's nose straight down and executed a no-flaps dive away from the lighter Zero. The 1,000-pound bomb Robinson had lugged out from Henderson Field was still aboard, and its weight helped raise the speed of the desperate breakaway dive. Only when the speed indicator registered 320 knots did Robinson begin to relax. But too soon; the Zero was still on his tail. Robinson executed a Split-S maneuver somewhere between 3,000 and 2,500 feet and dropped his air speed to 240 knots. The Zero was still there, so Robinson flathatted right between two rows of coconut palms on an island—Banika—that had suddenly loomed up in his field of vision. As Robinson pulled up to get over a hill, the Zero resumed firing from dead astern. Robinson dived as soon as he cleared the hill and then started back up toward the nearest cloud, which was only 500 feet above the water. Suddenly, the Zero rocked his wings and broke away, as clear a salute as any aerial combatant had ever received. When Len Robinson landed at Henderson Field after 1630, ground crewmen counted sixty-eight holes in his Dauntless. Neither Robinson nor his radioman-gunner was injured.

Unfortunately, Lt Vivien Welch, Lt(jg) Don Wakeham, and their gunners never returned. Ens Jeff Carroum and ARM3 Robert Hynson struck out together toward the Russell Islands, but the two eventually went their separate ways in the water. It took Carroum, who nearly perished from sunstroke and thirst, until late on November 17 to get ashore. He was eventually found by islanders and, in due course, rescued by his countrymen. Hynson must have died a lonely death in the water; his remains were never found.

༖

The sum of all the afternoon strikes was the outright loss of *Shinanogawa Maru* and *Arizona Maru*, which obliged Tanaka to leave behind destroyers *Naganami* and *Makinami* to rescue survivors. In addition, *Kumagawa Maru* was apparently so badly damaged that she was left behind, burning and dead in the water, with yet another destroyer in attendance. She never made it home.

༖

The last strike of the day was a mixed bag of Navy and Marine Dauntlesses and three bomb-equipped Torpedo-10 TBFs. Among the fighter pilots escorting the mission was LtCol Joe Bauer, the Cactus fighter commander. Bauer had commanded the first Marine fighter squadron to reach the New Hebrides in early 1942, and he had flown a number of missions as a guest of the squadrons deployed at Fighter-1 during the dark early days of the Guadalcanal campaign. On one of those missions, and again on the mid-October day his own squadron had been moved up to Cactus, Bauer had gotten four back-to-back kills. Those and other assorted victories had already gotten him written up for a Medal of Honor. However, almost as soon as Bauer's squadron, VMF-212, had set up housekeeping, Bauer had been relieved by his exec and given the newly created Fighter Command job. He had barely flown since, but he did manage to slip the leash long enough to lead the last fighter escort of the day aloft with the last bomber strike, which was commanded by the tireless Maj Joe Sailer. Flying on Bauer's wing was VMF-121's Capt Joe Foss, the Cactus Air Force's premier ace.

The mixed group of Navy and Marine Dauntlesses and three Navy TBFs found Tanaka's last five transports as the sunlight was fading. MTSgt Don Thornbury pointed the nose of his VMSB-142 Dauntless down at a small transport and almost immediately acquired a float Zero in his gunsight. Without deviating from his dive, Thornbury opened fire with his two cowl-mounted machine guns, then released his bomb and pulled out. He was almost immediately jumped by a land-based Zero, which got all over Thornbury's SBD before Thornbury could do much to evade. The Zero pilot was so good, in fact, that he prevented Thornbury from joining up on the re-forming dive-bomber formation. Attacks were made from dead astern, which tended to blank out the usefulness of Pvt John Audas's rear machine guns; they could not be fired if they were in danger of hitting the bomber's tail. The Zero pilot even pulled up abreast of Thornbury's Dauntless several times between firing passes, a rather galling expression of disdain. Meantime, Thornbury had put on full power and was surging along at 218 knots right over the water, a tactic that at least prevented the Zero from striking his unprotected belly. The Dauntless was steadily acquiring more and more holes from 7.7mm and 20mm rounds, but it remained flyable. Whenever the Zero concentrated on one wing or the other, Thornbury skidded out to the opposite side. Finally, the Zero pilot became overconfident and stayed in one place long enough for Private Audas to get in a long, continuous burst with his .30-caliber machine guns. Among other things, the burst, which was fired during a tight turn, blew a hole through the vertical stabilizer and jammed the SBD's rudder. As soon as Thornbury felt the controls go stiff, he turned to look for damage and was just in time to see the Japanese fighter cartwheel into the water. For all that, however, Audas was not given credit for even a probable kill.

Don Thornbury claimed a direct hit on the small transport and, indeed, the last Cactus strike of the day destroyed *Nako Maru*, a 7,000-ton cargoman that stayed afloat just long enough to allow destroyer *Suzukaze* to come alongside to rescue the survivors among her crew and passengers.

Though several Zeros certainly got through to the bombers, most were caught up in a swirling dogfight with the large portion of the fighter escort commanded by VMF-112's skipper, Maj Paul Fontana. By that time of the day, the Japanese were throwing in every type of fighter in their inventory. VMF-112's 2ndLt Leon

Clark, who had been downed by a friendly fighter early in the day and who was aloft on his fourth or fifth mission since sunrise, got his second kill of the day, a float biplane fighter out of Rekata Bay. SSgt Tom Hurst, also of VMF-112, also got a float biplane, but his Wildcat was so badly shot up in the duel that Hurst had to ditch over open water. He spent two days in a life raft and took several weeks to get home. (He eventually met up with Ens Jeff Carroum, of Bombing-10, and they returned together.) In all, eight Japanese fighters were shot down by the VMF-112 escorts, including a Zero and a float biplane by Major Fontana and two float biplanes by 2ndLt Ed Pedersen. In addition, a float biplane and a Zero were credited to two of the VMSB-132 radioman-gunners, one of whom had killed a Zero during one of the morning strikes. And a Torpedo-10 TBF gunner was given credit for one of the Zeros.

As Maj Joe Sailer led the bombers away toward home, LtCol Joe Bauer, Capt Joe Foss, and 2ndLt Tom Furlow broke away from the unengaged group of Wildcats providing top cover and descended to strafe one of the remaining transports. All day, on specific orders from BGen Lou Woods, Bauer had been admonishing his departing fighter jocks to eschew just such shenanigans because of the more or less constant presence of Japanese fighters. The strafing run went off without a hitch, but as the three Wildcats streaked for home right on the surface, two float Zeros from nearby Rekata Bay attacked Bauer from directly astern. Bauer was one of the best air-to-air combatants in the U.S. services; he had consummate faith in his own skill and no fear of the enemy. He smoothly turned into the Japanese attack and blew one of the float fighters out of the sky. As Bauer engaged the one Zero, Foss and Furlow engaged the other. However, the second amphibian fighter led the two Wildcats right over a destroyer, and antiaircraft gunfire forced them to break off the chase. When they recovered, they saw Bauer swimming out of the oil slick left by his downed and sunken Wildcat. Foss tried to release the life raft he had stored in a compartment behind his cockpit, but the effort failed. As Foss made another pass over the man all the pilots called the Coach, Bauer waved and pointed toward Guadalcanal; he apparently wanted Foss to hightail it for home and get help. Foss, who had been downed in the water near the start of his tour, fully understood the eloquent, wordless plea.

As soon as Foss landed his Wildcat at Henderson Field, he and Maj Joe Renner, a Cactus staffer, piled aboard a J2F Duck amphibian scout and taxied out to the main runway. However, before the Duck could get airborne, all takeoffs were delayed while a squadron of Army Air Forces B-26 medium bombers, the first to reach Cactus, arrived from Noumea. It was after dark by the time the Duck and two Wildcat escorts got airborne and, though several fighter pilots had risked running out of fuel to orbit over Bauer, the fighter commander could not be found by Renner and Foss. By the time the Duck arrived, all the orbiting fighters were gone. In the weird light cast by burning Japanese ships against the bottoms of low clouds, Renner and Foss and the two Wildcats flew back and forth in expanding circles around the spot at which Foss thought he had last seen Joe Bauer. At length, there was nothing to do except return home. The Coach was never found. It is a testimony to Joe Bauer's towering achievements as a man and a leader that no fighter pilot based at Cactus that week thought the destruction of six Japanese transports was worth the loss of the Coach.

卍

The score at sunset was six of twelve transports sunk, plus one damaged and retiring and one dead in the water and sinking. Of the four transports still able to steam toward Guadalcanal, several had certainly been damaged by bombs. They embarked about 8,000 of the 13,000 Imperial Army soldiers around whom the entire effort had been shaped. Of Tanaka's original eleven destroyers, seven had been left behind with cripples or sent north with survivors. Overall that day, the Marines claimed twenty-one Japanese fighters downed in air-to-air combat over the transports, and the various Navy squadrons turned in claims for seven kills, plus one patrol bomber downed near *Enterprise*. It had been one of the Cactus Air Force's highest scoring days. Finally, although over 5,000 Imperial Army soldiers had been embarked in the ships lost or left by the wayside, Admiral Tanaka later claimed that only 400 deaths resulted from the orgy of destruction meted out by the *Enterprise* air group and the Cactus Air Force. That number is simply not credible.

PART VII

Duel of the Dreadnoughts

41

The Japanese senior commanders in the region reacted to news of RAdm Hiroaki Abe's failure to bombard Henderson Field with extreme lethargy. It took nearly a full day from the time the news reached Combined Fleet headquarters at Truk for Adm Isoroku Yamamoto to decide to mount a major relief expedition to save *Hiei*, to support RAdm Raizo Tanaka's transports, and to bombard Henderson Field. Then it took many more hours to get the relief force underway.

Not until the middle of the morning of November 14 did VAdm Nobutake Kondo's Advance Force Main Body get underway from Ontong Java, an atoll about 500 miles east of Rabaul. By then, *Hiei* had been scuttled and Tanaka was already under continuous attack by the Cactus Air Force.

Initially, Kondo's force comprised two heavy cruisers, one light cruiser, and three destroyers. On the way, two destroyers from the carrier screen joined, and, finally, so did six of the battleworthy surviving ships of Abe's battered bombardment force—*Kirishima*, light cruiser *Nagara*, and destroyers *Asagumo*, *Teruzuki*, *Ikazuchi*, and *Samidare*.

Early on, long before Kondo sailed, it became clear that about the only service Kondo could render on November 14 was a distant support of Tanaka's transport force in the unlikely event it was engaged by an Allied naval surface force. If all went well on November 14, however, Kondo's formidable battle force would be in a position to support directly Tanaka's unloading operation and bombard Henderson Field through the night of November 14–15.

It is difficult to understand, in view of the tragic losses sustained by Tanaka's transports during November 14, why Tanaka's and Kondo's missions were not aborted. However, Admiral Yamamoto, who had played no active role in events until Kondo sailed, decided that the Imperial Army forces ashore had to be reinforced at all costs and that Tanaka had to sail on despite ongoing and massive losses.

The Japanese had never been particularly skilled at planning operations on the run, nor indeed of reacting coherently when plans went awry. VAdm Nobutake Kondo, who had been named the Combined Fleet's deputy commander-in-chief only two weeks earlier, was among the least flexible of senior Imperial Navy officers in this regard. As a matter of fact, Kondo's appointment to the newly created fleet post and as the on-the-scene commander of the emergency mission to Guadalcanal troubled many younger officers. They felt that his showing at Santa Cruz, where he held his powerful surface units back when they might have engaged American surface warships, rendered him unworthy for so important a task as securing the waters adjacent to Guadalcanal.

卍

Trout, a U.S. Navy fleet submarine on picket duty on the approaches to Guadalcanal, spotted the speeding Japanese surface force east of Santa Ysabel during the late afternoon of November 14. Although the submarine's main job was lying low and reporting the passage of Japanese ships, she fired three torpedoes, which all missed, and then broadcast a plain-language sighting message.

True to form, crack Japanese radio-direction-finding teams monitored *Trout*'s transmission and deduced that an approaching American surface battle force was among the recipients. Thus Admiral Kondo knew that his force might be challenged somewhere off Guadalcanal. As the afternoon wore on, sightings by Japanese picket submarines confirmed the presence of the American battle force and further indicated that it was comprised in part of heavy cruisers or battleships. In response to the sighting reports, Kondo divided his battle force into three groups—one for taking on the American surface force, one for bombarding Henderson Field, and one for covering Admiral Tanaka's diminished unloading operation.

It was nearly dusk by the time Kondo reacted to the last sighting report. By then, just as the day's last Cactus-based air strike was leaving the battered transport force, Admiral Tanaka simply lost heart and turned the surviving destroyers and transports away from Guadalcanal. However, Tanaka's attention was refocused by a dispatch direct from the Combined Fleet commander, Admiral Yamamoto: All the surviving Imperial Army troops aboard the transports were to be landed with their equipment and supplies at Guadalcanal. As Tanaka turned his diminished force back toward the objective, lookouts reported the approach of several destroyers whose decks were crowded with the hundreds of soldiers they had rescued from the sea. Soon after that, Tanaka was informed by radio that the Kondo force was closing on Guadalcanal at full speed in order to engage an American force that was also apparently closing on the island. And, finally, shortly before midnight, Tanaka's lookouts spotted the Kondo force dead ahead, leading the way toward Guadalcanal. The news completed the hours-long job of revitalizing the Japanese transport chief's spirits.

卍

By the late afternoon of November 14, the American commander—RAdm Willis Lee, embarked in the new fast battleship *Washington*—knew about as much as his adversary Kondo. Undoubtedly, *Trout's* sighting report had been authenticated and supplemented by the gleanings of the wide-ranging Allied radio-intelligence effort. Thus, Kondo's intentions were known insofar as the Japanese commander had articulated them in exchanges with Combined Fleet headquarters.

Admiral Lee's Task Force 64 had been formed on the run during the afternoon of November 13, as Task Force 16, the *Enterprise* force, was racing north from Noumea. Initially, it was hoped by VAdm Bill Halsey, the South Pacific Area commander, that Lee's force of two battleships and four destroyers could turn back the Mikawa bombardment force on the evening of November 13, before the Japanese cruisers and destroyers struck Henderson Field. However, Lee was too far south to arrive in time, so the plan was revised to get him to Guadalcanal early in the evening of November 14. Undoubtedly, Halsey's intelligence staff had received news of the formation and early intentions of the Kondo force by way of the Pacific Fleet intelligence center at Pearl Harbor.

That the only two Allied battleships in the region were being risked in a possible surface action in restricted waters reflected the all-or-nothing attitude of VAdm Bill Halsey, for the two dreadnoughts had been committed at his express command. However, on a more profound level, the creation and dispatch of Task Force 64 pointed up the desperate straits into which the American South Pacific war effort had been hurled as a result of the significant losses inflicted upon RAdm Dan Callaghan's surface battle force. Lee neither had a plan nor a cohesive force: His two battleships had never before operated together, nor had any of the four destroyers. Indeed, the four destroyers were from four separate squadrons, and no single officer had been placed in overall charge of them. Of the four, none was equipped with modern SG-type surface-search radar and two even lacked fire-control radar. In addition, battleship *South Dakota* had not yet gotten over the effects of a direct bomb hit on her forward 16-inch turret during the Santa Cruz carrier battle. Therefore, exactly half the American ships were in some manner crippled or inadequate for undertaking a night surface confrontation with the superior Japanese force.

42

After hovering about 100 miles south of Guadalcanal until sunset, VAdm Willis Lee's battleship task force dashed toward Savo and initially sniffed the western approaches to Ironbottom Sound from west of Savo. During the passage up Savo's western shore, the American lookouts were able to see the dim glare of fires well over the western horizon—Tanaka's burning transports. At 2100, November 14, after the four destroyers and two fast battleships had scouted along Savo's western shore, Admiral Lee ordered course shifted to a due easterly heading, directly across Savo's northern shore and directly through the northern entrance to Ironbottom Sound. If nothing was found north of Savo, Task Force 64 would head south and then west again.

Lee, whose orders from VAdm Bill Halsey freed him to undertake his own plan once he reached Savo, hoped to hit the main Japanese battle force first, then any possible covering forces, then the transports, then whatever the transports had already landed on the beaches. About all he had to go on, besides several radio-intelligence reports and one sighting report, was vague information concerning Japanese patterns gleaned from skimpy and haphazardly disseminated information from American commanders who had been involved in earlier actions around Savo. If anything, such gleanings could be more accurately described as lore rather than information. Even so, Lee was so fresh to the Pacific War that the skimpy lore helped fill in the voids.

Lee's departure from Noumea and then from Task Force 16 had been so hurried that he arrived off Guadalcanal without knowledge of recent events at the scene, without Guadalcanal's current radio recognition codes, without even his own radio call sign. Eager to get the latest word, the admiral simply broke into the radio frequency in use at Lunga that night and asked for information. The radio watch officer ashore had no knowledge of Lee or his force, so rejoined with a terse, "We do not recognize you!" Before that could be straightened out, Lee's radiomen picked up talk among three PT boats patrolling north of Savo. When one torpedo boat reported, "There go two big ones, but I don't know whose they are," Lee broke into the Cactus circuit again with, "Refer your big boss about Ching Lee; Chinese, catchee? Call off your boys!" The skipper of one of the PT boats replied that he knew who Lee was and that he was not after him. In response to Lee's earlier request for information, Cactus replied that it had none.

࿘

Everyone in authority in Task Force 64 was extremely uneasy about the venture, but all of them recognized the imperatives involved and, on balance, the imperatives won out over the valid concerns.

In addition to having no set plan he could impart to his six captains, Lee had not been able to establish any clear lines of authority between himself and his subordinate commanders. The senior destroyer skipper, Cdr Thomas Fraser, of *Walke*, had been placed in nominal command of all four destroyers, but he had a ship of his own to conn and no real means for guiding the others. Likewise, Lee was faced with the choice of dividing his own time between overseeing all six ships or simply guiding the two fast battleships. Of course, he chose the former, leaving the two battleship captains more or less to their own devices. Lee knew better than to line all his ships in one column, but the situation forced him to do just that. Thus, the four destroyers were deployed in a straight line ahead of the two battleships, which were also in line. It is possible that Lee did not even know that two of the destroyers had not yet been equipped with radar fire-control sets—that both might be pretty useless in a night battle.

The four destroyers had been selected for the mission because, of all the destroyers attached to Task Force 16, they had the most fuel aboard. That was the sole selection criterion; the four were from four separate squadrons and had never trained or operated together. *Walke* was selected as the makeshift destroyer division's nominal flagship because her skipper outranked his three fellow destroyer captains. Other than the fact that each destroyer was equipped with four 5-inch gun mounts, they shared no major fighting characteristics. Each was a different type from the others: *Walke* was a 1,570-ton *Sims*-class destroyer that had been launched in 1939; she mounted eight 21-inch torpedoes in two quadruple mounts. *Benham*, which was deployed next astern of *Walke*, was a 1,500-ton *Craven*-class destroyer launched in 1938; she had four quadruple torpedo mounts but no gunnery radar. *Preston*, which was third in line, was a 1,500-ton *Mahan*-class destroyer launched in 1936; she mounted three quadruple torpedo mounts but no gunnery radar. Finally, *Gwin* was a modern 1,630-ton *Benson*-class warship launched in early 1940; she mounted ten 21-inch torpedoes in a pair of quintuple mounts and was equipped with gunnery radar. However, as the last destroyer in line, *Gwin* had been designated the starshell ship, a role for which radarless *Benham* or *Preston* were manifestly better suited. It is doubtful that Admiral Lee knew or even thought that any of his ships lacked radar, and it is possible that *Walke*'s Commander Fraser did not know either, for if he or anyone else in authority had given the matter any thought at all, *Gwin* would certainly have been ordered to swap places with *Benham* or *Preston*.

Each of the battleships mounted nine 16-inch guns arrayed in three triple turrets; however two of the huge guns in *South Dakota*'s Turret-2 had been damaged by bomb shrapnel during the Santa Cruz carrier battle and they could not be used. *Washington*, a 35,000-ton *North Carolina*-class vessel launched in early 1940, also mounted twenty dual-purpose 5-inch guns in ten dual mounts, five to a side. *South Dakota*, the 35,000-ton namesake of her own class of ships, mounted sixteen 5-inch guns in eight dual mounts, four to a side.

The two ships had virtually identical surface-fighting characteristics. Both battleships also had excellent, modern FC and FD fire-control and fire-direction radar sets, and both had SG surface-search radars.

On the night of November 14, *Washington* and *South Dakota* were the most powerful—and were considered by many to be the most valuable—warships the U.S. Navy had afloat in the embattled South Pacific. Thus one of Admiral Lee's biggest concerns was simply taking the huge battleships into such restricted waters. The charts of the area in Task Force 64's possession had not been completely verified or updated and it was feared that unknown hidden obstacles abounded. *South Dakota,* which was somewhat shorter in length than *Washington,* had a slight advantage in that she could turn in less space than the flagship, but the advantage was considered moot in such restricted waters. What all the concern about the battleships really came down to was that the two represented the pinnacle of decades of naval thought, and it remained to be seen if such prestigious and expensive ships would really be risked in an uncertain night confrontation in restricted waters. No American or Japanese battleship had ever been put in such a position before the night of November 13, and details and an assessment of that episode were not known to Lee. He—and Halsey—were certainly committed to the notion of springing a pair of battleships on the Japanese force, but the idea of risking uncharted reefs was something else again. Everyone in authority aboard both dreadnoughts was extremely concerned with navigation, so all eyes were certainly not peeled in search of the enemy. Even the modern miracle of radar was encumbered by feedback from the land hemming in the potential battle arena. Returning radar emissions—the stuff of which radar "pictures" are made—carried back the outlines of coastlines often higher than the mastheads of Japanese ships that might be lurking in Ironbottom Sound. Radarmen, who were all new to their jobs, were having a terrifically hard time sorting all the "noise" from the picture they hoped to see. This only increased command paranoia.

꙲

All hands were weary. The grind of duty in the war zone—constant four-on and four-off shifts, a mind-numbing pattern alleviated only by endless continuous hours spent at General Quarters—had just about sapped the energy reserves of even the youngest, most resilient officers and crewmen aboard all the American warships. Some officers and sailors in Task Force 64 had been on continuous alert for over twenty-four hours, since the battleships and destroyers had arrived off Guadalcanal the night before, too late to intercept the Mikawa bombardment force that had struck Henderson Field and Fighter-1. The paranoia—the uncertainty of it all—was wearing everyone down even further. Much of the idle talk among the sailors in the six warships was in the form of verbal fantasies of home, good food, and liberty.

MM2 Jim McDermott, of *Walke*, had spent the afternoon fixing a leak in the ship's steam whistle and had barely had time to take a shower and wolf down the evening meal before going to his General Quarters station, a 20mm gun next to the after control station. McDermott's battle station was an unusual one for a machinist's mate, but the most recent draft of replacements had been composed entirely of sailors too short to fire the 20mm guns, so, at 5 feet 11 inches and 185 pounds, McDermott had been drafted. As Task Force 64 approached Savo, McDermott became engaged in conversation with *Walke*'s executive officer, LCdr Reader Scott, who wanted to talk about the effects of exploding depth charges on the survivors of sunken warships. Scott knew of several instances where such things had occurred, and he had worked out a scheme for avoiding the literally gut-wrenching effects of massive underwater explosions upon swimmers. He explained his theory to McDermott, who never for a moment believed they would ever have to put it to work.

While MM2 McDermott was listening to the exec, S2 J. O. Pinion, a sixteen-year-old lookout manning a post atop the after deckhouse, saw that the knot of warships was forming into a single column. As Pinion watched the phosphorescent wakes diverge, he saw one luminescent streak make its way slowly toward his own ship. He was about to yell a warning when the other ship pulled away.

Benham was operating under at least two distinct disadvantages. The first was technical; she had not yet been outfitted with gunnery radar, so the only means her director crew had of finding targets was stereoscopic optical sights. A night battle was the last place a ship as disadvantaged as *Benham* should have been heading. In addition, she had undergone a change of command immediately prior to sailing from Noumea with Task Force 16; an extremely successful, experienced, and popular skipper had been replaced on the eve of battle by a complete unknown. Worse yet, the change of command had accompanied a further gutting of the ship's cadre of experienced officers. In keeping with policies for crewing new ships, *Benham* had contributed, among others, her experienced gunnery officer, a lieutenant who might have found a way to overcome the lack of radar in a night action. Her new gunnery officer, a recent Annapolis graduate, was a smart, eager-to-learn youngster, but he did lack necessary know-how.

Withal, *Benham's* large battery of sixteen torpedo tubes, the largest battery aboard any of the four U.S. Navy destroyers, could be effectively employed at night. The torpedo officer was another youngster with no experience, but his second-in-command, a chief torpedoman, was one of the experienced old salts who was holding the destroyer's crew together. During the final approach on Savo, the chief visited each of the four quadruple torpedo mounts and steadied each two-man mount crew with technical talk and showed them a large rawhide mallet he said he would use to jar loose any recalcitrant fish.

For all the problems and potential problems topside, *Benham* was blessed with a savvy, well-honed engineering staff. One of the few battle lessons disseminated throughout the Pacific Fleet concerned the large number of hideous casualties resulting from inadequate dress during battles in which below-decks damage was sustained. *Benham's* engineering chiefs and senior petty officers strictly enforced the dress codes. Intentionally—indeed, ruthlessly —overlooking the fact that the firemen, machinist's mates, and watertenders would be subjected to hours of work in the relatively unventilated fire rooms and engine rooms, where temperatures rose to about 115 degrees, the chiefs made every man button his long shirtsleeves and collar, wear his bulky, confining kapok life jacket, and don his heavy denim fireproof trousers and hooded jacket.

Preston, the third destroyer in the American line, was also handicapped by lack of fire-control radar, but her officer cadre had not undergone nearly the turbulence experienced by *Benham's*. Indeed, her skipper, Cdr Max Stormes, was many years senior to *Benham's* new captain, and he had had many months aboard in which to hone his crew to a sharp fighting edge. *Preston's* lone edge in the area of seeing in the dark was a relatively unreliable SC radar set. However, even this small possible advantage was denied *Preston* by an order from *Washington* to turn it off because its return was interfering with the battleship's more sophisticated radar array.

Preston, which had been dispatched from Guadalcanal soon after her arrival there with the transports on November 12, had been a part of Cdr Murray Stokes's Destroyer Division 10, the unit that had included *Cushing*, *Laffey*, *Sterett*, and *O'Bannon*. Commander Stormes had received no firm details about the earlier night action, but there was an inchoate sense aboard *Preston* that the upcoming fight might be an opportunity to redress a balance made awry in the early hours November 13.

So far as LCdr William Cox was concerned, *Gwin* had a command problem similar to *Benham's*. Cox, the rear destroyer's exec, had been fleeted up from his longstanding job as gunnery officer at the same time the former exec had been fleeted up to command the modern warship. Cox's problem lay in the fact that the new skipper, LCdr John Fellows, was only a year senior to him and, at thirty-two, years younger than any other destroyer captain Cox knew of. Cox did feel that Fellows had the makings of a good destroyer skipper but that he lacked seasoning. Thus, as the American column entered the potential battle arena, Lieutenant Commander Cox left his post in the after control station and found an excuse to hang around the bridge. His conviction was simply that two inexperienced heads were better than one.

Gwin, which, like *Preston*, had been attached to Destroyer Division 10, was the newest and best-equipped of the four American destroyers. She had a good fire-direction radar set and her gun mounts were of the most modern design, capable of putting out more rounds faster than any of the other three. Though she had been a carrier escort during the Doolittle Raid on Toyko and had accompanied the fleet to Guadalcanal on D-Day, she had seen no direct action in the war, so her officers and crew were eager to put their long months of grueling training to use. However, for reasons that have never been made clear, and despite her modern gunnery array, *Gwin* was relegated to the task of providing illumination from all her guns for all the other ships.

During the long day of sailing in circles south of Guadalcanal, *Gwin* had girded for the upcoming battle. Under the stern eye of the exec, and despite *Gwin*'s ample need for a fresh paint job, all the ship's paint and solvents were jettisoned over the side, and all other potentially flammable supplies followed them. Watertight integrity was ensured by issuing dog wrenches to the ship's huskiest crewmen, who were overworked through the long afternoon. Every life jacket aboard the destroyer was inspected, and new batteries were inserted in all the ship's flashlights and life-jacket beacons. All hands were issued whistles to pin to their life jackets, and emergency kits of every sort were made ready and stowed where they could be reached. Every piece of equipment that would not be needed for the next twenty-four hours was stowed out of the way. All hands were advised to shower and don clean clothing, precautions that might save them from infection in case they were wounded. After the evening meal, which was served early, even food was locked away. All the cooks were sent to join damage-control parties after making up a supply of sandwiches and setting out urns of coffee in the galley. The furious activity did as much to allay active imaginations as it did to ready the ship for action.

South Dakota had something of a mixed record in the war. Upon her arrival in the South Pacific in early September, she had promptly damaged herself on a reef and had had to undergo extensive repairs to her outer hull. Upon returning to duty in time for the Santa Cruz battle, she had been hit atop her forward 16-inch turret by a large Japanese bomb. That turret had not been damaged, but shrapnel had disabled two of the big guns in Turret-2. More fallout from the bomb had severely wounded her skipper, Capt Tom Gatch, and only quick action by a corpsman had prevented him from bleeding to death. Gatch had refused relief despite his serious wounds, and he was going into action this night swathed in bandages and with one arm in a sling.

Despite the heavy armor surrounding most of the work spaces aboard the two battleships, many battleship sailors, particularly those stationed deep in the dreadnoughts' bowels, were openly fearful of the vaunted Japanese Long Lance torpedoes. Most of the men sealed into spaces below decks had given hours of thought to possible routes of escape in the event their ship was severely damaged and they had to abandon it. Unlike destroyer sailors, whose ships were extremely vulnerable but who had easier access to the outside, the battleship sailors were well protected but much farther from the open decks. In fact, the men in the battleships' fire rooms and engine rooms had been sealed in beneath hatches dogged down with the aid of sledgehammers; there was no way out in the event of a direct hit. Everyone knew that, for escape was a well-worn subject of the imagination, though it was not a topic of open discussion, except with one's closest comrades.

Not unexpectedly, there was a big difference between the way the men below decks and the men topside reacted to the impending battle. The topside areas of both battleships were quiet—eerily silent—while the crowded and noisy engineering spaces were filled with raucous, nervous laughter and loud banter. It was as if the men stationed topside did not want to be heard by the enemy while such thoughts could never occur to men in the noisy, throbbing hearts of the ships.

The sweet smell of tropical flowers, which had been so deeply engraved upon the memories of battle-bound sailors two nights earlier, totally suffused the air around and throughout the six ships of Task Force 64. Even the men in the battleships' dank, overheated engineering spaces—six decks down—detected the sick-sweet smell of rotting vegetation and blossoming flowers carried to them by an offshore breeze. Landward, there was both life and death, all mixed together.

卍

The Japanese were out there, operating in four groups. The transports and their remaining escorts, several of which were loaded with rescued soldiers, had dropped back to await the outcome of warship sweeps through the southern entrance to Ironbottom Sound. VAdm Nobutake Kondo's flagship, heavy cruiser *Atago*, was teamed with her sister, *Takao*, and mighty *Kirishima*; they were ready to run in and bombard Henderson Field once the two patrolling units ahead gave the word that the entrance and approaches were clear. RAdm Susumu Kimura, aboard light cruiser *Nagara*, one of the most effective Japanese ships during the November 13 melee, was overseeing a mixed group of six destroyers charged with providing a close-in screen for the heavies. RAdm Shintaro Hashimoto, embarked in light cruiser *Sendai*, was 3 miles ahead of Kimura with three destroyers from his own Destroyer Squadron 3; Hashimoto's outer screen was looking for the American battle force reportedly guarding the approaches to Henderson Field.

If no Americans were found on the way to Lunga Point, the three heavies and several of the smaller vessels would open a shattering bombardment timed to coincide with the arrival of Admiral Tanaka's Reinforcement Group off Cape Esperance. If the way to Lunga Point was barred, Tanaka would drop farther back and all the warships would attack from several directions in accordance with long-established, repeatedly successful night-battle doctrine —torpedoes followed, when they struck, by gunfire.

卐

To the 46 inferior torpedoes mounted aboard the four American destroyers, the Japanese had as many as 122 at the ready, plus reloads. Even the four Japanese cruisers mounted numerous torpedo tubes—16 each aboard the heavy cruisers and 8 each aboard the light cruisers. To 16 5-inch guns aboard the American destroyers and 36 5-inch and 16 operable 16-inch guns aboard the American battleships, the Japanese arrayed 8 14-inch guns, 14 6-inch guns, and 8 5-inch guns aboard *Kirishima*; a total of 20 8-inch guns and 16 5-inch guns aboard the two heavy cruisers; a total of 14 5.5-inch and 4 3-inch guns aboard the two light cruisers; and a total of 45 5-inch and 8 3.9-inch guns aboard the nine destroyers.

卐

A quarter moon was showing and visibility around Savo was quite good. There was some cloudiness, which cast shadows, but the darker spots actually helped lookouts because ships sailing between them would show up in contrasting shades.

The Japanese were ready for a fight and, for once, so were the Americans.

43

Light cruiser *Sendai*, flying the flag of RAdm Shintaro Hashimoto and leading three destroyers, was well ahead of Admiral Kondo's main body when, at 2210, her lookouts spotted "two enemy cruisers and four destroyers" north of Savo. When the sighting was made, Hashimoto's Sweeping Unit was steaming south along a course that would take it about 6 miles east of Savo. Hashimoto immediately dispatched destroyers *Ayanami* and *Uranami* to the southwest to look for more U.S. Navy ships west of Savo while *Sendai* and destroyer *Shikinami* attempted to close on the American column from the rear, along the original southerly course and east of Savo.

As soon as Hashimoto's sighting report reached Kondo, who was aboard heavy cruiser *Atago*, the force commander contacted RAdm Susumu Kimura, who was aboard light cruiser *Nagara*, and ordered him to turn directly south toward Cape Esperance with four of his six destroyers. Kimura ordered destroyers *Shirayuki*, *Ikazuchi*, *Hatsuyuki*, and *Samidare* to remain with *Nagara* and left *Teruzuki* and *Asagumo* to guard Kondo's two heavy cruisers and *Kirishima*. As soon as Kimura completed his arrangements, he turned south along a course that would take him within about 4 miles of

Savo's western shore. He hoped to intercept Task Force 64 from ahead somewhere south of Savo. Kondo, with *Atago, Takao, Kirishima,* and the two destroyers, turned southwest behind Kimura along a slightly diverging course that would take them to within about 10 miles of Savo's western shore.

Admiral Kondo and his subordinates had cannily split the Japanese bombardment and sweeping forces into four independent elements that could take on the single American column from several directions at once. Of course, Kondo had no way of being certain that there was just one American force, or that the early disclosure of his own presence had not led to similar American moves. But Japanese doctrine and training covered most eventualities so Kondo and his subordinates were confident of a positive outcome.

卐

The quarter moon was setting behind the mountains around Cape Esperance at 2252 when Lee's Task Force 64 completed the search leg east of Savo and turned due west to patrol south of the conical island. Three minutes later, *Washington's* SG surface-search radar pinpointed a firm target about 18,000 yards to the northwest, well off the flagship's starboard bow. This was *Sendai*.

Lee's initial reaction was to withhold his fire while the battleship radars and lookouts searched for additional targets. They had to be out there, and Lee did not want to give away his position by prematurely firing the battleship's main guns. The target was plotted onto the main-battery fire-direction charts and regularly monitored by the radar. Meantime, additional targets were sought.

Lee maintained his silence for twenty-four minutes as he sought additional targets and waited for the Japanese light cruiser (and her initially unperceived destroyer escort) to close range. Then, at 2312, *Washington's* main-battery director officer reported that he had visually sighted the target through his spotting telescope. *South Dakota,* which was astern the flagship, reported by TBS radio that she also had obtained a visual sighting. Admiral Lee waited four more minutes for other targets to turn up, then transmitted a simple order to all ships over the open TBS circuit, "Open fire when you are ready."

Washington's first salvo of nine 16-inch rounds was sent on its way at 2317. Range from the flagship was 11,000 yards. Seconds later, three of the flagship's five starboard dual 5-inch antiaircraft mounts opened fire on *Shikinami* at a range of 15,000 yards. The flagship's first two 16-inch salvos straddled *Sendai*, but they did not harm her.

South Dakota joined in against *Shikinami* at 2318 from 15,700 yards with her seven operable 16-inch guns. Almost immediately, her skipper, Capt Tom Gatch, and many topside personnel gave themselves credit for a direct hit and sinking, but the Japanese destroyer was not touched. Nevertheless, transmissions on the Japanese voice-radio circuit, which *South Dakota* had been monitoring for hours, became numerous and sounded extremely excited. The battleship's radio-direction-finding team was thus able to deduce the presence of at least thirteen separate ships, which was short by just one.

As soon as Admiral Hashimoto saw *Washington*'s second salvo fall on the opposite side of his ship from the first salvo, he ordered *Sendai* and *Shikinami* to turn tail back to the north beneath a smoke screen of their own making. Within the half minute it took *Washington*'s gunners to reload and fire the main guns again, the two Japanese warships had run at high speed from direct view. The battleships continued to put out main-battery salvos until the targets were off the gunnery radar screens.

The two rear American destroyers had spotted *Sendai* and *Shikinami* moments after the battleships opened fire. *Benham* swung out her two starboard quadruple torpedo mounts, but the torpedo officer reported that the fish in them would hit Savo before reaching the Japanese ships. *Gwin*'s torpedomen swung out both of her quintuple torpedo mounts and entered a solution for a high-speed torpedo run, but it was obvious that *Sendai* was beyond range. MoMM2 Murray Stern happened to be on *Gwin*'s main deck, taking a break from his duties in the after fire room, when the action began. In fact, he was shooting the breeze with the torpedomen manning the after mount when orders to swing the mount out to bear on *Sendai* arrived. Suddenly, there was a great *whoosh*, and one of the five fish in the after mount was ejected into the water. When Stern asked the mount trainer how that had happened, the torpedoman told him that it had been fired automatically by the main director. In fact, there had been a malfunction; no one had intended to expend any torpedoes.

☙

Walke, whose lookouts were unable to see *Sendai* and *Shikinami* around the curve of Savo, remained on the alert for other targets closer in or approaching from other quadrants. Meantime, she increased speed from 17 to 26 knots at Admiral Lee's express order. The pensive wait was rewarded when *Walke*'s lookouts spotted destroyers *Ayanami* and *Uranami* dead ahead as the two lurked along Savo's southern shore. That was at 2322, five minutes after *Washington* fired her first main-battery salvo at *Sendai*.

Only a moment after her lookouts sang out their sighting reports, *Walke* opened fire at a range of about 11,000 yards. However, the targets were absolutely dead ahead, and that prevented *Walke*'s two after 5-inch mounts from bearing on them since their shells would not have cleared the superstructure. Since Mount-3 was the designated starshell mount, *Walke* had no means for illuminating her targets without halving her effective output of rounds, an unacceptable alternative.

Even worse than her temporary inability to bring two guns to bear or fire any illumination rounds, *Walke*'s gunnery radar was blinded by the radar return that included Savo's near shore, in whose shadow the two Japanese destroyers cannily remained. Neither *Benham* nor *Preston*, the two destroyers behind *Walke*, had gunnery radars and they did not fire because their lookouts and director trainers could see no targets. *Gwin*, whose gunnery radar return was also obscured by Savo, undertook her assigned mission and merely fired starshells. Despite that assist, the two Japanese destroyer captains so skillfully blended their ships into the shadowy background that the many salvos they pumped out were taken by observers aboard *Washington* and *Benham* to be flashes from several nonexistent shore-based field artillery batteries.

Gwin opened with a starshell salvo in compliance with her general mission order, but her captain, LCdr John Fellows, ordered his gunners to switch to high explosives after only two starshell salvos had been expended. *Gwin*'s gunnery radar was completely buffaloed by the return from Savo, and the SC search radar was unable to pinpoint targets with any degree of reliability, so Lieutenant Commander Fellows ordered his gunnery officer to try to get on target by visually estimating range and point of aim on the flashes of the Japanese guns. *Gwin* fired two salvos of 5-inch antiaircraft rounds at one of the Japanese destroyers, but her gunnery officer realized that the range to the targets was too great and that all he was doing was drawing attention to his ship. *Gwin* thus checked fire within two minutes of opening with her first starshell salvo.

When several rounds put out by either *Ayanami* or *Uranami* fell into *Benham*'s wake and the ship did not return the fire, an overexcited sailor manning a 20mm gun on the main deck cut loose at the distant targets until he was forcibly squelched by officers who were certain that the muzzle flashes from his gun would help the Japanese pinpoint their ship. Moments later, however, *Benham*'s new skipper, LCdr John Taylor, awoke to the fact that the distant gun flashes were from moving ships, and not stationary shore batteries, so he ordered his own guns into action against the nearer target. An attempt was made to get the range by means of the SC search radar and the point of aim by means of visual estimates on the gun flashes. However, before *Benham*'s guns could be fired, the target merged with Savo.

卍

Several minutes after *Walke* got her first 5-inch salvo away at *Ayanami* or *Uranami*, her vigilant lookouts perceived a shadowy fresh target as it emerged from the gloom directly off her starboard bow. She briefly checked fire as all her guns came around on the new target, which was estimated to be 7,500 yards away. Shortly after *Walke* resumed firing, several of her rounds appeared to straddle the new target. However, just as lookouts were reporting that flames were erupting from solid hits, the target disappeared from view around a point of land to the northwest.

Benham, which was 300 yards astern of *Walke*, opened fire on what, at first, LCdr John Taylor took to be the rightmost of several darkened ships that were emerging from behind Savo. However, after *Benham* had already committed herself, a ship even farther to the right opened fire on one of the other American destroyers. *Benham* was having a great deal of difficulty keeping her guns on the moving target she had already selected, so Lieutenant Commander Taylor decided to leave the newly revealed Japanese ship for a better-equipped friendly destroyer. *Benham's* torpedo officer reported that he was ready to fire all eight starboard torpedoes at the target, but Taylor, who had deduced that his ship's target was a destroyer, decided to save the fish for a larger target. Taylor's pronouncement stunned the torpedomen manning the starboard mounts.

Radarless *Preston* did not fire at *Ayanami* and *Uranami*. However, when her lookouts distinctly saw a large moonlit ship emerging from behind Savo, Cdr Max Stormes ordered his gunnery officer to lay his guns by means of the ship's optical range-finding equipment. The director crew estimated the range at 9,000 yards, the mounts were locked in train, and only moments after the captain gave the order *Preston* fired her first four-gun salvo. The target was so clearly visible in the moonlight that *Preston* did not need to fire any starshells. Lookouts and the director crew agreed that the splashes were short of the target but on the correct heading. Several additional salvos, each longer than the preceding, quickly brought the guns right on target, and then the destroyer's main battery went to full automatic. Though the target—probably *Nagara*—soon merged with a dark shadow, *Preston's* gunnery team could not be deterred. Indeed, the very next salvo appeared to draw blood. *Nagara* returned *Preston's* fire with several of her 5.5-inch guns and what appeared to be automatic weapons. The large shells missed, but a stream of 25mm bullets passed through the after damage-control party and felled a ship's cook. By then, *Preston's* guns were pumping salvo after salvo into the Japanese light cruiser and had clearly set her afire in several places. As *Preston's* guns were being shifted to another target, a dark shadow set into Savo's darker silhouette, topside observers noted that a destroyer-size Japanese warship was also burning as a result of hits scored by another U.S. warship.

One of *Gwin's* lookouts spotted *Nagara* and her accompanying destroyers at 2326, as they emerged from behind Savo. With that, the rear American destroyer's 5-inch guns were relaid on the rightmost target. That ship—*Nagara*—was almost 10,000 yards due north of the rear American destroyer. Apparently surprised by her unexpected meeting engagement with *Walke* and *Preston*, *Nagara* was already turning away in a counterclockwise direction. By the time *Gwin* got her first salvo away, RAdm Susumu Kimura's well-blooded destroyer-squadron flagship appeared to be in flames from hits scored by the American destroyers ahead.

Then it all started going bad for the American destroyers.

44

FC3 Jim Cook, a member of *Preston*'s gun-director crew, had about the worst seat in the house—facing backward, to port, away from the direction the guns were firing. However, Cook was in on the excitement as he worked to hold all four of *Preston*'s guns on target despite the roll and pitch of the ship. Though *Preston* was solely reliant upon her optical director sights, which were inadequate for night work, Cook distinctly heard the rangefinder operator exclaim, "It's burning!" Then the gunnery officer, ordered him to "Pick up another target." Thus, so far as Cook could tell, *Preston* had been scoring ample hits on a Japanese vessel or vessels despite her lack of gunnery radar.

However, *Nagara*'s gunners, who also lacked radar, finally got *Preston* firmly in their sights. At about 2336, two of the Japanese light cruiser's 5.5-inch rounds simultaneously struck *Preston* from starboard. One of them penetrated the overhead shared by both fire rooms and instantly killed every man in both compartments. Bricks from the boilers and other assorted debris were hurled onto the main deck, where further injuries were incurred. A fire that was ignited by the debris cooked off the TNT charge in a torpedo warhead that had already been burst open by the force of the blast just beneath its mount. Finally, the after stack was toppled by the blast, and it carried away the searchlight, which in turn toppled over the starboard torpedo mount. The second round struck *Preston* just aft of Mount-2, but it did not explode. Nevertheless, the dud killed one sailor and injured another, tore a large hole in the deck, and severed the power cable and intercom link to both forward mounts.

Seconds after the two 5.5-inch rounds struck *Preston*, FC3 Jim Cook, who was facing away from the action to starboard, out the back of the gun director, saw three large splashes suddenly appear on *Preston*'s unengaged port side.

RT2 Willard Peterson was standing on the after portion of the bridge, right outside the radar-sonar shack, which had been shut down by order of Admiral Lee because *Preston*'s SC radar was ostensibly interfering with the flagship's SG radar return. Smarting from what he thought was an unnecessary order—*Preston*'s radar had operated many times while battleships were using their sets—Peterson's full attention was suddenly riveted by splashes from several large shells striking the water to port. But before Peterson could act or speak, several large greenish flashes engulfed the entire after part of his ship.

Undetected by anyone aboard *Preston*, one of the Japanese heavy cruisers had slid out of the murk to port and laid on a full ten-gun salvo of 8-inch rounds from extremely close range. At least three of the 8-inch rounds struck the destroyer, leaving the entire ship aft of the after stack a flaming shambles. One of the 8-inch rounds penetrated the after engine room and detonated right on the generators, another detonated between Mount-3 and the after control station, and the third scored a direct hit on Mount-4. Personnel losses were catastrophic; nearly everyone aft of the after deckhouse was killed, including the executive officer.

The captain's talker, MM2 Gordon Klopf, was busily relating a blow-by-blow account of the action to the men in the engineering spaces when the 8-inch shells hit. Klopf was struck in the leg by a sliver of shrapnel and the force of the blast tore off his helmet and battle phones, made him bite his tongue, and slammed him into a bulkhead so hard that five ribs were broken.

FC3 Jim Cook could only watch in helpless awe from his place high up in the gun director. Suddenly, something large and hard struck Cook's helmet, and then something else. As Cook pulled his head in between his shoulders as far as it would go, he saw potatoes and onions on the director deck. The ship's spud locker had been blown up and its contents were raining down on the entire ship. Several feet away from Cook, in the front of the director, the gunnery officer was trying to fight back. Despite the pummeling his ship was taking and the obvious loss of both after mounts, the gunnery officer tried to bring Mount-1 and Mount-2 to bear on the heavy cruiser to port. However, neither could be guided from the director due to the loss of power and communications to the 5.5-inch dud.

RM3 Myron Lindley was in the radio shack with nothing to do because *Preston* was observing radio silence. Suddenly, without warning, the steady rhythm of the destroyer's 5-inch guns was interrupted by a terrific jolt. All the dust that had accumulated in the radio shack over the years was blown into the air, and the emergency lights came on. There was another great jolt and the entire deck shivered and shimmied for several seconds. RM3 Lindley ran to the passageway outside the blind compartment to see what was going on, but by then the ship was already beginning to list to starboard. Certain the ship was going down, Lindley told the others in the radio shack to run for their lives and then headed for the nearest rail.

At 2337, within the same minute *Preston* had been mortally damaged by at least five direct hits, Cdr Max Stormes turned to his talker, MM2 Gordon Klopf, and ordered, "All hands, abandon ship." But Klopf's battle phones had been torn off by concussion and nearly all the men with whom he had been communicating were dead anyway. Other members of the bridge watch who heard the captain passed the final command by shouting it at the tops of their voices. Then they all moved to obey the command and their most vital instincts. By then, *Preston* was listing sharply to starboard and rapidly settling by the stern.

As soon as FC3 Jim Cook heard, "Abandon Ship," he hurtled out of the gun director and climbed and fell all the way to the main deck. Cook caught a momentary glimpse of Commander Stormes heading aft, but by the time Cook was able to follow, the ship was rolling onto her side. As the deck canted out from under Cook's feet, he had to grab a life line—which was dangling from over his head—in order heave himself up to the net railing. One of Cook's feet became entangled in the mesh, but he was able to rid himself of the encumbered shoe and get up onto the hull of the ship, which was by then fully exposed. Finally, Cook sprinted down the hull in the opposite direction of the roll and ran straight into the water.

RT2 Willard Peterson heard the shouted order to abandon ship, but he was temporarily rooted to his spot on the after part of the bridge by a potentially fatal error he had made earlier. After the ship's SC radar had been shut down, Peterson had stepped out of the radar-sonar shack and reconnected his battle phones to a bulkhead socket. Minutes later, when the action started, Peterson had tied the ties of his hot, bulky life jacket, a device he usually left open when he was in the confined radar-sonar shack. Thus, when Peterson tried to leave the bridge, he found himself arrested by the phone cord, which was screwed into a socket on the bulkhead. It took precious seconds for Peterson to figure out how he was trapped, and by then his fear robbed his fingers of the dexterity required to quickly unscrew the phone cord. Peterson was thus by far the last man off the bridge. Once free, he worked his way down two starboard-tilting portside ladders to the main deck and then slid down the exposed hull most of the way to the keel. On the way, barnacles on the hull badly cut his hands, which he was using as brakes. Somewhere along the way, Peterson also apparently suffered a broken neck, which he did not feel and which did not impede his progress through the water. What did impede him as he stroked away from the ship with all his energy was his life jacket, which persistently and maddeningly floated most of the way over his head.

MM2 Gordon Klopf, the captain's talker, made it from the bridge to the main deck despite a shrapnel wound in the leg and five broken ribs. However, just as Klopf stepped off the port side of the ship into the water, the SC radar antenna rolled on top of him and pushed him beneath the surface. Klopf struggled mightily to free himself, but the effects of his injuries, fear, and shock caused him to pass out. When he came to seconds later, his head was above water; his life jacket had somehow overcome the weight of the radar antenna.

Miraculously, five men emerged alive from the shattered engineering spaces, all from the after engine room. One was MM1 Al Thrift, who had been knocked from his feet by the initial blast while standing on the throttle platform. The two throttlemen also survived, though one had received a blow to the head that would ultimately prove mortal. Though still shaky from the effects of the blast, Thrift stayed below to look for wounded survivors even after hearing the abandon-ship order. However, all the fallen men he checked were dead, so he left by way of the port hatch, right behind MM1 Dick Simmons, the severely dazed but uninjured steam-condenser operator. Simmons and Thrift were both scalded as they climbed through a 3-foot layer of superheated steam that had collected against the overhead around the hatch. Though the ship was rapidly twisting away beneath his feet, MM1 Simmons refused to leave without a life jacket. MM1 Thrift, whose own life jacket had been damaged by the blast below, wasted no time arguing; he simply pushed Simmons over the side and towed him away from the ship as fast as he could in order to avoid being pulled under by the suction.

Less than thirty seconds after the abandon-ship order was passed from the bridge, *Preston* rolled over on her starboard side and raised her bows vertically in the air. And there she hung, precariously balanced atop a pocket of air.

卍

FC3 Jim Cook had just hit the water when he heard a cry for help. He swam only a few feet before colliding with the ship's chief radioman, who asked Cook to stay with him in the water. Cook agreed and the two held themselves together as Japanese shells continued to burst around them. When Cook chanced a look around, a huge shell-lighted shadow—*South Dakota*—was bearing straight down on him and the chief radioman. At the last moment, the great ship turned a bit to starboard, no doubt to avoid *Preston*'s standing bows.

As soon as MM2 Gordon Klopf came to on the surface, he heard a fellow survivor cry out that part of his arm had been torn off. Klopf was dog-paddling toward the injured man when he was overtaken by *South Dakota*'s bow wave. He grabbed the wounded man and tried to drag him out of the way while yelling for someone aboard the passing battleship to drop life rafts. Several of the battleship's life rafts were dropped, but none of them fell near Klopf.

Ens Ted Marx, *Preston's* torpedo officer, had left the bridge with Commander Stormes and both had entered the water together from the port side. Marx, who swam to the right, looked up just as *South Dakota's* bow wave descended on him. He rode the wave away from the passing behemoth and was nearly brained by a cork life ring someone threw over the side. Commander Stormes, who swam to the left, was never seen again.

South Dakota barely avoided running down a score of swimmers on the port side of *Preston's* bows—MM1 Al Thrift and MM1 Dick Simmons were only yards from *Preston* when they were lifted many feet off the surface by *South Dakota's* huge bow wave—but she undoubtedly killed survivors who had gone off the starboard side of the ship, and her great roiling wake undoubtedly claimed others, probably including Commander Stormes. Just as the battleship cleared the swimmers, her main turret fired a salvo directly over her fantail, and many of the swimmers saw a huge conflagration engulf her airplane hangar.

Moments after *South Dakota* passed, a shark attacked MM2 Gordon Klopf and the sailor whose arm had been severed. The bleeding man was pulled under and apparently consumed, but Klopf, who was thoroughly panicked, fought off at least one shark by furiously kicking and splashing, though the sharp ends of his five broken ribs released waves of agony every time he moved.

Preston's bows hung vertically out of the water for about ten minutes. Then the ship continued her final plunge to the bottom.

45

The gun duel between the American destroyers and *Nagara* and the Japanese destroyers remained inconclusive well past 2330, when *Ayanami* and *Uranami* fired many torpedoes at the passing American column. These torpedo spreads were bolstered at 2335 when Admiral Kimura's *Nagara* force also loosed an immense spread of deadly Long Lance torpedoes.

At about 2340, *Walke* was turning to port so that her torpedo crews could launch their own fish to starboard. As the lead American destroyer turned, she was straddled twice by Japanese shells from an undetermined source or sources. Seconds later, lookouts warned that a torpedo wake was heading right for the ship. S2 J. O. Pinion, the starboard lookout on the after deckhouse, did not see the torpedo because he was too busy peering over the 20mm ready ammunition box at the colorful 5-inch and 5.5-inch tracer rounds burning through the night sky. Pinion was pulled back when the ship's exec, LCdr Reader Scott, yelled, "Get down!" No sooner had Pinion spread-eagled himself on the deck than *Walke* was struck on her starboard side, just below Mount-2, by one torpedo.

The flash of the torpedo detonation had not quite dissipated when the Japanese ship or ships that had laid on the straddles put a full salvo right on the mark. Rounds went into the radio shack and foremast and all around Mount-3.

The torpedo blast blew the forecastle and a section of the superstructure completely off the ship as far back as the bridge, and fires throughout the forward part of the ship instantaneously detonated the 20mm magazine. The force of the torpedo blast raised the main deck amidships and buckled the forward bulkhead of the forward fire room, thus destroying watertight integrity amidships.

S2 J. O. Pinion rode out the bucking aftermath of the torpedo blast and then tried to get up. However, he was driven back down to the deck by a cascade of hot water and fuel oil.

Cox Peter Trella, the Mount-3 gun captain, had been knocked unconscious by the force of the torpedo blast and thus did not see or feel the mortal blow. When Trella came to an instant after the blast, he stood up to look over the edge of the topless mount, but like S2 Pinion, he was driven to the deck by tons of falling seawater and liberated fuel oil. Trella, who was certain that the entire ship was already underwater, yelled, "Let's get out of here!" Another gunner obligingly opened the rear hatch and the entire gun crew bolted.

Lt Jack Walsh, *Walke's* communications officer, had had a feeling about this action. Though blooded at the Coral Sea, Walsh had never before taken the precautions he did this night; he had never worn a steel helmet in action before, and had never inflated his life belt before. When the torpedo detonated ahead of the bridge, Walsh was bodily lifted from the deck of the charthouse and rammed into an angle iron welded to the overhead. The impact broke his fifth cervical vertebra. Then Walsh came down hard, tearing ligaments in his left leg and shattering his left kneecap.

MM2 Jim McDermott, who was standing by his 20mm gun next to the after control station, was also thrown to the deck by the force of the blast, and so was nearly everyone else in the vicinity. When the bucking ship finally settled down, McDermott saw huge fires billowing from around and forward of the bridge. By then, also, it seemed to McDermott that the forward part of the ship was driving *into* the water at an acute angle.

EM3 George Behrens, a member of the after damage-control party, instinctively ran forward to help with the wounded. When

Behrens reached the spot where Mount-2 should have been—right over the spot where the torpedo had detonated—all he could find was a round hole in the deck; the mount and all the men in it were gone. Behrens was so thoroughly nonplussed that he ran to the fantail and hid beneath the depth-charge rails.

Lt Jack Walsh was groping around the deck of the bridge for a handhold when a large-caliber shell—probably an 8-incher from one of the Japanese heavy cruisers, which were just arriving on the scene—struck *Walke's* pilothouse, just below. The entire steel surface beneath the injured communicator bobbed and rolled as though alive. When Walsh tasted a wet, sticky substance that had covered him, he was relieved to find it was —not blood!—merely fuel oil.

Cox Peter Trella, formerly the Mount-3 gun captain, began looking for his brother, Paul, a first-class fireman, as soon as he climbed down to the main deck. Paul, a talker with the after damage-control party, was uninjured. The two had just gotten together when another sailor yelled, "Let's abandon ship." Everyone seemed ready to go, but CBM John Bussard was having no part in it. *Walke's* chief boatswain's mate cast a look of derision at the younger sailors and announced that he was going forward to the galley to get a cup of coffee. As soon as Chief Bussard left, the Trella brothers and several other sailors ran to the fantail and jumped straight into the water. Chief Bussard's act of sangfroid, the province of chief petty officers from time immemorial, was to cost him his life, for *Walke* was indeed only moments away from sinking.

As the ship's very speed drove her gutted bows deeper into the water, and as Japanese shells continued to plunge through her hull and upper works, Cdr Thomas Fraser remained on the bridge pending a full assessment of the damage. When all the relevant news was in, Commander Fraser immediately ordered, "Abandon ship!" No one ever saw Fraser again after he gave the order.

EM3 George Behrens, who had hidden beneath the depth-charge rails, regained his composure as soon as he heard the abandon-ship order. He came out onto the fantail deck and moved to open a hatch leading up from the Mount-4 handling room. Before

Behrens could complete the act, however, the hatch was heaved open from the other side and Behrens was nearly trampled in the stampede that ensued.

When the talker in the after steering-engine room announced the order to abandon ship, MM1 Jack Strickland asked for a confirmation. The talker tried to comply, but the battle phones were dead, so Strickland ordered the compartment cleared. As Strickland moved to leave, he fell or was blown to the deck and injured his right kidney across the lip of a manhole. He experienced such intense pain that he had to be helped to the main deck.

Though EM3 George Behrens could plainly see that the ship was still taking hits from Japanese shells, he was sufficiently in control of himself to help pass out life belts to sailors who did not have them and to help wounded shipmates climb over the side. However, when the water on the fantail reached up over Behrens's knees, he knew it was time to leave and so he waded off the side of the ship.

Rather more calmly than he desired, MM2 Jim McDermott carefully removed his heavy protective antiflash jacket, neatly folded it, and placed it on the deck. Then he pulled off his steel helmet and placed it on top of the jacket. Then he helped others release the after port life raft. Only then did McDermott jump over the side to help pull the raft away from the doomed ship.

MM1 Jack Strickland, who had been painfully injured while leaving the after steering-engine room, also helped cut the after port life raft away. However, as soon as Strickland followed the raft into the water, he was nearly drowned as a score of hitherto passive onlookers suddenly came to life and rushed right over him to get to the raft.

Lt Jack Walsh, the severely injured communicator, was on the ladder to the director deck, over the bridge, when the abandon-ship order arrived. As Walsh made his way to the nearest rail with another officer, he was amazed to see that Mount-4 was still putting out rounds. The two officers were all set to leap when a rift in the smoke and flames revealed a 70-foot drop directly into a jagged hole in the destroyer's canted flank. "For God's sake," Walsh screamed, "don't jump!" At that instant, several lookouts hurtled from above, directly into the hole. Walsh beat off the flames that were blistering his arms and legs and painfully climbed over the side. Only then did he realize that he had earlier been blown clear out of his shoes. When he removed his helmet, he found that his earlier encounter with the overhead had creased the steel pot down the center, turning it into a steel fedora. Lieutenant Walsh could see that the ship was still sliding forward as survivors kicked aftward to reclaim the two rafts they had just released overboard. Shells were flying overhead, from every direction it seemed. With that, Walsh and the other officer jumped into the water.

卍

As the raft they had released drifted aft, MM2 Jim McDermott, MM1 Jack Strickland, and their comrades began gathering in wounded and burned swimmers and placing each of them in the raft until it was overfilled. At 2342, just as the life raft cleared the stern of the ship, *Walke* stood straight up out of the water, hung for a few seconds, and then disappeared from view, stern last.

All the sailors manning Mount-1 and its upper handling room were dragged down with the ship, but they received a second lease on life when *Walke*'s bow section twisted loose from the remainder of the ship and bobbed back to the surface. All the trapped sailors who could reach safety streamed out of the gun mount directly into the water. The bows, which remained afloat, provided a safe haven for a score of the survivors.

As soon as the ship disappeared from view, MM2 Jim McDermott heaved himself high out of the water, onto the side of the balsa raft. He had been warned earlier in the evening that so far in the war many shipwrecked destroyer sailors had been killed by their own depth charges. LCdr Reader Scott, *Walke*'s exec and the man who had told McDermott what to do, was right next to McDermott when the ship sank. Ironically, Lieutenant Commander Scott did not follow his own advice; he remained low in the water while McDermott porpoised up the side of the raft—just in time. At 2343, numerous depth charges detonated directly beneath the struggling swimmers, killing or mortally injuring many of them. Lieutenant Commander Scott and others were fated to die painful lingering deaths; the pressure from the explosion knotted their intestines and trapped the gases in them, and their only hope was immediate corrective surgery. Miraculously, S2 J. O. Pinion, who was hanging on to the side of the raft near Lieutenant Commander Scott, was not harmed by the continuous rolling blast, though he remained immersed in the water to his neck. Lt Jack Walsh, who was adrift in the open, sustained severe injuries to his lungs and would be coughing blood for a month.

No sooner had things settled down a bit than *Washington* arrived on the scene. The huge battleship was unable to turn away from the survivors and thus ran over them, but her topside crewmen managed to cut away several life rafts during the passage. *South Dakota* followed the flagship by several minutes, but she managed to avoid the swimmers. And that was the last the dazed and reeling *Walke* survivors saw of any friendly ships that night. The scene around *Walke*'s bows became quiet, except for the calls and pleas and oaths shouted and whined and muttered by the fewer than seventy sailors and officers left alive in the water.

46

As *Benham*'s gunnery officer, Lt(jg) Rollo Mayer, sought visible targets for his radarless 5-inch guns, LCdr John Taylor noticed that his ship had worked over about 300 yards to the right of *Walke*'s track. In order to avoid running into the lead destroyer's line of fire, Taylor ordered his helmsman to bring *Benham* 30 degrees to the left, to resume station directly astern of *Walke*. At that point, shell splashes from at least two ships were observed as they walked toward *Benham*. Taylor also observed a "small cruiser" abaft the port beam—it was certainly a destroyer, probably *Ayanami*—as it fired on the two American rear destroyers. As Taylor watched the action behind his ship, he saw that one of the trailing American destroyers had its guns right on the Japanese "light cruiser," which appeared to burst into flames.

Benham reached a position directly behind *Walke*, but she continued to swing farther to the left, to the due-westerly course last ordered by Admiral Lee. As Lieutenant Commander Taylor scanned the area around his ship, he saw a fire erupt aboard *Walke* and had to veer sharply to port to avoid hitting the suddenly slowing vanguard destroyer. By the time *Benham* came abreast of *Walke*, the lead destroyer was well down by the head and scores of men were taking to the water.

Seconds after *Benham* passed *Walke*, she was struck by a torpedo on the starboard side only a few yards from the tip of her bows, which were blown off as far back as the forward bulkhead of the Mount-1 magazine. The entire ship immediately rose about 4 feet out of the water, heeled slightly to port, rolled back over 30 degrees to starboard, settled by the head, and slowly righted herself. The shock of the detonation created a whipsaw effect down the entire length of the main deck and throughout all her internal compartments. The quake was so violent that virtually no one aboard the destroyer was left standing in its wake. *Benham*'s speed through the water abruptly dropped from about 27 knots to just 5 knots, and that in itself added to the effects of the blast by buckling hull plates and the longitudinal frames tying the ship together. Indeed, it was very likely the cause of the shock that broke *Behnam*'s back and created a crack across her main deck right above her forward fire room.

The huge volume of seawater thrown into the air by the combined force of the detonation and the sudden loss of speed—it rose at least 20 feet higher than Lt(jg) Rollo Mayer's gun director—descended with great force and caused further damage and personnel injuries. The greatest volume of water fell on the after portion of the ship, which settled deeply. The crewmen manning Mount-4 were immersed in water to their waists. CTM John Chapman was washed overboard by the deluge, and several torpedomen working on the tubes or among the depth charges were injured, as were the ship's chief machinist's mate, the chief boatswain's mate, and several other members of the after damage-control party. Injuries included several broken arms, legs, and shoulders, severe scalp wounds, a ruptured kidney, and a puncture wound of the abdomen.

F1 Bob Townsend, the forward fire room's oil king, would have been thrown from his feet with everyone else if he had not happened to be hanging on to a valve wheel when the ship bucked beneath him. Suddenly, through a stupor he shared with nearly all hands, Townsend realized that the lights in the fire room were out and that he could hear a great deal of water pouring down from above. Worse, he thought he could see shells passing across the sky—a sight he should never have experienced from within the supposedly enclosed fire room. As Townsend's partner scuttled up a ladder to the port escape trunk, he was thrown back to the deck by the descending water. He was up in a flash and ran right over Townsend, knocking him aside on his way up the starboard ladder. Townsend remained rooted to his place, stunned and bewildered by the intermittent views of the sky and the persistent flashes of blue light caused by electrical wires short-circuiting against the hull plates. Finally, the sound of running water snapped F1 Townsend's internal light back on. He pulled himself together, checked the water levels in both boilers, and began yelling for help. He then noticed several weak lights emanating from battery-operated battle lanterns located in the compartment below his own. When someone below yelled, "Who's up there," Townsend peered down through the steel grating on which he was standing and saw the ship's chief watertender wading around aimlessly in knee-deep water. He yelled down to tell the chief he was there, on duty, but the chief was by then off in his own world, mumbling over and over, "Where are my men? Where are my men?" With that, Townsend climbed down to help the chief, but the first man he found was a first-class watertender who was standing upright by the forced-air blower; he was just staring straight ahead and not moving a muscle. When Townsend went to retrieve the battle phones to make a report, he found that the talker had vacated the compartment with such alacrity that all he had left behind was a dangling, broken phone cord. Acting on his own, F1 Townsend secured one boiler, which had lost most of its feed water. The other boiler was okay except for the fact that its burner had gone out. The job was too big for one man working alone, so Townsend grabbed the internal telephone and tried to call the bridge. No one answered, so he called the forward engine room to tell them why they had no power and to ask for help. Someone told him that he would send help, but no help arrived.

The ship was nearly dead in the water, chaos was rampant, and a very large Japanese ship was emerging from the darkness off the port quarter. Fearful of being attacked while in so vulnerable a position, Lieutenant Commander Taylor ordered his somewhat dazed helmsman to make right standard rudder. Then he rang up the after engine room, which was connected to the operating after fire room, and ordered the port engine ahead at standard speed. These maneuvers swung the ship sharply to the right, away from the action. Taylor held *Benham* in a circle until she was heading due east, back the way she had come. However, when *Washington* passed her on an opposite heading, Taylor circled farther to the right, until he was heading west again. By the time *Benham* limped through the complete circle, the battle had passed her by.

꽃

Once she switched from firing starshells to radar-directed high-explosive rounds, *Gwin* gave an excellent accounting of herself. A Japanese destroyer to starboard that had been firing steady four-gun salvos at one of the American destroyers ahead was cleanly struck by two of *Gwin*'s full four-gun salvos, and when the smoke cleared only one of her guns was still firing. In fact, everything seemed to be going so well from the perspective of *Gwin*'s bridge watch that it stunned them to a man when the American destroyers in column ahead started burning and blowing up. Indeed, almost within the same moment *Preston* appeared to blow up 300 yards dead ahead, *Gwin* was hit for the first time.

The 5-inch round penetrated the starboard side of the after engine room about 4 feet above the waterline. All five engineers working on the upper level of the engine room were killed by the blast and a man on the lower level was mortally scalded by steam from a ruptured line. Superheated steam was blown into the 20mm clipping room and the Mount-4 handling room, where all hands were forced to evacuate to avoid being cooked alive. The lights on Mount-3 and Mount-4 went out, but emergency battle lanterns flickered on, and neither gun's ability to fire was impaired. The after repair party moved swiftly to the after engine room and doused all fires within a minute.

The blast in the engine room also broke all the shear pins holding the torpedoes in the forward mount; one fish slid out of its tube and hit the weather deck rail before plunging into the water, two others slid straight over the rail into the water, and the last two came to rest partway out of their tubes.

As *Gwin* passed *Preston*, both ships were rocked by a heavy explosion. LCdr William Cox, *Gwin*'s exec, saw a great yellow flame erupt around *Preston*'s torpedo tubes and was sure the source of the blast had been the torpedoes themselves. *Gwin* was so close to *Preston* when the latter blew up that one of her torpedomen caught a pair of dungarees around his neck, and other debris fell across her upper works.

In the midst of the blast, *Gwin*'s skipper, LCdr John Fellows, ordered, "Left full rudder," a standard and long-practiced emergency procedure that obliged odd-numbered ships in a column to veer to starboard while the even-numbered ships veered to port. However, Lieutenant Commander Fellow's knee-jerk reaction would have run *Gwin* directly into *Preston*. Without seeking permission, Lieutenant Commander Cox, the exec, jumped to the helmsman's side and yelled, "Hard right! Hard right!" The helmsman instantly responded to Cox as the exec turned to the captain and begged forgiveness for usurping his authority. Fellows had the good grace to let the incident pass without further mention.

Right after passing *Preston*, and only a minute after the 5-inch hit that destroyed her after engine room, *Gwin* was struck a glancing blow near her starboard depth-charge rack. The shell, which might have been a ricochet off the surface of the water, did not explode, but if left a jagged 2-foot hole in the deck, distorted the starboard depth-charge rack, and burst open two 600-pound depth charges, whose volatile contents spilled out onto the deck.

During the ensuing minute, as *Gwin*'s guns kept up a steady fire at *Ayanami* or *Uranami*, it was noted that *Benham* had disappeared from the American formation. Two minutes after that, *Gwin* ceased firing; she could find no suitable targets.

47

fter *Sendai* and *Shikinami* turned away from their guns, the two American battleships, huge and ponderous in a sea of midgets, fought a battle far different from the one that engulfed their four destroyer consorts.

Following the withdrawal of *Sendai* and *Shikinami*, *Washington*'s main battery remained inactive while her radarmen tried to sort through the profusion of targets and separate them from the confusing echoes of nearby land masses. *South Dakota*, trailing the flagship by more than a mile, withheld all her fire because her skipper, Capt Tom Gatch, feared hitting friendly vessels.

The only guns aboard the flagship that remained active were the ten 5-inchers arrayed in the five dual mounts on *Washington*'s starboard side. All five mounts poured out streams of 5-inch anti-aircraft tracer rounds, right into Savo's shadow, in an attempt to blanket the area from which *Ayanami* and *Uranami* were sniping at the passing vanguard destroyers. Suddenly the forward battery commander, Lt George Matton, noticed that the guns in one of his three mounts were firing high. Matton passed the word to Sky Control. Immediately, the other two mounts, which were still on target, were shifted to the control of the starboard after 5-inch battery director. With nothing else to do, Matton scanned the entire scene. As Japanese starshell rounds burst eerily over the destroyers ahead of *Washington* and as gouts of tracer flew out from unseen warships ahead and well to starboard, Matton witnessed the unmistakable signature of first one, and then two, and finally three of the vanguard destroyers falling victim to Japanese torpedoes and high-explosive rounds. In rapid succession, *Washington* brushed past each of the wounded, dead, and dying warships, and Matton was able to peer down at the bewildered survivors clinging to wreckage and rafts or thrashing about in the water for a safe purchase. Lieutenant Matton did not see that shipmates farther aft released two life rafts over the heads of a group of survivors that was being halved by *Washington*'s passage.

After *Washington* raced through the *Walke* survivors, as fiercely burning *Ayanami* and damaged *Uranami* receded, all the flagship's guns went silent for lack of suitable targets. *Nagara* had already turned away from the battle, and she and her four destroyer consorts had disappeared around a point of land jutting out from Savo's shore.

🎏

Seconds after *South Dakota* had fired her thirteenth and final 16-inch salvo after retreating *Sendai* and *Shikinami*, her main circuit breakers had jumped out, thus closing down her surface and gunnery radars and effectively disabling all her guns. That had been at 2333, and *South Dakota* would remain blind and toothless until her electricians and radar technicians figured out how to restore the power. By 2340, all four of the American vanguard destroyers had been destroyed or disabled. Thus, for critical minutes, only *Washington* was capable of putting up a fight against what many aboard her feared were several converging Japanese battle groups.

🎏

South Dakota's power was fully restored just as she cleared the scene of *Preston*'s demise, and her gun directors immediately began swinging to and fro in search of a target. Within seconds, the main battery director was arrested in its search by a small, well-lighted target in the middle distance directly astern of her fantail. Instantly,

424

the fast battleship's 16-inch turrets swung to match bearings on the director, but only the after turret could actually be brought on the target.

MoMM2 Murray Stern, of *Gwin*, was helping his ship's torpedomen push two loose torpedoes back into their tubes when he felt the hot glow of a searchlight on his back. Stern looked back over his shoulder and saw a huge ship bearing down on him. The source of the light was *Kirishima*, but the source of the three large-caliber near misses that nearly swamped *Gwin* was *South Dakota*, which had reflexively fired at the only lighted target her main battery director could find. *Gwin*'s signalmen instantly flashed the evening's color-coded recognition signals, and *South Dakota* stopped firing. However, for several scary seconds, MoMM2 Stern watched as three more of the battleship's huge tracer rounds fell in an arc toward his ship. All missed.

When *South Dakota*'s after turret first fired on *Gwin*, the muzzle flash from the three huge guns ignited volatile fuel vapors in and around two scout planes deployed on catapults on the fantail aft of the turret. The multiple fires, which could be seen from many angles and great distances, including by numerous *Preston* sailors who had just survived the battleship's turbulent passage, was completely doused within a half minute when the passage of the second salvo aimed at *Gwin* blew both burning scout planes overboard. Within a minute of the first salvo, two repair parties converged on the fantail to douse several small remaining fires and restore order.

The small fires remaining on *South Dakota*'s fantail were easily quenched, but not so the suspicion among *South Dakota*'s gunners that the main-battery radar was feeding them erroneous range information. The gunnery officer asked that the secondary-battery radars take over the task of directing the main battery, but that led to the discovery that two of the 5-inch directors were out and that the state of the other two was "doubtful." Electricians and radar technicians converged on the errant circuits in a frantic effort to restore *South Dakota*'s erratic night vision.

As soon as *South Dakota* revealed herself by setting her own scout planes afire, word of her position was passed to Admiral Kondo, on *Atago*'s flag bridge, and he ordered all ready torpedoes—at least thirty-four—fired at the American super-heavy. Then

Kondo entered the fight with his main force: heavy cruisers *Atago* and *Takao*, battleship *Kirishima*, and destroyers *Asagumo* and *Teruzuki*. Their first act, at 2348, was to bathe *South Dakota* in the scalding light of two pairs of large searchlights, one each from *Atago* and *Takao*, the first and second ships in the Japanese column. The distance to *South Dakota* from both heavy cruisers was only 5,000 yards.

Undetected and some 8,000 yards ahead of *South Dakota*, *Washington* had already plotted the Japanese formation on her radar and thus was able to open fire as soon as their searchlights found *South Dakota*. It took nearly thirty seconds after the lights went on for *South Dakota*'s secondary battery to get its first salvo away and for the after starboard 5-inch director to assume control of the main battery. As soon as *South Dakota*'s eight starboard 5-inch guns opened fire on the lights, the lights were doused. However, almost immediately, the third ship in the Japanese column—*Kirishima*—reilluminated *South Dakota* with her searchlight array. *South Dakota* responded with her first main-battery salvo of this phase of the fray, and then another, at a range of 9,800 yards. *Kirishima*, which was hit squarely by several of the 16-inch rounds, obligingly doused her lights.

South Dakota sustained her first hit at 2349, when a medium-caliber shell struck the foremast. Admiral Lee, who saw the bright flash of the hit, queried Capt Tom Gatch by TBS radio: "Are you all right?" Gatch's response: "Everything seems okay." But, within the minute, Gatch and the bridge crew felt the impact of several more hits they were unable to locate.

South Dakota's after main-battery director came back on line at 2351, and its crew oversaw the laying of the entire main battery on the third ship in the Japanese column, *Kirishima*, which was by then only 6,500 yards away and on an opposite-course heading. The main battery opened fire at the Japanese battleship on continuous automatic and got away up to seven shells at a time about every fifteen seconds.

At 2353, *South Dakota*'s SG radar located several small ships rounding Savo at a range of about 11,000 yards. These ships, or perhaps others, immediately began putting rounds into *South Da-*

kota's foremast structure. At 2355, the starboard forward 5-inch director, located above and abaft the bridge, was put out of action when a 5.5-inch or 6-inch round passed through the wiring trunk below the director. An intense electrical fire immediately erupted and, though the director crew was in extreme danger, all hands remained at their posts, trying to hold the starboard forward 5-inch gun group on target. The fire abated on its own within seconds, but the director was inoperable.

At 2356, a hit in the 1.1-inch clipping room located in the foremast structure killed the entire crew of one of the high 1.1-inch gun mounts and ignited fires in the clipping room itself. The survivors fought the fires to a standstill within minutes.

At 2357, *South Dakota*, which had not fired any of her 16-inch guns for several minutes, slowed from an undetermined top speed to 26 knots and began casting around in the dark to find *Washington*, which was completely hidden from the view of her radars and lookouts. As *South Dakota* was slowing, a 6-inch round from *Kirishima* passed through the radar plotting room, killing one officer and demolishing a steam line passing beside the compartment. Almost immediately after the first shell struck, a second 6-inch round detonated at virtually the same spot.

As *South Dakota*'s secondary battery continued to bear the entire burden of the response, three Japanese rounds exploded in and around Battle-2 and killed or wounded a half-dozen officers and sailors. Several more men in the area were scalded by high-pressure steam that was released from ruptured lines to the steam whistle and steam siren. Damage to ladders throughout the area rendered access to the casualties and several fires difficult for repair and rescue teams.

Sky Control sustained a direct hit at 0002 and several key officers and sailors were killed. The system overseeing the secondary batteries was shut down by the hit and all the engaged starboard mounts had to go to local control. When Captain Gatch learned that Sky Control had been demolished, he ordered his engineers to put on all the speed they could find.

At 0004, an 8-inch round from one of the Japanese heavy cruisers glanced off Mount-5, the center starboard 5-inch mount, passed through a signal storeroom, streaked across the superstructure, and came to rest in Mount-4, on the port side of the ship. The shell, a dud, was eventually recovered and thrown over the side.

A plea for help transmitted to *Washington* at 0005 went nowhere; the radio antenna had been shot away, leaving *South Dakota* voiceless as well as virtually sightless. Her main battery fired one full salvo at 0007, but the target was indistinct and no results were observed. A minute later, at 0008, Captain Gatch ordered all guns to cease firing for lack of targets.

↻

Many aboard *South Dakota* were certain that *Washington* had fled from the scene before the Japanese searchlights came on. But the flagship had not fled; she had been in continuous and extremely effective action against the Japanese heavies from precisely the moment the lights came on. But neither *South Dakota* nor the Japanese were able to see her, though how everyone missed the glare of her incessant firing is beyond comprehension. The secret of *Washington*'s success was undoubtedly her quiet passage through the battered, dying American vanguard during the ten minutes following her distant engagement with *Sendai* and *Shikinami*. The Japanese were apparently overly attentive to the American destroyers during that interval, and *South Dakota*'s magnificent opener—in which she set herself afire—further obscured the presence of the American flagship.

From her place at no time nearer than 8,000 yards ahead of *South Dakota*, *Washington* fired salvo after salvo from her entire main battery and her ten starboard 5-inch guns. During the one-sided firing exercise, *Kirishima* sustained numerous direct 16-inch hits while *Washington* remained utterly undetected as she pumped at least nine 16-inch and forty 5-inch shells into *Kirishima* alone. In addition to destroying one of the Japanese battleship's after 14-inch turrets, wrecking numerous areas topside and scything down scores of Japanese officers and sailors, the American flagship damaged the Japanese battleship's steering, a fatal blow in itself. In addition, *Atago* and *Takao* were hit many times over by both American battleships.

Washington received absolutely no damage. The closest Japanese shells landed 200 yards away, though one salvo narrowly missed striking her main mast while passing over the ship. Several torpedo wakes also passed close enough to her to be seen. Except for the persistent problem with one of her starboard forward 5-inch mounts, which continued to fire high, *Washington* suffered no breakdowns or problems with her gunnery or radar systems. It was, for her, a perfect baptism.

South Dakota sustained severe damage and heavy casualties, including at least fifty killed or mortally wounded. At least two 14-inch shells and as many as thirty-five smaller rounds struck her during the furious twenty-minute slugfest. The battleship's communications were totally disrupted, and her gunnery department sustained numerous casualties among key control personnel. Fires were sweeping her superstructure when Captain Gatch finally ordered his navigator to steer a course away from the scene of the fight.

Moments after *South Dakota's* guns went silent, Admiral Lee ordered *Washington* to steer to the northwest, toward the Russell Islands, in the hope of drawing the Japanese away from the American cripples. Admiral Kondo left his cripples—*Kirishima* and *Ayanami*—to fend for themselves and chased *Washington* with the two heavy cruisers and two destroyers under his immediate command. In the end, Kondo gave up the chase without launching the mass torpedo attack he originally envisioned. However, RAdm Raizo Tanaka, who had been drawn into the chase with destroyers *Hayashio*, *Kagero*, and *Oyashio*, continued to trail Lee all the way to the Russells, as did *Nagara* and several of RAdm Susumu Kimura's destroyers. Tanaka's and Kimura's ships got close enough to launch torpedoes up *Washington's* wake, but none of the deadly Long Lances found the target.

Thus ended the first battleship-versus-battleship confrontation undertaken in the twentieth century by the U.S. Navy. Admiral Lee claimed a victory on three counts: He kept Admiral Kondo from bombarding Henderson Field, he delayed the landing of troops from Admiral Tanaka's transports, and he mortally wounded a Japanese battleship.

And, indeed, dawn over Guadalcanal on November 15, 1942, was very much an American dawn.

48

Ayanami, battered by numerous shell hits and on fire down her entire length, was abandoned and scuttled shortly after the Americans left. Those in her crew who had survived were removed by *Uranami*, which sailed north alone.

Kirishima emerged from her ordeal with her rudder destroyed, fires raging down her main deck, and taking huge amounts of water through holes blasted in her hull by American 16-inch shells. No effort was expended in saving *Hiei*'s sister. Her crew was removed by *Asagumo*, *Teruzuki*, and *Samidare* and all her sea cocks were opened. She sank several miles northwest of Savo several hours before sunrise.

After giving up the fruitless chase to bring *Washington* to heel, Admiral Kondo ran for home with *Atago* and *Takao*, both of which wound up in Japan to undergo repairs of the extensive damage suffered at the hands of the American battleships. Likewise, *Nagara*, which had weathered hits in two consecutive night actions, was sent to Japan for repairs.

In all, the Imperial Navy lost 249 officers and men killed and 84 wounded in action that night.

On the American side, *Washington* and *South Dakota* joined up and headed for Noumea together. *South Dakota*, severely damaged by a bomb at Santa Cruz and by numerous Japanese shells off Savo, was sent home for repairs; *Washington* remained, temporarily the only new fast battleship in the Pacific Fleet.

Grievously wounded *Benham* found moderately wounded *Gwin* after sunrise and they set sail together for Espiritu Santo. Through the day, *Benham*'s crew did everything it could to overcome their ship's broken back and cracked main deck; hundreds of 5-inch rounds and other heavy loads were jettisoned over the side, and steel plates were welded across the break in the main deck. However, as the daytime's calm sea picked up a bit toward the late afternoon, as the ship's gingerly progress prevented her from making landfall by sunset, as constant flexing and straining brought on by even the lightest swell inexorably weakened the thin skin that was holding her two parts together, *Benham*'s chances of survival waned. In the end, her entire crew was evacuated to *Gwin*, and she was scuttled by gunfire. *Gwin* made it home with her double crew.

In a bizarre postscript, *Benham* was initially declared lost with all hands, and condolence letters arrived at the homes of her crewmen before letters from the survivors. The cause of the misunderstanding arose when CTM John Chapman was fished from the waters near Savo by friendly rescue craft. Chapman had been blown off *Benham*'s main deck by the torpedo blast that ultimately destroyed his ship. When a head-count ashore revealed that Chapman was the only *Benham* survivor to reach the Lunga Perimeter, the local authorities assumed that he was the ship's only survivor, period. There was nothing in Chief Chapman's recent experience to disabuse him of that terrible notion, so he went along with the finding. And so the sad telegrams went out. In fact, no member of *Benham*'s crew died that night, and only nine were injured.

※

The bulk of the *Walke* and *Preston* survivors were a pathetic lot of desperate men adrift in enemy waters, their prospects for rescue diminishing as a persistent tide carried them closer and closer through the dark hours toward the enemy-held shore near Cape

Esperance. After contending with the deadly passage of friendly battleships and vigorous attacks by bloodthirsty sharks, the various groups of swimmers and floaters beat feebly against the tide to put off their inevitable collision with land. There was little more they could do until it was light enough for rescuers to find them.

The *Walke* survivors, numbering about seventy, were well scattered in several groups, the largest of which was safely out of the water, perched atop their ship's bow section, which remained afloat and pointing toward the sky throughout the terrible night. As was the case with hundreds of shipwrecked sailors only two nights earlier, most of the survivors were coated with thick fuel oil and full to brimming with unavoidable gulps of seawater. Many had been wounded in the furious fight or critically injured by *Walke*'s own depth charges. Where possible, the casualties were lifted aboard the two life rafts that had been cast adrift from the sinking vessel, but many had to ride things out immersed in the water.

A bizarre incident occurred about an hour after *Walke* sank. S2 J. O. Pinion was one of the first in his raft-borne group, numbering about fifteen, to sense the submarine that surfaced only 50 feet away. Pinion heard the squeak of a hatch being undogged and the sound of footsteps on a deck. LCdr Reader Scott, *Walke*'s mortally injured exec, was the first to react: "Bow your heads," he whispered in a nonetheless peremptory tone, "No talking!" All hands instantly obeyed.

From the corner of his eye, S2 Pinion saw two Japanese sailors walk forward to the tip of the submarine's bows. Suddenly, a dim blue light reached out from the two submariners and swept over the raft and the men in the water. MM2 Jim McDermott, who was beside Lieutenant Commander Scott, reflexively hunched his head into his shoulders; he was convinced that the Japanese were going to machine-gun him and his shipmates. McDermott released his life belt and prepared to let go of the raft; if the Japanese opened fire, he was going to dive deep.

A group of *Preston* survivors, too far to be seen or heard by the *Walke* group, was close enough to see the blue light and wonder what was going on.

The blue light went off after two sweeps, and the two Japanese briefly conversed in low tones. There was the sound of footsteps again, and then the creaking of the hatch. The submarine eased well away from the castaways and submerged.

Later, about an hour before dawn, a relay of the able-bodied *Walke* survivors was trying to tow the raft away from the beach—they were actually losing ground despite heroic efforts—when two extremely noisy ships passed close by the raft and anchored several hundred yards out from the nearby beach. These were two of RAdm Raizo Tanaka's four surviving transports and cargomen.

While many of the *Preston* and *Walke* survivors tried to get away from Guadalcanal, FC3 Jim Cook and five other *Preston* survivors tried to swim to the island. One of the six, a quartermaster, was convinced that the nearest beach was in friendly hands. Fortunately, they saw the anchored Japanese transports and cargomen at first light and reversed course before they were seen.

MM2 Gordon Klopf's small group of *Preston* swimmers also tried to swim ashore. Klopf, who had five broken ribs and other assorted injuries, felt that becoming a prisoner was better than drowning, and apparently the others agreed. However, when Japanese soldiers ashore fired on the swimmers, it was decided that the risk of drowning was preferable to the certainty of being shot to death. The group slowly kicked back out of rifle range and waited for something to happen.

卐

The four Japanese transports and cargomen were found by Army Air Forces Capt Jim Jarman, skipper of the 67th Pursuit Squadron. Jarman, who was flying a P-39 on one of the first missions ever launched from Fighter-2, passed over the four ships at 1,200 feet but saw no signs of life. The ships appeared to be anchored several hundred yards off the beach, and it was by no means clear to Jarman whose they were; he had been at Guadalcanal for months and had seen stranger things than U.S. ships standing off a Japanese-held beach. During a second pass at only 400 feet, Jarman also saw several life rafts and groups of swimmers, but, again, he had no idea whose they were. As he came back over the ships, one of them slipped her anchor and got underway, making straight for the beach. With that, all four ships began slinging antiaircraft rounds at the low, slow P-39, thus resolving all doubts about their identity. Jarman's radio was not tuned to the set in the Henderson Field tower, so he flew straight to Fighter-1 and reported his findings in person.

As soon as Jarman's report was in, Marine Maj Joe Sailer led the first of daylong strikes against the Japanese transports in Doma Cove. Captain Jarman joined Sailer's strike with three other bomb-equipped P-39s. By the time the Cactus aircraft reached Doma Cove, all four ships had nosed into the beach and troops were streaming into the nearby trees. The Marine and Navy SBDs got two direct hits and a near miss on three of the transports and the four Army fighter-bombers not only bombed all four transports but worked them over in relays with their 20mm cannon and .30- and .50-caliber machine guns. On the way back to Fighter-1, Captain Jarman led his P-39s around Savo and, on the way, saw *Walke's* floating bows, a huge oil slick, and a great deal of floating debris. However, he did not know what to make of the find.

The beached and burning transports at Doma Cove and several large supply dumps the Japanese established just behind the tree line were mercilessly attacked throughout the entire day by a continuous stream of every type of aircraft operating from Henderson Field and the fighter strips. Many of the Japanese soldiers in the four ships were killed, and most of the 1,500 bags of rice and other assorted supplies were destroyed, and so were all four of the ships. Additional Cactus aircraft bypassed the beached vessels and beat north to search for Japanese cripples; they sank two of Tanaka's burning and abandoned transports in the Slot.

卐

The *Walke* and *Preston* castaways had ringside seats for the continuous bombing and strafing of Admiral Tanaka's four beached transports, but, strangely, they were not seen or recognized as friendly survivors by any of the scores of passing pilots or aircrewmen. At one point, S2 J. O. Pinion distinctly saw a crewman aboard a B-17, directly overhead, lean out an open hatch to take pictures of the burning transports, but the man did not seem to notice the frantic waves for attention.

After participating in several strafing sorties in the morning and early afternoon, Capt Jim Jarman followed a late-dawning hunch and returned to investigate a patch of sea in which he had earlier seen the flotsam and jetsam of the night's naval contest. What he found—and finally recognized—at about 1430 were living sailors, most of the 264 officers and men who had survived the sinking of *Preston* and *Walke*, men who for nearly fifteen hours had been feebly beating against the tide with their hands, men whose only hope was Jim Jarman and the boats he called to rescue them, men who would have died of injuries or exhaustion or been driven ashore in Japanese territory in a matter of a few hours. After two passes without eliciting any notice from destroyer *Meade*, Jarman actually had to fire his 20mm cannon and all his machine guns in front of the destroyer's bows to divert her from the pressing business of shelling the beached transports, a job she had been undertaking within sight of the survivors since midmorning.

When MM1 Jack Strickland, a strong swimmer, volunteered to try to make it all the way to Lunga, three other *Walke* survivors clambered to join him. At about the time Captain Jarman was trying to waylay *Meade*, and long after MM1 Strickland and his companions had struck for Lunga, a floatplane found them. The plane, one three *San Francisco* scouts that had been flown to Tulagi on November 12, was providing spotting information to *Meade* when her pilot happened to see the swimmers. He circled overhead once, landed nearby, and taxied up to the oil-covered survivors. Before anyone had an opportunity to speak, the airplane's crewman climbed out onto the wing and leveled a Thompson submachine gun on one of the four water-logged sailors, a Filipino mess attendant. A great deal of shouting finally convinced the crewman that the four were indeed friends. MM1 Strickland explained that the two life rafts he and the others had left earlier were filled with sick and injured men who were in danger of perishing if they did not get help soon. The pilot agreed to fly on to locate them and then get word to *Meade* to pick them up. Then the crewman handed over a lift raft—the tiny floatplane could not take any passengers aboard —and the pilot took off. The rafts were found by *Meade*, but, by then, two of the survivors had died from their burns. A short time later, the destroyer picked up MM1 Strickland and his companions.

Late in the afternoon, after nearly sixteen hours adrift, MM2 Jim McDermott saw a distant destroyer make a firing pass at the beach. Though McDermott's eyes were burning from the effects of salt water, fuel oil, and the glaring sun, and despite his weakened condition brought on by thirst, hunger, hypothermia, and exhaustion, he decided to swim to the ship to elicit some help for his shipmates, most of whom were in even worse shape. Before leaving, it finally occurred to McDermott to protect himself from the sun. He removed his undershorts, wiped as much oil and gunk off his face as he could, and placed the shorts on his head to ward off the direct rays of the sun. Then he and another sailor struck out for the distant friendly warship. Fortunately, the two had gone only a few hundred yards when they were seen by the crew of a ramped landing boat out of Kukum. After McDermott and his companion were taken aboard and had pointed out the raft full of men they had just left, the landing boat took everyone else aboard and ran straight to *Meade*.

MM1 Al Thrift's group of *Preston* survivors was getting close to the beach when the *San Francisco* floatplane landed nearby and taxied up to them. After the oil-covered sailors identified themselves as Americans, the aircrewman told them to grab the pontoon for a tow out to safer waters. The floatplane pulled the swimmers about a mile farther from the beach and then, with a promise to send help, cast them off next to a much larger group. *Meade* arrived in good time and took everyone aboard. MM1 Thrift was able to pull himself up the cargo net rigged to *Meade*'s side, but, like many other swimmers, he was unable to stand up because the blood had stopped circulating in his legs. As Thrift and others in similar condition were forced to walk up and down the deck to restore their circulation, he asked the time. It was about 1700; he and his fellow survivors had been adrift since before midnight.

Cox Peter Trella, his brother, F1 Paul Trella, and *Walke*'s boilermaker, did not find a raft, but they did manage to stay together through the dark hours. The boilermaker had a small waterproof container filled with cigarettes and candy which the three consumed between short catnaps. One side of Peter Trella's inflatable Mae West life jacket had been punctured while he was leaving

Walke, so he had to blow it up from time to time to remain afloat. The three watched the incessant air attacks upon the Japanese ships on the nearby beach, and they saw *Meade* arrive to shell the ships and beachside supply dumps. *Meade's* gig picked up a nearby raft-load of *Walke* survivors the three swimmers had not even seen, but it turned back toward the destroyer without picking them up. The three frantically waved and shouted to attract attention, and the gig finally turned back to retrieve them too. One of the boat crewmen asked the three if they needed help getting aboard, but Peter Trella said he was fit enough to do the job himself. He no sooner reached out to grasp the gunwale than his lights went out. The next thing he knew, he was in a clean bunk aboard *Meade*, accepting a cup of hot coffee.

By the time *Meade* found MM2 Gordon Klopf, of *Preston*, his tongue was so swollen that he had to hold his fingers in his mouth to keep from gagging whenever he vomited seawater, which was often. By then, Klopf's only response to his agony, brought on as much by severe dehydration as severe injuries, was to mutter the Twenty-third Psalm over and over. He was barely aware of his rescue and drifted off to sleep as soon as he was led to a bunk.

FC3 Jim Cook, of *Preston*, had just climbed aboard *Meade* and was standing in an internal passageway, in the act of pulling his life preserver over his head, when a Japanese Zero fighter running from an American Wildcat fighter banked sharply and strafed the destroyer. The precipitous attack came as a complete surprise, and no one had time to react before the Zero had already opened fire. MM1 Al Thrift, also of *Preston*, was in the same internal passageway when the Zero pounced. He heard the General Quarters klaxon only a moment before bullets pierced the bulkhead and bathed him in the blood of the sailor just ahead of him. That was FC3 Jim Cook, who saw 20mm tracer rounds exploding against the bulkhead and felt sharp stings in his left arm and left calf and a warm sprinkle of blood on his face. Two *Meade* crewmen and three *Walke* survivors were killed in the attack, and several *Walke* and *Preston* survivors were wounded. *Meade* claimed credit for downing the Zero.

The *San Francisco* floatplane, which was so instrumental in the rescue of so many *Walke* and *Preston* survivors, crashed into the sea late in the afternoon. The wreckage was located by *Meade*, but the pilot and aircrewman had been killed.

卍

Bombing and strafing attacks continued throughout the day, reducing supply dumps and all four beached transports to rubble, extinguishing the last faint Japanese hope that anything of value might be salvaged from so thorough a defeat.

The Imperial Navy had been beaten at Guadalcanal, and even it could no longer avoid that stark truth.

Epilogue

he U.S. Navy lost more ships than the Imperial Navy did
during the Naval Battle of Guadalcanal, yet the U.S. Navy
has been declared the winner. This is because the Japanese
were kept from *all* their vital missions during the course of two
furious night surface engagements and the Cactus Air Force's full
day of stupendously successful air attacks upon Japanese warships
and transports in the Slot. Even more than this technical victory—
for it is technically accurate to decide a battle simply in terms of
whose *will* prevailed—was the ultimate strategic decision that fa-
vored the U.S. Navy in the wake of the two night battles off in
mid-November 1942.

The loss of two precious battleships—the crown jewels of
1942's world-class navies—combined with the loss of a heavy
cruiser, three destroyers, and eleven transports, plus severe damage
to numerous other warships, caused the Imperial Navy to pull in its
horns at Guadalcanal. The decision was irrevocable. After November 15, 1942, no Japanese warship larger than a destroyer was ever
again risked in the waters off Guadalcanal or, indeed, within range
of American shore-based aircraft. After November 15, the Japanese
admirals simply lost their will to risk their largest ships. This—

combined with the halting output of Japan's shipyards and the dazzling output of America's shipyards, which in late 1942 had yet to hit their stride—is what defeated the Imperial Navy in the Pacific War. There is no sense having a navy if it is not committed to battle in a war of national survival, which is precisely how the Japanese viewed the Pacific War.

Notwithstanding the Imperial Navy's moral defeat at Guadalcanal, it is true that Japanese tactics at sea continued to dominate well into 1943. Indeed, the U.S. Navy suffered a major and extremely humiliating defeat at the hands of eight of RAdm Raizo Tanaka's troop-carrying transports on the night of November 30— within sight of the four burned-out hulks run up on the beach at Doma Cove. However, in time, the U.S. Navy abandoned its outmoded tactics and learned to win toe-to-toe battles with Japanese surface ships. Ironically, there were precious few such battles after mid-1943, and the burgeoning U.S. surface-battle fleet was mainly used for shore bombardment and in antiaircraft-defense roles. But that in itself is an outcome of the two November night battles off Savo.

The inability of the Imperial Navy to overcome the Cactus Air Force by any means—in the air or by bombarding its base—was the ultimate cause of Japan's defeat at Guadalcanal. So long as Henderson Field and its satellite fighter strips were in operation, the Imperial Navy would be incapable of lifting in the numbers of troops and amounts of supplies required to win the battle ashore. Unable even to feed his starving troops, much less supply them with overwhelming firepower, the Imperial Army commander on Guadalcanal was immediately obliged to cede the initiative and go over to a three-month-long battle of attrition. During that battle, many thousands of Japanese soldiers were killed in battle, and many thousands more died from disease and hunger. In the end, in early February 1943, the Imperial Navy retrieved only 13,000 of the 50,000 soldiers it had carried to Guadalcanal between late August and late November 1942.

In direct contrast to the Imperial Navy's inability to resupply and adequately reinforce Japanese ground forces at Guadalcanal, the technical and moral victory in mid-November permitted a hitherto beleaguered and virtually defeated U.S. Navy to bring in adequate supplies for the first time since the August 7 landings. By late December, U.S. Navy transports had carried in fresh regiments amounting to two fresh divisions.

After its brilliant, decisive contribution toward defeating Admirals Abe, Kondo, and Tanaka in mid-November, the Cactus Air Force was able to devote less of its energies to defending itself and more of its energies to supporting the land offensive that ultimately scoured Japanese ground forces from the island. Yet more important from a strategic viewpoint was the Cactus Air Force's role in clearing the way for Allied invasions further up the Solomons chain. In fact, the first missions of the nascent strategic air offensive in the Solomons began within days of the mid-November naval and air battles.

For all the good that came from so many deaths, so many ships lost, so many risks taken, there is no telling what chaos a clear defeat might have imposed. The U.S. Navy in the Pacific was about out of fighting ships; it would be months before the Pacific Fleet again had as many operational warships on hand as it did on November 12. Would equal or greater losses for smaller gains have been acceptable or even sustainable? Like the Japanese, the U.S. Navy reached a low moral ebb in mid-November; the dispatch of first Callaghan and then Lee into the treacherous waters around Savo were acts of desperation. But they were also acts of an area commander, Bill Halsey, both new to his job and undefeated in his thinking. It was the early and decisive victories under Halsey's stewardship—off Savo in mid-November, and off the Santa Cruz Islands earlier, in late October—that both set the tone for the remainder of the Pacific naval war and raised Halsey and like-minded leaders to key fighting commands as the war grew and spread. If one wonders at Halsey's good fortune in arriving on the scene at a pivotal moment, wonder no more; his presence, his combative brand of leadership, as much as anything, affected the outcome of those battles. For at both Santa Cruz and off Savo it was Halsey's orders that caused his fleets to stand and fight. Halsey's place in history was not a fluke brought on by his arrival at a lucky moment but upon the aggressive acts of will he imposed upon events occurring at the critical moment that coincided with his arrival.

Perversely, in an age still dominated by the thinking of battleship admirals and surface-warfare strategists, the twin surface victories off Savo provided Halsey and his caste of air-minded senior admirals with a platform from which they could make their views on the use of carrier-based air power stick.

Though they did not recognize it in those terms, the Japanese surface admirals gave up in the face of the ascendancy of U.S. air power at Guadalcanal. After November 15, 1942, they withheld their capital ships from battles that might have seriously influenced the outcome of the war because they feared air power. In their minds, the worst blow ever to befall the Imperial Navy was the loss of *Hiei*, an outmoded, thirty-year-old battleship. Land-based air sank *Hiei* in a place from which she might have been towed and at a time when she might have been salvaged. Two nights later, the quick scuttling of *Kirishima* was an echo of the final destruction of *Hiei* by Cactus-based bombers. In addition, the last Japanese heavy cruiser lost while the ultimate outcome of the war might have been changed was *Kinugasa*—another victim of American air power. After that, except for *Kirishima*, *Atago*, and *Takao*, which were already in motion, no Japanese battleship or heavy cruiser was ever again sent into a battle that might have had serious strategic consequences.

On November 12, 1942, the Imperial Navy had the better ships and the better tactics. After November 15, 1942, its leaders lost heart and it lacked the strategic depth to face the burgeoning U.S. Navy and its vastly improving weapons and tactics. The Japanese never got better while, after November 1942, the U.S. Navy never stopped getting better.

Afterword

This note is for naysayers who do not feel, as I feel, that the job of studying history is an elastic, ongoing enterprise that can be influenced by new advice, new information, new insights, and more careful readings of the old records.

This volume is not your standard recitation of the Naval Battle of Guadalcanal. What you have read is often at direct variance with what has become accepted in constant iterations of what I believe to be both an incorrect reading of extant official documents and an unwillingness by any earlier chroniclers to seriously engage survivors of all ranks and stations in the information-gathering process. Thus, I have created the potential for controversy—perhaps even bitter controversy—in both my presentation of new evidence and in my reading of and conclusions drawn from old evidence.

To follow my reasoning, if you are interested in why the old conclusions do not hold up under careful scrutiny, you must first accept the conclusion—inevitable if you were to read the action reports of various ships—that every ship in action on the night of November 13, 1942, was operating on a time line somewhat removed from the time lines of every other ship. That is, no two clocks were set to the same standard; the clocks were not synchronized. Most of the errors of earlier chroniclers stem from this simple fact. (I had precisely the same difficulty, stemming from the same fact, in reconciling the flow of events presented in the second volume in this series, *Guadalcanal: The Carrier Battles*. However, there was not as much going on at a given moment and fewer erroneous conclusions had been drawn by earlier chroniclers.) It is also relevant to note that no one developed any of these naval actions fully in a book-length study before I undertook the job. Thus, no one had reason to examine the evidence as closely as I have been forced to do. This condition did not in itself confer greater wisdom upon me, but it certainly focused my attention upon detail.

Second, you must accept the notion that the Navy of 1942 reserved no place in its thinking for the observations—much less the opinions—of enlisted personnel or even junior officers. Quite simply, no one asked such people what they saw or what they thought about what they saw unless they were the only witnesses to an important event or the only survivors of a ship that was lost. I have done so partly because it is my firm policy to seek the advice of a wide spectrum of participants, and also because the passing years have placed most such people in the majority of survivors. Of course, I find that information from living sources is often in error and that accounts published over the intervening decades have colored the recollections of many. But, on balance, the information proves to be sound. I know this is the case because so very much of it agrees with information from other sources and other people.

In just one small example, we have an answer to the question, "Who ran down the survivors of USS *Barton* moments after their ship was sunk?" Everyone who tried to answer the question has concluded that USS *Monssen* was the culprit. Impossible! A careful reading of the action reports indicates that *Monssen* was abreast of *Barton* when the latter was torpedoed, and that she passed from the scene before the survivors were in the water. But that does not answer the question; it merely tells who did *not* do it. Two sequences give us the answer. In the action report submitted by USS *O'Bannon*, we find reference to the fact that (a) the bow section of a U.S. destroyer was seen sticking straight up out of the water, that (b) *O'Bannon* turned hard left to avoid the debris and thus ran over men in the water, and (c) that *O'Bannon* was thrown into the air by a large detonation directly beneath her keel as she was overrunning the survivors. Also contained in the report is the guess that the sunken ship was USS *Laffey*. For years, chroniclers have taken the final guess as proof and, in so doing, concluded that *Laffey* survivors were subjected to the terror of being engulfed in the detonation of their ship's depth charges. No one who was in the water around *Laffey* agrees, but everyone I found who was in the water around *Barton* tells me that (a) their ship's bows protruded above the waves for several minutes, that (b) they were immediateley overrun by a destroyer, and (c) their ship's depth charges immediately detonated beneath them. Even more compelling are two last-minute letters from survivors who clearly read the numerals "450" on the passing destroyer's bow in the light of starshells. *O'Bannon* was far from where she thought she was; no one thought to question the guess contained in that ship's action report; and, certainly, no one ever asked for details from the *Barton* survivors who read *O'Bannon*'s bow number as that ship ran over them.

I have pieced together scores of other incidents in similar fashion.

For those readers interested in checking my conclusions regarding the November 13 night action against the official records, it will be helpful to know that I imposed order upon various chronologies by establishing firm times for three events referenced in all reports and for one event common to at least four of the last five ships in the U.S. column. After careful examination of the records, I concluded that *Akatsuki* opened her searchlight shutters at 0150, that Admiral Callaghan transmitted his open-fire order at 0152, that Callaghan transmitted his cease-fire order at 0158, and that *Barton* was torpedoed at 0200. Objectively, the sequence might be off by one minute in either direction, but the time *between* the events is firm. Almost everything contained in reports that seriously purport to be accurate—many do not—falls into place if these intervals are rigidly regarded. (Of course, a minute is a minute long, so some variance must be tolerated in timings based on these base points.)

I do not claim to have reached perfectly accurate conclusions. People who might have changed my thinking are dead, could not be found, or would not help. However, based on a massive effort to gather new materials and insights, and upon a careful blending of official records and credible new material, new connections can be made, old conclusions need to be adjusted or discarded, and a more complete, cetrtainly more accurate story can emerge.

As to the efficacy of the new sources, the most important standard I have imposed with regard to information concerning substantive events is that I ignored what someone told me about what others saw or said they did; I only used first-hand information that was applied to a new source's own actions. This standard was applied with somewhat less rigor in cases concerning anecdotal material. The qualifier "probably" appears in the text far more than I would have hoped, particularly in light of the probability that this will be the last study to which the aging survivors will make direct contributions. Sadly, and maddeningly, "probably" is often the only word that can be fairly used with respect to the identities and actions of and consequences to Japanese ships.

Having written all of the above, let it be noted that portions of the brief account of these night battles appearing in my *Guadalcanal: Starvation Island* are in error precisely because I fell into the trap of accepting the gleanings of conventional wisdom before I had fully studied the extant documents or collected new materials from living sources for this volume. Errors of this nature occur quite often, but it is rare for an author to be given the opportunity to correct a small part of one book by means of writing a whole new book.

In closing, I feel obliged to recognize the outstanding efforts of a singular individual whose unfailing support was vital to the outcome of this effort. He is VAdm Edward N. "Butch" Parker, whose clarity of purpose and vision that dark night in 1942 did as much as anything to snatch victory from the jaws of defeat. His clarity of mind in 1987 did as much as anything to educate this landsman. Scores of others, too numerous to list in this manner, gave willingly of their time and memories. Though I have singled out only one man, let it be said that every scrap provided was in its way essential to my comprehension of those long-ago events.

APPENDIX A

U.S. FORCES

Task Force 67   RAdm Richmond K. Turner

Task Group 67.1   Capt Ingolf N. Kiland
  Transport Division 2
    McCawley (AP) (FF)   Capt Charlie McFeaters
    Crescent City (AP)   Capt John R. Sullivan
    President Adams (AP)   Cdr Frank H. Dean
    President Jackson (AP)   Cdr Charles W. Weitzel

Task Group 67.4   RAdm Daniel J. Callaghan
  San Francisco (CA) (F)   Capt Cassin Young
  Cruiser Division 4   RAdm Mahlon S. Tisdale
    Pensacola (CA) (F)*   Capt Frank L. Lowe
    Portland (CA)   Capt Laurance T. DuBose
    Helena (CL)   Capt Gilbert C. Hoover
    Juneau (CLAA)   Capt Lyman K. Swenson
    Barton (DD)   LCdr Douglas H. Fox
    Monssen (DD)   LCdr Charles E. McCombs

---

*Detached November 12 to join Task Force 16

Destroyer Division 10 — Cdr Thomas M. Stokes
  Cushing (DD) — LCdr Edward N. Parker
  Laffey (DD) — LCdr William E. Hank
  Sterett (DD) — Cdr Jesse G. Coward
  O'Bannon (DD) — Cdr Edwin N. Wilkinson
  Shaw (DD) — Cdr Wilbur G. Jones
  Gwin (DD)* — LCdr John B. Fellows
  Preston (DD)* — Cdr Max B. Stormes
  Buchanan (DD) — Cdr Ralph E. Wilson

Task Group 62.4 — RAdm Norman Scott
  Atlanta (CLAA) (F) — Capt Samuel P. Jenkins
  Destroyer Division 12 — Capt Robert G. Tobin
  Aaron Ward (DD) (F) — Cdr Orville F. Gregor
  Fletcher (DD) — Cdr William N. Cole
  Lardner (DD) — Cdr William M. Sweetser
  McCalla (DD) — LCdr William G. Cooper
  Attack Cargo Ships
  Libra (AKA) — Cdr William B. Fletcher, Jr.
  Betelgeuse (AKA) — Cdr Harry D. Power
  Zeilin (AKA) — Capt Pat Buchanan

Task Force 16 — RAdm Thomas C. Kinkaid

  Enterprise (CV) (F) — Capt Osborne Hardison
  Air Group 10 — Cdr Richard K. Gaines
  VF-10 — LCdr James H. Flatley, Jr.
  VB-10 — LCdr James A. Thomas
  VS-10 — LCdr James R. Lee
  VT-10 — Lt Albert R. Coffin

Cruiser Division 5 — RAdm Howard H. Good
  Northampton (CA) (F) — Capt Willard A. Kitts, III
  San Diego (CLAA) — Capt Benjamin F. Perry
  Destroyer Squadron 2 — Capt Harold R. Holcomb
  Clark (DD) (F) — LCdr Lawrence H. Martin
  Anderson (DD) — LCdr Richard A. Guthrie
  Hughes (DD) — Cdr Donald J. Ramsey
  Destroyer Division 4 — Cdr Arnold E. True
  Morris (DD) (F) — LCdr Randolph B. Boyer
  Mustin (DD) — Cdr Wallis F. Petersen
  Russell (DD) — Cdr Glenn R. Hartwig

Task Force 64   RAdm Willis A. Lee

Battleship Division 6
  Washington (BB) (F)   Capt Glenn B. Davis
  South Dakota (BB)   Capt Thomas L. Gatch
Destroyer Screen
  Walke (DD)   Cdr Thomas E. Fraser
  Benham (DD)   LCdr John B. Taylor

Task Force 63   RAdm Aubery W. Fitch

Cactus Air Force   BGen Louis E. Woods
  VT-8   Lt Harold H. Larsen
  67th Pursuit
    Squadron   Capt James T. Jarman
  339th Fighter
    Squadron   Maj Dale D. Brannon
  11th Heavy Bomb
    Group   Col La Verne G. Saunders
  Marine Air Group 14   LtCol Albert D. Cooley
    VMF-112   Maj Paul J. Fontana
    VMF-121   Maj Leonard K. Davis
    VMF-122   Capt Nathan T. Post, Jr.
    VMSB-131   LtCol Paul Moret
    VMSB-132   Maj Joseph K. Sailer, Jr.
    VMSB-141   1stLt Robert M. Patterson
    VMSB-142   Maj Robert H. Richard
    VMF-212   Maj Frederick R. Payne, Jr.
    VMO-251   Maj Charles H. Hayes
  Marine Air Group 25   LtCol Perry K. Smith
    VMJ-152   Maj Elmore W. Seeds
    VMJ-253   Maj Henry C. Lane

JAPANESE FORCES

COMBINED FLEET	Adm Isoroku Yamamoto (At Truk)
Advance Force	VAdm Nobutake Kondo (In *Atago*)

Raiding Group   VAdm Hiroaki Abe
  Battleship Division 11
    Hiei (BB) (F)
    Kirishima (BB)
    Destroyer Squadron 10   RAdm Susumu Kimura
    Nagara (CL) (F)
    Akatsuki (DD)
    Amatsukaze (DD)
    Ikazuchi (DD)
    Inazuma (DD)
    Teruzuki (DD)
    Yukikaze (DD)
  Sweeping Unit   RAdm Tamotsu Takama
    Destroyer Squadron 4
    Asagumo (DD) (F)
    Harusame (DD)
    Murasame (DD)
    Samidare (DD)
    Yudachi (DD)
  Patrol Unit   Capt Yasuhide Setoyama
    Destroyer Division 27
    Shigure (DD) (F)
    Shiratsuyu (DD)
    Yugure (DD)

Main Body   VAdm Nobutake Kondo

  Bombardment Unit
    Atago (CA) (FF)
    Takao (CA)

Sweeping Unit   RAdm Shintaro Hashimoto
  Destroyer Squadron 3
    Sendai (CL) (F)
    Ayanami (DD)
    Shikanami (DD)
    Uranami (DD)

Carrier Support Group   VAdm Takeo Kurita

Supporting Unit
  Battleship Division 6
    Kongo (BB) (F)
    Haruna (BB)
    Tone (CA)
Air Striking Unit   RAdm Kakuji Kakuta
  Carrier Division 2
    Junyo (CV)
    Hiyo (CVL)
Screening Unit
  4–8 destroyers

Outer Seas Force   VAdm Gunichi Mikawa
                       (CinC 8th Fleet)

Support Group   VAdm Gunichi Mikawa
Main Unit
    Chokai (CA) (FF)
    Kinugasa (CA)
    Isuzu (CL)
    Arashio (DD)
    Asashio (DD)
Bombardment Unit   RAdm Shoji Nishimura
    Suzuya (CA) (F)
    Maya (CA)
    Tenryu (CL)
    Kazagumo (DD)
    Makigumo (DD)
    Michishio (DD)
    Yugumo (DD)

Reinforcement Group   RAdm Raizo Tanaka
  Escort Unit
    Destroyer Squadron 2
      Hayashio (DD) (F)
      Amagiri (DD)
      Kagero (DD)
      Kawakaze (DD)
      Makinami (DD)
      Mochizuki (DD)
      Naganami (DD)
      Oyashio (DD)
      Suzukaze (DD)
      Takanami (DD)
      Umikaze (DD)
  Transport Unit
    Arizona Maru
    Brisbane Maru
    Canberra Maru
    Hirokawa Maru
    Kinugawa Maru
    Kumagawa Maru
    Nako Maru
    Niagara Maru
    Sado Maru
    Shinanogawa Maru
    Yamaura Maru
    Yamatsuki Maru

Land-Based Aircraft   VAdm Jinichi Kusaka
  11th Air Fleet
  (at Rabaul)
    25th Air Flotilla
    26th Air Flotilla

Advance Expeditionary Force

VAdm Teruhisa Komatsu
(CinC 6th Fleet, at Truk)

Patrol Group
  I-15
  I-16
  I-17
  I-20
  I-24
  I-26
  I-122
  I-172
  I-175
  RO-34
Scouting Group
  I-7 (off Santa Cruz)
  I-9 (off San Cristobal)
  I-21 (off Noumea)
  I-31 (off Suva)

APPENDIX B

NAVAL BATTLE ORGANIZATION

November 13, 1942

U.S. BATTLE FORCE	*JAPANESE BATTLE FORCE*
Cushing (DD)	*Hiei* (BB)
Laffey (DD)	Kirishima (BB)
Sterett (DD)	Nagara (CL)
O'Bannon (DD)	*Akatsuki* (DD)
Atlanta (CLAA)	Amatsukaze (DD)
San Francisco (CA)	Asagumo (DD)
Portland (CA)	Harusame (DD)
Helena (CL)	Inazuma (DD)
Juneau (CLAA)	Ikazuchi (DD)
Aaron Ward (DD)	Murasame (DD)
Barton (DD)	Samidare (DD)
Monssen (DD)	Teruzuki (DD)
Fletcher (DD)	Yukikaze (DD)
	Yudachi (DD)

*Sunk or scuttled.

November 15, 1942

U.S. BATTLE FORCE	*JAPANESE BATTLE FORCE*
Walke (DD)	*Kirishima* (BB)
Benham (DD)	Takao (CA)
Preston (DD)	Atago (CA)
Gwin (DD)	Nagara (CL)
Washington (BB)	Sendai (CL)
South Dakota (BB)	Asagumo (DD)
	*Ayanami (DD)
	Hatsuyuki (DD)
	Ikazuchi (DD)
	Samidare (DD)
	Shikanami (DD)
	Shirayuki (DD)
	Teruzuki (DD)
	Uranami (DD)

*Sunk or scuttled.

APPENDIX C

CHARACTERISTICS OF PARTICIPANTS

U.S. WARSHIPS

Aaron Ward

Type: Destroyer
Class: *Benson*
Bow Number: DD 483
Commissioned: 11/22/41
Displacement: 1,630 tons
Speed: 37 knots
Crew: 250
Armaments: Four 5-inch DP (4 × 1)
                     Four 1.1-inch AA (1 × 4)
                     Four 20mm AA
                     Five 21-inch torpedoes (1 × 5)

Atlanta

Type: Light Antiaircraft Cruiser
Class: *Atlanta*
Bow Number: CL(AA) 51
Commissioned: 9/6/41
Displacement: 6,000 tons

Speed: 33 knots
Crew: 810
Armaments: Sixteen 5-inch AA (8 × 2)
                      Sixteen 1.1-inch AA (4 × 4)
                      Eight 21-inch torpedoes (2 × 4)

Barton

Type: Destroyer
Class: *Benson*
Bow Number: DD 599
Commissioned: 1/31/42
Displacement: 1,630 tons
Speed: 37 knots
Crew: 250
Armaments: Four 5-inch DP (4 × 1)
                      Eight 20mm AA
                      Ten 21-inch torpedoes (2 × 5)

Benham

Type: Destroyer
Class: *Craven*
Bow Number: DD 397
Commissioned: 4/16/38
Displacement: 1,500 tons
Speed: 36.5 knots
Crew: 250
Armaments: Four 5-inch DP (4 × 1)
                      Five 20mm AA
                      Sixteen 21-inch torpedoes (4 × 4)

Cushing

Type: Destroyer
Class: *Mahan*
Bow Number: DD 376
Commissioned: 12/31/35
Displacement: 1,465 tons
Speed: 36.5 knots
Crew: 172
Armaments: Four 5-inch DP (4 × 1)
                      Eight 20mm AA
                      Twelve 21-inch torpedoes (3 × 4)

Fletcher

Type:	Destroyer
Class:	*Fletcher*
Bow Number:	DD 445
Commissioned:	5/3/42
Displacement:	2,050 tons
Speed:	37 knots
Crew:	300
Armaments:	Five 5-inch DP (5 × 1)
	Two 40mm AA (1 × 2)
	Six 20mm AA
	Ten 21-inch torpedoes (2 × 5)

Gwin

Type:	Destroyer
Class:	*Benson*
Bow Number:	DD 433
Commissioned:	5/25/40
Displacement:	1,630 tons
Speed:	37 knots
Crew:	250
Armaments:	Four 5-inch DP (4 × 1)
	Eight 20mm AA
	Ten 21-inch torpedoes (2 × 5)

Helena

Type:	Light Cruiser
Class:	*Brooklyn*
Bow Number:	CL 50
Commissioned:	8/27/38
Displacement:	10,000 tons
Speed:	34 knots
Crew:	1300
Armaments:	Fifteen 6-inch (5 × 3)
	Eight 5-inch AA (4 × 2)
	Sixteen 40mm AA (4 × 4)
	Seven 20mm AA
	Four SOC aircraft

Juneau

Type:	Light Antiaircraft Cruiser
Class:	*Atlanta*
Bow Number:	CL(AA) 52
Commissioned:	10/25/41
Displacement:	6,000 tons
Speed:	33 knots
Crew:	810
Armaments:	Sixteen 5-inch AA (8 × 2)
	Sixteen 1.1-inch AA (4 × 4)
	Eight 21-inch torpedoes (2 × 4)

Laffey

Type:	Destroyer
Class:	*Benson*
Bow Number:	DD 459
Commissioned:	10/30/41
Displacement:	1,630 tons
Speed:	37 knots
Crew:	250
Armaments:	Four 5-inch DP (4 × 1)
	Four 1.1-inch AA (1 × 4)
	Five 20mm AA
	Five 21-inch torpedoes (1 × 5)

Monssen

Type:	Destroyer
Class:	*Benson*
Bow Number:	DD 436
Commissioned:	5/16/40
Displacement:	1,630 tons
Speed:	37 knots
Crew:	250
Armaments:	Four 5-inch DP (4 × 1)
	Eight 20mm AA
	Ten 21-inch torpedoes (2 × 5)

O'Bannon

Type:	Destroyer
Class:	*Fletcher*
Bow Number:	DD 450
Commissioned:	3/14/42
Displacement:	2,050 tons
Speed:	37 knots
Crew:	300
Armaments:	Five 5-inch (5 × 1)
	Eight 20mm AA
	Ten 21-inch torpedoes (2 × 5)

Portland

Type:	Heavy Cruiser
Class:	*Portland*
Bow Number:	CA 33
Commissioned:	5/21/32
Displacement:	9,800 tons
Speed:	33 knots
Crew:	1150
Armaments:	Nine 8-inch (3 × 3)
	Eight 5-inch AA (8 × 1)
	Sixteen 1.1-inch AA (4 × 4)
	Twenty-two 20mm AA
	Three SOC aircraft

Preston

Type:	Destroyer
Class:	*Mahan*
Bow Number:	DD 379
Commissioned:	4/22/36
Displacement:	1,500 tons
Speed:	36.5 knots
Crew:	172
Armaments:	Four 5-inch DP (4 × 1)
	Six 20mm AA
	Twelve 21-inch torpedos (3 × 4)

San Francisco

Type:	Heavy Cruiser
Class:	*New Orleans*
Bow Number:	CA 38
Commissioned:	2/10/34
Displacement:	9,950 tons
Speed:	33 knots
Crew:	1,050
Armaments:	Nine 8-inch (3 × 3)
	Eight 5-inch AA (8 × 1)
	Sixteen 1.1-inch AA (4 × 4)
	Nineteen 20mm AA

Three SOC aircraft

South Dakota

Type:	Battleship
Class:	*South Dakota*
Bow Number:	BB 57
Commissioned:	7/6/41
Displacement:	35,000 tons
Speed:	28 knots
Crew:	2,500
Armaments:	Nine 16-inch (3 × 3)
	Sixteen 5-inch DP (8 × 2)
	Sixteen 1.1-inch AA (4 × 4)
	Three SOC aircraft

Sterett

Type:	Destroyer
Class:	*Craven*
Bow Number:	DD 407
Commissioned:	10/27/38
Displacement:	1,500 tons
Speed:	36.5 knots
Crew:	250
Armaments:	Four 5-inch DP (4 × 1)
	Six 20mm AA
	Eight 21-inch torpedoes (2 × 4)

Walke

Type:	Destroyer
Class:	*Sims*
Bow Number:	DD 416
Commissioned:	10/20/39
Displacement:	1,570 tons
Speed:	38 knots
Crew:	250
Armaments:	Four 5-inch DP (4 × 1)
	Six 20mm AA
	Eight 21-inch torpedoes (2 × 4)

Washington

Type:	Battleship
Class:	*North Carolina*
Bow Number:	BB 56
Commissioned:	1/6/40
Displacement:	35,000 tons
Speed:	28 knots
Crew:	2,500
Armaments:	Nine 16-inch (3 × 3)
	Twenty 5-inch DP (10 × 2)
	Sixteen 1.1-inch AA (4 × 4)
	Three SOC aircraft

JAPANESE WARSHIPS

Akatsuki

Type:	Destroyer
Class:	*Akatsuki*
Commissioned:	5/7/32
Displacement:	2,090 tons
Speed:	38 knots
Crew:	200
Armaments:	Four 5-inch DP (2 × 2)
	Fourteen 25mm AA (7 × 2)
	Four 13mm AA
	Nine 24-inch torpedoes (3 × 3)

Amatsukaze

Type:	Destroyer
Class:	*Kagero*
Commissioned:	10/19/39
Displacement:	2,033 tons
Speed:	35.5 knots
Crew:	240
Armaments:	Six 5-inch DP (3 × 2)
	Four 25mm AA
	Three 13mm AA
	Eight 24-inch torpedoes (2 × 4)

Asagumo

Type:	Destroyer
Class:	*Asashio*
Commissioned:	11/5/37
Displacement:	1,961 tons
Speed:	35 knots
Crew:	200
Armaments:	Six 5-inch DP (3 × 2)
	Four 25mm AA
	Eight 24-inch torpedoes (2 × 4)

Atago

Type:	Heavy Cruiser
Class:	*Takao*

Commissioned:	6/16/30
Displacement:	13,160 tons
Speed:	34 knots
Crew:	773
Armaments:	Ten 8-inch (5 × 2)
	Eight 5-inch AA (4 × 2)
	Eight 25mm AA
	Four 13mm AA
	Sixteen 24-inch torpedoes (4 × 4)
	Three aircraft

Ayanami

Type:	Destroyer
Class:	*Fubuki*
Commissioned:	10/5/29
Displacement:	2,090 tons
Speed:	34 knots
Crew:	197
Armaments:	Six 5-inch DP (3 × 2)
	Two 13mm AA
	Nine 24-inch torpedoes (3 × 3)

Harusame

Type:	Destroyer
Class:	*Shiratsuyu*
Commissioned:	9/21/35
Displacement:	1,580 tons
Speed:	34 knots
Crew:	180
Armaments:	Five 5-inch DP (2 × 2, 1 × 1)
	Four 25mm AA
	Two 13mm AA
	Eight 24-inch torpedoes (2 × 4)

Hatsuyuki

Type:	Destroyer
Class:	*Fubuki*
Commissioned:	9/29/27
Displacement:	2,090 tons
Speed:	34 knots
Crew:	197

Armaments:	Six 5-inch SP (3×2)
	Two 13mm AA
	Nine 24-inch torpedoes (3×3)

Hiei

Type:	Battleship
Class:	*Kongo*
Commissioned:	11/21/12
Displacement:	31,720 tons
Speed:	30.5 knots
Crew:	1,437
Armaments:	Eight 14-inch (4×2)
	Fourteen 6-inch (14×1)
	Eight 5-inch AA (4×2)
	Twenty 25mm AA
	Three aircraft

Ikazuchi

Type:	Destroyer
Class:	*Akatsuki*
Commissioned:	10/22/31
Displacement:	2,090 tons
Speed:	38 knots
Crew:	200
Armaments:	Four 5-inch DP (2×2)
	Fourteen 25mm AA
	Four 13mm AA
	Nine 24-inch torpedoes (3×3)

Inazuma

Type:	Destroyer
Class:	*Akatsuki*
Commissioned:	2/25/32
Displacement:	2,090 tons
Speed:	38 knots
Crew:	200
Armaments:	Four 5-inch DP (2×2)
	Fourteen 25mm AA
	Four 13mm AA
	Nine 24-inch torpedoes (3×3)

Kirishima

Type:	Battleship
Class:	*Kongo*
Commissioned:	12/1/13
Displacement:	31,980 tons
Speed:	30.5 knots
Crew:	1,437
Armaments:	Eight 14-inch (4 × 2)
	Fourteen 6-inch (14 × 1)
	Eight 5-inch AA (4 × 2)
	Twenty 25mm AA
	Three aircraft

Murasame

Type:	Destroyer
Class:	*Shiratsuyu*
Commissioned:	6/20/35
Displacement:	1,580 tons
Speed:	34 knots
Crew:	180
Armaments:	Five 5-inch DP (2 × 2, 1 × 1)
	Four 25mm AA
	Two 13mm AA
	Eight 24-inch torpedoes (2 × 4)

Nagara

Type:	Light Cruiser
Class:	*Nagara*
Commissioned:	4/24/21
Displacement:	5,170 tons
Speed:	36 knots
Crew:	438
Armaments:	Seven 5.5-inch (7 × 1)
	Two 3-inch AA (2 × 1)
	Eight 24-inch torpedoes (4 × 2)
	One aircraft

Samidare

Type:	Destroyer
Class:	*Shiratsuyu*

Commissioned: 6/7/35
Displacement: 1,580 tons
Speed: 34 knots
Crew: 180
Armaments: Five 5-inch DP (2 × 2, 1 × 1)
                   Four 25mm AA
                   Two 13mm AA
                   Eight 24-inch torpedoes (2 × 4)

Sendai

Type: Light Cruiser
Class: *Sendai*
Commissioned: 10/30/23
Displacement: 5,195 tons
Speed: 35 knots
Crew: 450
Armaments: Seven 5.5-inch (7 × 1)
                   Two 5-inch DP (2 × 1)
                   Four 25mm AA
                   Six 13mm AA
                   Eight 24-inch torpedoes (4 × 2)
                   One aircraft

Shikinami

Type: Destroyer
Class: *Fubuki*
Commissioned: 6/22/29
Displacement: 2,090 tons
Speed: 34 knots
Crew: 197
Armaments: Six 5-inch DP (3 × 2)
                   Two 13mm AA
                   Nine 24-inch torpedoes (3 × 3)

Shirayuki

Type: Destroyer
Class: *Fubuki*
Commissioned: 3/20/28
Displacement: 2,090 tons
Speed: 34 knots
Crew: 197

Armaments: Six 5-inch SP (3 × 2)
Two 13mm AA
Nine 24-inch torpedoes (3 × 3)

Takao

Type: Heavy Cruiser
Class: *Takao*
Commissioned: 5/12/30
Displacement: 13,160 tons
Speed: 34 knots
Crew: 773
Armaments: Ten 8-inch (5 × 2)
Eight 5-inch AA (4 × 2)
Eight 25mm AA
Four 13mm AA
Sixteen 24-inch torpedoes (4 × 4)
Three aircraft

Teruzuki

Type: Antiaircraft Destroyer
Class: *Akitsuki*
Commissioned: 11/21/41
Displacement: 2,701 tons
Speed: 33 knots
Crew: 200
Armaments: Eight 3.9-inch AA (4 × 2)
Four 25mm AA
Four 24-inch torpedoes (1 × 4)

Uranami

Type: Destroyer
Class: *Fubuki*
Commissioned: 11/29/28
Displacement: 2,090 tons
Speed: 34 knots
Crew: 197
Armaments: Six 5-inch SP (3 × 2)
Two 13mm AA
Nine 24-inch torpedoes (3 × 3)

Yudachi

Type: Destroyer

Class: *Shiratsuyu*
Commissioned: 6/21/36
Displacement: 1,580 tons
Speed: 34 knots
Crew: 180
Armaments: Five 5-inch DP (2×2, 1×1)
                Four 25mm AA
                Two 13mm AA
                Eight 24-inch torpedoes (2×4)

Yukikaze

Type: Destroyer
Class: *Kagero*
Commissioned: 3/24/39
Displacement: 2,033 tons
Speed: 35.5 knots
Crew: 240
Armaments: Six 5-inch DP (3×2)
                Four 25mm AA
                Three 13mm AA
                Eight 24-inch torpedoes (2×4)

BIBLIOGRAPHY

BOOKS

Becton, RAdm F. Julian, with Joseph Morchauser, III. *The Ship That Would Not Die*. New York: Prentice-Hall, 1980.

Bulkley, Capt Robert J., Jr. *At Close Quarters*. Washington: Office of Naval History, 1962.

D'Albas, Capt Andrieu. *Death of a Navy*. New York: The Devin-Adair Company, 1957.

Dull, Paul S. *A Battle History of the Imperial Japanese Navy (1941–1945)*. Annapolis: Naval Institute Press, 1978.

Hammel, Eric. *Guadalcanal: Starvation Island*. Crown Publishers, 1987.

———. *Guadalcanal: The Carrier Battles*. Crown Publishers, 1987.

Hara, Tameichi, with Fred Saito and Roger Pineau. *Japanese Destroyer Captain*. New York: Ballantine Books, 1961.

Holbrook, Heber A. *The History of the U.S.S. San Francisco in World War II*. Dixon, California: Pacific Ship and Shore, 1981.

Horan, James D. *Action Tonight*. New York: G. P. Putnam, 1945.

Hough, LtCol Frank O., Maj Verle E. Ludwig, and Henry I. Shaw. *U.S. Marine Corps Operations in World War II*, Vol. I: *Pearl Harbor to Guadalcanal*. Washington: U.S. Government Printing Office, 1958.

Johnston, Stanley. *The Grim Reapers*. New York: E. P. Dutton & Co., 1943.

Lenton, H. T. *American Battleships, Carriers, and Cruisers*. Garden City: Doubleday & Co., 1968.

Miller, John, Jr. *Guadalcanal: The First Offensive. The U.S. Army in World War II*. Washington: U.S. Government Printing Office, 1949.

Miller, Thomas G., Jr. *The Cactus Air Force*. New York: Harper & Row, 1969.

Morison, RAdm Samuel Eliot. *History of United States Naval Operations in World War II*, Vol. V.: *The Struggle for Guadalcanal*. Boston: The Atlantic Monthly & Little Brown, 1962.

Musicant, Ivan. *Battleship At War: The Epic Story of the U.S.S. Washington*. New York: Harcourt Brace Jovanovich, 1986.

Olynyk, Dr. Frank J. *USMC Credits for the Destruction of Enemy Aircraft in Air-to-Air Combat: World War II*. Aurora, Ohio: Frank J. Olynyk, 1982.

————. *USN Credits for the Destruction of Enemy Aircraft in Air-to-Air Combat: World War II*. Aurora, Ohio: Frank J. Olynyk, 1982.

Potter, E. B. *Nimitz*. Annapolis: Naval Institute Press, 1976.

Roscoe, Theodore. *United States Destroyer Operations in World War II*. Annapolis: Naval Institute Press, 1953.

Silverstone, Paul H. *U.S. Warships of World War II*. Garden City: Doubleday & Co., 1966.

Simmons, Walter. *Joe Foss: Flying Marine*. New York: E. P. Dutton & Co., 1943.

Stafford, Cdr Edward P. *The Big E: The Story of the U.S.S. Enterprise*. New York: Random House, 1978.

Tillman, Barrett. *The Wildcat in WWII*. Annapolis: Nautical & Aviation Publishing Company of America, 1983.

————. *The Dauntless Dive Bomber in World War II*. Annapolis: Naval Institute Press, 1976.

Toland, John. *The Rising Sun: The Decline and Fall of the Japanese Empire*. New York: Random House, 1970.

Watts, Anthony J. *Japanese Warships of World War II*. Garden City: Doubleday & Co., 1966.

Wolfert, Ira. *Torpedo 8*. Boston: Houghton Mifflin Company, 1943.

INDEX

473